7-95

FOR REFERENCE

This book cannot
be checked out

Great Women
Mystery Writers

Great Women Mystery Writers

CLASSIC TO CONTEMPORARY

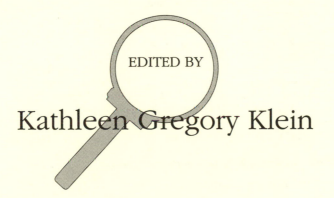

EDITED BY

Kathleen Gregory Klein

GREENWOOD PRESS
Westport, Connecticut • London

Library of Congress Cataloging-in-Publication Data

Great women mystery writers : classic to contemporary / edited by
  Kathleen Gregory Klein.
      p.   cm.
    Includes bibliographical references (p.   ) and indexes.
    ISBN 0–313–28770–8 (alk. paper)
    1. Detective and mystery stories, English—Women authors—Bio-
bibliography.   2. Detective and mystery stories, American—Women
authors—Bio-bibliography.   3. Detective and mystery stories,
American—Women authors—Dictionaries.   4. Detective and mystery
stories, English—Women authors—Dictionaries.   5. Women authors,
American—Biography—Dictionaries.   6. Women authors, English—
Biography—Dictionaries.   I. Klein, Kathleen Gregory.
PR830.D4G74   1994
823'.0872099287—dc20   94–16123

British Library Cataloguing in Publication Data is available.

Library of Congress Catalog Card Number: 94–16123
ISBN: 0–313–28770–8

First published in 1994

Greenwood Press, 88 Post Road West, Westport, CT 06881
An imprint of Greenwood Publishing Group, Inc.

Printed in the United States of America

The paper used in this book complies with the
Permanent Paper Standard issued by the National
Information Standards Organization (Z39.48–1984).

10 9 8 7 6 5 4 3 2 1

THIS BOOK IS DEDICATED TO
THE DETECTIVE FICTION CAUCUS
AND,
AS ALWAYS, TO RICK KLEIN

CONTENTS

PREFACE

Great Women Mystery Writers is a dictionary of classic and contemporary women mystery authors organized alphabetically according to the best-known name under which the writer publishes. The Author/Pseudonym Index lists each author's legal name and all names under which she publishes mystery fiction; the index refers users to the name under which the entry can be found: e.g., Vine, Barbara. *See* Rendell, Ruth. All authors cited in the text are included in this index.

The entries, each by a scholar-critic in the field, contain the following: available biographical information, a critical analysis of the fiction, recommendations (e.g., best books, whether to read a series in a particular order), other writers whose work is related, a complete mystery bibliography, and a selected critical bibliography.

Mystery bibliographies are organized by the name/pseudonym under which the works were published and further divided into nonseries and series books. Short story collections are included with novels; uncollected short stories are not listed. Original British and U.S. publication information is given, while books first published elsewhere include that original publication information.

The appendixes provide additional information useful to readers and reference librarians. They include descriptions of the Edgar and Agatha awards, with lists of women writers who were nominated and those who won; a brief history of Sisters in Crime; a description and listing of fan-author-centered and academic conferences; subscription information on fan, review, and academic publications about mystery fiction; access information for DO-ROTHYL, the electronic billboard for mystery fans; and a list of North American bookstores specializing in mystery fiction. A category listing of novels by popular subgenres (classical, hard-boiled, police procedural, soft-boiled, cozy, etc.) is also included. The two indexes cover author/pseudonym listings and the titles of works mentioned in the critical essays.

ACKNOWLEDGMENTS

I would like to thank Barbara Rader of Greenwood Press, who first thought of this book and invited me to edit it; the contributors who wrote entries, suggested authors to include, and recommended other contributors; the English Department of Southern Connecticut State University for timely assistance; and, especially, my husband for his continuing support.

Great Women
Mystery Writers

INTRODUCTION

Mystery fiction is the single most popular type of reading shared by women and men. Statistics from the past twenty years show that over 20 percent of all books sold are mystery novels—whether called detective fiction, crime novels, thrillers, or mysteries. Accounting for this popularity is a complicated process that is not made easier by oversimplified explanations based on needs for entertainment, reassurance, or escape. Readers are difficult to categorize: some read only Sherlock Holmes stories, hard-boiled private eye novels, or Golden Age mysteries, while others lean toward police procedurals, lighthearted comic capers, or village mysteries. Still others browse by historical period, favorite author, or setting. Finally, some people read everything they can find.

Since its beginnings, the genre has offered ample variety for its diverse readers. Although some critics have argued that *mystery* is an expansive term, with stories of crime to be found as easily in the Bible, Greek tragedy, and Shakespeare as in contemporary hard-boiled or cozy novels, most historians have agreed that mystery or detective fiction finds its beginnings in the nineteenth century. Preceding the more clearly defined examples of Edgar Allan Poe, who is generally credited with the first mystery-detective short stories, are three phenomena. First, from late-seventeenth-century Britain came the *Newgate Calendar* and its imitators, which included the life histories and confessions of condemned prisoners, often embellished by editorial comment. Then, eighteenth-century English literature contributed the gothic tales of Horace Walpole and, especially, Ann Radcliffe. Finally, from France in 1828 came the first account of a real-life professional detective, the *Memoirs* of Eugene François Vidoc, who founded the French Sûreté. Drawing on all these sources, the mystery-detective fiction of nineteenth-century Britain and the United States included moralistic tales of criminals, adventure stories of thief-takers, sensational novels of women in danger, and accounts of clever investigators, both in and out of the relatively new police forces.

From the outset, women as well as men were the creators and the subjects of this emerging fictional form. During the nineteenth century, British and American women were sufficiently prolific producers of fiction for an exasperated Nathaniel Hawthorne to label his writing competition as "those damned scribbling women." The women persisted nonetheless. In her history of the detective novel, A. E. Murch notes that the criticism of sensational fiction in Britain in the 1850s and '60s focused on its female authorship. "Publishers," she says, "seemed to feel there was something peculiarly indelicate about tales of crime or criminals being written by a woman, and were reluctant to print them" (1968, p. 152). However, as the scope of *Great Women Mystery Writers* makes clear, women write about crime and criminals very well indeed.

Women writers made their most significant contributions to the emerging field of mystery-detective fiction in the extraordinarily popular sensational novels. Best known, both in their own time and now, are Mrs. Henry Wood and Mary Elizabeth Braddon, both extremely prolific writers, with Braddon doubling Wood's total of forty published novels. Just twenty years after the publication of Poe's "Murders in the Rue Morgue," they each published the novels for which they continue to be known. Along with Wilkie Collins, they are considered the originators of this influential subgenre. The importance of sensational fiction, in its own right and as a predecessor of mystery-detective fiction, is the emphasis that the predominantly women writers placed on secrets, sensational crimes, some attention to investigation, and what Maureen Reddy describes as "women's position in society[:] . . . the terrifying underbelly of the apparently placid domestic haven idealized by official culture" (1988, p. 8). Elaine Showalter, in *A Literature of Their Own*, insists that the sensationalists articulated and shared the fantasies of protest and escape held by their middle-class female readers; furthermore, she adds: "The sensationalists made crime and violence domestic, modern, and suburban; but their secrets were not simply solutions to mysteries and crimes; they were the secrets of women's dislike of their roles as daughters, wives, and mothers" (1977, p. 158). Moreover, Showalter assesses this fiction as "genuinely radical and experimental . . . feminine domestic realism" (p. 181).

East Lynne, by Mrs. Henry Wood (who is never known by her own given name), was a best-selling novel and popular stage melodrama. Its overarching story tells of Lady Isabel Carlyle who deserts her passionless marriage and two children only to be similarly deserted by her caddish lover. Punished for her sins, she is badly disfigured in a train wreck, which also kills her illegitimate child. Returning to her husband's house (and his second wife, her greatest enemy), she secretly becomes governess to her own children. Embedded within this romance is the now-familiar story of a man falsely convicted of a crime, new evidence brought to light, and an alibi proven false. The happier outcome to this unjust imprisonment demonstrates Mrs. Wood's familiarity with points of evidence and her accurate presentation of the law.

Mary Elizabeth Braddon's *Lady Audley's Secret* was even more popular: with eight editions printed during its first year of publication, the novel was never out of print in her lifetime. Into this tale of double identity, bigamy, attempted murder, and possible madness—all by an innocent-looking woman—Braddon introduces the male detective figure of Robert Audley, a former victim who solves the mystery more by coincidence than plan. Several of Braddon's subsequent novels pay particular attention to the detection of what Murch (1968) calls "ingenious" crimes, as women writers moved the genre of mystery fiction closer to its more explicit form.

The early U.S. proponents of the genre made their mystery-detective fiction debuts in novels that borrowed equally from their sensational sisters in England and their mysterious, gothic countryman at home, Edgar Allan Poe. First off the marks was Meta Victoria Fuller Victor, writing as Seeley Regester, who was conveniently married to Orville Victor, the dime novel creator and Beadle and Adams editor. Borrowing liberally from all her predecessors, Regester published what must now be acknowledged as the first full-length detective novel in English. In this she predated Fergus Hume's *The Mystery of the Hansom Cab*, Anna Katharine Green's *The Levenworth Case*, and the first of Arthur Conan Doyle's Sherlock Holmes novels. As B. J. Rahn (1988) aptly demonstrates, Regester's novel meets all the criteria later recognized as part of the formula; in *The Dead Letter*, she follows the conventions of murder, inept police, a gifted amateur detective, and investigation and solution of the crime mystery. However, it is Anna Katharine Green who is widely acknowledged as the Mother of Detective Fiction for the considerable popularity of her novels, especially *The Levenworth Case*. Barrie Hayne attributes her importance to two elements: "her consolidation of the detective novels as a realistic art form, and her contribution to the development of the detective hero" (1981, p. 154). Minimizing the sensational elements, Green moved the detective novel toward its emphasis on a character's explanation of a mystery through his or her intellect. Green began with the creation of a male police officer in the investigator's role, but later invented both Amelia Butterworth, an amateur spinster detective, and Violet Strange, an early paid detective.

The importance of these nineteenth-century innovators was overshadowed in the last decade by two rising trends—the increasing popularity of short stories over novels and the emergence of the scientific detective. Both these factors are represented in Conan Doyle's creation of Sherlock Holmes. Nonetheless, conventional histories of the genre that leap from Poe to Conan Doyle—omitting the early women writers and their particular combination of romance, sentimentalism, sensationalism, domesticity, and realism—miss a vital link between the reading public and the development of the most popular genre of fiction.

Bridging the gap between the early women writers and the Golden Age of detective fiction, with its five female stars, was the well-published American author Mary Roberts Rinehart, who became famous for her "Had-I-But-Known" heroines. Her use of what Jan Cohn calls the "buried story" links Rinehart's fiction with the secret agendas that Showalter (1977) finds in sensational fiction. Rinehart clearly did not write the British country-house mysteries or the hard-boiled novels that dominated the market during most of her career, but she continued to develop complex and varied narratives of mystery, secrets, and suspense through the first half of the twentieth century.

In what has come to be known as the Golden Age of detective fiction, women writers undoubtedly took top honors. Although the male writers are hardly unknowns—including Freeman Wills Crofts, H. C. Bailey, Anthony Berkeley, Ronald Knox, Rex Stout, S. S. Van Dine, and Ellery Queen—the quintet of Agatha Christie, Dorothy L. Sayers, Josephine Tey, Margery Allingham, and Ngaio Marsh have come to be known as the quintessential authors of this glittering era. The Golden Age covers a chronological period (1920 to 1939), a historical period (the time between World War I and World War II), and a fictional period. The detective fiction of this age—and similar fiction since—is variously called classical, traditional, or cozy, as well as village mystery, domestic malice, or Golden Age mystery. In its own time, such a novel would have focused on a crime (typically murder) and criminal, a victim, and a detective who resolves the crime through deduction, an examination of clues, and, often, a reconstruction. This is primarily a puzzle or intellectual game where minimal attention is paid to the sufferings of the victim or even the probable fate of the criminal. Above all, the author is expected to "play fair" with the readers, providing them with the clues necessary to solve the puzzle-mystery along with the detective. Founded in 1927 in London, the Detection Club established mock-serious rules for its members that required them to forswear "Jiggery-Pokery, Coincidence or the Act of God"; nonetheless, the very stereotyped expectations developed by these rules provided authors with legitimate tricks to play on their audiences.

There is no question of the preeminence of Agatha Christie in both the Golden Age and our own. Her books have been published, translated, purchased, and read more than any others except the Bible, and *The Mousetrap* continues as the longest-running play in London. Around the world, her name is the automatic corollary to the term *mystery fiction*, and even critics who do not appreciate her narrative style or character development acknowledge Christie's position in the canon. John Cawelti summarizes her achievement:

Christie's ability to design an unusually complex and well-balanced detection-mystification structure and to set it forth with enough character and atmosphere to give it some flesh but not enough to distract from the chain of inquiry . . . has made her the most successful living writer of the classical detective formula. (1976, p. 119)

No less important is Christie's flexibility in creating multiple, successful examples of the Golden Age's eccentric detective. Eschewing the upper-class, Oxbridge-educated, socially prominent, male detective, Christie offers an egg-shaped, retired Belgian policeman; an elderly, English spinster; and a scatterbrained middle-aged woman novelist, in addition to a cluster of lesser figures. In Hercule Poirot, Jane Marple, Ariadne Oliver, Tuppence and Tommy Beresford, Parker Pyne, Harley Quin, and others, she avoids the heroic male model of Sherlock Holmes (or Peter Wimsey and Roderick Alleyn) except in such stolid Watson-figures as Captain Hastings. Her detectives ground Christie's novels in the bourgeois middle-class world of her readers, satisfying their quest for a comic ending which returns their world to its secure and familiar status quo.

By contrast, the upper-class, Oxbridge-educated, socially prominent, eccentric, heroic male detective is at the heart of the Golden Age detective fiction of Dorothy L. Sayers and Margery Allingham. Lord Peter Wimsey and Albert Campion stand as independent of their creators as does Sherlock Holmes in the tradition of the Great Detective. Both novelists move their characters from "silly ass about town" status to depictions as more thoughtful and introspective men. Both characters are wisely affiliated with official policemen—Charles Parker and Charlie Luke—although the latter does take center stage, while the former is always ancillary to Lord Peter. Sayers and Allingham give their detectives one other crucial characteristic in common—an intelligent, independent wife. Although Allingham wrote just short of twice Sayers's output over almost three times as many years, both marked and helped define the Golden Age.

In the project of defining this crucial period of mystery writing by women, the British authors Christie, Sayers, and Allingham were joined by New Zealand writer Ngaio Marsh and Scottish-born Josephine Tey. The latter two have in common the creation of the important police detectives of the Golden Age. In Roderick Alleyn, Marsh invented a police (British Criminal Investigations Division) version of Wimsey and Campion: he is well born, well educated, socially prominent, and part of the male heroic role. Called "the Cid" for his looks and his profession by a young Watson-like figure, Alleyn eschews the eccentricities and early foolishness of the titled amateur detectives. However, he does marry a woman as independent and intelligent as either Harriet Vane Wimsey or Amanda Fitton Campion. Not of this mold is Tey's police inspector Alan Grant, who appears in five of her eight novels. Although he shares the financial independence and eccentricities—he displays a certain "flair"—of his counterparts, he lacks the charisma of a great detective. A more ordinary mortal, Grant suffers from claustrophobia and a decided inability to settle down with any of his fascinating and independent love interests.

The Golden Age of detective fiction was hit hard by the emergence of the American-based hard-boiled school of writing, particularly in Raymond Chandler's essay, "The Simple Art of Murder." Chandler's emphasis on the necessary masculinity of the detective in a milieu of obligatory violence was a direct challenge to the women writers who were dominating the field and their unmistakably gentlemanly male heroes (Ariadne Oliver and Miss Marple's undoubtedly lady-like behavior were apparently less threatening to Chandler and his colleagues). The hard-boiled writers' disgust with bodies in the library and their valorization of knight errants in the mean streets was undoubtedly overstated to make a point. Furthermore, one of the submerged implications was that certain kinds of mystery/detective fiction could be identified by the gender of their writers, and, indeed, male writers of Golden Age fiction suffered challenges to their masculinity as the hard-boiled novels trumpeted their connection to the machismo of Ernest Hemmingway. Not until the 1980s did women writers in any significant numbers find ways to remake the hard-boiled style into their own.

Throughout the war years of the late 1930s and '40s, detective fiction of all kinds flourished; for example, racks of books were kept at the entrances to the underground bomb shelters in London. Copies were printed in England and the United States despite the war-related paper shortages. Then, and during the decades that followed, women writers were important in both the continuation and the changes of the genre. Even a cursory examination of the better-known writers who began often-lengthy careers in the decades between 1940 and the early '70s makes for astonishing reading. Novelists first published in the 1940s include Christianna Brand, Elizabeth Daly, Frances Crane, Margaret Scherf, Doris Miles Disney, E. X. Ferrars, Margaret Millar, Charlotte Armstrong, and Patricia Highsmith. The latter three are especially known for their suspenseful writing. In the postwar period of the 1950s, readers were introduced to Gwendoline Butler/Jennie Melville, Dorothy Salisbury Davis, Patricia Moyes, and the team of Mildred and Gordon Gordon. In the 1960s, with Dorothy Uhnak and Lillian O'Donnell, policewomen in procedural novels by women made their first real appearance. Elizabeth Linington and the team of Maj Sjowall and Per Wahloo continued the male-centered police procedural novel. In addition, P. D. James, Ruth Rendell, Amanda Cross, Dorothy Gilman, Jane Langton, Elizabeth Lemarchand, and Joyce Porter all published their first novels in the '60s. The following decade saw the introduction—among others—of Marian Babson, Margot Arnold, Anne Morice, Antonia Fraser, Lucille Kallen, Ellis Peters, Anne Perry, Elizabeth Peters, Charlotte Mac-

Leod, Gwen Moffat, and June Thomson. The Victorian novels of Elizabeth Peters and Anne Perry and the medieval novels of Ellis Peters touched off a wave of historically based tales of murder and detection.

For all the underlying continuity, the history of detective fiction is also one of variation and change. The increase in popularity of novels over short stories; the development of hard-boiled, soft-boiled, and police procedural novels; and the growth of espionage, thrillers, and antiheroic fiction all demonstrate the genre's enormous flexibility and its readers' voracious appetites. In the late 1970s and '80s another wave of change, which had begun earlier, came to maturity; this development can be found not in the introduction of a new form so much as in the conscious manipulation of the existing ones. The very formulae that authors and readers had come to know (and, as in Agatha Christie's *The Murder of Roger Ackroyd*, to mistrust) became the underlying agenda of mystery/detective fiction.

One of the markers of this new approach to mystery fiction is the emergence of a different kind of detective. Although the preceding years had hardly seen a homogenous breed of crime solvers, the '80s introduced such variety as to create a new critical mass. Most prominent are the women detectives: not just amateurs but also private investigators (P.I.s) and police detectives in numbers heretofore unimaginable. With this breach in the model of the heroic male detective (whether classic gentleman, macho P.I., or basic cop), authors also offered African-Americans, Native Americans, gays, lesbians, rabbis, priests and nuns, Armenians, Asians, Russians, and a woman working in partnership with a 400-year-old vampire: in short, a kind of variation not seen since the days of the American dime novels of detection (1880–1910), with their Bowery detectives, lady detectives, boy detectives, and dog detective. Moreover, for at least the first of these—the women detectives—women authors played the leading role. For example, between 1980 and 1993, sixty-eight women private eyes appeared in print, sixty-four of which were created by women. The impact of women writing about women has not been negligible. In an unprecedented performance, Margaret Maron's novel *Bootlegger's Daughter* won all the major 1993 U.S. awards for mystery: the Edgar, the Agatha, the Macavity, and the Anthony for best novel of the year. Maron's protagonist is Judge Deborah Knott in the new Colleton County series; the hero of her earlier series is Lt. Sigrid Herald of the New York Police Department.

Founded in 1986 as an advocacy group for women (writers, readers, editors, reviewers, and booksellers), Sisters in Crime is the first organization to take a leading role in examining the conditions of women writers and the treatment of women characters. Sisters in Crime now has over 2,200 members throughout the world (primarily in the United States). The 1993–94 president, Linda Grant, wrote of the organization's goals: "Books help to define our reality; they have the power to validate our experience and to expand our concept of the possible. If women's voices are not heard, possibilities shrink for all of us" (1993, p. 1). In isolation, no woman's voice—indeed, no single voice—carries sufficient weight, but the community of voices and the support that collective effort provides can encourage change and growth.

In 1993, women writers winning major awards for mystery fiction in addition to Margaret Maron included Barbara Neely (Anthony, Agatha, and Macavity for *Blanche on the Lam*), Marele Day (Shamus for *The Last Tango of Delores Delgado*), Anne Perry (American Mystery Award for *Defend and Betray*), Sue Grafton (American Mystery Award for *"I" Is for Innocent*), Mary Higgins Clark (American Mystery Award for *All around the Town*), Jaye Maiman, Elizabeth Pincus (Lambda Literary Award for *Crazy for Loving* and *Two-Bit Tango*), and Marcia Muller, the first woman to receive "The Eye," the lifetime achievement award of the Private Eye Writers of America. Seeley Regester would be impressed—I know I am.

BIBLIOGRAPHY

Cawelti, John G. *Adventure, Mystery, and Romance: Formula Stories as Art and Popular Culture*. Chicago: University of Chicago Press, 1976.

Cohn, Jan. "Mary Roberts Rinehart." In *Ten Women of Mystery*, ed. Earl F. Bargainnier. Bowling Green, Ohio: Popular Press, 1981, pp. 183–224.

Grant, Linda. "More Than a Trend." *Sisters in Crime Newsletter*, 5, no. 4 (Dec. 1993): 1, 4.

Hayne, Barrie. "Anna Katharine Green." In *Ten Women of Mystery*, ed. Earl F. Bargainnier. Bowling Green, Ohio: Popular Press, 1981, pp. 153–82.

Murch, A. E. *The Development of the Detective Novel*. Westport, Conn.: Greenwood Press, 1968.

Rahn, B. J. "Seeley Regester: America's First Detective Novelist." In *The Sleuth and the Scholar*, eds. Barbara A. Rader and Howard G. Zettler. Westport, Conn.: Greenwood Press, 1988, pp. 47–62.

Reddy, Maureen. *Sisters in Crime*. New York: Continuum, 1988.

Showalter, Elaine. *A Literature of Their Own: British Women Novelists from Brontë to Lessing*. Princeton, N.J.: Princeton University Press, 1977.

SUGGESTIONS FOR FURTHER READING

This reading list is limited to books that include substantial information about women mystery writers. There are, of course, many more books about the mystery genre as a whole.

Bakerman, Jane, ed. *And Then There Were Nine: More Women of Mystery*. Bowling Green, Ohio: Popular Press, 1984.

Bargainnier, Earl F., ed. *Ten Women of Mystery*. Bowling Green, Ohio: Popular Press, 1981.

Benstock, Bernard, ed. *Essays on Detective Fiction*. London: Macmillan, 1983.

Bloom, Clive, ed. *Twentieth-Century Suspense: The Thriller Comes of Age*. London: Macmillan, 1990.

Budd, Elaine. *13 Mistresses of Murder*. New York: Ungar, 1986.

Carr, Helen, ed. *From My Guy to Sci-Fi: Genre and Women's Writing in the Post-modern World.* London: Pandora Press, 1989.

Carr, John C. *The Craft of Crime: Conversations with Crime Writers.* Boston: Houghton Mifflin, 1983.

Cooper-Clark, Diana. *Designs of Darkness: Interviews with Detective Novelists.* Bowling Green, Ohio: Popular Press, 1983.

Craig, Patricia, and Mary Cadogan. *The Lady Investigates: Women Detectives and Spies in Fiction.* New York: St. Martin's, 1982.

Cranny-Francis, Anne. *Feminist Fiction: Feminist Uses of Generic Fiction.* New York: St. Martin's, 1990.

DellaCava, Frances A., and Madeline H. Engel. *Female Detectives in American Novels.* New York: Garland, 1993.

Fleenor, Juliann, ed. *The Female Gothic.* Montreal, Canada: Eden Press, 1983.

Henderson, Lesley, ed. *Twentieth Century Crime and Mystery Writers.* 3rd ed. Chicago and London: St. James, 1991.

Herbert, Rosemary. *The Fatal Art of Entertainment.* New York: G. K. Hall, 1994.

Irons, Glenwood, ed. *G Is for Genre Bending.* Toronto, Canada: University of Toronto Press, forthcoming.

Klein, Kathleen Gregory. *The Woman Detective: Gender and Genre.* Urbana: University of Illinois Press, 1988; Tokyo: Shobun Sha, 1994. Rev. ed., 1995.

———. *Woman Times Three: Writers, Detectives, Readers.* Bowling Green, Ohio: Popular Press, forthcoming.

Mann, Jessica. *Deadlier Than the Male: Why Are Respectable English Women So Good at Murder?* New York: Macmillan, 1981.

Mason, Bobbie Anne. *The Girl Sleuth: A Feminist Guide.* Old Westbury, N.Y.: Feminist Press, 1975.

Murch, A. E. *The Development of the Detective Novel.* Westport, Conn.: Greenwood Press, 1968.

Nichols, Victoria, and Susan Thompson. *Silk Stalkings: When Women Write of Murder.* Berkeley, Calif.: Black Lizard, 1988.

Reddy, Maureen. *Sisters in Crime: Feminism and the Crime Novel.* New York: Continuum, 1988.

Reilly, John, ed. *Twentieth Century Crime and Mystery Writers.* 1980. New York: St. Martin's; London: Macmillan. 2nd ed., 1985.

Slung, Michelle, ed. *Crime on Her Mind: Fifteen Stories of Female Sleuths from the Victorian Era to the Forties.* New York: Pantheon, 1975.

Swanson, Jean, and Dean James. *By A Woman's Hand.* New York: Berkeley, 1994.

Winn, Dilys, ed. *Murderess Ink: The Better Half of the Mystery.* New York: Workman, 1979.

KATHLEEN GREGORY KLEIN

❦ A ❦

CATHERINE AIRD (1930–)

Catherine Aird was born Kinn Hamilton McIntosh in Huddersfield, York-shire, England, on June 20, 1930. She now lives in Canterbury, Kent, where she has served as both a local historian and an aide to her father, a phy-sician. She has edited a number of local history and biographical publications and authored "son et lumière" productions and a local history video. She has written sixteen mystery novels, numerous uncollected short stories, and several articles about other mystery writers. Her services to the Girl Guides Association led to her being made a member of the prestigious Order of the British Empire (MBE). She also received an honorary M.A. from the University of Kent at Canterbury. From 1990 to 1991 she served as the chair of the Crime Writers' association. Her mystery novel *Henrietta Who* was filmed in the Netherlands, and many of her works appear in translation in various countries throughout the world.

Like Agatha Christie, Aird locates her works largely in the English coun-tryside, and specifically, in Calleshire County, whose towns and villages encompass the tangled histories, human relationships, and family secrets that provide a rich source of motives for murder most foul. The country is large enough to allow a variety of settings, including stately homes, a uni-versity, an agricultural school, a high-tech firm, and even a convent. Such diversity allows for a varied cast of characters as well, ranging from farmers to learned dons.

Her victims are a similarly mixed lot, including a nun, whose body is found at the bottom of the convent stairs; a village nurse; an industrialist; a headless, naked corpse; and a librarian-archivist. There are even skele-tons: in *Some Die Eloquent*, when the skeleton of an apparent victim of the blitz is discovered thirty years later, signs of a pregnancy supply a possible motive for murder. In *A Most Contagious Game*, the only book featuring an amateur detective, the discovery of a century-old hidden skeleton vies for interest with the recent murder of a beautiful young bride. The use of archives and other historical documents to provide the solution to the mystery not only suggests Aird's interest in local history and genealogy but also recalls Josephine Tey's *Daughter of Time*, in which both the mystery and its solution lie in the past.

Despite the multiplicity of plotters and victims, the regular cast is small. Although joined occasionally by other recurrent characters, only four—Detective Inspector C. D. Sloan, Constable Crosby, Superintendent Leeyes, and Dr. Dabbe—appear (in all but one book) throughout the series. Despite their frequent appearances, however, Aird provides only scant information about her characters' lives outside their work. Sloan, the central figure in this group, is the only series character who is at all developed. A rose grower, he is married, and events surrounding the birth of his son in *Some Die Eloquent* not only provide interesting glimpses into his domestic relations but also intertwine with the mystery surrounding the murder of an elderly science teacher. Although Sloan has had only a village education, his fondness for literary allusion suggests a deeper, more philosophically inclined character than is revealed. Leeyes is demanding, fond of cliché, and a devotee of Adult Education Courses, whose precepts he applies, often irrelevantly and frequently amusingly (to the readers if not to his underlings), to the case at hand. Dr. Dabbe, the pathologist, is characterized by his mordant humor, vast technical knowledge, and apparent unshockability. Crosby, whose promotion from patrolman is rumored to be the result of a typist's error, provides most of the humor that permeates Aird's work, along with most of Sloan's exasperation. Nicknamed the "defective constable" by his colleagues, Crosby's penchant for fast driving, schoolboy wit, and the ill-placed remark routinely collide with Sloan's methodical, fundamentally serious approach to his work.

Aird uses a variety of methods to tell her stories. The repetition of pieces of information and short, fragmented sentences can sometimes be irritating but more frequently serves to draw the reader into involvement with the events and characters about whom she writes. Her plotting is imaginative and unforced, her red herrings are used judiciously, and her wit is dry and clever. *Henrietta Who*, one of her most interesting novels, gives a strong sense of Aird's method of characterization, scene setting, and plot development, and *The Stately Home Murders* (published in *The Complete Steel*) provides not only a stately home, but also dotty relatives, assorted day-trippers and a butler as suspects.

Readers who enjoy police procedurals tempered by English village cozy will find Aird a good addition to their reading lists; they might also enjoy works by others, like Ngaio Marsh, Josephine Tey, and Dorothy Simpson, who write in a similar vein.

MYSTERY FICTION

A Most Contagious Game. New York: Doubleday; London: Macdonald, 1967.

Inspector C. D. Sloan Series

The Religious Body. London: Macdonald; New York: Doubleday, 1966.

Henrietta Who? London: Macdonald; New York: Doubleday, 1968.

The Complete Steel. London: Macdonald, 1969; as *The Stately Home Murders*. New York: Doubleday, 1970.

A Late Phoenix. London: Collins; New York: Doubleday, 1971.

His Burial Too. London: Collins; New York: Doubleday, 1973.

Slight Mourning. London: Collins, 1975; New York: Doubleday, 1976.

Parting Breath. London: Collins, 1977; New York: Doubleday, 1978.

Some Die Eloquent. London: Collins, 1979; New York: Doubleday, 1980.

Passing Strange. London: Collins, 1980; New York: Doubleday, 1981.

Last Respects. London: Collins; New York: Doubleday, 1982.

Harm's Way. London: Collins; New York: Doubleday, 1984.

A Dead Liberty. London: Collins; New York: Doubleday, 1986.

The Body Politic. London: Collins; New York: Doubleday, 1990.

A Going Concern. London: Collins; New York: Doubleday, 1993.

After Effects. forthcoming.

CRITICAL BIBLIOGRAPHY

Friedenthal, Martin. "The Calleshire Chronicles." *The Armchair Detective*, 20, no. 2 (1987): 138–45.
Salwak, Dale. "Interview with Catherine Aird." *Clues*, 5, no. 1 (1984): 73–90.

THERESA PERRI AMMIRATI

MARGERY ALLINGHAM (1904–1966)

Margery Allingham, one of the Golden Age mystery writers, was born May 20, 1904, in London, to Emily Jane (Hughes) and Herbert Allingham. Since both her parents were journalists, she learned about writing early; her father set her to writing when she was seven. Her formal education came at Endsleigh House School, Colchester; the Perse School, Cambridge; and the Regent Street Polytechnic, London. In 1927 she married Philip Youngman Carter, beginning a long and fruitful collaboration. Carter finished the last of her novels, *Cargo of Eagles*, and wrote two Campion books, *Mr. Cam-*

pion's Farthing and *Mr. Campion's Quarry*, from ideas Allingham had left in notes. In addition to the Campion series, she wrote a number of short stories, several other novels, three under the pseudonym of Maxwell March, and numerous reviews and articles. She died of cancer on June 30, 1966.

Allingham's non-Campion novels, with the exception of *Black Plumes*, are undistinguished. Her chief claim to fame and her best work, the Campion series, began with the appearance of Albert Campion as a major supporting character in *The Crime at Black Dudley*. The series spans his long career, allowing Allingham to develop her character from his first appearance as a flippant adventurer of mysterious antecedents into a mature detective whose aristocratic connections need not be hidden. The series includes both thrillers and detective stories, with several novels partaking of both types. The novels are third-person narratives, with the exception of *The Case of the Late Pig*. Generally, the point of view is Campion's, but use of the third person allows Allingham to move away from her protagonist at times, a technique that is especially valuable in *The Tiger in the Smoke*, *The Beckoning Lady*, and *The Mind Readers*.

Over the course of the series, Campion falls in love and is rejected, marries, begets a son, and ages. Allingham provides him with a growing family: a formidable mother and a mysterious brother, neither of whom ever appears; a fashion-designer sister; two cleric uncles; his talented aircraft-designer wife, the Lady Amanda Fitton; his son, Rupert; and most notably, his valet and jack-of-all-trades, Maggersfontein Lugg. Campion's associations with official law officers include close relationships with three Scotland Yard inspectors, Yeo (briefly), Oates, and the charismatic Charlie Luke who, besides Campion, is the most fully developed and important character in the series. Over the course of the series there is a notable change in Campion's connection with his own family. In the early novels it is important that he is the scapegrace son of aristocracy, probably a ducal family. Later, especially in the postwar novels, the Wimseyesque connection with the aristocratic relatives becomes less important and Campion's association with his "middle-class" relatives, such as Canon Avril and younger, professional nephews and nieces, is emphasized instead.

In addition to the cast of continuing characters, Allingham develops a series of delightful eccentrics in the novels. These eccentrics, who are both city- and country-bred, male and female, young and old, are one of the strongest aspects of the series. It is evident from *The Oaken Heart*, her book-length personal essay about village life during World War II, that many of the rural eccentrics in Allingham's novels drew inspiration from real life. The elderly female characters are of special interest. They range from titled ladies to a retired dance hall performer; from the gentle but strong, through the iron-willed, to the slightly ditzy but well-intentioned. Campion's ability to work with and through these characters is one of his strongest features as a puzzle solver, for often, the eccentrics hold the key to the mystery. A number of the villains are also eccentric, and their very eccentricity adds to their villainy, most notably in the case of the supremely evil Jack Havoc of *The Tiger in the Smoke*. Opposite Havoc is Campion's equally eccentric cleric uncle, the remarkably wise and innocent Canon Avril, whose presence brings an allegorical quality to *The Tiger in the Smoke* and *The Mind Readers*.

Allingham also displays a keen sense of scene, adeptly using both urban and rural settings to enhance the action of her novels. London is the setting for nearly half the novels, either in total or in part, and she makes good use of the "villages" of this "city of villages." *More Work for the Undertaker* explores a lower-class neighborhood that has fallen from better times. *Death of a Ghost* uses the artsy world of Little Venice. *The Fashion in Shrouds* and *Coroner's Pidgin* are set in the chic world of the club scene, both before and during World War II. London becomes more than a setting, serving almost as a character in *The Tiger in the Smoke*. In this novel, which is generally considered Allingham's best, the city takes on a life of its own, shrouded in fog (the smoke of the title) in which the characters play out their roles. The pastoral world of rural England is another favorite setting. Several of the early Campion novels, *Mystery Mile*, *Look to the Lady*, and *Sweet Danger* in particular, are set in pastoral villages inhabited by somewhat shabby gentry and their rustic loyal retainers. Allingham's personal favorite of the series, *The Beckoning Lady* (a postwar novel) is the most pastoral of the later works. Coming soon after the dark and brooding *Tiger*, it is a charming romp in a world seemingly untouched by the ravages visited upon London during the blitz, although the ominous presence of the Inland Revenue in the background belies an ideal world.

World War II and its aftermath are very important in the Campion series. None of the novels deals directly with the war, but several employ it as background. *The Fashion in Shrouds*, written in 1938, alludes to the trouble brewing in Europe, both through the importance of aircraft engineering and through the club scene, which has Isherwood-like overtones. This club scene is used again in *Coroner's Pidgin*, in which Campion has returned from a mysterious and lengthy mission in Europe toward the end of the war. He finds a ravaged London, which he hardly recognizes, where Lugg is fondly nurturing a pig. London's destruction also appears in *Traitor's Purse*. Only the beginnings of the bombing are evident, but they give a sense of foreboding to this novel, which is concerned with German espionage. In *The Tiger in the Smoke* and *The China Governess*, Allingham deals with the human side of the war's aftermath, with people who have, in various ways, been displaced physically and emotionally by the war. These late novels demonstrate Allingham's development from a writer of thrillers to a novelist capable of serious consideration of the human dimension of the characters she creates.

Allingham's novels need not be read in sequence, although it is interesting to see how she develops Campion over nearly forty years and a score of novels. Jumping into some of the later novels can be confusing because of established identities and relationships. *The Tiger in the Smoke*, *The Beckoning Lady*, and *The Fashion in Shrouds* are perhaps the novels that best stand alone. Conversely, *Traitor's Purse* gains depth when read in conjunction with *The Oaken Heart*.

Readers who like Allingham will also appreciate contemporary novelists such as Amanda Cross, Ruth Rendell, and Elizabeth George, as well as other Golden Age writers like Dorothy L. Sayers, Josephine Tey, Ngaio Marsh, and Agatha Christie.

MYSTERY FICTION

Writing as Margery Allingham

The White Cottage Mystery. London: Jarrolds, 1928; New York: Penguin, 1978.
Black Plumes. London: Heinemann, 1940; New York: Penguin, 1950.
Wanted: Someone Innocent. London: Pony Books, 1946.
Deadly Duo. New York: Doubleday, 1949; as *Take Two at Bedtime*. London: World's Work, 1950.
No Love Lost. London: World's Work, New York: Doubleday, 1954.

Albert Campion Series

The Crime at Black Dudley. London: Jarrolds, 1929; as *The Black Dudley Murder*. New York: Doubleday, 1930.

Mystery Mile. London: Jarrolds; New York: Doubleday, 1930.

Look to the Lady. London: Jarrolds, 1931; as *The Gyrth Chalice Mystery*. New York: Doubleday, 1931.

Police at the Funeral. London: Heinemann, 1931; New York: Doubleday, 1932.

Sweet Danger. London: Heinemann, 1933; as *Kingdom of Death*. New York: Doubleday, 1933; as *The Fear Sign*. New York: MacFadden, 1961.

Death of a Ghost. London: Heinemann; New York: Doubleday, 1934.

Flowers for the Judge. London: Heinemann; New York: Doubleday, 1936; as *Legacy in Blood*. New York: Mercury 1949.

Dancers in Mourning. London: Heinemann; New York: Doubleday, 1937; as *Who Killed Chloe?* New York: Avon, 1943.

The Case of the Late Pig. London: Hodder and Stoughton, 1937.

Mr. Campion: Criminologist. New York: Doubleday, 1937.

The Fashion in Shrouds. London: Heinemann; New York: Doubleday, 1938.

Mr. Campion and Others. London: Heinemann, 1939. Rev. ed. New York: Penguin, 1950.

Traitor's Purse. London: Heinemann; New York: Doubleday, 1941; as *The Sabotage Murder Mystery*. New York: Avon, 1932.

Coroner's Pidgin. London: Heinemann, 1945; as *Pearls before Swine*. New York: Doubleday, 1945.

The Case Book of Mr. Campion. London: Spivak, 1947.

More Work for the Undertaker. London: Heinemann, 1948; New York: Doubleday, 1949.

The Tiger in the Smoke. London: Chatto and Windus; New York: Doubleday, 1952.

The Beckoning Lady. London: Chatto and Windus, 1955; as *The Estate of the Beckoning Lady*. New York: Doubleday, 1955.

Hide My Eyes. London: Chatto and Windus, 1958; New York: Penguin, 1960; as *Tether's End*. New York: Doubleday, 1958; as *Ten Were Missing*. New York: Dell, 1961.

The China Governess. New York: Doubleday, 1962; London: Chatto and Windus, 1963.

The Mind Readers. New York: Morrow; London: Chatto and Windus, 1965.

Cargo of Eagles. London: Chatto and Windus; New York: Morrow, 1968.

The Allingham Casebook. London: Chatto and Windus; New York: Morrow, 1969.

The Allingham Minibus. London: Chatto and Windus; New York: Morrow, 1973.

Writing as Maxwell March

Other Man's Danger. London: Collins, 1933; as *The Man of Dangerous Secrets*. New York: Doubleday, 1933.
Rogues' Holiday. London: Collins, 1933; New York: Doubleday, 1935.
The Shadow in the House: London: Collins; New York: Doubleday, 1936.

CRITICAL BIBLIOGRAPHY

Cox, J. Randolph. "Miss Allingham's Knight: The Saga of Albert Campion." *The Armchair Detective*, 15 (1982): 86–91.
Gaskill, Rex W. "Margery Allingham." In *And Then There Were Nine: More Women of Mystery*, ed. Jane S. Bakerman. Bowling Green, Ohio: Popular Press, 1985, pp. 30–57.
Huey, Talbott W. "Mr. Campion and the Survival of the Great Detective." *Clues: A Journal of Detection*, 3 (1982): 90–104.
Martin, Richard. *Ink in Her Blood: The Life and Crime Fiction of Margery Allingham*. Ann Arbor, Mich.: UMI, 1988.
Pike, B. A. *Campion's Career: A Study of the Novels of Margery Allingham*. Bowling Green, Ohio: Popular Press, 1987.

PAULA M. WOODS

CHARLOTTE ARMSTRONG (1905–1969)

Charlotte Armstrong was born May 2, 1905, in the small mining town of Vulcan, Michigan. She attended the University of Wisconsin until transferring to Barnard College, because, she said, "I knew that I must get to New York, somehow." She then became "an avid New Yorker, haunting the Village and seeing all the plays on Broadway." After graduating, she went to work for the *New York Times*, where she met Jack Lewi. They married in January 1928, and she had her first child in December of that year.

Her first three novels featured amateur detective MacDougal Duff, a likable history professor. However, Duff is less interesting and developed than Armstrong's other characters. Armstrong centers on, but also disposes of, Duff in the third novel by making him the hero and bundling him off into a happily ever after ending.

Her fourth novel, and her first suspense work, *The Unsuspected*, is a tale of a highly respected, charismatic philanthropist who secretly schemes to get his ward's fortune. When this novel was bought for the movies, the Lewi family moved to California and Armstrong wrote the screenplay, which starred Claude Raines. Her sixth novel, *Mischief*, also became a movie under the title *Don't Bother to Knock*, starring Anne Bancroft, Richard Widmark, and Marilyn Monroe (in her first major role, as the psychopathic babysitter).

These early novels show trends that appear in the rest of her work. Armstrong was always stretching the boundaries and conventions of the genre. For example, the reader often learns both the identity and motivation of the villain right at the beginning. The suspense lies not in wondering "who dunit" but in watching the characters trying to solve a puzzle while in the background a clock ticks away inexorably toward some catastrophe. *The Chocolate Cobweb* has a most unlikely villain. As soon as the basic exposition is laid out, the third-person narrator goes inside the villain's mind to discover that she killed the artist's first wife and now plans to do in his son.

Armstrong's characters are quintessentially average Americans, as familiar as a next-door neighbor. Most protagonists are women, and the stories are usually told from their perspectives. Armstrong's heroines are average (white) women. Sometimes they are pretty, even beautiful, but more often they are ordinary in appearance and intelligence and traditional in occupation. Often they are young and innocent. What they all have are absolute integrity and the willingness to persevere against all opposition.

The villains are also familiar, seemingly ordinary: loving relatives, trusted friends, or respected public figures. Underneath this type of placid exterior, however, lies a terrifying, black pit of evil and depravity. The villains are almost uniformly influential and well-to-do (sometimes rich). They are more articulate and credible than the heroines, who are usually relatively friendless and powerless. Thus, in addition to struggling with the villains, protagonists often must also struggle against an indifferent, insensitive, or unresponsive system, which is typically allied with the villain. For example, in *The Turret Room*, two innocents are pitted against a wealthy and influential family. Harold, an ex-husband of the family's (evil) "golden girl," and Edith, a poor relative, struggle to get the police to believe them despite the wealthy family's attempts to blame them.

Armstrong's villains are often aided and abetted by passively evil people who, for their own selfish or greedy motivations, are willing to let matters take their course, even at times helping things along, and always justify their own motives.

Offsetting this cluster of primary and secondary villains and an establishment arrayed against the protagonists are the kind, ethical "passing strangers"—ordinary people willing to get involved. Often these chance-met strangers play crucial roles. One of Armstrong's most charming stories, *A Dram of Poison*, has an unlikely pair of protagonists: Mr. Gibson, a middle-aged bachelor who marries Rosemary, the awkward, thirty-two-year-old daughter of a dead friend. Their tentative steps toward love and happiness are so destroyed by his sister's pompous meddling that Gibson decides to commit suicide, stealing—and then losing—a bottle of poison. The rest of the book details the comical chase to find the poison before it kills someone else. In the course of the day, Gibson and Rosemary pick up various well-wishers: a bus driver, a Parent-Teacher Association (PTA) president, a painter, and a nurse. The unlikely crew becomes friends and partisans of Gibson and Rosemary.

Children often appear in Armstrong's novels as well-rounded characters acting with courage and resourcefulness. Armstrong was proud to be both a successful mother and a novelist, and in the preface to *The Innocent Flower* she said that the characters of three children in the story were drawn from those of her own children.

Although Armstrong's novels have had both critical and commercial success, winning many Edgar awards, she is less well known than some writers, perhaps partly because she chose not to develop a series. Moreover, because her work stretches the genre's limits, it sometimes eludes labels. Although Armstrong used Gothic elements (sparingly) in her novels, she was likely to use them ironically, and nothing could be less Gothic than her mood and tone.

Like Alfred Hitchcock, she delighted in seeing ordinary people transcend their limitations when placed in jeopardy, and like science-fiction writer Ray Bradbury, she painted a cozy, homey picture of ordinary people and places only then to raise the hair on the back of the reader's neck by lifting the mask and showing the alien hiding underneath. Readers who like this type of mystery might be interested in the annual Malice Domestic™ convention.

MYSTERY FICTION

Writing as Charlotte Armstrong

The Unsuspected. New York: Coward-McCann, 1946; London: Harrap, 1947.

The Chocolate Cobweb. New York: Coward-McCann, 1948; London: Davies, 1952.

Mischief. New York: Coward-McCann, 1950; London: Davies, 1951.

The Black-Eyed Stranger. New York: Coward-McCann, 1951; London: Davies, 1952.

The Better to Eat You. New York: Coward-McCann; London: Davies, 1954; as *Murder's Nest.* New York: Pocket Books, 1955.

The Dream Walker. New York: Coward-McCann; London: Davies, 1955; as *Alibi for Murder.* New York: Pocket Books, 1956.

A Dram of Poison. New York: Coward-McCann; London: Davies, 1956.

The Albatross. New York: Coward-McCann, 1957.

Duo: The Girl with a Secret/Incident at a Corner. New York: Coward-McCann, 1959; London: Davies, 1960.

The Seventeen Widows of Sans Souci. New York: Coward-McCann; London: Davies, 1959.

Something Blue. New York: Ace, 1962.

Then Came Two Women. New York: Ace, 1962.

A Little Less than Kind. New York: Coward-McCann, 1963; London: Collins, 1964.

The Mark of the Hand. New York: Ace, 1963.

The One-Faced Girl. New York: Ace, 1963.

Who's Been Sitting in My Chair? New York: Ace, 1963.

The Witch's House. New York: Coward-McCann, 1963; London: Collins, 1964.

The Turret Room. New York: Coward-McCann, 1965; London: Collins, 1965.

Dream of Fair Woman. New York: Coward-McCann; London: Collins, 1966.

I See You. New York: Coward-McCann, 1966.

The Gift Shop. New York: Coward-McCann; London: Collins, 1967.

Lemon in the Basket. New York: Coward-McCann, 1967; London: Collins, 1968.

The Balloon Man. New York: Coward-McCann; London: Collins, 1968.

Seven Seats to the Moon. New York: Coward-McCann; London: Collins, 1969.

The Protégé. New York: Coward-McCann; London: Collins, 1970.

MacDougal Duff Series

Lay On, MacDuff! New York: Coward-McCann, 1942; London: Gifford, 1943.

The Case of the Weird Sisters. New York: Coward-McCann; London: Gifford, 1943.

The Innocent Flower. New York: Coward-McCann, 1945; as *Death Filled the Glass.* London: Cherry Tree Books, 1945.

Writing as Jo Valentine

Catch-As-Catch-Can. New York: Coward-McCann, 1952; London: Davies, 1953; as *Walk Out on Death.* New York: Pocket Books, 1954.
The Trouble in Thor. New York, Coward McCann; London: Davies, 1953; as *And Sometimes Death.* New York: Pocket Books, 1955.

CRITICAL BIBLIOGRAPHY

Cleveland, Carol. "Armstrong, Charlotte." In *Twentieth Century Crime and Mystery Writers*, ed. Lesley Henderson. 3rd ed. Chicago: St. James, 1991, pp. 30–31.

MYRA HUNTER JONES

MARGOT ARNOLD (1925–   )

Margot Arnold was born Petronelle Cook in Devon, England, on May 16, 1925. She studied archaeology at Oxford, where she earned an honors B.A. (1946) and an honors M.A. (1950), but her promising professional career (she once worked with the famous husband-and-wife team of Louis and Mary Leakey) was cut short in 1950 when she married a young American teacher who soon after joined the diplomatic service. Because of her husband's frequent assignments overseas, she spent extended periods in Africa, Europe, and the Middle East, locations she has used as settings in her mysteries and thrillers. Her position as a diplomat's wife and mother of three young children precluded her pursuing a career, and in the mid-1950s, while living in South Africa, Arnold began writing short stories for amusement. Her first story, a tale of horror, appeared in the *London Mystery Magazine*. Her preferred genre in her early years as a writer was the escapist romance, in part because her manuscripts were subject to the scrutiny and veto of the U.S. State Department. These pressures led to her holding the manuscript of her first novel, *The Officer's Woman*, for seven years until a friend, having read it for amusement while visiting Arnold in Paris, took it to England and arranged for its publication. It was published under a pseudonym, as have been all her subsequent works of fiction, to protect her husband's career. She chose the pseudonym Margot Arnold as a combination of her middle name (Margaret) and the memory of Benedict Arnold, a distant ancestor of her husband (whom she has since divorced). A number of successful historical romances followed the publication of *The Officer's Woman*. In 1979, after the publication of a book on Marie the

Voodoo Queen of New Orleans, her agent suggested a series of murder mysteries as a possible venture, and Arnold, who was an enthusiastic reader of detective fiction, began work on the Penny Spring and Sir Toby Glendower series.

Arnold's reputation as a mystery writer rests on the Penny Spring/Toby Glendower stories, eleven of which have been published thus far. From the first, *Exit Actors, Dying* to her latest, the recently published *Dirge for a Dorset Druid*, Arnold has used her archeological background and knowledge of history and anthropology as the backbone of the series. The novels are lightly sprinkled with arcane facts about civilizations both ancient and modern and interesting insights into cultures as diverse as those of ancient Greece, Rome, England, and Hawaii.

The charm of the series, however, lies in the developing relationship between the two protagonists, fellow Oxford tutors who encounter a series of murders in distant spots around the world. The characters are taken from life and are based on two of Arnold's tutors at Oxford who were, as the author claims, exactly as she has depicted them in the books (he is totally neurotic and a bit of a misogynist, while she is a small, plain, spinsterish woman). The two tutors had a very close relationship, devoid of any romantic notions but more intense than many marriages, which Arnold recreated in the relationship of their fictional counterparts. Most of the dialogue in the series, for example, is based on Arnold's projections of what the old tutors would have said to each other in similar circumstances.

The Spring/Glendower tales are classic mysteries following very similar narrative patterns: one or the other of the detective twosome is reluctantly drawn into the investigation of a murder in an exotic setting and summons the other to his or her assistance. As murder follows upon murder, they pursue an investigation in which archeological and anthropological data play a prominent role until, as they near a resolution, one of them is lured into a deadly trap from which he or she must be rescued by the other. As the series has progressed, the younger generation (represented by Peggy's son Alexander and his young wife, Sonya, who is also Toby's recently discovered Russian ballerina daughter) have started to play prominent roles in the investigations. Arnold had recently concluded that her aging sleuths need help with the legwork and can no longer credibly sustain the punishment and injuries inflicted on them in earlier works.

The series is also notable for its subtle humor, which is the result of slightly improbable settings and circumstances, somewhat caricaturesque characters, and a veiled element of parody in the use of the traditional elements of the genre. The series is best read in the order of its publication, as its success is somewhat dependent on the reader's familiarity with the characters as their relationships develop from one novel to the next.

Readers who enjoy the Penny Spring/Toby Glendower series may also appreciate Agatha Christie's "partners-in-crime" series featuring Tommy and Tuppence Beresford, as well as Christie's archaeological mysteries. Arnold, now a naturalized American citizen living in Bethlehem, Pennsylvania, is planning a new series featuring a new set of partners in detection.

MYSTERY FICTION

Penny Spring and Sir Toby Glendower Series

Exit Actors, Dying. New York: Playboy Press Paperbacks, 1979.

The Cape Cod Caper. New York: Playboy Press Paperbacks, 1980; Bath, England: Chivers Press, 1982.

Zadok's Treasure. New York: Playboy Press Paperbacks, 1980; Bath, England: Chivers Press, 1982.

Death of a Voodoo Doll. New York: Playboy Press Paperbacks, 1982.

Death on the Dragon's Tongue. New York: Playboy Press Paperbacks, 1982.

Lament for a Lady Laird. New York: Playboy Press Paperbacks, 1982.

The Menehune Murders. Woodstock, Vt.: Countryman Press, 1989.

Toby's Folly. Woodstock, Vt.: Countryman Press, 1990.

The Catacomb Conspiracy. Woodstock, Vt.: Countryman Press, 1991.

The Cape Cod Conundrum. Woodstock, Vt.: Countryman Press, 1992.

Dirge for a Dorset Druid. Woodstock, Vt.: Foul Play Press, 1993.

CRITICAL BIBLIOGRAPHY

Nichols, Victoria, and Susan Thompson. "Dr. Penelope Spring and Sir Tobias Glendower." In *Silk Stalkings.* Berkeley, Calif.: Black Lizard, 1988, pp. 5–6.

LIZABETH PARAVISINI-GEBERT

❦ B ❦

MARIAN BABSON (?–   )

Marian Babson was born in New England, but since 1960 she has lived as a transplanted American in London. She is the author of over thirty mystery novels, most of which feature a cozy British setting. For ten years, Babson served as the secretary of the British Crime Writers Association, and her novel *The Cruise of a Deathtime* (1983) won the first Poisoned Chalice Award, which is given for a mystery involving the greatest number of bizarre murders.

Babson's first mystery, *Cover-Up Story* (1971), introduced the public relations team of Perkins and Tate, amateur detectives she would eventually feature in three other novels. This first work, about the representation of an American hillbilly singing group on tour in England, introduced Babson's humorous take on the typical British cozy novel. The other Perkins and Tate novels, *Murder on Show*, *In the Teeth of Adversity*, and *Tourists Are for Trapping*, highlight humorous antics and conversation over complex plotting and suspense. This emphasis on humor is also repeated in one of Babson's best novels, *Reel Murder*, about two aging movie stars reunited for a revival of their best films. The behind-the-screen rivalry and evocation of the old world of movies are superbly and humorously handled by Babson. She employs the knack for parodying a certain industry and its vain workers again in *Death in Fashion*, where a small fashion house is beset by artistic espionage and murder.

Marian Babson channels the creativity of her characters into bizarre plots featuring multiple murders. In several of her novels, Babson pokes fun at classic detective fiction by choosing extreme settings and odd means of murder. In *The Twelve Deaths of Christmas*, London falls prey to a yuletide killer who changes weapons with each killing. One victim even dies when fake snow is sprayed into his nose and mouth. Another Babson highlight is *The Cruise of a Deathtime*, in which the crew and guests are alternately killed in ever-increasing groups. For example, first, three crew members playing cards are killed, and then a group of four passengers. By the end of the novel, readers might wonder if anyone will disembark.

Babson's humorous romps highlight just one aspect of her detective writing. Since her first novel, she has also written about some more serious themes, including the conflict between American and British sensibilities. As an American living in London, Babson brings her insight and experience to this tension in several of her novels. *Death Swap*, which is narrated by an American woman who has traded her New Hampshire home for summer in England, constantly remarks not only on the geographical and climatic differences but on the social ones as well. Her English counterpart, speaking in the companion novel, *A Trail of Ashes*, does the same with the strange customs and freedoms that she finds in New England. The Perkins and Tate mystery *Tourists Are for Trapping* features a troop of touchy Americans in England for a bus tour. Much of the tension in each of these novels results from the struggles of outsiders trying to adapt to their temporary home.

Babson often swaps the humorous approach for the serious, psychological side of crime. *The Lord Mayor of Death* is a superb account of psychological drama as several characters hasten to capture a man intent on bombing a crowded London parade. *Pretty Lady* combines a vengeful wife who uses an unsuspecting, slightly retarded man to help her murder her husband. *So Soon Done For* pits the residents of an exclusive neighborhood against squatters whom they are unable to remove legally. Babson shows her skill at psychological suspense and depiction of pressing social problems in these works.

However, Babson never sacrifices the surprise revelation of the classic mystery. One of her best novels, *Murder Sails at Midnight*, shows Babson in top form: it tells the story of an unidentified paid assassin following an unidentified victim on an Atlantic passage of the *Beatrice Cenci*, a luxury Italian cruise ship. Babson nimbly keeps the victim, perpetrator, and motive hidden until the climactic ending scene when the ship passes a sister cruiser, which is a cause for a celebration of bells, whistles, and fireworks. The ending is surprising and believable, and in this work, Babson replicates the classic detective novel superbly.

Whether she is writing a slapstick mystery or one dealing with the mind of the murderer, Babson repeatedly presents fresh scenes and satisfying endings. She takes us into the worlds of catering, fashion, newspapers, department stores, tours, dentists, boarding houses, and cat shows, all with equal finesse concerning detail and dialogue. While Babson's novels do not involve deep character studies nor intricate plots, they are neatly crafted and entertaining mysteries. British writer Anne Morice works in the same vein as Babson, while Americans Joan Hess and Susan Dunlap provide similar humor in transatlantic settings.

MYSTERY FICTION

Pretty Lady. London: Collins, 1973; New York: Walker, 1990.

The Stalking Lamb. London: Collins, 1974; New York: Bantam, 1990.

Unfair Exchange. London: Collins, 1974; New York: Walker, 1986.

Murder Sails at Midnight. London: Collins, 1975; New York: Bantam, 1989.

There Must Be Some Mistake. London: Collins, 1975; New York: St. Martin's, 1987.

Untimely Guest. London: Collins, 1976; New York: St. Martin's. 1987.

The Lord Mayor of Death. London: Collins, 1977; New York: Walker, 1979.

Murder, Murder, Little Star. London: Collins, 1977; New York: Walker, 1980.

Tightrope for Three. London: Collins, 1978; New York: Walker, 1989.

So Soon Done For. London: Collins, 1979; New York: Walker, 1988.

The Twelve Deaths of Christmas. London: Collins, 1979; New York: Walker, 1980.

Dangerous to Know. London: Collins, 1980; New York: Walker, 1981.

Bejewelled Death. London: Collins, 1981; New York: Walker, 1982.

Queue Here for Murder. London: Collins, 1981; as *Line Up for Murder.* New York: Walker, 1981.

Death beside the Sea. London: Collins, 1982; New York: Walker, 1983.

Death Warmed Up. London: Collins, 1982; New York: Walker, 1982.

The Cruise of a Deathtime. London: Collins, 1983; New York: Walker, 1984.

A Fool for Murder. London: Collins, 1983; New York: Walker, 1984.

Death Swap. London: Collins, 1984; New York: Walker, 1985.

A Trail of Ashes. London: Collins, 1984; New York: Walker, 1985.

Death in Fashion. London: Collins, 1985; New York: Walker, 1986.

Weekend for Murder. London: Collins, 1985; as *Murder on a Mystery Tour.* New York, Walker, 1987.

Reel Murder. London: Collins, 1986; New York: St. Martin's, 1986.

Fatal Fortune. London: Collins, 1987; New York: St. Martin's, 1991.

Guilty Party. London: Collins, 1988; New York: St. Martin's, 1991.

Encore Murder. London: Collins, 1989; New York: St. Martin's, 1990.

Past Regret. London: Collins, 1990; New York: St. Martin's, 1992.

Shadows on Their Blood. New York: St. Martin's, 1993.

Nine Lives to Murder. London: Collins, 1992; New York: St. Martin's, 1994.

Perkins and Tate Series

Cover-Up Story. London: Collins, 1971; New York: St. Martin's, 1988.

Murder on Show. London: Collins, 1972; as *Murder at the Cat Show.* New York: St. Martin's, 1989.

Tourists Are for Trapping. London: Collins; New York: St. Martin's, 1989.

In the Teeth of Adversity. London: Collins; New York: St. Martin's, 1990.

CRITICAL BIBLIOGRAPHY

DeMarr, Mary Jean. "Advent of Mystery: Pre-Christmas Rituals and Customs in Novels by Marian Babson, Carol Ann O'Marie and Isabelle Holland." *Clues,* 14, no. 1 (1993): 49–68.

————. "Marian Babson, American/English Mystery Novelist." *Clues*, 3, no. 1 (1989): 63–74.

THOMAS MAVOR

NIKKI BAKER (1962–   )

Born in 1962, Nikki Baker grew up in a stable, upper-middle-class, black family. After attending public high school, she earned a B.S. degree in mechanical engineering and an M.B.A. in economic and finance from large, prestigious, midwestern universities. She worked briefly as an engineer, and then settled into a career in financial services in northern California. Despite a demanding career, she has also published three mystery novels in three years. Her belief in the importance of minority voices in fiction motivates her writing.

Baker's mystery novels all feature Virginia Kelly, a young, black, lesbian financial analyst in Chicago. Each novel focuses on Virginia's personal rather than professional life. In each mystery, Virginia happens on a murder arising out of a particular social situation. A friend or acquaintance is killed and, though not a professional detective, Virginia is curious, concerned, and intelligent. She follows her instincts and, through a combination of logic and happenstance, unmasks the murderer.

The first novel, *In the Game*, is straightforward first-person narration by Virginia who, like Baker, is a successful, well-educated, young, black lesbian with a career in financial services. Although the plots are clearly fictional, Baker writes out of the experience of being black, lesbian, and female in a social, political, and economic culture that favors heterosexual white men. Virginia is politically and socially aware, but due to her family's influence, the dominant values that she is beginning to question are materialistic. The mystery in *In the Game* arises from Virginia's concern for an old friend who suspects her lover, Kelsey, of infidelity. When Kelsey turns up brutally murdered behind a women's bar, the police and the lesbian subculture suspect a hate crime. Already in possession of some inside information, Virginia doubts this too-obvious conclusion and follows her own trail, which leads her somewhere where she least expected to find the murderer.

In The Lavendar House Murder, Virginia is on vacation with her friend Naomi in Provincetown on Cape Cod. They stay at Lavendar House, a renovated Victorian guest house favored by lesbians. More structurally complex than the first, this novel consists of short chapters, and begins with an italicized and dated excerpt from a venomous note, apparently written by the murderer to the victim. Such italicized notes recur, interspersed with Virginia's first-person narration, to provide clues to the identity of Joan Di Maio's murderer. A series of flashbacks reveal details about Virginia's relationship with Joan and other vacationing lesbians, throwing suspicion on several and maintaining the suspense to the end.

Baker's third mystery, *Long Goodbyes*, takes Virginia back to her midwestern hometown for a high school reunion. Again focusing on relationships, this time including Virginia's parents, old friends, and teachers, Virginia deals with personal issues, including her family's attitudes toward her sexuality. The book begins with a first-person monologue in which a killer describes the murder of an unidentified victim. We next find Virginia engaged in an unsatisfying sexual encounter with Rosalee Paschen. When Virginia awakens to find Rosalee gone, she begins a search that unexpectedly becomes a murder investigation. As in Baker's other novels, the mystery arises out of the ordinary social activity of the protagonist, and the writer provides interesting motivation for the murderers, who are ordinary people having extreme responses to extraordinary circumstances.

Readers who enjoy the Virginia Kelly mysteries might also enjoy works by Katherine V. Forrest, Claire NcNab, Barbara Wilson, Val McDermid, and Sarah Dreher.

MYSTERY FICTION

Virginia Kelly Series

In the Game. Tallahassee, Fla.: Naiad Press, 1991.
The Lavendar House Murder. Tallahassee, Fla.: Naiad Press, 1992.
Long Goodbyes. Tallahassee, Fla.: Naiad Press, 1993.

ANN MARTIN SCOTT

LINDA BARNES (1949–   )

Linda Joyce Appelblatt Barnes was born June 6, 1949, in Detroit. She received her B.F.A. in 1971 from Boston University. She married Richard Barnes on June 7, 1970; they have one son and live in Boston, where she sets her Michael Sprague and Carlotta Carlyle series. Barnes worked as a software engineer prior to becoming a novelist. In 1986, she won the Anthony for her short story "Lucky Penny." She won an Edgar (1987) and an American Mystery Award (1988) for her first Carlotta Carlyle novel, *A Trouble with Fools*.

Barnes has created two separate series. From 1982 to 1986, she wrote the Michael Sprague series, featuring a private eye turned actor who still does favors for his friends. In 1987, she began her ongoing series featuring a female detective, Carlotta Carlyle. Both series are centered in Boston and draw Barnes into comparison with Robert B. Parker, whose Spenser series is also set there. Although the Sprague series featured Boston, Sprague traveled elsewhere for some of his cases. *Bitter Finish* shows his attempt to salvage his investments in a California vineyard operated by a former lover, while *Cities of the Dead* has him traveling with his aunt to New Orleans to clear the family cook of a murder charge.

The Michael Sprague series is bland compared to the Carlotta Carlyle titles. Michael Sprague is a rich, young detective who is obliged to work neither as a private eye nor as an actor. His wealthy connections provide a vital focus for the novels. In *Dead Heat*, they allow him to work for a wealthy politician and run in the Boston Marathon. Sprague is, however, more interested in people, as most of his cases involve helping a friend rather than serving a client.

Only two connections exist between the two series. First, Barnes creates strong-willed aunts for both Sprague and Carlyle, and second, Barnes uses her B.F.A. training to make literary allusions. *Blood Will Have Blood* (Sprague) relies heavily on a knowledge of Macbeth and the theatrical jinx associated with the play, while *A Trouble with Fools* (Carlyle) establishes a Yeatsean allusion in that money supposedly supplied to the Irish Republican Army (IRA) is really a ruse for drug running, with "Maud Gonne" or "Maudie" as the operation's name.

The Michael Sprague series appears to have been a warm-up for the Carlotta Carlyle novels, which set Barnes squarely in the hard-boiled female tradition. To some extent her character is typical of those created by Sue Grafton and Sara Paretsky, for Barnes creates a divorced female private eye who has worked in law enforcement and is independent. Like her contemporaries, Carlotta values her extended family. Carlotta is 6'1" tall with flaming red hair; she owns her own home, which she inherited from her aunt. Carlotta also works part time as a cab driver to supplement her income and to have an inconspicuous way to follow clients. She hates exercise and plays volleyball at the YMCA as her only means of staying in shape.

Barnes always features the importance of friendship and shows Sprague's concern for other people. Carlotta shows a deep commitment to both friends and clients. In *A Trouble with Fools*, Carlotta hires Roz to clean Margaret Devlin's home after thugs have destroyed it while searching for money. *Snake Tattoo* shows Carlotta committed to clearing the name of her former boss and finding a teenage runaway who had been sexually abused by her father. *Coyote* and *Snapshot* also show Carlotta working for clients who are dead or missing. Throughout the series, Carlotta finds herself helping her "little sister," Paolina, cope with her family troubles, and in *Snapshot*, Carlotta makes contact with Paolina's father, a drug lord who sends financial aid for the girl.

Barnes's focus on people also allows her to explore male-female relationships. Carlotta continuously has to decide about the nature of her relationship with Mooney, her former boss. She also finds herself attracted to what she calls the "wrong" men in *Coyote* and *Snapshot*. Barnes allows Carlotta a recurring love interest in Sam Gianelli, a mob boss's son and part owner of the cab company where she works. In *Steel Guitar*, Carlyle briefly resumes a sexual relationship with her ex-husband.

Barnes frequently places Carlyle in conflict with corruption. With Carlotta dating Gianelli, mob presence is always a factor, although Sam claims to be free of the family business. However, in *A Trouble with Fools* and *Steel Guitar*, Carlotta comes in conflict with the family's illegal drug sales and laundering of money. In *A Trouble with Fools*, Barnes has Carlotta and Mooney tricking the Federal Bureau of Investigation (FBI), which had illegally tapped her phone. *Snake Tattoo* has a conflict with a corrupt policeman, while *Coyote* depicts an Immigration official illegally selling "green cards." *Snapshot* has a hospital chief of pharmacy selling bootleg drugs to Third World countries.

Violence is not a problem for Barnes or Carlotta. In *A Trouble with Fools*, Flaherty is shot and killed, perhaps by a member of the Gaelic Brotherhood, while in *Snake Tattoo*, Carlotta herself kills Valerie Haslam's father. In *Steel Guitar*, Carlotta is implicated in the death of Dee Willis's road manager.

Barnes generates her plots from timely topics like AIDS, sexual abuse, money laundering, runaways, illegal immigration, and corruption in the music world. Her handling of plots occasionally seems superficial, but in each case, her focus is on the effect that these problems have on individuals.

The series appears to focus on a few personal characteristics of Carlotta's, like refusing to smoke because her father died of lung cancer. Carlotta also attempts to blend her ethnic background with her life-style. With an Irish father and Jewish mother, she loves bacon but celebrates Passover. Despite her own casual appearance, she has kept the Victorian house and furnishings of her Aunt Bea, which causes a client's misconception of her.

Barnes is able, however, to portray a detective who is sensitive, people-oriented, feminist, and ethnic. Although Carlotta does not preach feminism extensively, she is always battling for women who, because of their sex or race, are being abused by the system. Such is the case with Marta, Paolina's mother who, because she is poor, Hispanic, and female, cannot even repair her home in the projects. *Coyote* also focuses on women who are sexually harassed and economically abused. In *Steel Guitar*, Dee Willis cites her problems in music as due to being a woman. Barnes's women are occasionally arrogant and stubborn, but they are usually strong.

Readers of the hard-boiled tradition will find Barnes's best work in *A Trouble with Fools* and *Coyote*. Readers who like the Carlotta Carlyle series will also enjoy the works of Marcia Muller, Sue Grafton, and Sara Paretsky.

MYSTERY FICTION

Michael Sprague Series

Blood Will Have Blood. New York: Avon, 1982.

Bitter Finish. New York: St. Martin's; London: Severn House, 1993.

Cities of the Dead. New York: St. Martin's; London: Severn House, 1994.

Dead Heat. New York: St. Martin's; London: Severn House, 1994.

Carlotta Carlyle Series

A Trouble with Fools. New York: St. Martin's, 1987; London: Hodder and Stoughton, 1988.

Snake Tattoo. New York: St. Martin's; London: Hodder and Stoughton, 1989.

Coyote. New York: Delacorte, 1990; London: Hodder and Stoughton, 1991.

Steel Guitar. New York: Delacorte, 1991; London: Hodder and Stoughton, 1992.

Snapshot. New York: Delacorte, 1993.

CRITICAL BIBLIOGRAPHY

Nichols, Victoria, and Susan Thompson. "Michael Sprague." In *Silk Stalkings*. Berkeley, Calif.: Black Lizard, 1988, pp. 101–2.
Semple, Linda. "Barnes, Linda." In *Twentieth Century Crime and Mystery Writers*, ed. Lesley Henderson. 3rd ed. Chicago and London: St. James, 1991, pp. 64–65.

DONNA WALLER HARPER

J. S. BORTHWICK (1923–   )

J. S. Borthwick is the pseudonym of Jean Scott Creighton. Born in Buffalo, New York, on September 26, 1923, Creighton attended boarding school at Miss Porter's School in Farmington, Connecticut. After briefly pursuing her interest in theater, she attended the University of Buffalo (now the State University of New York at Buffalo), where she enrolled in a premedical program. Her studies were interrupted by World War II, during which she undertook nursing duties at an army hospital. Marriage and the births of her three children followed the completion of her B.A., but she eventually returned to SUNY-Buffalo for graduate study in English. After years of summering in Maine, she has lived there full time since 1976. She volunteers in local public schools, offering writing workshops and lecturing, in addition to her writing.

The five novels in Borthwick's Sarah Deane series (a sixth is forthcoming) present a heroine who solves mysteries almost despite herself. In the first two novels, Sarah is a teacher and graduate student of English literature in Boston, whose summer vacations—birding in Texas in *The Case of the Hook-Billed Kites* and working at a museum and then an art gallery in coastal Maine in *The Down East Murders*—are interrupted by the appearance of a number of corpses. By the time of *The Student Body*, Sarah is a teaching fellow at "Bowmouth College" in Maine, continuing her graduate studies while teaching, and still finding her routines interrupted by sudden deaths.

In the first novel, Sarah begins, haltingly, a romantic relationship with a physician, Dr. Alex McKenzie. Their romance grows over the course of *The Down East Murders*, and in *The Student Body*, she and Alex are living together at the Camden Hills of Maine while Sarah teaches at Bowmouth and Alex is on the staff at Mary Starbox Memorial Hospital. Borthwick's inclusion of Dr. McKenzie as a regular character in the series enables her to introduce a range of medical information into the narrative, and Alex's appointment as a county medical examiner helps cement the forensic aspects of the plots. When the setting changes from Texas to Maine, in the middle three novels, Borthwick also introduces two more regular characters, Detective Sergeant George Fitts of the Criminal Investigation Department of the Maine State Police and Mike Laaka, a deputy sheriff. These two characters have almost diametrically opposed natures. Fitts not only appears, literally, to be an egghead but is, in fact the typical intellectual, unemotional, and detached investigator; Laaka, by contrast, embodies small-town geniality and gossip; he is knowledgeable about the ways of the local people, although more often he is focused on his next bet on a horse rather than on a murder investigation. By using this group of characters over the course of several novels, Borthwick offers the stable, cozy atmosphere associated with traditional village or rural mysteries, with their closed circle of suspects, while she keeps the freedom to change the local venue with each novel. In this tradition, Borthwick is careful to restrict the cast of characters in each of her novels. In the first novel, she focuses on visitors to a Texas wildlife sanctuary; in the second, she focuses on a small island off the coast of Maine and on those inhabitants of the adjacent coastal town with personal connections to the island. Bowmouth College faculty and students provide the cast for *The Student Body*; passengers and crew of a luxury schooner cruising the coast of Maine are suspects in *Bodies of Water*; and vacationers at the pretentious Rancho del Gato Blanco resort in Arizona come under suspicion in *Dude on Arrival*.

In seeking motives for murder, Borthwick tends to the traditional as well. Whereas the hard-boiled detective novel presumes that corruption is endemic in society—that society itself is the real culprit—Borthwick returns to the more personal motives of Golden Age mysteries, and most often to a greed that leads the villains to live false lives in order to protect their reputations and standing in the community while covertly indulging their extravagant tastes. On a more contemporary note, Borthwick's obvious interests in the outdoors appear in her novels in descriptions of sailing, skiing, and bird watching. Alex McKenzie consistently demonstrates his outdoor skills, while Sarah Deane struggles, usually comically, to stay afloat or on her skis. This enthusiasm for the outdoors translates into a more general concern for the environment. Borthwick creates casts of characters who naturally articulate a range of views on environmental questions, and her love of the outdoors and respect for nature permeate her novels without heavy-handed editorializing.

Sarah Deane is a far "softer" investigator than the hard-boiled women created recently by authors like Sara Paretsky and Sue Grafton. As an unwilling amateur, she is far more eager to shake off her reputation as a sleuth than to pursue such a line of work professionally. She is also more interested in creating a traditional home for herself than a character like Paretsky's V. I. Warshawski. While she clearly has a mind of her own, controlling, for example, the development of her relationship with Alex, she comes to be fully committed to a partnership with him; she is an equal partner, but she clearly wants—and needs—a man in her life in ways that would seem alien to Warshawski.

Although it is not necessary to read the series in order, the novels seems richer when one can watch the characters growing more complex from book to book. Those who enjoy Borthwick's novels might also appreciate the novels of Jane Langton and, of course, the classic works of Dorothy L. Sayers.

MYSTERY FICTION

Sarah Deane Series

The Case of the Hook-Billed Kites. New York: St. Martin's, 1982; London: Gollancz, 1983.

The Down East Murders. New York: St. Martin's, 1985.

The Student Body. New York: St. Martin's, 1986.

Bodies of Water. New York: St. Martin's, 1990.

Dude on Arrival. New York: St. Martin's, 1992.

The Bridled Groom. New York: St. Martin's, forthcoming.

CRITICAL BIBLIOGRAPHY

Pike, B. A. "Borthwick, J. S." In *Twentieth Century Crime and Mystery Writers*,
    ed. Lesley Henderson. 3rd ed. Chicago and London: St. James, 1991,
    pp. 110–11.

ROBERT P. WINSTON

ELISABETH BOWERS (1949–   )

Elisabeth Bowers was born October 10, 1949, in Vancouver, British Columbia; she currently lives with her partner and her daughter on the Gulf
Islands off the West Coast of British Columbia. Bowers studied at the University of British Columbia. In addition to writing, she has made a living
as a bakery worker, reporter, tree planter, teacher, library technician, and
postal worker.

Both Bowers's novels, *Ladies' Night* and *No Forwarding Address*, are
set in Vancouver, B.C., and feature Meg Lacey, a full-time detective and
divorced mother, which is an unusual combination that even Meg suggests
some readers may find "indigestible." Through first-person narration, the
reader learns much about Meg's children as Meg ponders their lives and
her part in them. Meg also has a lover, Tom; in *Ladies' Night,* the problems
in a nontraditional relationship, especially one in which the female partner
is a detective, play an important role. In the second book, less action and
narration are spent on this relationship.

The feminist point of view taken by Meg Lacey grows out of the path
she has followed in becoming a detective. In both books Meg tells the
reader how being raped forced her out of the traditional role of a suburban
housewife with a husband and two children. Meg's feminist view is also
seen through the role of lesbians; lesbian relationships appear in both cases,
and these relationships are accepted by Meg without comment.

The search motif is prominent in both Meg Lacey books. In her first
case, she is searching for missing children. Further investigation reveals a
child pornography operation that ultimately puts Meg in the middle of a
murder investigation and on opposite sides from the police. In the tradition
of the adversarial relationship between the hard-boiled detective and the
police, the police suspect Meg of withholding information. The intense police interrogation she undergoes, especially at the hands of Inspector Di-
keakos (who appears in both novels), enhances the mutual distrust between
the police and Lacey.

This police interrogation regarding withheld information is reminiscent of the experience of Cordelia Gray in P. D. James's *An Unsuitable Job for a Woman*. Also reminiscent of James's novel is the manner in which Lacey inherits her own detective agency. After Meg's partner, George, dies from alcoholism, she becomes the sole owner of a faltering detective agency.

The case under investigation in the second Meg Lacey novel, *No Forwarding Address*, again involves a search for a missing person. Vicky Fischer hires Meg to find her sister Sherry, who suddenly left her husband with her four-year-old son, Mark, in tow. Because of her concern for others, particularly those most lacking power, Meg finally agrees to look for Sherry. The suspense in this novel is intense, with Meg Lacey's danger being primarily physical rather than emotional, as it was at the end of the first book. In both novels, Meg's own search for herself and her place in the world acts as a parallel to the searches that she undertakes as a detective.

Although both books are effective and enjoyable, the writing style is perceptibly improved in the second one. In *No Forwarding Address*, Bowers gives the reader more about the Vancouver locale, similar to the way in which Sara Paretsky immerses the reader in Chicago. Another quality that connects this book in a stylistic manner with Paretsky's work is Lacey's dreaming. Similar to other women detectives, Meg Lacey has physical attributes that enable her to perform a job that is often physically demanding. Meg is trained in Aikado, and in both novels she uses this skill in the line of duty. Like Sue Grafton's Kinsey Milhone or Sara Paretsky's V. I. Warshawski, who use running to unwind and help them focus, Lacey relaxes with Aikado.

Readers who enjoy the work of Sara Paretsky or Marcia Muller should certainly enjoy Elisabeth Bowers's Meg Lacey novels.

MYSTERY FICTION

Meg Lacey Series

Ladies' Night. Seattle, Wash.: Seal Press, 1988; London: Virago, 1990.

No Forwarding Address. Seattle, Wash.: Seal Press, 1991.

CRITICAL BIBLIOGRAPHY

Bakerman, Jane S. "Elisabeth Bowers' *Ladies Night*." *Clues*, 13, no. 2 (1992): 61–70.

BONNIE C. PLUMMER

MARY ELIZABETH BRADDON (1835–1915)

Mary Elizabeth Braddon was born on October 4, 1835, and died on February 4, 1915. Braddon wrote over eighty novels, numerous short stories, and several essays throughout her career. Her father's irresponsibility and infidelity led to the separation of Braddon's parents when she was four. The difficult living circumstances of the mother and children after the parents' separation probably contributed to Braddon's negative portrait of upper-class and aristocratic families in her novels.

To support herself and her mother, Mary went on the stage, using the stage name of Mary Seyton, and acted primarily in melodramas. This experience doubtless trained her ear and talent for sensation fiction.

In 1860 Braddon quit the stage for a full-time literary career. Her first novel, *Three Times Dead*, remains ignored. However, her fourth novel, *Lady Audley's Secret*, was so popular that she earned enough money to keep herself and her mother comfortably for the rest of their lives. This novel is the prototype for the literary trend of sensation novels. *Lady Audley* created a literary scandal with its tale of a blond "angel in the house" who is actually a bigamist and twice-attempted murderer. Readers were outraged at this subversion of literary and social convention. Many writers hinted that the immorality of the novel was to be expected of someone of Braddon's "questionable morals": Braddon moved in with the publisher John Maxwell in 1861, before the publication of *Lady Audley*. They could not marry because Maxwell's wife was alive, living in a mental institution. Braddon cared for Maxwell's five children, and the couple had six children of their own (only five survived infancy). In 1874 they were married. Two of their sons became novelists, also.

Aurora Floyd involves blackmail, murder, and horse racing, and is a galloping good read. The defiant Aurora tries to manage her way out of difficulties without enlisting male aid. Although a detective is introduced, he fails to capture the criminal. Instead, one of the principal characters finds the villain. The detective's portrait is interesting because the detective comes into the country from Scotland Yard but does not collaborate with the local police. Instead, he competes with them as a free-lance detective rather than as a police employee. Braddon also gives readers a glimpse of the early incarnations of Scotland Yard.

Not all Braddon's novels contain detective work, but even her historical novels, such as *London Pride* (set in Restoration England), include attempted crimes and a trial scene. It is very hard to declare, then, which books are crime novels.

French writers such as Honoré de Balzac, Gustav Flaubert, and Emile Zola and British writers such as Wilkie Collins, Charles Dickens, and Ed-

ward Bulwer-Lytton heavily influenced Braddon's writing. *Rough Justice*
serves as an example of these influences. A young man is wrongly accused
of the murder of a poverty-stricken, but good, woman. All the evidence
points to his guilt. Braddon portrays the poverty that he and the young
woman had shared years before. Their life together and then her life alone
recalls a realism that the French writers first employed. The murderer is
caught but not given to the police after a labyrinth of circumstances is
unraveled by the falsely accused person and a detective. The murderer uses
the money he receives after the victim's death for good social causes, such
as homes for fallen women, and becomes a member of Parliament because
of his money and the marriage it enables him to make. He is idolized as
a good man. His theory is that the killing of one life is justified if it saves
so many other people. The novel is a compelling puzzle about the relentless power of money and good works in *fin de siècle* London. The complexity of the plot, its social and ethical issues, and the vivid writing are
representative of Braddon's mature style. Readers may also wish to read
*The Doctor's Wife, Dead Love Has Chains, The Lady's Mile, The Lovels
of Arden*, and *The Fatal Three*. Writers such as Charles Dickens, William
M. Thackeray, Robert Louis Stevenson, William E. Gladstone, and Henry
James were among several of her contemporary writers who admired
Braddon's work.

Readers wishing to read more sensation fiction would enjoy the novels
of Mrs. Henry Wood (especially her famous *East Lynne*), Ouida (Marie
Louise de la Ramée, an antifeminist), and Rhoda Broughton. In contrast
to Braddon, both Wood and Ouida were conservative writers who were
fearful of the rise of the working classes.

Readers should not regard this bibliography as a record of every book
written by Braddon nor, since I have not read each book, should they
regard it as listing of strictly criminous books.

MYSTERY FICTION

Writing as Mary Elizabeth Braddon

Three Times Dead. London: W. & M. Clark; Beverley, England: Empson, 1860.
    Repr. 1861; As *Trail of the Serpent* [with U.S. subtitle]. London: Ward,
    1861. In United States with subtitle, *or the Secret of the Heath*. New York:
    Dick, 1864.
Lady Audley's Secret. London: Tinsley, 1862; New York: Dick, 1863. London and
    New York: Dover, 1974. Oxford: Oxford University Press, World Classics,
    1987.
The Lady Lisle. London: Ward, Lock, and Tyler, 1862; New York: Dick, 1863.
Aurora Floyd. London: Tinsley, 1863; New York: Harper, 1863. London: Virago
    Press, 1984.

Captain of the Vulture. London: Ward, Lock, and Tyler, 1863; as *Darrell Markham; or, The Captain of the Vulture*. New York: Dick, 1863.

Eleanor's Victory. London: Tinsley, 1863; New York: Harper, 1863.

John Marchmont's Legacy. London: Tinsley, 1863; New York: Harper, 1863.

The Doctor's Wife. London: Maxwell, 1864; New York: Dick, 1864.

Henry Dunbar; the Story of an Outcast. London: Maxwell, 1864; New York: Dick, 186[?].

Only a Clod. London: Maxwell, 1865; New York: Dick, 1865.

Sir Jasper's Tenant. London: Maxwell, 1865; New York: Dick, 1865.

The Lady's Mile. London: Ward, Lock, and Tyler, 1866; New York: Dick, 1878.

Birds of Prey. London: Ward, Lock, and Tyler, 1867; New York: Harper, 1867.

Rupert Godwin. London: Ward, Lock, and Tyler, 1867; New York: Dick, 1867.

Charlotte's Inheritance. London: Ward, Lock, and Tyler, 1868; New York: Harper, 1868.

Dead Sea Fruit. London: Ward, Lock, and Tyler, 1868; New York: Harper, 1868.

Run to Earth. London: Ward, Lock, and Tyler, 1868.

Fenton's Quest. London: Ward, Lock, and Tyler, 1871; New York: Harper, 1871.

The Lovels of Arden. London: Maxwell, 1871; New York: Harper, 1872.

Robert Ainsleigh. London: Maxwell, 1872; as *Bound to John Company; or, The Adventures and Misadventures of Robert Ainsleigh*. New York: Harper, 187[?].

To the Bitter End. London: Maxwell, 1872; New York: Harper, 1875.

Lucius Davoreen; or, Publicans and Sinners. London: Maxwell, 1873; as *Publicans and Sinners; or, Lucius Davoreen*. New York: Harper, 1874.

Strangers and Pilgrims. London: Maxwell, 1873; New York: Harper, 1873.

Lost for Love. London: Chatto and Windus, 1874; New York: Harper, 1875.

Taken at the Flood. London: Maxwell, 1874; New York: Harper, 1874.

Hostages to Fortune. London: Maxwell, 1875; New York: Harper, 1875.

A Strange World. London: Maxwell, 1875; New York: Harper, 1875.

Dead Men's Shoes. London: Maxwell, 1876; New York: Harper, 1876.

The Black Band; or, the Mysteries of Midnight. London: Vickers, 1877; New York: DeWitt, 1869.

Milly Darrell and Other Tales. London: Maxwell, 1873. London: Carleton, 1877; as *Meeting Her Fate*. London: Carleton, 1881.

Weavers and Weft and Other Tales. London: Maxwell, 1877; New York: Harper, 1877.

An Open Verdict. London: Maxwell, 1878; New York: Harper, 1878.

The Cloven Foot. London: Maxwell (J & R), 1879; New York: Harper, 1879.

Vixen. London: Maxwell (J & R), 1879; New York: Harper, 1879.

Just as I Am. London: Maxwell (J & R), 1880; New York: Harper, 1880.

The Story of Barbara. London: Maxwell (J & R), 1880; as *Barbara; or, Splendid Misery*. New York: Harper, 1880.

Asphodel. London: Maxwell (J & R), 1881; New York: Harper, 1881.

Flower and Weed (And Other Stories). New York: Harper, 1882; London: Maxwell, 1884.

Mount Royal. London: Maxwell (J & R), 1882; New York: Harper, 1882.

The Golden Calf. London: Maxwell (J & R), 1883; New York: Lovell, 1883.

Phantom Fortune. London: Maxwell (J & R), 1883; New York: Harper, 1883.

Under the Red Flag. (And Other Stories). New York: Harper, 1883; London: Maxwell, 1886.
Wyllard's Weird. London: Maxwell (J & R), 1885; New York: Harper, 1885.
Mohawks. London: Maxwell (J & R), 1886; New York: Harper, 1886.
One Thing Needful, and Cut by the County. London: Maxwell (J & R), 1886; New York: Harper, 1885. as *Penalty of Fate; or, The One Thing Needful*. [New York?]: Illustrated Publishing, 1886.
Like and Unlike. London: Spencer Blackett, 1887; New York: Munro, 1887.
The Fatal Three. London: Simpkin, Marshall, 1888; New York: Harper, 1888.
The Day Will Come. London: Simpkin, Marshall, 1889; New York: Harper, 1889.
One Life, One Love. London: Simpkin, Marshall, 1890.
Gerard; or, The World, the Flesh, and the Devil. London: Simpkin, Marshall, 1891.
The Venetians. London: Simpkin, Marshall, 1892; New York: Harper, 1892.
All along the River. London: Simpkin, Marshall, 1893; New York: Cassell, 1893.
Thou Art the Man. London: Simpkin, Marshall, 1894.
Sons of Fire. London: Simpkin, Marshall, 1895.
Rough Justice. London: Simpkin, Marshall, 1898.
His Darling Sin. London: Simpkin, Marshall, 1899.
The Infidel. London: Simpkin, Marshall, 1900; New York: Harper, 1900.
The Conflict. London: Simpkin, Marshall, 1903.
A Lost Eden. London: Hutchinson, 1904.
The Rose of Life. London: Hutchinson, 1905; New York: Brentano's, 1905.
The White House. London: Hurst and Blackett, 1906.
Dead Love Has Chains. London: Hurst and Blackett, 1907.
Her Convict. London: Hurst and Blackett, 1907.
During Her Majesty's Pleasure. London: Hurst and Blackett, 1908.
Our Adversary. London: Hutchinson, 1909.
Beyond These Voices. London: Hutchinson, 1910.
The Green Curtain. London: Hutchinson, 1911.
Miranda. London: Hutchinson, 1913.
Mary. London: Hutchinson, 1916.

Writing as Babington White

Circe. London: Ward, Lock, and Tyler, 1867.
Ralph the Bailiff & c. London: Ward, Lock, and Tyler, 1867; as *Dudley Carleon*. New York: Dick, 1864.

CRITICAL BIBLIOGRAPHY

Hughes, Winifred. *The Maniac in the Cellar: Sensation Novels of the 1860s*. Princeton, N.J.: Princeton University Press, 1980.
Wolff, Robert Lee. *Sensational Victorian: The Life and Fiction of Mary Elizabeth Braddon*. New York: Garland, 1979.

CATHERINE ELIZABETH HOYSER

CHRISTIANNA BRAND (1907–1988)

Brand is the best-known pseudonym of Mary Christianna Lewis, née Milne. The daughter of a rubber planter, Brand was born in Malaya on December 7, 1907, and spent her early childhood in India. She was educated in a Franciscan convent in England and worked as a governess, nightclub dancer, secretary, model, dress packer, and salesperson before marrying Roland Lewis, a doctor, in 1939. At the time of her death on March 11, 1988, Brand had authored seventeen mystery novels and three anthologies of short stories. She served as chair of the Crime Writers Association in 1972–73 and was honored twice for her short fiction by the Mystery Writers of America.

Called "the best puzzle-maker of her generation of crime writers" by Robert Barnard, Brand published in a number of subgenres, but her fame rests primarily on her series of classical-style novels featuring Inspector Cockrill of rural Kent. Though he is a policeman who draws on the resources of the constabulary, Cockrill fits more squarely in the tradition of the eccentric individual investigator; like his fictional precursor Hercule Poirot, Cockrill's humorous mannerisms, oddball tastes, and testy vanity belie his perceptivity and acumen.

From his introduction in *Heads You Lose* to his final appearance in *Tour de Force*, Brand's sleuth brings his ordered intellect and moral insight to bear on the pathologies that give rise to crime. Though not infallible, Cockrill is portrayed as a man of psychic stability and ethical discernment in a world of seething passions gone awry. Brand is chiefly concerned with demonstrating the lethal effects of obsession, the theme that governs her mystery milieu.

Cockrill's skills are put to the test in the six novels in which he is featured. *Heads You Lose* is set in a country village where two grisly murders (both of women) have been committed. Cockrill must maneuver his way through a morass of deceptions and covert liaisons to single out the murderer, and in so doing, he exposes the violent consequences of emotional inhibition and misguided chivalry.

Green for Danger, which is arguably Brand's best novel and certainly her most celebrated, is set in a World War II hospital ward, a domain Brand knew well from her experience as a doctor's wife. In the novel, wartime tensions exacerbate the raw nerves caused by conflicting romantic entanglements among the medical staff, and Cockrill is called in to ferret out a murder from among them. Here, Brand explores the dark undercurrents of filial, as well as sexual, love, and again shows the damaging effects of male prerogative and restrictive social attitudes on women.

Crime passionel is reprised in *The Crooked Wreath, Death of Jezebel,* and *London Particular*. *Jezebel* may be Brand's least successful Cockrill novel owing to an improbable *modus operandi* and a rather tedious resolution. *Particular* is more successful, however. It features another of her compulsive culprits, whose stifled desires and Victorian prudery have pushed him over the homicidal edge. Again, Brand offers astute commentary on the dangers of psychic repression and the misogynist subtext of patriarchal culture.

The final Cockrill novel, *Tour de Force*, is the lightest and most humorous of the series; *Tour* is also among the most cleverly plotted, and its poignant resolution highlights Cockrill's compassionate sensibility.

Brand wrote other classical novels of detection, but later in her career she turned to Gothic thrillers where she revisited the subject of emotional mania in new story structures.

First-time readers might begin with *Green for Danger*; there is no need to read the Cockrill stories in chronological order. *Cat and Mouse* is also a compelling introduction to the author. Brand's stories of traditional detection will appeal to admirers of Agatha Christie, Margery Allingham, and Ngaio Marsh, while her Gothic mysteries invite comparisons with Phyllis A. Whitney and Mary Higgins Clark. Brand's exploration of psychological themes and incipient treatment of feminist issues give her fiction a contemporary appeal, and her stylistic elegance continues to gratify audiences.

MYSTERY FICTION

Writing as Christianna Brand

Cat and Mouse. London: Michael Joseph; New York: Knopf, 1950.

The Three-Cornered Halo. London: Michael Joseph: New York: Scribner's, 1957.

What Dread Hand? London: Michael Joseph, 1968.

Court of Foxes. London: Michael Joseph, 1969; Northridge, Calif.: Brooke House, 1976.

Brand X. London: Michael Joseph, 1974.

A Ring of Roses. London: W. H. Allen, 1977. (Also as by Mary Ann Ashe.)

The Honey Harlot. London: W. H. Allen, 1978.

The Brides of Aberdar. London: Michael Joseph, 1982; New York: St. Martin's, 1983.

Buffet for Unwelcome Guests: The Best Short Stories of Christianna Brand. Ed. Francis M. Nevins, Jr., and Martin H. Greenberg. Carbondale: Southern Illinois University Press, 1983.

Crime on the Coast, and No Flowers by Request. London: Gollancz, 1984.

Inspector Cockrill Series

Heads You Lose. London: John Lane; New York: Dodd, Mead, 1942.

Green for Danger. New York: Dodd, Mead, 1944; London: John Lane, 1945.

The Crooked Wreath. New York: Dodd, Mead, 1946; as *Suddenly at His Residence*. London: John Lane, 1947.

Death of Jezebel. New York: Dodd, Mead, 1948; London: John Lane, 1949.

London Particular. London: Michael Joseph, 1952; as *Fog of Doubt*. New York: Scribner's, 1953.

Tour de Force. London: Michael Joseph; New York: Scribner's, 1955.

Inspector Charlesworth Series

Death in High Heels. London: John Lane, 1941; New York: Scribner's, 1954.

The Rose in Darkness. London: Michael Joseph, 1979.

Writing as Mary Ann Ashe

Alas, for Her that Met Me! London: Star Books, 1976.
A Ring of Roses. London: Star Books, 1976. (Also as by Christianna Brand.)

Writing as China Thompson

Starrbelow. London: Hutchinson; New York: Scribner, 1958.

CRITICAL BIBLIOGRAPHY

Babener, Liahna. "Christianna Brand's 'Cockie' Cockrill." In *Cops and Constables: American and British Fictional Policemen*, ed. Earl Bargainnier. Bowling Green, Ohio: Popular Press, 1986, pp. 125–42.
Barnard, Robert. "The Slightly Mad, Mad World of Christianna Brand." *The Armchair Detective*, 19, no. 3 (1986): 238–43.
Penzler, Otto. "Introduction." In Christianna Brand, *Green for Danger*. San Diego: University of California Extension, 1978, pp. vi–xii.

LIAHNA BABENER

LILIAN JACKSON BRAUN (?–   )

Lilian Jackson Braun was born in Massachusetts but later moved to Michigan where, at age fifteen, she began writing. When the Depression prevented her from attaining a college education, she continued her work with newspapers by writing advertising copy, a job she held for fifteen years. She also worked for thirty years as an editor for the *Detroit Free Press*. She currently divides her time between Michigan and North Carolina.

Her writing career began in the mid-1960s when she wrote "The Sin of Madame Phloi" to help recover from the death of her Siamese cat. *Ellery Queen Mystery Magazine* published that story and five others, and Dutton selected two stories for their Best Mystery Stories of the year (1963–66).

She parlayed the stories into her novel writing, but after her first three in "The Cat Who" series, her publisher declined the fourth. Braun then ceased writing until her second husband, Earl Bettinger, encouraged her to resubmit the fourth novel.

Braun's first three novels are set "Down Below," which is a generic name for a big city. Her amateur detective, Jim Qwilleran, is a reformed alcoholic and prizewinning journalist. He inherits two Siamese cats whom he spoils with gourmet foods but who, in turn, help him solve crimes. After Braun's hiatus from writing, she resumed her series with the Down Below setting but eventually moved Qwilleran to Pickax, a secluded rural area where he inherits the Klingenshoen fortune with a stipulation that he live in Pickax for five years. Braun, who tries to write two novels a year, admits that many readers are drawn to the series by her feline sleuths, but she also tries to create a plot line for those readers who are less than interested in cats. Nonetheless, her knowledge and love of cats clearly helped create the felines KoKo and Yum Yum. When she learned that Siamese are prone to eat wool, she made that fact the focus of *The Cat Who Ate Danish Modern*. Cats' propensity for adhesive became the core of *The Cat Who Sniffed Glue*, while their playful snatching and hiding of objects became focus in both *The Cat Who Went Underground* and *The Cat Who Knew a Cardinal*. In all novels, the capricous antics of the cats develop the plots.

Braun utilizes her other interests as well. Her detective, Arch Riker, and Junior Goodwinter are all created from her knowledge of newspaper work. She blends her knowledge of rural Michigan and the Blue Ridge Mountains, where she owns homes, to create Pickax County. Her interest in interior decorating was important to both *The Cat Who Ate Danish Modern* and *The Cat Who Turned On and Off*. Her husband's theatrical background is used in several books and incorporated as one of Qwilleran's interests. Mountain lore and Scottish lore play important parts in *The Cat Who Moved a Mountain* and *The Cat Who Wasn't There*, respectively. One of Braun's novels, *The Cat Who Went Underground*, allows her to dabble with topics like the occult, UFOs, and serial killing.

Braun's strengths show in her plots and eccentric characters—some of whom have recurring roles. Iris Cobb's problems with husbands—three, all of whom died—bring her to Pickax to cook for Qwilleran and the cats. Braun's creation of an eccentric bookseller, Bedington Smith, and the cantankerous Amanda Goodwinter are examples of her recurring eccentrics, as is the bagpipe-playing sheriff.

Braun creates romantic tension by having various characters interested in Qwilleran. The love interest with Iris Cobb ends with her death in *The Cat Who Talked to Ghosts*, and the long-running interest of Melinda Goodwinter ends in *The Cat Who Wasn't There*. Braun appears to have settled Qwilleran into romantic interests with librarian Polly Duncan, a stout matron his own age. The tension arises with her devotion to Bootsie, her male Siamese, and Qwilleran's hostility toward the cat.

Braun's novels are usually upbeat and positive, but she is able to generate bleakness in her more recent works. The sinister turn of Melinda Good-winter is a prime example; Melinda turned from a pleasant doctor to a woman who would murder Polly in order to marry Qwilleran for his money. The positive nature of the novels is seen in the antics of the felines, who are always romping and ordering Qwilleran around. Braun also demonstrates a positive note by showing how Qwilleran spends the Klingenshoen fortune to establish the "Mooseville Something," a community college, and a museum for town artifacts. He makes his money available to assist any townspeople who need it.

Braun's mysteries will be enjoyed by animal lovers and people who enjoy quaint settings or eccentric characters. Readers who like Braun will also enjoy Charlotte MacLeod and Alisa Craig.

MYSTERY FICTION

The Cat Who Series

The Cat Who Could Read Backwards. New York: Dutton, 1966; London: Collins, 1967.

The Cat Who Ate Danish Modern. New York: Dutton, 1967; Bath, England: Chivers, 1991.

The Cat Who Turned On and Off. New York: Dutton, 1968; London: Headline, 1991.

The Cat Who Saw Red. New York: Putnam, 1986.

The Cat Who Played Brahms. New York: Putnam, 1987.

The Cat Who Played Post Office. New York: Putnam; London, Curley, 1987.

The Cat Who Had 14 Tales. New York: Jove, 1988; Bath, England: Chivers, 1991.

The Cat Who Knew Shakespeare. New York: Putnam, 1988; Bath, England: Chivers, 1990.

The Cat Who Sniffed Glue. New York: Putnam, 1988; Bath, England: Lythway, 1990.

The Cat Who Went Underground. New York: Putnam, 1989.

The Cat Who Talked to Ghosts. New York: Putnam, 1990; London: Headline, 1991.

The Cat Who Lived High. New York: Putnam, 1990; London: Headline, 1991.

The Cat Who Knew a Cardinal. New York: Putnam, 1991; London: Headline, 1992.

The Cat Who Moved a Mountain. New York: Putnam; London: Headline, 1992.

The Cat Who Wasn't There. New York: Putnam, 1992; London: Headline, 1993.

The Cat Who Went into the Closet. New York: Putnam, 1993.

The Cat Who Came to Breakfast. New York: Putnam, 1994.

CRITICAL BIBLIOGRAPHY

Nelson, Catherine. "The Lady Who." *The Armchair Detective* 24, no. 4 (Fall 1991): 388–98.

DONNA WALLER HARPER

GWENDOLINE BUTLER (1922–   )

Gwendoline Williams Butler was born in Blackheath, Southeast London. In 1944, she enrolled at Oxford's Lady Margaret Hall as a history student, and in 1949, she was awarded a B.A. in history. Also in 1949, she married Lionel Butler, and they had one daughter. Until the mid-1950s, Butler taught medieval history "in a very modest kind of way," as she put it, at Oxford for her college, Somerville, and St. Anne's. She also lectured at Westfield College, University of London.

Butler published her first novel, *Receipt for Murder*, in 1956. Since then, she has gone on to write more than fifty more. As Gwendoline Butler, she created police inspector John Coffin; as Jennie Melville, she created another police detective, this time a woman, Charmian Daniels. In addition to the novels that feature her series detectives, Butler has also written some non-series detective novels and some novels that fall into the romantic genre.

In 1973, Butler won the Crime Writers Association's Silver Dagger Award for *Coffin for Pandora*. In 1981, she received the Romantic Novelists Association Award for *The Red Staircase*, and she has also won the Ellery Queen Short Story Award for a piece called "The Sisterhood." She has served as chairwoman of the Crime Writers Association's Gold Dagger Award Committee. She has contributed forewords for several titles in the Black Dagger Series of Reissued Crime Classics; in addition, Butler is a frequent lecturer on crime fiction. In the fall of 1993, she was a Celebrity Lecturer on the eastward crossing of the *Queen Elizabeth II*, speaking on "Women and Crime Fiction."

Butler turned to writing crime novels after her husband received an appointment as the Chair of Medieval History at St. Andrew's University in Scotland. She comments, "I gave him all my small history library and turned to crime. After a bit I had enough intellectual energy to spin off another persona, Jennie Melville, which was my grandmother's name, and I went on from there." Butler's John Coffin novels and the Charmian Daniels books, which she writes as Jennie Melville, are police procedurals, yet they frequently fit into the soft-boiled or psychological categories of detective fiction as well.

Unlike many writers whose work tends to become stale as they age,

Butler's writing continues to evolve. Her later novels are as good as—and in many cases better—than her earlier ones. Both Coffin and Daniels grow over the years. Whereas the first Coffin or Daniels novels were about crime and its solution, the later ones seem largely to be about detectives and how crime and the crime-solving job affect them.

In the earlier novels, John Coffin appears as a cardboard figure of a character. He is often called on for particular kinds of cases, usually those that involve a great deal of psychological analysis of the characters' minds, including Coffin's. Many cases involve families—husbands and wives, parents and children, brothers and sisters. Coffin faces difficulties in his own marriage, which ultimately ends in divorce. He also finds that instead of being an only child, as he had thought for many years, he has two half-siblings. The discovery of his family members opens the already thoughtful Coffin to even more introspection.

Charmian Daniels grows in much the same way as Coffin. When first introduced, Daniels seems to be a hard-bitten and driven young police-woman. She, too, seems to attract a certain kind of case; her special cases involve violent crimes committed by and toward women. The Charmian Daniels novels offer an interesting insight into women in the police force. When Daniels begins her career, she is one of a very few policewomen, and although by the time of her latest appearance the police departments have become more modernized and include women in many capacities, she finds that there are still many obstacles to overcome along the way. Daniels's love life—or, at times, lack thereof—is one of the obstacles. Here, Melville presents the quandary of the twentieth-century career woman: how to combine a relationship and a career and be happy in both.

In general, Butler's pervasive theme involves human relationships. The cases of both Coffin and Daniels often go far to prove the maxim that those we love will most often be the ones who hurt us. John Coffin and Charmian Daniels also illustrate the basic human struggle to find the perfect person with whom to spend one's life. Neither has succeeded so far, but neither has given up yet, either. In their isolation and questioning, their lives and those of the people they encounter in their cases mirror the lives of people around the globe.

One of the most severe frustrations in dealing with Butler's work is its lack of availability. It is worthwhile to search bookstores—used and new—for Butler/Melville's works, even though locating them is difficult. Many of her older books are no longer in print, and even a university-size inter-library loan department cannot locate all of them. Generally, her books are "easy reads"; that is, in an afternoon or evening of uninterrupted reading one can finish a Coffin or Daniels novel. I would recommend that a reader begin with the books from the 1970s rather than those from the beginning. Coffin and Daniels become much more compelling characters as they age than they were as they began their careers.

MYSTERY FICTION

Writing as Gwendoline Butler

Receipt for Murder. London: Bles, 1956.

The Interloper. London: Bles, 1959.

The Vesey Inheritance. New York: Coward McCann, 1975; London: Macmillan, 1975.

The Brides of Freiberg. London: Macmillan, 1977; as *Meadowsweet*. New York: Coward McCann, 1977.

The Red Staircase. New York: Coward McCann, 1979; London: Collins, 1980.

John Coffin Series

Dead in a Row. London: Bles, 1957.

The Dull Dead. London: Bles, 1958; New York: Walker, 1962.

The Murdering Kind. London: Bles, 1958; New York: Roy, 1964.

Death Lives Next Door. London: Bles, 1960; New York: St. Martin's, 1992; as *Dine and Be Dead*. New York: Macmillan, 1960.

Make Me a Murderer. London: Bles, 1961.

Coffin in Oxford. London: Bles, 1962.

Coffin for Baby. London, Bles, 1963; New York: Walker, 1963.

Coffin Waiting. London: Bles, 1963; New York: Walker, 1965.

Coffin in Malta. London: Bles, 1964; New York: Walker, 1965.

A Nameless Coffin. London: Bles, 1966; New York: Walker, 1967.

Coffin Following. London: Bles, 1968.

Coffin's Dark Number. London: Bles, 1969.

A Coffin from the Past. London: Bles, 1970.

A Coffin for Pandora. London: Macmillan, 1973; as *Olivia*. New York: Coward McCann, 1974.

A Coffin for the Canary. London: Macmillan, 1974; as *Sarsen Place*. New York: Coward McCann, 1974.

Coffin on the Water. London: Collins, 1986; New York: St. Martin's, 1989.

Coffin in Fashion. London: Collins, 1987; New York: St. Martin's, 1990.

Coffin Underground. London: Collins, 1988; New York: St. Martin's, 1989.

Coffin in the Black Museum. London: Collins, 1989; as *Coffin in the Museum of Crime*. New York: St. Martin's, 1990.

Coffin and the Paper Man. London: Collins, 1990; New York: St. Martin's, 1991.

Coffin on Murder Street. London: Collins, 1991; New York: St. Martin's, 1991.

Cracking Open a Coffin. New York: St. Martin's, 1992.

Writing as Jennie Melville

The Hunter in the Shadows. London: Hodder and Stoughton, 1969; New York: McKey, 1970.

The Summer Assassin. London: Hodder and Stoughton, 1971.

Ironwood. London: Hodder and Stoughton, 1972; New York: McKay, 1972.

Nun's Castle. New York: McKay, 1973; London: Hodder and Stoughton, 1974.

Raven's Forge. London: Macmillan, 1975; New York: McKay, 1975.

Dragon's Eye. New York: Simon and Schuster, 1976; London: Macmillan, 1977.

Axwater. London: Macmillan, 1978; as *Tarot's Tower*. New York: Simon and Schuster, 1978.

The Painted Castle. London: Macmillan, 1982.

The Hand of Glass. London: Macmillan, 1983.

Listen to the Children. London: Macmillan, 1986.

Death in the Garden. London: Macmillan, 1987; as *Murder in the Garden*. New York: St. Martin's, 1990.

A Cure for Dying. London: Macmillan, 1989.

Witching Murder. London: Macmillan, 1990.

Charmian Daniels Series

Come Home and Be Killed. London: Joseph, 1962; New York: British Book Centre, 1964.

Burning Is a Substitute for Loving. London: Joseph, 1963; New York: British Book Centre, 1964.

Murderer's Houses. London: Joseph, 1964.

There Lies Your Love. London: Joseph, 1965.

Nell Alone. London: Joseph, 1966.

A Different Kind of Summer. London: Joseph, 1967.

A New Kind of Killer, an Old Kind of Death. London: Hodder and Stoughton, 1970; as *A New Kind of Killer*. New York: McKay, 1971.

Murder Has a Pretty Face. London: Macmillan, 1981; New York: St. Martin's, 1989.

Windsor Red. London: Macmillan, 1988; New York: St. Martin's, 1988.

Footsteps in the Blood. London: Macmillan, 1990; New York: St. Martin's, 1993.

Making Good Blood. New York: St. Martin's, 1990.

Dead Set. London: Macmillan, 1992; New York: St. Martin's, 1993.

Whoever Has the Heart. London: Macmillan, 1992; New York: St. Martin's, 1993.

CRITICAL BIBLIOGRAPHY

Craig, Patricia. "Butler, Gwendoline." In *Twentieth Century Crime and Mystery Writers*, ed. Lesley Henderson. 3rd ed. Chicago and London: St. James, 1991, pp. 159–60.

Nichols, Victoria, and Susan Thompson. "Charmian Daniels." In *Silk Stalkings*. Berkeley, Calif.: Black Lizard, 1988, pp. 54–55.

GWENDOLYN WHITEHEAD

❧ C ❧

P. M. CARLSON (1940–   )

Patricia McElroy was born in Guatemala City on February 3, 1940. She earned her B.A., M.A., and Ph.D. degrees from Cornell University. Like Sara Paretsky, she is married to a professor (M. A. Carlson). She taught as an instructor and lecturer in psychology and human development at Cornell. She was also the chairperson of the Ithaca, N.Y., Environmental Commission from 1975 to 1978 and a member of the board of directors of Bloomington Restorations, Inc., and Historic Ithaca. In addition to writing about the development of language in children, she writes mysteries as P. M. Carlson. Her writing has been a critical as well as popular success, earning her Edgar, Anthony, and Macavity nominations for her novels and short stories. She is past president of Sisters in Crime.

Carlson has created two amateur detectives, Bridget Mooney and Maggie Ryan, and one professional, Deputy Sheriff Marty Hopkins. Bridget Mooney is an actress in a touring company and is portrayed in a series of short stories set in late-nineteenth-century America. Real people often interact with the character; for example, she helps Lillie Langtry foil a kidnapping plot and takes Jesse James as her lover. Mooney is more emancipated than a suffragette as a result of her difficult childhood. At one stage she was a prostitute being pimped by her aunt. Mooney is totally self-absorbed and filters all thoughts and actions through the litmus of the query, "What good will this do me?"

The Mooney stories are written in the first person, so readers learn about her through her own thoughts and rationalizations as well as through her actions. Mooney can be considered an antihero in that she manages to profit from the crimes of others. In the denouement of "Death Scene: The Moor of Venice," she steals an emerald necklace from its thief, rationalizing that she has earned it by having entertained the owner years ago. As an independent woman concerned with her own survival, she chooses not to be bound by societal conventions.

The second amateur detective is Margaret Mary (Maggie) Ryan. Carlson's detective stories about Ryan show both a murder case and a character study as Ryan moves through her life in each book, which is written from the omniscient point of view. Ryan meets Nick O'Connor, who will become her husband; she attends graduate school; she works in Manhattan and buys a brownstone in Brooklyn; she returns to her alma mater as a Ph.D. to do some statistical work for a faculty member; and she achieves psychological closure by establishing a relationship with a child she had given up for adoption.

The time frame is very important to this series. The works span the late 1960s and 1970s, a period of great turmoil and change. The Vietnam War forms a backdrop for the books—it is mentioned in conversations, seen on television newscasts, read about in newspaper and magazine articles, and protested by Ryan and other students. When the war ends, it remains present in the form of its consequences: posttraumatic stress disorder suffered by soldiers and nurses and the strain between proponents of the pro-war and anti-war positions.

Gravestone begins a new series, involving Deputy Sheriff Marty (Martine) Hopkins. Written from the omniscient point of view, this novel takes place in Indiana and concerns two crimes: the racially motivated slaying of a Jewish musician married to a black woman and the death of a judge's daughter, whose skeleton Hopkins discovers laid out in a coffin and buried in a cave. As she tries to solve both cases, she has to cope with being virtually a single parent and the only woman on the force.

All three characters are feminists. Mooney acknowledges the difficulty of being an independent career woman in the late 1800s. She can conform to the conventional image of women, but she does not hesitate to defend herself or take revenge if need be. Ryan is an example of the young liberated woman of the 1970s. She works at being a good student and creating a career for herself, and her marriage with Nick is a relationship of equals. Hopkins has been a single parent to her child because her husband Brad is often away, trying to become a success as a disk jockey (and believing that all he needs is a gimmick). She has to defend herself in the office from the chauvinism of the male sheriffs, and she often feels she has to prove her worth and abilities.

Carlson's personal background appears in the stories. For example, her academic experiences form the backdrop of *Audition for Murder, Murder Is Academic, Murder Is Pathological*, and *Murder Misread*. Her portraits of undergraduate and graduate students as well as the battle for tenure and issues involved in educational and psychological experimentation are vivid and realistic. Her acting background serves as the framework for all the Mooney stories as well as *Audition for Murder, Murder Is Academic*, and

Rehearsal for Murder. Audition for Murder is a detailed description of all the work that goes into putting on a play, in this case *Hamlet*. The time the author spent living in Bloomington, Indiana, can be seen in the Indiana setting for *Gravestone*.

Readers of Carlson will probably also enjoy the works of Susan Dunlap, Nancy Picard, and Anne Perry.

MYSTERY FICTION

Maggie Ryan Series

Audition for Murder. New York: Avon Books, 1985.

Murder Is Academic. New York: Avon Books, 1986.

Murder Is Pathological. New York: Avon Books, 1987.

Murder Unrenovated. New York: Bantam Books, 1988.

Rehearsal for Murder. New York: Bantam Books, 1990.

Bad Blood. New York: Doubleday Books, 1991.

Murder in the Dog Days. New York: Bantam Books, 1991.

Murder Misread. New York: Bantam Books, 1991.

Marty Hopkins Series

Gravestone. New York: Pocket Books, 1993.

Bloodstream. New York: Pocket Books, 1994.

Bridget Mooney Series

"Father of the Bridge; or A Fate Worse than Death." In *Mr. President Private Eye*, ed. Martin Greenberg. New York: Random House, 1988.

"Death Scene; or The Moor of Venice." In *Sisters in Crime 2*, ed. Marilyn Wallace. New York: Berkeley Books, 1990.

"The Dirty Little Coward That Shot Mr. Harriet; or Such Stuff as Dreams Are Made On." In *Sisters in Crime 5*, ed. Marilyn Wallace. New York: Berkeley Books, 1992.

"The Jersey Lily; or, Make Me Immortal with a Kiss." In *Malice Domestic*, ed. Elizabeth Peters. New York: Pocket Books, 1992.

LINDA R. HARRIS

VERA CASPARY (1904–1987)

Very Caspary was born in Chicago, Illinois, on November 13, 1904. After working as a stenographer and in advertising agencies, she began free-lance writing and writing screen plays. She won the Screen Writers Guild Award in 1950. Caspary died in 1987.

Late in Caspary's novel *Laura*, the pompous and prolix Waldo Lydecker gives the reader an insight into Laura's romantic inclinations: "Always the same pattern, isn't it? A lean, lithe body is the measure of masculinity. . . . Let a man be hard and spare and you clothe him in the garments of Romeo, Superman, and Jupiter disguised as a bull." Although he is motivated by sexual jealousy, he has shrewdly discovered the key to her character—and, incidentally, the organizing principle of Caspary's fiction. Caspary's psychothrillers often reveal more than she intended. Although most of her novels end happily—with the murderer discovered and the women married to the men "of their dreams"—Caspary does not go far enough in analyzing why, in the first place, these women love the men they do.

Caspary shapes her novels around women loving misogynistic men. In *Laura*, the protagonist is sexually attracted to socially constructed images of masculinity; her actual lovers seem largely irrelevant to her needs. For example, at the novel's beginning, she is engaged to Shelby Carpenter, a southern aristocrat who refashions Laura into a sheltered southern belle, the type of woman he "knew" best. However, she is "rescued" from this marriage by the novel's tough-guy detective, Mark McPherson, who thinks of women as "dolls and dames," and who seems similarly dismissive of a woman's needs. Nonetheless, he receives Laura's highest encomium: "He's a man." He is more like Shelby than their physical resemblance suggests, for psychologically, both refashion Laura and love her image. Like Shelby, he falls in love with an imagined character when he romantically worships Laura's portrait before even meeting her.

The question must puzzle the reader even as it plagues her best friend, Waldo: why is "the measure of masculinity" so irresistible for Laura? Her male friends (she seems to have no female friends) continually refigure her, so that her own character is lost in their image building. Waldo also loves a manufactured image of Laura to compensate for his (presumed) homosexuality; like the other men in the novel, Waldo is concerned about Laura's image—and his supposed devotion to her is evidenced in his promise that he will create in his newspaper column a public relations fabrication to exonerate her. However, Laura returns his affection, too. Like most of Caspary's women characters, she has internalized society's definition of power relations between the sexes. Not recognizing the disparity of power between the sexes in society, Laura is attracted to male power, to the image of strength—"the measure of masculinity"—that she thinks will fulfill her, even if it dehumanizes her.

Writing before feminist analyses of gender relations in society, Caspary herself seems unaware of the underlying sexual dynamics in *Laura* (and in most of her novels). Laura's presumptive marriage to McPherson is presented as a very positive ending. In other novels, Caspary explores unhappy marriages based on sadomasochism. In *The Man Who Loved His Wife*, for example, all Elaine's friends are mystified by her deep attraction to Fletcher, the wealthy, powerful, and crude businessman who marries her. To Elaine, "Fletch" is "the measure of masculinity." His loss of the symbols of masculinity, however, leads to disaster for their marriage. Suffering from cancer of the larynx, Fletch loses his voice and—as a consequence of depression—his sexual potency. Because he has become emasculated in both his own and Elaine's eyes, Fletch sets in motion a diabolic plot to possess Elaine even after his death—one that Elaine cannot foil, even with the assistance of her hyper-masculinized lover, a doctor.

The narrative ends with Elaine being "punished" more for her adultery than for Fletch's murder. However, the plot alone does not provide justification for her misery at the novel's conclusion: the reader must consider the psychodynamics of her self-lacerating pain, which lies in her unconsciously instilled gender stereotypes. For Elaine, a woman's happiness is contingent on making a man happy; the fulfillment of her sexuality depends on the expression of his own. Thus, Elaine can never be happy: her sexual "failure" with Fletch dooms her. Perhaps unknowingly, Caspary's actual subject in this and other novels is the self-destructiveness of gender relations in a patriarchal society.

Like Elaine, Jean McVeigh of *The Husband* directs her life according to the desires of a man. A wealthy heiress, Jean is attracted to the misogynistic Stuart Howell, a handsome con man who marries her, robs her, and then tries to kill her. Although the novel's premise is that Jean has much more sense than she realizes, the plot is built on implausbilities and contradictions, which can be resolved if viewed within the context of gender relations. Jean is not gullible; she is "in love" with "the measure of masculinity" that Stuart self-consciously manufactures. Jean is complemented by Valerie, a would-be starlet who is also taken in by Stuart's image; like Jean, Valerie is fooled because Stuart's image accentuates a social construction of masculinity.

Readers should begin Caspary's work by reading *Laura*, on which the wonderful Hollywood film was based. They will find, in Waldo's words, "always the same pattern" in Caspary's other works. Those who enjoy her psychothrillers might also turn to the novels of Ruth Rendell.

MYSTERY FICTION

Laura. Boston: Houghton Mifflin, 1943; London, Eyre and Spottiswoode, 1944.
Bedelia. Boston: Houghton Mifflin; London: Eyre and Spottiswoode, 1945.
The Murder in the Stork Club. New York: Black, 1946; as *The Lady in Mink*. London: Gordon Martin, 1946.
Stranger Than Truth. New York: Random House, 1946; London: Eyre and Spottiswoode, 1947.

The Weeping and the Laughter. Boston: Little, Brown, 1950; as *The Death Wish.*
    London: Eyre and Spottiswoode, 1951.
Thelma. Boston: Little, Brown, 1952; London: W. H. Allen, 1953.
False Face. London: W. H. Allen, 1954.
The Husband. New York: Harper; London: W. H. Allen, 1957.
Evvie. New York: Harper; London: W. H. Allen, 1960.
A Chosen Sparrow. New York: Putnam; London: W. H. Allen, 1964.
The Man Who Loved His Wife. New York: Putnam; London: W. H. Allen, 1966.
Rosecrest Cell. New York: Putnam, 1967; London: W. H. Allen, 1968.
Final Portrait. London: W. H. Allen, 1971.
Ruth. New York: Pocket Books, 1972.
Elizabeth X. London: W. H. Allen, 1978; as *The Secret of Elizabeth.* New York:
    Pocket Books, 1979.

CRITICAL BIBLIOGRAPHY

Bakerman, Jane S. "Caspary, Vera." In *Twentieth Century Crime and Mystery
    Writers,* ed. Lesley Henderson. 3rd ed. Chicago and London: St. James,
    1991, pp. 178–79.
————. "Vera Caspary's Fascinating Females: Laura, Evvie and Bedelia." *Clues,* 1,
    no. 1 (1980): 46–52.

GARY STORHOFF

SARAH CAUDWELL (1939–   )

Born Sarah Cockburn in London in 1939, the daughter of writer Claud
Cockburn studied the classics before taking up law at St. Anne's College,
Oxford, and eventually being called to the Chancery Bar. After several
years' practice as a barrister, she joined the Trust Division of Lloyd's Bank,
Ltd., where she specialized in international tax planning. She chose the
pseudonym Sarah Caudwell when she began her writing career in 1981. In
addition to her own three novels, Caudwell is one of five mystery writers
who collaborated with *Harper's* editor Jack Hitt in writing *The Perfect
Murder.* She is also a sometime contributor to the *New York Times.*

   Caudwell draws on her own experience at Lincoln's Inn to establish the
locus of the novels—legal chambers at 62 New Square—and the central
cast of young barristers who work there. Housed in an area called the
Nursery, these junior members of chambers consist of Selena Jardine, a
most persuasive advocate; Desmond Ragwort, a paragon of unassailable
virtue; Michael Cantrip, his breezy antithesis; and Timothy Shepherd, a
slightly older, and thus slightly busier, lawyer. The group is rounded out
by Julia Larwood, from next door at no. 63. Julia's expertise in tax matters
is balanced by her ineptitude in almost everything else.

To this quintet is added Hilary Tamar, an Oxford don and Timothy's former tutor. Hilary has maintained contact with Timothy since their university days and drops in when in London. Though a member of the Faculty of Laws, Hilary is a historian whose specialty in medieval law gives little insight into current legal practice. Explanations from the others about estate planning, tax avoidance, and capital transfer laws serve to enlighten the reader on some of the legal technicalities essential to the plots.

After helping solve the first mystery, Hilary is called in to help with others, while always being careful to avoid Henry, the clerk at no. 62, who considers Hilary a bad influence on the young. They tend to spend too much time chatting over coffee, drinking wine at the Corkscrew, or dining at Guido's when he (or she) is around. An unresolved mystery concerns Hilary's gender, which is never revealed.

Although all the novels are narrated by Hilary, each incorporates letters from another character. In *Thus Was Adonis Murdered*, Julia's friends know of her difficulties before her letters from Venice start to arrive in chambers. The details of events leading up to the murder, when read after the fact, add a chilling suspense to the novel. Selena's letters from Greece in *The Shortest Way to Hades* and Cantrip's telexes from the Channel Isles in *The Sirens Sang of Murder* move those plots in more traditional ways but are no less effective.

Caudwell's writing style is so witty and pleasurable that one looks for a listener to whom the novels can be read aloud. Hilary is a master of understatement and occasional hyperbole. Julia's and Selena's letters are consistent with the writers' personalities but no less ironic than Hilary's narration. Cantrip, however, is given to slang and malapropism. Hilary excuses him because of his "inferior education" (he went to Cambridge rather than Oxford).

Humor lies, not only in expression and in circumstance, but in the third novel, in a book that Julia and Cantrip are trying to write as a get-rich-quick scheme. Naming it *Chancery* and making their characters idealized versions of themselves, they use their own experiences as bases for their plot. Since the reader sees both the real incidents and the exaggerations that accrue with the telling, the contrast makes for great hilarity. The writing is also painfully bad, in careful imitation of the popular romances that Julia and Cantrip aspire to emulate.

Caudwell's novels are classical mysteries in the sense that they are solved through the processes of rational thought. Hilary sees each one as the scholar's search for truth. Just as Selena uses her courtroom skills to outwit and outtalk a murderer, others contribute their knowledge of the Finance Act or the practice of "teasing the Revenue" (or confronting the income tax officials) to piece together the puzzles. In the second novel, Hilary applies the techniques of textual criticism to solve the mystery.

A reader familiar with the classics and European travel will find particular delight in these novels, but such acquaintance is not essential. Hilary, who is ever the teacher, is careful to explain any necessary allusions, as well as those aspects of the British legal system that tend to confuse Americans who are not fans of John Mortimer's *Rumpole of the Bailey*. Rumpole devotees should enjoy these books, as should Michael Innes and V. C. Clinton-Baddeley readers.

MYSTERY FICTION

Hilary Tamar Series

Thus Was Adonis Murdered. London: Collins; New York: Scribner, 1981.

The Shortest Way to Hades. London: Collins, 1984; New York: Scribner, 1985.

The Sirens Sang of Murder. London: Collins; New York: Delacorte, 1989.

CRITICAL BIBLIOGRAPHY

DeCandido, GraceAnne, and Helga Borck. "Caudwell, Sarah." In *Twentieth Century Crime and Mystery Writers*, ed. Lesley Henderson. 3rd ed. Chicago and London: St. James, 1991, pp. 179–80.

MARCIA J. SONGER

AGATHA CHRISTIE (1890–1976)

Agatha Christie was born September 15, 1890, in Torquay, England, the daughter of an American, Frederick Alvah Miller, and his English wife, Clarissa ("Clara") Boechmer. Christie received most of her education at home, later attending Paris finishing schools. In 1914 Agatha married Archibald Christie, who served in the Royal Flying Corps during World War I, while Agatha worked as a volunteer nurse and later as a pharmaceutical dispenser. In 1919, Christie gave birth to her only child, Rosalind.

In response to a challenge from her sister Madge, Christie wrote a detective novel, *The Mysterious Affair at Styles*, which was published in 1921 by John Lane. It was the first of her 97 published books. In 1926, Christie's mother died, Archie Christie asked for a divorce, and *The Murder of Roger Ackroyd* became a press sensation—which led Christie to disappear for ten days as the result of stress-induced amnesia.

After her divorce in 1928, Christie traveled to the Middle East. There she met archaeologist Max Mallowan, whom she married in 1930. At this time, in addition to writing mysteries, she began writing a series of psychological novels under the name Mary Westmacott, as well as mystery plays, both adaptations and original scripts. Her sales soaring, Christie won honors in Britain and the United States. In 1954 she became the first writer to receive the Mystery Writers of America's Grand Master Award. In 1956 she became a Commander of the British Empire and in 1971, a Dame of the British Empire.

When Christie died, on January 12, 1976, her books had sold over 400 million copies worldwide and her play *The Mousetrap*, which opened in 1952, was still playing in London's West End, making it the longest running play ever produced. Since 1976, Christie has become even more popular due to film and television versions of nearly all her novels and stories and the availability of paperback editions of all her books. *The Mousetrap* celebrated its fortieth anniversary and still attracts audiences. Christie's books have sold over 1 billion copies in English and have been translated into more languages than Shakespeare's works. Not simply a writer, Agatha Christie has become a phenomenon.

Christie's readers knew little about her during her life, except through her 1946 memoir, *Come, Tell Me How You Live*. We now have access to her *Autobiography* (1977), *Mallowan's Memoirs* (1977), and Janet Morgan's authorized biography (1985). Christie's Mary Westmacott novels, and particularly the largely autobiographical *Unfinished Portrait*, reveal Christie's psyche and beliefs. Her mysteries reveal much about their writer as well: her views on being a mystery writer (via alter ego Ariadne Oliver), her love of dogs and gardens, her favorite music and literature, and her keen sense of justice.

Agatha Christie's influence on the detective fiction genre is universally acknowledged. Christie was one of the British writers who shaped the classic whodunit formula in the 1920s and 1930s. Along with Dorothy L. Sayers, G. K. Chesterton, and others, Christie was a member of the Detection Club, which established strict rules for writing detective stories that were designed to give readers a fair chance of solving the puzzles. Although praised as a master puzzler, Christie became as famous for breaking the rules as for creating them.

Christie helped popularize other aspects of the classic murder mystery formula: the great and eccentric detective, the dim sidekick, the old lady sleuth, murder in a closed society (a country estate, a train, a village), familiar characters (boring retired colonels, absent-minded clergy, miserly patriarchs), and mysteries that are solved more by rationalization than by legwork.

Contemporary feminist crime writers owe Christie a debt. Besides creating older women amateur detectives in Jane Marple and Ariadne Oliver, Christie created many brave, intelligent young women adventurers/investigators, such as Emily Trefusis and Lady Eileen Brent. In the Miss Marple stories especially, Christie suggests the difficulty of being a woman in a society that keeps women poor, excludes them from education and meaningful work, judges them on their beauty, and teaches them that love is the aim of life.

Why is Christie so popular? Admirers and detractors have their theories. The popularity and variety of her detective heroes is a factor. Readers love Hercule Poirot, the dapper Belgian who uses his "little grey cells" to outsmart the official police, and Jane Marple, the fluffy village spinster whose vast knowledge of human nature makes her an effective, if unlikely, nemesis. Christie created other detectives. This diverse lot includes Superintendent Battle, Tommy and Tuppence Beresford, Parker Pyne, and Harley Quin.

Christie is the cleverest whodunit plotter ever, and is known for fair but surprising endings. Readers love to suspect each character and develop their own theories, only to discover that they have been bamboozled again. Christie is described as using the gimmick of the "least likely person," but her murderers are seldom the butler or the mysterious stranger. They are more likely to be obvious suspects whom readers have eliminated because of plausible alibis, skilled misdirection, or manipulation of our assumptions about people and the genre.

Christie's fiction contains wonderful details of English life from 1920 through the mid-1970s. Many readers associate Christie with the period, sentimentally pictured in "The Adventure of the Christmas Pudding," when prosperous families lived in large country estates with well-tended gardens and hosts of servants. However, Christie's work also shows the social and economic upheavals resulting from two World Wars, the decline of the empire, and economic hard times. In her later books, the old houses and gardens, like England itself, are badly in need of care and cash. Nonetheless, despite her realistic view of changing times, Christie's stories represent to many a pleasantly nostalgic view of English character and values.

Christie's plain style—called "flat" or "uninspired" by some reviewers—has made her writing easy to translate. While the descriptions of places are few, Christie is skilled at dialogue, letting her characters reveal themselves through their words. A storyteller par excellence, Christie creates suspense that enthralls readers. Christie's ability to paint individualized character portraits in a few sentences is another aspect of her style that has captivated her readers, if not always her reviewers.

While praising her plotting, reviewers have often demeaned Christie's skill with characterization. Character types reappear tiresomely in the Christie canon, but she often manipulates these stereotypes to fool us, causing us to question our assumptions about apparently devoted husbands, dedicated doctors, and similar characters. Christie did create memorable, unstereotypical characters, who were often women, including Lucy Eyelesbarrow, Griselda Clement, Miss Blacklock, Henretta Savernake, and Mrs. Boynton. Christie's popularity across cultures can be attributed to her emphasis on universal human traits such as jealousy, spite, greed, loneliness, and arrogance.

Christie's work is uneven. Most readers prefer the detective stories to the thrillers, and nearly everyone concedes that her last books (not including *Curtain* and *Sleeping Murder*, which were written during World War II) show a marked decline. Nonetheless, it is an achievement that Christie produced so many mysteries and innovations within the formulas that she used. The large and varied Christie canon is a rich feast for hungry readers.

Where should a new reader begin? Some become "hooked" by reading her most famous puzzle novels, such as *And Then There Were None*, *The Murder of Roger Ackroyd*, and *The Murder on the Orient Express*. A more systematic approach is to read the first novel and/or short story collection about each of her detectives, which are all vintage Christie. My favorite Christie novels—*The Moving Finger*, *Murder in Retrospect*, and *A Murder Is Announced*—I have come to appreciate after having read both the more dramatic and the more pedestrian of her works. After reading all the Christie novels (several times), I enjoyed reading the Mary Westmacott novels, which reveal much about their writer and develop themes that were only glanced at in her detective stories. Readers who like Christie's mysteries often delight in the works of Christie's British contemporaries, Dorothy L. Sayers, Josephine Tey, Ngaio Marsh, and Margery Allingham.

MYSTERY FICTION

Writing as Agatha Christie

The Man in the Brown Suit. New York: Dodd, 1924; London: Lane, 1924.

Murder at Hazelmoor. New York: Dodd, 1931; as *The Sittaford Mystery*. London: Collins, 1931.

The Hound of Death and Other Stories. London: Collins, 1933.

The Listerdale Mystery. London: Collins, 1934.

The Boomerang Clue. New York: Dodd, 1935; as *Why Didn't They Ask Evans?* London: Collins, 1934.

And Then There Were None. New York: Dodd, 1940; as *Ten Little Niggers*. London: Collins, 1939. (Also titled *Ten Little Indians* and *The Nursery Rhyme Murders*.)

Death Comes as the End. New York: Dodd, 1944; London: Collins, 1945.

Remembered Death. New York: Dodd, 1945; as *Sparkling Cyanide*. London: Collins, 1945.

The Witness for the Prosecution and Other Stories. New York: Dodd, 1948.

Crooked House. New York: Dodd, 1949; London: Collins, 1949.

They Came to Baghdad. New York: Dodd, 1951; London: Collins, 1951.

So Many Steps to Death. New York: Dodd, 1955; as *Destination Unknown*. London: Collins, 1954.

Ordeal by Innocence. New York: Dodd, 1959; London: Collins, 1958.

The Pale Horse. New York: Dodd, 1962; London: Collins, 1961.

Endless Night. New York: Dodd, 1968; London, Collins, 1967.

Passenger to Frankfurt: An Extravaganza. New York: Dodd, 1970; London: Collins, 1970.

The Golden Ball and Other Stories. New York: Dodd, 1971.

Hercule Poirot Series

The Mysterious Affair at Styles. New York and London: Lane, 1921. (Note: 1920, the copyright date, is usually cited as the publication date for *Styles*. However, the novel was released in February 1921 in London and New York.)

Murder on the Links. New York: Dodd, 1923; London: Lane, 1923.

Poirot Investigates. New York: Dodd, 1925; London: Lane, 1924.

The Murder of Roger Ackroyd. New York: Dodd, 1926; London: Collins, 1926.

The Big Four. New York: Dodd, 1927; London: Collins, 1927.

The Mystery of the Blue Train. New York: Dodd, 1928; London: Collins, 1928.

Peril at End House. New York: Dodd, 1932; London: Collins, 1932.

Thirteen at Dinner. New York: Dodd, 1933; as *Lord Edgware Dies.* London: Collins, 1933.

Murder in the Calais Coach. New York: Dodd, 1934; as *Murder on the Orient Express.* London: Collins, 1934.

Murder in Three Acts. New York: Dodd, 1934; as *Three Act Tragedy.* London: Collins, 1935.

Death in the Air. New York: Dodd, 1935; as *Death in the Clouds.* London: Collins, 1935.

The A.B.C. Murders. New York: Dodd, 1936; London: Collins, 1936.

Murder in Mesopotamia. New York: Dodd, 1937; London: Collins, 1936.

Cards on the Table. New York: Dodd, 1937; London: Collins, 1936.

Dead Man's Mirror and Other Stories. New York: Dodd, 1937; as *Murder in the Mews.* London: Collins, 1937.

Death on the Nile. London: Collins, 1937; New York: Dodd, 1938.

Poirot Loses a Client. New York: Dodd, 1937; as *Dumb Witness.* London: Collins, 1937.

Appointment with Death. New York: Dodd, 1938; London: Collins, 1938.

Murder for Christmas/A Holiday for Murder. New York: Dodd, 1939; as *Hercule Poirot's Christmas.* London: Collins, 1938.

The Regatta Mystery and Other Stories. New York: Dodd, 1939.

Sad Cypress. New York: Dodd, 1940; London: Collins, 1940.

Evil under the Sun. New York: Dodd, 1941; London: Collins, 1941.

The Patriotic Murders/An Overdose of Death. New York: Dodd, 1941; as *One, Two, Buckle My Shoe.* London: Collins, 1940.

Murder in Retrospect. New York: Dodd, 1943; as *Five Little Pigs*. London: Collins, 1943.

Murder after Hours. New York: Dodd, 1946; as *The Hollow*. London: Collins, 1946.

The Labors of Hercules. New York: Dodd, 1947; London: Collins, 1947.

There Is a Tide. New York: Dodd, 1948; as *Taken at the Flood*. London: Collins, 1948.

The Underdog and Other Stories. New York: Dodd, 1951.

Mrs. McGinty's Dead. New York: Dodd, 1952; London: Collins, 1952.

Funerals Are Fatal. New York: Dodd, 1953; as *After the Funeral*. London: Collins, 1953.

Hickory, Dickory, Death. New York: Dodd, 1955; as *Hickory, Dickory, Dock*. London: Collins, 1955.

Dead Man's Folly. New York: Dodd, 1956; London: Collins, 1956.

The Adventure of the Christmas Pudding and A Selection of Entrees. London: Collins, 1960.

Cat among the Pigeons. New York: Dodd, 1960; London: Collins, 1959.

Double Sin and Other Stories. New York: Dodd, 1961.

The Clocks. New York: Dodd, 1964; London: Collins, 1963.

Third Girl. New York: Dodd, 1967; London: Collins, 1966.

Hallowe'en Party. New York: Dodd, 1969; London: Collins, 1969.

Elephants Can Remember. New York: Dodd, 1972; London: Collins, 1972.

Hercule Poirot's Early Cases. New York: Dodd, 1974; as *Poirot's Early Cases*. London: Collins, 1974.

Curtain. New York: Dodd, 1975; London: Collins, 1975.

Tommy and Tuppence Beresford Series

The Secret Adversary. New York and London: Lane, 1922; New York: Dodd, 1922.

Partners in Crime. New York: Dodd, 1929; London: Collins, 1929.

N or M? New York: Dodd, 1941; London: Collins, 1941.

By the Pricking of My Thumbs. New York: Dodd, 1968; London: Collins, 1968.

Postern of Fate. New York: Dodd, 1973; London: Collins, 1973.

Superintendent Battle Series

The Secret of Chimneys. New York: Dodd, 1925; London: Lane, 1925.

The Seven Dials Mystery. New York: Dodd, 1929; London: Collins, 1929.

Cards on the Table. New York: Dodd, 1937; London: Collins, 1936.

Easy to Kill. New York: Dodd, 1939; as *Murder Is Easy.* London: Collins, 1939.

Towards Zero. New York: Dodd, 1944; London: Collins, 1944.

Harley Quin Series

The Mysterious Mr. Quin. New York: Dodd, 1930; London: Collins, 1930.

Jane Marple Series

Murder at the Vicarage. New York: Dodd, 1930; London: Collins, 1930.

The Tuesday Club Murders. New York: Dodd, 1933; as *The Thirteen Problems.* London: Collins, 1932.

The Body in the Library. New York: Dodd, 1942; London: Collins, 1942.

The Moving Finger. New York: Dodd, 1942; London: Collins, 1943. (The U.S. edition is slightly condensed.)

A Murder Is Announced. New York: Dodd, 1950; London: Collins, 1950.

Three Blind Mice and Other Stories/The Mousetrap and Other Stories. New York: Dodd, 1950.

Murder with Mirrors. New York: Dodd, 1952; as *They Do It with Mirrors.* London: Collins, 1952.

A Pocket Full of Rye. New York: Dodd, 1954; London: Collins, 1953.

What Mrs. McGillicuddy Saw! New York: Dodd, 1957; as *4:50 from Paddington.* London: Collins, 1957.

The Mirror Crack'd. New York: Dodd, 1963; as *The Mirror Crack'd from Side to Side.* London: Collins, 1962.

A Caribbean Mystery. New York: Dodd, 1965; London: Collins, 1964.

At Bertram's Hotel. New York: Dodd, 1966; London: Collins, 1965.

Nemesis. New York: Dodd, 1971; London: Collins, 1971.

Sleeping Murder. New York: Dodd, 1976; London: Collins, 1976.

Miss Marple's Final Cases and Two Other Stories. London: Collins, 1979.

Parker Pyne Series

Mr. Parker Pyne, Detective. New York: Dodd, 1934; as *Parker Pyne Investigates.* London: Collins, 1934.

Writing as Mary Westmacott

Giant's Bread. New York: Doubleday, 1930; London: Collins, 1930.

Unfinished Portrait. New York: Doubleday, 1934; London: Collins, 1934.

Absent in the Spring. New York: Farrar, 1944; London: Collins, 1944.

The Rose and the Yew Tree. New York: Rinehart, 1948; London: Heinemann, 1948.

A Daughter's a Daughter. London: Heinemann, 1952; New York: Dell, 1963.
The Burden. London: Heinemann, 1956; New York: Dell, 1963.

MYSTERY PLAYS BY AGATHA CHRISTIE OR BASED ON AGATHA CHRISTIE'S FICTION

1928   *Alibi.* (Adapted by Michael Morton from *The Murder of Roger Ackroyd.*)

1930   *Black Coffee.* (An original play by Christie.)

1936   *Love from a Stranger.* (Adapted by Frank Vosper from "Philomel Cottage.")

1937   *Akhnaton.* (An original play by Christie; never produced.)

1940   *Peril at End House.* (Adapted by Arnold Ridley.)

1943   *Ten Little Niggers/Ten Little Indians.* (Adapted by Christie.)

1945   *Appointment with Death.* (Adapted by Christie.)

1946   *Hidden Horizon/Murder on the Nile.* (Adapted by Christie from *Death on the Nile.*)

1949   *The Murder at the Vicarage.* (Adapted by Moie Charles and Barbara Toy.)

1951   *The Hollow.* (Adapted by Christie.)

1952   *The Mousetrap.* (Adapted by Christie from "Three Blind Mice.")

1953   *Witness for the Prosecution.* (Adapted by Christie.)

1954   *Spider's Web.* (An original play by Christie.)

1956   *Towards Zero.* (Adapted by Christie, with Gerald Verner.)

1958   *Verdict.* (An original play by Christie.)

1958   *The Unexpected Guest.* (An original play by Christie.)

1960   *Go Back for Murder.* (Adapted by Christie from *Murder in Retrospect.*)

1962   *Rule of Three.* (Three original one-act plays by Christie: "The Rats," "Afternoon at the Seaside," and "The Patient.")

1972   *Fiddlers Three.* (Original play by Christie.)

1977   *A Murder Is Announced.* (Adapted by Leslie Darbon.)

1981   *Cards on the Table.* (Adapted by Leslie Darbon.)

PUBLISHED PLAYS

Akhnaton. New York: Dodd, 1973; London: Collins, 1973.
The Mousetrap and Other Plays. New York: Dodd, 1978.

COLLABORATIVE MYSTERIES WRITTEN BY THE DETECTION CLUB (WITH CONTRIBUTIONS BY AGATHA CHRISTIE)

Anthony Berkeley, Agatha Christie, G. K. Chesterton, M. Cole, Freeman Wills Croft, Selwyn Jepson, Milward Kennedy, Ronald Knox, John Rhode, Dorothy L. Sayers, and Henry Wade. *The Floating Admiral.* New York, Doubleday, 1931; London: Hodder, 1931.

E. C. Bentley, Anthony Berkeley, Agatha Christie, Freeman Wills Croft, Ronald
    Knox, Dorothy L. Sayers, and Valentine Williams. *"The Scoop" and "Be-
    hind the Screen."* New York: Harper, 1983; London: Gollancz, 1983.

CRITICAL BIBLIOGRAPHY

Bargainnier, Earl F. *The Gentle Art of Murder: The Detective Fiction of Agatha
    Christie.* Bowling Green, Ohio: Popular Press, 1980.
Barnard, Robert. *A Talent to Deceive: An Appreciation of Agatha Christie.* New
    York: Dodd, 1980.
Feinman, Jeffrey. *The Mysterious World of Agatha Christie.* New York: Award,
    1975.
Fitzgibbon, Russell H. *The Agatha Christie Companion.* Bowling Green, Ohio: Pop-
    ular Press, 1980.
Gill, Gillian. *Agatha Christie: The Woman and Her Mysteries.* New York: Free
    Press, 1990.
Haining, Peter. *Agatha Christie: Murder in Four Acts.* London: Virgin, 1990.
Hart, Anne. *The Life and Times of Hercule Poirot.* New York: Putnam's, 1990.
————. *The Life and Times of Miss Jane Marple.* New York: Dodd, 1985.
Keating, H.R.F., ed. *Agatha Christie: First Lady of Crime.* New York: Holt, 1977.
Maida, Patricia D., and Nicholas B. Spornick. *Murder She Wrote: A Study of Aga-
    tha Christie's Detective Fiction.* Bowling Green, Ohio: Popular Press, 1982.
Morgan, Janet. *Agatha Christie: A Biography.* New York: Knopf, 1985.
Murdoch, Derrick. *The Agatha Christie Mystery.* Toronto, Canada: Pagurian,
    1976.
Osborne, Charles. *The Life and Crimes of Agatha Christie.* Chicago: Contemporary
    Books, 1990.
Ramsey, G. C. *Agatha Christie: Mistress of Mystery.* New York: Dodd, 1967.
Riley, Dick, and Pam McAllister, eds. *The Bedside, Bathtub and Armchair Com-
    panion to Agatha Christie.* New York: Ungar, 1979.
Robyns, Gwen. *The Mystery of Agatha Christie.* New York: Doubleday, 1978.
Sanders, Dennis, and Len Lovallo. *The Agatha Christie Companion: The Complete
    Guide to Agatha Christie's Life and Work.* Rev. ed. New York: Berkley,
    1989.
Shaw, Marion, and Sabine Vanacker. *Reflecting on Miss Marple.* London: Rou-
    tledge, 1991.
Toye, Randall, comp. *The Agatha Christie Who's Who.* New York: Greenwich, 1980.
Underwood, Lynn, ed. *Agatha Christie: Official Centenary Edition, 1890–1990.*
    New York: Harper, 1990.
Wagoner, Mary S. *Agatha Christie.* Boston: Hall, 1986.
Wynne, Nancy Blue. *An Agatha Christie Chronology.* New York: Ace, 1976.

MARTY S. KNEPPER

MARY HIGGINS CLARK (1929–   )

Mary Higgins Clark was born in New York City on December 24, 1929,
and grew up in the Bronx. While working as a Pan Am airline stewardess,

she married Warren Clark in 1949. After he died in 1964, she wrote radio scripts to support her five children until she sold her first novel, *Where Are the Children?* With ten bestselling suspense novels to date, Clark has been crowned "Queen of Suspense." A grandmother of five, she resides in Saddle River, New Jersey.

Right from the beginning, Clark established herself as anything but a mere spinner of suspense novels about distraught heroines menaced by villains and rescued by Mr. Right. In her very first novel, *Where Are the Children?* Clark introduced the kind of heroine who was to dominate her work: an independent, resourceful woman who knows exactly what she is up against and what she has to do to survive. In her early novels, the heroine is an ordinary woman driven by terrifying circumstances to do extraordinary things. For example, the heroine of her second novel, *A Stranger Is Watching*, is a housewife who outwits a ruthless killer who is holding her and a small child hostage deep in the bowels of Grand Central Station.

Unfortunately, the heroine of *A Cry in the Night*, Clark's fourth novel, is more damsel-in-distress than feisty adversary. In this novel, a poor, deceived young woman is swept off her feet by a "Prince Charming" and transported to a remote Minnesota farm where she finds her days filled with loneliness and her nights with terror. Clark, who works best in an urban setting, and preferably New York, is out of her element here.

Beginning with *A Cry in the Night*, Clark embarked on a series of experimental novels in which she tried her hand at types of mystery fiction usually associated with other popular writers. *A Cry in the Night* is a Gothic tale reminiscent of Daphne du Maurier, while *The Cradle Will Fall* is a medical thriller in the tradition of Robin Cook. However, in this novel Clark is back in stride with clearly defined adversaries, a tenacious heroine, and page-turning suspense. In *Stillwatch*, a political thriller set in Washington, D.C., Clark invades territory that is familiar to readers of Margaret Truman. In competition with such a formidable rival, Clark succeeds admirably by positing not one, but two strong women protagonists, one a senator about to be appointed vice-president, and the other, a television producer assigned to film a special on the senator. Not the least fascinating element of this intriguing novel is the interweaving of the lives and fates of these two determined, but vulnerable, women. *Weep No More, My Lady* is a "celebrity" mystery, a popular genre that was once the exclusive domain of Thomas Tryon (*Crowned Heads*). Unfortunately, Clark strains credulity with both her setting, a posh California health spa, and her heroine, a young woman who is reluctantly drawn into investigating the murder of her sister, a glamorous movie star.

Having challenged other turf with mixed results, Clark returned to New York in her next four novels, each of which shows Clark in top form. Although the metropolitan setting and a taut story line account for much of this success, what really clinches it is a savvier breed of heroine whose relationships on all levels are more fully realized. Beginning with *While My Pretty One Sleeps*, which is set in the world of high fashion, Clark's protagonists tend to be professional women who move in sophisticated circles. Furthermore, the interactions between people, especially within families, are based on a value system that Clark clearly supports. In this novel, for example, the relationships that the heroine maintains with her father and her fiancé are positive and reassuring.

In her later novels, Clark also reveals adroitness at tackling contemporary issues. *Loves Music, Loves to Dance* is a novel about the risk involved when people use the personal ads to find romance. In this case, two Manhattan career women find themselves pursued by a psychopath when, to help a friend with his research, they agree to place ads in personal columns. How they become aware and fight back is a lesson in urban survival.

Clark combines the issue of child abuse with the enigma of multiple personalities in *All around the Town*, another thriller right out of today's headlines. In this one, Clark blends psychological insight with classic suspense to solve the crime by first solving the mystery of her main character's complex identity. Clark treats sensitive issues with candor but without sensationalism. She is equally up-to-date in *I'll Be Seeing You*, a carefully crafted thriller in which she places a cast of wildly different characters in a network of intrigue involving scandal at a fertility clinic, a bigamist, a stalker, and an imposter—all orchestrated to produce a conclusion that is both totally surprising and thoroughly convincing.

Readers who are new to Mary Higgins Clark are advised to start with either the very early or the very recent novels.

MYSTERY FICTION

Where Are the Children? New York: Simon and Schuster; London: Talmy Franklin, 1975.
A Stranger Is Watching. New York: Simon and Schuster, 1977; London: Collins, 1978.
The Cradle Will Fall. New York: Simon and Schuster; London: Collins, 1980.
A Cry in the Night. New York: Simon and Schuster, 1982; London: Collins, 1983.
Stillwatch. New York: Simon and Schuster; London: Collins, 1984.
Weep No More, My Lady. New York: Simon and Schuster; London: Collins, 1987.
The Anastasia Syndrome and Other Stories. New York: Simon and Schuster, 1989; London: Century, 1990.
While My Pretty One Sleeps. New York: Simon and Schuster; London: Century, 1989.
Loves Music, Loves to Dance. New York: Simon and Schuster, 1991; London: Chivers, 1992.
All around the Town. New York: Simon and Schuster; London: Century, 1992.
I'll Be Seeing You. New York: Simon and Schuster, 1993.
Remember Me. New York: Simon and Schuster, 1994.

CRITICAL BIBLIOGRAPHY

Freeman, Lucy. "Mary Higgins Clark." *The Armchair Detective*, 18, no. 3 (1985): 228–37.

Hoch, Edward D. "Clark, Mary Higgins." In *Twentieth Century Crime and Mystery Writers*, ed. Lesley Henderson. 3rd ed. Chicago and London: St. James, 1991, pp. 210–11.

THOMAS WHISSEN

ANNA CLARKE (1919–   )

Anna Clarke was born in Cape Town, South Africa, on April 28, 1919. Educated in South Africa, Montreal, Oxford, and London, she had decided on studying mathematics at the university, but a severe illness made this impossible. In 1945 Clarke earned a B.Sc. in economics at the University of London. Afterwards, she worked as a private secretary for the publishers Victor Gollancz and Eyre & Spottiswoode. From 1956 to 1962 Clarke was administrative secretary to the British Association for American Studies. Clarke published her first mystery in 1968, turning to this genre after attempting nonmystery novels. She began writing to escape the tedium of her job and a restricted physical life. In 1973, Clarke earned a B.A. from Open University in London and in 1975, an M.A. from Sussex University in literature.

Clarke studied literature to learn more about the creative process but found that it remained a mystery. For her, it was "fascinating, but insoluble." The sources of her stories are many and often unexpected, sometimes originating from a single sentence that came to mind. While Clarke described her works as unplanned and written without any preestablished routine, her novels are tightly plotted and psychologically convincing.

Clarke describes herself as a feminist, but a humanist first. Her novels are set in the recognizable world of modern Britain, frequently in the academic world of London University or the suburbs or countryside outside London. However, the sense of familiarity soon slips away as outwardly conventional characters reveal their quirky and highly emotional inner selves. Clarke specializes in revealing disturbed psyches hidden behind nondescript and outwardly normal appearances. Because the world she describes seems so ordinary, murder appears out of place, yet many accidental deaths turn out to have been carefully planned murders. Frequently, murderers give themselves away by repeating their crimes once too often, revealing a pattern behind the deaths.

Clarke's characters are frequently warped by others' attempts to control them or by their need to control other people. A recurring character in

Clarke's novels is a physically and psychologically crippled woman who thrives on manipulating others. Such a figure appears in *Murder in Writing*, *The Poisoned Web*, and *A Mind to Murder*. Other characters rebel against those who take their passionate devotion for granted, as happens in *Poison Parsley*, *The End of a Shadow*, *The Lady in Black*, and *Last Judgement*. In Clarke's work, the more hidden the relationship, the more passionate the feelings underlying it.

Although Clarke believes that her gender has made little difference in her own life, her novels demonstrate an interest in examining women's lives from different perspectives. Many women in her novels are insane to some degree, which often drives them to murder. Women who were driven to madness by men appear in *Desire to Kill*, *One of Us Must Die*, *Legacy of Evil*, *Last Judgement*, and *Game, Set and Danger*. Troubling childhood memories make Ruth, in *My Search for Ruth*, and Sally Livingstone, in *Last Voyage*, struggle against the possibility of insanity and those who try to control their memories of the past.

Clarke's interest in literature surfaces in her fiction in several ways. Often, her novels focus on literary artifacts such as letters or manuscripts. Several look at the process of writing and its relation to life. Authors, critics, and publishers make frequent appearances as characters. *Soon She Must Die* openly analyzes the relation of its plot to Henry James's *Wings of the Dove*. One of Clarke's frequent themes is that people need to create fictions in order to live their lives. Her novels demonstrate that life and fiction are difficult to separate.

Seven of Clarke's novels focus on the character of Dr. Paula Glenning, a university professor of literature whose curiosity and desire to help others involve her in uncovering mysteries. Paula is a woman of good sense as well as good heart, and her sanity prevents her from being drawn into fictions spun by less unbalanced minds. Paula has a network of friends and lovers. In particular, as Paula's relationship with Professor James Goff deepens from friendship into a long-term commitment, Goff plays an increasingly prominent role in solving the mysteries. Glenning and Goff often stumble on their solutions; their lack of expertise makes them realistic figures. In tracing Goff's development from a selfish young man into a considerate companion, Clarke has drawn one of the more realistic pictures of a relationship to be found in detective fiction.

Clarke is often compared to Ruth Rendell and Dorothy Salisbury Davis. Glenning is reminiscent of Kate Fansler in the novels of Amanda Cross.

Readers would do well to begin with the first Paula Glenning novel, *Last Judgement*, or the nonseries works, *The Poisoned Web* and *My Search for Ruth*, which will quickly engage readers.

MYSTERY FICTION

The Darkened Room. London: Long, 1968; New York: Berkley, 1991.
A Mind to Murder. London: Chatto & Windus, 1971; New York: Berkley, 1991.

The End of a Shadow. London: Chatto and Windus, 1972; New York: Berkley, 1991.

Plot Counter-Plot. London: Collins, 1974; New York: Walker, 1975.

My Search for Ruth. London: Collins, 1975; New York: Richardson Steirman Black, 1988.

The Deathless and the Dead. London: Collins, 1976; as *The Downhill Path*. New York: McKay, 1977.

Legacy of Evil. London: Collins, 1976; New York: Berkley, 1991.

The Lady in Black. London: Collins, 1977; New York: McKay, 1978.

Letter from the Dead. London: Collins, 1977; New York: Doubleday, 1981.

One of Us Must Die. London: Collins, 1977; New York: Doubleday, 1980.

The Poisoned Web. London: Collins, 1979; New York: St. Martin's Press, 1982.

Poison Parsley. London: Collins, 1979; New York: Berkley, 1992.

Last Voyage. London: Collins, 1980; New York: St. Martin's Press, 1982.

Game, Set, and Danger. New York: Doubleday, 1981; London: Hale, 1983.

Desire to Kill. New York: Doubleday, 1982; London: Hale, 1983.

We the Bereaved. New York: Doubleday, 1982; London: Hale, 1984.

Soon She Must Die. New York: Doubleday, 1984; London: Hale, 1985.

Paula Glenning Series

Last Judgement. New York: Doubleday, 1985; London: Hale, 1986.

Cabin 3033. New York: Doubleday, 1986; Bath, England: Chivers, 1988.

The Mystery Lady. New York: Doubleday, 1986; London: Severn House, 1988.

Last Seen in London. New York: Doubleday, 1987; Bath, England: Chivers, 1992.

Murder in Writing. New York: Doubleday, 1988.

The Whitelands Affair. New York: Doubleday, 1989.

The Case of the Paranoid Patient. New York: Doubleday, 1991.

CRITICAL BIBLIOGRAPHY

Douglas, Kristen V. "Anna Clarke." In *Critical Survey of Mystery and Detective Fiction*, ed. Frank N. Magill. Pasadena, Calif.: Salem Press, 1988, pp. 354–59.

Grimes, Larry E. "Clarke, Anna." In *Twentieth Century Crime and Mystery Writers*, ed. Lesley Henderson. 3rd ed. Chicago and London: St. James, 1991, pp. 211–13.

"It's Never Too Late." *Ladies Home Journal*, 103 (January 1986): 86.

MARILYN RYE

LIZA CODY (1944–   )

Liza Cody was born on April 11, 1944. She studied painting, sculpture, etching, and engraving at the City and Guilds of London Art School and qualified for a Certificate of Merit upon completion of her coursework. At graduation in 1964, she was awarded a scholarship to study in Italy and later was given a place at the Royal Academy School of Art.

At the end of her first year at the Royal Academy, she married a sculptor, and in 1966 she gave birth to a daughter. In 1974, she traveled in Africa for six months and was unwillingly swept up in the Ethiopian revolution. Her experiences are recorded in a riveting novel called *Rift*.

When Cody returned to England, she tried her hand at story telling. Although she admired the work of Dashiell Hammett and Raymond Chandler, Cody felt she could not deal with a male protagonist, nor with a loner: "Because I am a woman, I understand women better. I think women are more complex; they have more layers." Moreover, she did not find the portrayal of women—especially working women—in mainstream fiction or detective fiction particularly realistic. Anna Lee is based on English women that Cody observed in the military and police forces who are somewhat damaged by their professional training (i.e., by trying to fit into a traditional, male-dominated occupation). As a result, they become somewhat "masculine," bossy, and defensively competent.

Liza Cody's Anna Lee is one of a small group of fictional female P.I.'s in England. Anna Lee was preceded by P. D. James's Cordelia Gray and has recently been joined by Sarah Dunant's Hannah Wolfe and Val McDermid's Kate Brannigan. By contrast with Cordelia Gray, Anna Lee and the other investigators seem more mature and woman-like, perhaps because they are more sexually experienced. Certainly they are "tougher" in their worldview. In the conventional P.I. tradition, all of them can survive on the mean streets, and all can—and do—"take a beating." Also traditionally, their "victory" is often incomplete or tarnished in some way.

Cody claims that Anna Lee is not a professed feminist; rather, she is an apolitical figure, a woman who merely wants to do a job well, not to change the system. Cody herself does want to change the system by pointing out its inequities, but she decided very early on that her books should "show" rather than "tell" of women's second-class status. They record the gross inequities of entrenched male privilege, the cozy but exclusive camaraderie of male bonding, and the unconscious arrogance and condescension expressed by men in their treatment of women in countless daily interactions. The calm assumption of women's incompetence and inherent inferiority is registered in numerous put-downs: from failing to introduce women to ignoring them in conversation or talking about them in the third person as if they were absent or deaf; from making denigrating casual remarks to the habitual use of status-lowering diminutives or outright abuse; and from the universal assumption that the bottom line of a woman's worth is her sexual attractiveness.

Anna is part of the small staff of five men and two women that constitutes the Brierly Security Agency, which is owned and managed by Martin Brierly. Although he employs her, Brierly continues to regard Anna as not

entirely trustworthy and constantly questions her judgment and unorthodox methods, while profiting from her results. In *Dupe*, after Anna has
solved a difficult case against great odds and sustained personal injury as
well as damage to her home, and at a time when she deserves not only to
be praised but to be comforted, Brierly nearly fires her after confiscating a
cash reward she has won. In *Stalker*, after she has been forced off the road
and her car is wrecked while on a job, Brierly insists it is Anna's fault for
not following instructions. No matter how well she performs or how much
she earns for Brierly, she never receives anything more than grudging approval.

In five of the six Anna Lee novels, Anna is the lowest in the pecking order
at the agency. Except for Bernie Schiller, an older man who respects and
befriends her, Anna is merely tolerated rather than accepted by the other
(male) investigators—Johnny Crocker, Phil Maitland, and Tim Baker. The
only other female in the office is Beryl Doyle, the office manager, a woman
who "blooms most richly in all male company." Like many women who
have conceded power to the male gender, Beryl resents women who successfully compete with men professionally and refuses to grant Anna equal
respect with the men because to do so would be to acknowledge her own
second-class status.

In five of the six Anna Lee novels, Anna is hired to locate, rescue, and/
or exonerate a young woman who is in jeopardy. In most of them, moreover, the victim has been betrayed by a man in her first sexual encounter,
although she contributes to her own predicament in trusting the wrong
man due to lack of sexual experience and because she seeks sexual initiation
without fully understanding the risks involved. In most cases, she is betrayed by an older man who exploits her for selfish reasons or fails to
realize her vulnerability among experienced adults. Catastrophe results in
either case. Anna's job is to retrieve the situation insofar as she is able, but
her assistance is not usually welcomed by the victim. Furthermore, in many
instances—do what she will—she is unable to win the confidence of the
victim or effectually mend the damage. Cody stated: "The Anna Lee books
are about failed responsibility. Anna tries to take responsibility but she
fails."

Anna left school at sixteen with a high enough examination score to
qualify for the police force, where she spent five years prior to joining
Brierly Security. She occupies the upstairs flat in a house on the cusp between Shepherds Bush and Notting Hill in London. She is friendly with her
neighbors in the downstairs flat, Bea and Selwyn Price, who function as a
surrogate family. Anna performs small household chores like mending the
lawnmower and cutting the grass, and in exchange, Bea often invites her
over for meals. Anna has lovers from time to time but no permanent relationship. Of course, what she observes in her daily experience would not
tend to encourage a belief in love's permanency.

In her most recent novel, *Bucket Nut*, Cody introduces a new protagonist, Eva Wylie, the "London Lassassin." An aspiring female wrestler who earns her living as a one-woman security agency, Armour Protection, and lives in a second-hand trailer in the used car and wrecker's yard she guards, Eva is not really a detective at all. Although *Bucket Nut* is a crime novel, it is not a murder mystery but rather is closer to the thriller in that the central character becomes unwittingly swept up in violent action and must save herself. Because she runs errands part time for Mr. Cheng, who operates a protection racket, and hires herself out as a bouncer (euphemistically labeled "crowd control"), and because she frequently "borrows" cars and "boosts" merchandise, wallets, or whatever she needs at the moment, Eva cannot turn to the police for help. Moreover, she loathes the "polizei" because of her hostile adolescent encounters with them, and in any case, would consider it demeaning to ask anyone for help.

With her large physical frame and self-sufficient life-style, Eva violates every aspect of what is conventionally considered feminine and sexually attractive and is rejected by both men and women as a grotesque. She has developed a tough, aggressive personality in order to survive in an unkind world. A misfit without friends, she secretly longs for affection and companionship. Like Anna, Eva tries to protect a young woman in trouble but fails. Eva is as engaging as she is ingenious—a true original—and *Bucket Nut* is a brilliant contribution to the genre.

Cody won the John Creasey Award for *Dupe* as the best first crime novel in 1980; the Crime Writers Association's Silver Dagger Award in 1992 for *Bucket Nut*; and the Anthony Award in 1992 for a short story, "Lucky Dip."

Readers who are most interested in Anna's professional exploits will find her in top form as detective cum unwelcome surrogate mother in *Bad Company*, *Headcase*, and *Backhand*. *Dupe*, *Stalker*, and *Headcase* furnish the most background on her personal life.

MYSTERY FICTION

Anna Lee Series

Dupe. London: Collins, 1980; New York: Scribners, 1983.

Bad Company. London: Collins; New York: Scribners, 1982.

Stalker. London: Collins; New York: Scribners, 1984.

Headcase. London: Collins, 1985; New York: Scribners, 1986.

Under Contract. London: Collins, 1986; New York: Scribners, 1987.

Backhand. London: Chatto, 1991; New York: Doubleday, 1992.

Eva Wylie Series

Bucket Nut. London: Chatto, 1992; New York: Doubleday, 1993.

Monkey Wrench. London: Chatto, 1994.

CRITICAL BIBLIOGRAPHY

Bakerman, Jane S. "Cody, Liza." In *Twentieth Century Crime and Mystery Writers*, ed. Lesley Henderson. 3rd ed. Chicago and London: St. James, 1991, pp. 220–21.
Nichols, Victoria, and Susan Thompson. "Anna Lee." In *Silk Stalkings*. Berkeley, Calif.: Black Lizard, pp. 214–15.

B. J. RAHN

SUSAN CONANT (?–   )

Susan Conant was born and raised in Merrimack Valley, Massachusetts. She graduated from Radcliffe College and the Harvard Graduate School of Education with a Ed.D. in human development. Her husband is a clinical psychologist and practices in Cambridge, Massachusetts. They have been married for twenty-four years and have one daughter. Like Holly Winter, her novels' character, Conant owns two Alaskan Malamute dogs as well as two cats. She is the Massachusetts coordinator of the Alaskan Malamute Protection League, edits *Pawprints*, the newsletter of the New England Dog Training Club, and trains with the New England and Charles River Dog Training Clubs.

Conant is the recipient of a 1991 Maxwell Award for Fiction Writing. Her work has been published in *Pure-Bred Dogs/American Kennel Gazette* and *Dog World*. There are obvious correspondences between Conant's life and that of her fictional character, the dog-loving Holly Winter.

Holly Winter is introduced in *A New Leash on Death* as a single, thirty-year-old writer for "*Dog's Life*" magazine, who mourns the recent loss of her beloved golden retriever and is haunted by the memory of her mother, who died several years before. Her father is a loving but seemingly eccentric dog fanatic who shares his home in Maine with an ever-growing number of wolf-dogs. Winter's parents raised her to love and respect dogs and to be independent, and she learned both lessons well. Winter is not characterized after the ubiquitous "Eccentric Sleuth" of Charles Dickens, Wilkie Collins, and Arthur Conan Doyle. Rather, she is sociable and self-reliant— and she buys her clothes from the L. L. Bean store.

Fate alone introduces Winter to crime solving when, one night at the Cambridge Dog Training Club, a fellow trainer disappears. Each subsequent novel in the series revolves around the suspicious death of a "dog person." Winter's concern for the victims and their dogs incites her to bypass the traditional methods of the local police and initiate investigations of her own. Single by choice, she dodges the advances of her next-door neighbor (a local Irish cop named Kevin Dennehy, with whom she otherwise maintains a friendship), partly for friendship's sake and partly for the information she can extract from him concerning the murder investigations. She has an ongoing—and casual—sexual affair with her veterinarian, Steve Delaney. They share a passion for dogs and an occasional weekend together, but there is no commitment between them and Winter prefers to keep it that way.

Winter's independent nature, coupled with her keen understanding of dogs and the nature of their owners, enables her to run circles around the slow, methodical, and usually ineffective tactics employed by police investigators. The murders and subsequent investigations happen locally. Though not intimately acquainted with the victims, she knows them through dog clubs and colleagues and is deeply affected when owners are murdered and their dogs are orphaned. By the conclusion of the third novel, *A Bite of Death*, Winter has "adopted" two Alaskan Malamutes, Rowdy and Kimi, from their murdered owners.

Of her six novels, Conant's *A Bite of Death* deals most completely with women's issues. Psychologist Elaine Walsh is found dead of an apparent drug overdose. However, the story revolves primarily around Joel and Kelly Baker, a couple who appear to have a perfect marriage by conventional standards. However, the Bakers have remained in the closet in terms of their sexual identity, and the pretense of their lives combined with the shame of their secret drives them to murder, suicide, and ultimate exposure. The novel bitterly illustrates what happens when the individual denies his or her own convictions in exchange for the acceptance and approval that come from adhering to the established social order. The emphasis is on the female experience of such self-denial and prescribed behavior: "This is a world that makes it difficult for women to act directly, and people prevented from acting directly become people who find it difficult to play fair." The conclusion offers little hope of any liberation from such stifling, and indeed deadly, social values. In the midst of a comparatively light and easygoing canine mystery, Conant manages to give the reader abstruse and valuable issues to consider.

Winter grows and expands as a character from the first novel on, and much of her current status and attitudes can be grasped only by backtracking to *A New Leash on Death*, the earliest novel. The first chapter of each story offers a short biographical rundown on Winter and may see the reader through sufficiently, but with the sacrifice of witnessing character development. For that reason, I strongly suggest reading the novels in their sequential order.

Diehard dog haters, or those who are thoroughly indifferent to the species, will nonetheless find themselves fascinated by and drawn to the beautiful world of dogs as it is played against the terror and mystery of death and Holly Winter's challenge of the conventional modes of thinking.

Although not broadly represented, the world of animals has begun to appear as a background for mystery and detective stories. For those readers who wish to explore further, I recommend Dick Francis or Lillian Jackson Braun, both of whom use the animal world as a background for murder.

MYSTERY FICTION

Holly Winter Series

Dead and Doggone. New York: Berkley Publishing Group, 1990.

A New Leash on Death. New York: Berkley Publishing Group, 1990.

A Bite of Death. New York: Berkley Publishing Group, 1991.

Paws before Dying. New York: Berkley Publishing Group, 1991.

Bloodlines. New York: Doubleday, 1992.

Gone to the Dogs. New York: Doubleday, 1992.

Ruffly Speaking. New York: Doubleday, 1994.

BARBARA DOUGLAS

PATRICIA D. CORNWELL (1956–   )

Patricia D. Cornwell was born in Miami, Florida, in 1956 and grew up in that state. She graduated from Davidson College in North Carolina in 1979 with a degree in English and subsequently became an award-winning police reporter for the *Charlotte Observer*. In 1981, she moved to Richmond, Virginia, with her then-husband, a Davidson professor who had enrolled in Union Theological Seminary. In 1983 she published *A Time for Remembering*, a biography of Ruth Bell Graham, the wife of the evangelist Reverend Billy Graham. After her divorce, in preparation for writing crime novels, Cornwell became a volunteer police officer in Richmond and was employed as a computer analyst in the chief medical examiner's office. She continues to live in Richmond, where she serves as a consultant to the chief medical examiner. She is committed to authenticity in her crime fiction. To date, she has published four crime novels: *Postmortem*, which won the Edgar, Creasy, Anthony, and Macavity awards; *Body of Evidence*; *All That Remains*; and *Cruel and Unusual*.

All her novels are set in Richmond, the city with—as is pointed out in *Postmortem*—the second highest per-capita homicide rate in the United States. Kay Scarpetta, chief medical examiner of Virginia and a forty-year-old divorcee, narrates the stories and is the protagonist. A great deal of emphasis is placed on forensic medicine and computer programming, making the novels unusual contributions to crime fiction and resulting in an unusual subgenre of the police procedural.

Both a lawyer and doctor, Scarpetta possesses a formidable intelligence. As a professional woman committed to her career, she must confront the prejudices of a male-dominated justice system. Her relationship with Marino, the police detective with whom she works in all the novels, is shown to evolve. In the first novel, their relationship is tense because of his suspicion and distrust of her, but in the third book, *All That Remains*, mutual respect, sympathy, and even affection have replaced the tension. Scarpetta is attempting to balance commitment to career with her personal life, and when it is revealed in *All That Remains* that Marino's wife has left him because of his obsession with his work and his neglect of her, Kay and Marino recognize that they confront similar problems and draw closer together personally.

The crimes in all the novels are multiple killings, often with women as the primary victims. In her novels, Cornwell emphasizes violence, but not through describing the violence as it occurs. Rather, she focuses on medical details to convey the effects. Kay is an excellent medical detective able to look objectively at the details of the cases, but she is also sensitive and becomes emotionally involved, sometimes placing herself in physical jeopardy as a result. Because of Kay's character, the novels convey a sense of fear, isolation, and loss.

All That Remains seems to place less emphasis on forensic detail and shows more interest in the psychology of Kay Scarpetta. In the second novel, Mark James, a former lover when they were in law school together, reappears in Kay's life. Mark is an FBI agent who is committed to his career, so while he and Kay clearly love one another, in the third novel tension exists between them as they try to balance commitment to their respective careers and to one another. The most recent novel reveals that Mark has been killed by a terrorist bomb. Unable to deal with that death, Kay retreats within herself and begins to have difficulty relating to others. One would expect the focus on Kay's personal life to continue in future novels.

Although readers can best gain a clear sense of Kay's development thus far by reading all the novels in sequence, I would recommend *All That Remains* for an introduction to Cornwell's crime fiction.

MYSTERY FICTION

Kay Scarpetta Series

Postmortem. New York: Scribner's, 1990; London: Macdonald-Futura, 1991.
Body of Evidence. New York: Scribner's; Toronto: Collier-Macmillan, 1991.

All That Remains. New York: Scribner's; Toronto: Maxwell-Macmillan, 1992.

Cruel and Unusual. New York: Scribner's; Toronto: Maxwell-Macmillan, 1993.

ESSAY

"Having Something to Say." *The Writer*, 104 (December 1991): 18–20.

CRITICAL BIBLIOGRAPHY

Herbert, Rosemary. "All That Remains." *The Armchair Detective*, 25, no. 4 (1993): 388.

Tangorra, Joanne. "PW Interviews: Patricia D. Cornwell." *Publishers Weekly*, 238 (February 15, 1991): 71–72.

FRANK W. SHELTON

AMANDA CROSS (1926–   )

Amanda Cross, a pseudonym of Carolyn Heilbrun, was born in East Orange, New Jersey, on January 13, 1926. She grew up in New York City, graduated from Wellesley College, and received her M.A. and Ph.D. from Columbia University. After twelve years teaching at Brooklyn College, she returned to Columbia, where she taught English, humanities, and Women's Studies for the next twenty years. She was Avalon Professor of the Humanities when she resigned in 1992. A literary critic, she began writing detective novels in 1963, using a pseudonym to protect herself since she was an assistant professor working toward tenure. She married James Heilbrun and has three children.

Her first novel, *In the Last Analysis*, received a scroll from the Mystery Writers of America as one of the best first novels of 1964 and was nominated for an Edgar, also for best first novel. *Death in a Tenured Position*, her sixth novel, received the 1981 Nero Wolfe Award for mystery fiction.

Amanda Cross's detective Kate Fansler is a tall, thin, witty literary critic and feminist in the classic amateur detective mold. In her mid- to late thirties, she is independently wealthy and works as a tenured associate professor in the English graduate studies division of a well-known Manhattan university. Established as a keen mind and a wit through scholarly publications and her teaching reputation, she first finds herself involved in murderous pursuits when she helps an old friend and former lover in *In the Last Analysis*, sorts out a publisher's library of letters, in *The James Joyce Murder*, pinch-hits at her old school in *The Theban Mysteries*, or accompanies a colleague on a seemingly innocent jaunt in *The Question of Max*. These rambles lead to chaos and confusion, death, murder, and mayhem.

Family associations, a wide circle of friends, and reasonable fame in her field of literary criticism also place Kate—"an aging Nancy Drew"—at the scene of the crime, and often, in fact, as one of the chief suspects. Her academic credentials and Noel Cowardesque comedic repartee generally bewilder, befuddle, or infuriate the police; consequently, it is very fortunate that she has maintained a long relationship with Reed Amhearst, an assistant district attorney who connects her to the legal apparatus and whom she later marries. Her expert scholarship makes Kate a good detective and a persistent one, with an eye for the particular unobtrusive, seemingly insignificant detail that is in fact the key to the case. Moreover, her ability to synthesize that key into a complex and complicated narrative matrix not only solves the crime but make sense of it as well.

Fansler might have continued as only a mannered, witty, and charming character had not Cross placed her squarely in the middle of radical university politics. In the third book, *Poetic Justice*, when the university is "occupied by students," Kate finds herself defending a nontraditional student bastion. While accumulating doubt about her world perspective, Kate Fansler changes: she not only proposes to Reed—risking marriage—but extends that risk to other openly political and private causes.

Cross and Fansler have a love of, and special gift for, dialogue and elegance of language. The novels turn on exchanges of ideas and discussions of human and literary issues. This talk enriches every book, but it also demonstrates the importance of knowledge, literature, and thought. Another impressive motif in the novels is Cross's definition of thought and knowledge as developed via Kate's experiences. While Fansler may try to be rational in the traditional sense, her knowledge and thinking are repeatedly shown to be a synthesis of knowledges—acquired in learning, through lived experience, by age, with emotional commitment, and in sensitivity to vibrations in the web of living. Fansler's conversations are simultaneously research and laboratories for detection.

Cross creates her academic setting vividly and accurately, and her university is much more than a backdrop; for the intricacies of academic relationships and culture seethe with those passions, hatreds and pettinesses that serve as fertile ground for vengeful angers and murderous acts. Clearly, for Cross, academia contains no sacred cows. While many of the characters build on fairly familiar academic types, Cross complicates and illuminates their personae precisely, sometimes humorously but always with devastating clarity.

Cross writes detective novels of character and manners, or perhaps her characters believe they are in a novel of manners until they fall across a dead body somewhere in the middle of the novel. Then, her revelations peel away the layers of the most ordinary, familiar, or loved. Her characters and the novels themselves are rich in comedic range, human foible and eccentricity, philosophical conundrum, and murder puzzle.

Notably, however, in *The Question of Max*, Cross turns to a subject that occupies her attention in her later novels—"the woman question:" in particular, the lives, biographies, and autobiographies of women—their relationships, class status, choices in a patriarchal culture, professional possibilities, and private realities. Women's biography becomes the context for investigations of whatever crisis led to death. Kate uses her wit and insight to piece together the life before the death in a biography of sorts, and her solution depends on understanding the life and the people in it. To this end, Cross treats women as human beings who have been the subjects of silences and of unwritten narratives. Her last novel, *The Players Come Again*, tackles these speaking silences in a rich texture of friendship, marriage, and various documents. Fansler's compassion brings a special vividness to the structures of women's lives, particularly in their conflicted private multiplicity, but also in the public dissensions among feminists and feminisms, the clashes within professions—and ultimately, the confusions and dangers of being a woman in a male culture.

In her concern for women's lives, Cross explores the conflicts women face when teaching in universities that are given over to male bureaucrats, the profit motive, and administrations that pander to corporate money while advocating humanitarian and egalitarian ideals.

Kate becomes a strong "insider" advocate for women and other marginalized groups. Her later cases explore and expose the subtleties of disadvantage with which women cope every day, and Fansler's frustrations dramatize the elusive nature of the women in the case. Cross obviously perceives that women's lives, as obscured by simultaneous and multiple public personae, make excellent detective fiction material. As a good detective, Kate Fansler reconstructs what happened to the victim but in addition, and perhaps more important to her (and more satisfying to her fans), is the fact that Fansler and Cross give women life, even in death.

Certainly, Kate Fansler and company will grow on the reader if the books are read in order, but for those who are interested in a literary mystery combined with a screwball comedy, *The James Joyce Murder* is a good introduction to the range of characters in the Cross canon. For intricacy, fun, and action, I recommend *The Question of Max*; and for one of the funniest academic scenes in literature, see the dissertation examination in *Poetic Justice*. The latter novel is also a fascinating portrayal of academic politics. Finally, for those interested in biography—as issue, research dilemma, and life story—Cross's *The Players Come Again* is brilliant and absolutely engrossing.

Readers captured by the Kate Fansler novels might also enjoy Jane Langton, Charlotte MacLeod, Elizabeth Peters, Margot Arnold, Anne Perry, Ellis Peters, and Carole Nelson Douglas.

MYSTERY FICTION

Kate Fansler Series

In the Last Analysis. New York: Macmillan; London: Gollancz, 1964.

The James Joyce Murder. New York: Macmillan; London: Gollancz, 1967.

Poetic Justice. New York: Knopf; London: Gollancz, 1967.

The Theban Mysteries. New York: Knopf; London: Gollancz, 1971.

The Question of Max. New York: Knopf, 1976; London: Virago, 1984.

Death in a Tenured Position. New York: Dutton, 1981; as *Death in the Faculty.* London: Virago, 1981.

Sweet Death, Kind Death. New York: Dutton, 1984; London: Gollancz, 1986.

No Word from Winifred. New York: Dutton, 1986; London: Virago, 1987.

A Trap for Fools. New York: Dutton; London: Chivers, 1989.

The Players Come Again. New York: Random House, 1990; London: Virago, 1991.

CRITICAL BIBLIOGRAPHY

Barasch, Frances K. "Faculty Images in Recent American Fiction." *College Literature*, 10, no. 1 (Winter 1983): 28–37.

Berkley, Miriam. "PW Interviews: Carolyn Heilbrun/Amanda Cross." *Publishers Weekly*, 235 (April 14, 1989): 47–48.

Carter, Steven R. "Amanda Cross." In *Ten Women of Mystery*, ed. Earl F. Bargainnier. Bowling Green, Ohio: Bowling Green State University Popular Press, 1981, pp. 269–96.

Heilbrun, Carolyn. *Hamlet's Mother and Other Women.* New York: Ballantine, 1990.

Knepper, Marty. "Who Killed Janet Mandelbaum and India Wonder? A Look at the Suicides of Token Women in Amanda Cross's *Death in a Tenured Position* and Dorothy Bryant's *Killing Wonder*." *Clues: A Journal of Detection*, 13, no. 1 (Spring-Summer 1992): 45–58.

Lussier, Mark, and Peggy McCormack. "Heilbrun: An Interview." *New Orleans Review*, 13, no. 4 (Winter 1986): 65–73.

Mann, Judy. "Heilbrun vs. the Hierarchy." *Washington Post*, 26 June 1992, sec. E:3.

Matthews, Anne. "Rage in a Tenured Position." *New York Times Magazine*, 8 November 1992, sec. 6:47.

Michie, Helena. "Murder in the Canon: The Dual Personality of Carolyn Heilbrun." *Massachusetts Studies in English*, 9, no. 3 (1984): 1–12.

Mills, Kay. "Life after a Tenured Position." *Los Angeles Times Magazine*, 19 July 1992, p. 13.

Reddy, Maureen T. "The Feminist Counter-Tradition in Crime: Cross, Paretsky, and Wilson." In *The Cunning Craft: Original Essays on Detective Fiction and Contemporary Literary Theory*, ed. Ronald G. Walker and June M. Frazer. Macomb: Western Illinois University Press, 1990, pp. 174–87.

Roberts, Jeanne Addison. "Feminist Murder: Amanda Cross Reinvents Womanhood." *Clues: A Journal of Detection*, 6, no. 1 (Spring-Summer 1985): 2–13.

Schleh, Eugene. "Character Development of Kate Fansler in the Amanda Cross Novels." *Clues: A Journal of Detection*, 13, no. 1 (Spring-Summer 1992): 73–79.

Wilt, Judith. "Feminism Meets the Detective Novel." *Clues: A Journal of Detection*, 3, no. 2 (Fall-Winter 1982): 47–51.

DENISE M. MARSHALL

❦ D ❦

ELIZABETH DALY (1878–1967)

Elizabeth Teresa Daly was born in New York City in 1878. Of a distinguished family, she attended Miss Baldwin's School, received her B.A. from Bryn Mawr College in 1901, and earned her M.A. from Columbia University in 1902. She taught at Bryn Mawr from 1904 to 1906. From her undergraduate days on, she was involved in producing amateur theater. This interest is not surprising: her uncle, Augustin Daly, was a major force in the American theater as well as an avid book collector who owned a Shakespeare first folio. Remarkably, Daly published her first and second mystery novels only in 1940—at the age of sixty-one. In 1960, the Mystery Writers of America awarded her an Edgar. She died in 1967.

If there are more satisfying classic murder mysteries than those of Elizabeth Daly, I have yet to find them. Her plots are beautifully constructed, their resolutions surprising but—once explained—impeccably logical. She writes with grace and economy, handling both dialogue and description with finesse, even as the narrative proceeds apace. For today's reader, Daly's novels offer the added pleasure of imaginative participation in the lives of uppercrust New Yorkers in the 1940s. In all, Elizabeth Daly writes thoroughly civilized mysteries, tales in which the most ruthless criminals dress for dinner and violent death is no excuse for breaches of decorum.

Much of the books' sensibility arises from the continuing character of the sleuth Henry Gamadge. Initially, Gamadge might seem an unlikely detective. Frequently characterized as "amiable," he is also described as "rather colorless," "thinnish, tallish," and "a little stooped from his sedentary occupation." Although of independent means, Gamadge consults professionally on dubious rare books and manuscripts. As he says in *Unexpected Night*, "If somebody wants to sell you a rare old pamphlet about Nell Gwyn, with Charles the Second's autograph on the flyleaf and marginal notes by Louis the Fourteenth, I'll perhaps be able to tell you whether it was made later than 1900 and what part of Michigan it came from." Sometimes, his specialized knowledge leads him to criminal investigation. For example, in *The Book of the Lion*, he is asked to appraise the correspondence of a minor poet, and several murders ensue. More often, people seek his help because he is known to be clever, discreet, and intrigued by the unusual; he tells his client in *Somewhere in the House*, "Strangeness is a recommendation to me, you know." However he becomes involved in a case, he is likely to uncover a bibliographic clue. Daly skillfully presents Gamadge's expertise in terms accessible to the general reader; her books are—in her own words of advice to an aspiring writer—"literate, but not literary."

Combining scholarly logic with a thoroughgoing understanding of human nature, Gamadge is as skilled at spotting an inheritance scam as detecting a forged folio. He is absolutely attuned to social gradations, but he never confuses them with moral status. Despite the gentility of their milieu, Daly's novels are admirably free of the snobbery that pervades so many Golden Age detective stories. For example, in *Death and Letters*, the Gamadges' nanny finds her employers to be eccentric: "It didn't matter to Miss Mullins that they ate their meals wherever they happened to sit down, and had no dining-room, and treated their animals like people and treated people all alike."

Through the novels, a picture of Gamadge emerges. He lives in an inherited brownstone house, which has been remodeled to include a laboratory. Like many a bachelor detective in fiction, he meets his wife in the course of detecting. Clara is fourteen years younger than Henry and generally a minor figure in the novels, although she can serve as an able assistant when called on. For example, in *The House without the Door*, she stealthily searches her hostess's upstairs, while downstairs, Henry keeps the conversation flowing. In *Evidence of Things Seen*, Clara sees a ghost and becomes the chief suspect in a locked-room murder. Although her husband solves the mystery, Clara's poise under pressure certifies her as a worthy match for Henry.

Daly's novels can be read in any order. It is true that a later book may refer in passing to a character from a previous one, but a prodigious memory would be required for these references to be distracting. Too, the circumstances of continuing characters do change: Harold Bantz (Henry's assistant) gets married, Robert Schenck goes from insurance investigator to FBI agent, and Gamadge himself marries and becomes a father. However, these changes are incidental to the plot of any given novel. Daly does not probe individual personalities; rather, she explores complex webs of relationships, often within extended households only some of whose inhabitants are related by blood. Thematically, Daly's novels turn on her finely calibrated depiction of the ties that bind, of the infinitely variable bonds and obligations that—whether large or small, honored or betrayed—engage us in one another's fate. Quite typical, and among my favorites, are *Nothing Can Rescue Me* and *Arrow Pointing Nowhere*.

Although all Daly's books have appeared in paperback over the years, she is overdue for a complete set of reprints. (Thorndike Press has recently reissued several of her novels in large-print editions.) Eleanor Boylan, Daly's niece, carries on the family tradition with a new series of mysteries featuring Clara Gamadge (now widowed) as sleuth. Other writers that Daly aficionados are likely to enjoy include Catherine Aird, Jane Langton, and Anne Morice.

MYSTERY FICTION

Henry Gamadge Series

Deadly Nightshade. New York: Farrar and Rinehart, 1940; London: Hammond, 1948.

Unexpected Night. New York: Farrar and Rinehart; London: Gollancz, 1940.

Murders in Volume 2. New York: Farrar and Rinehart, 1941; London: Eyre and Spottiswoode, 1943.

The House without the Door. New York: Farrar and Rinehart, 1942; London: Hammond, 1945.

Evidence of Things Seen. New York: Farrar and Rinehart, 1943; London: Hammond, 1946.

Nothing Can Rescue Me. New York: Farrar and Rinehart, 1943; London: Hammond, 1945.

Arrow Pointing Nowhere. New York: Farrar and Rinehart, 1944; London: Hammond, 1946; as *Murder Listens In*. New York: Bantam, 1949.

The Book of the Dead. New York: Farrar and Rinehart, 1944; London: Hammond, 1946.

Any Shape or Form. New York: Farrar and Rinehart, 1945; London: Hammond, 1949.

Somewhere in the House. New York: Rinehart, 1946; London: Hammond, 1949.

The Wrong Way Down. New York: Rinehart, 1946; London: Hammond, 1950; as *Shroud for a Lady*. New York: Spivak, 1956.

Night Walk. New York: Rinehart, 1947; London: Hammond, 1950.

The Book of the Lion. New York: Rinehart, 1948; London: Hammond, 1951.

And Dangerous to Know. New York: Rinehart, 1949; London: Hammond, 1952.

Death and Letters. New York: Rinehart, 1950; London: Hammond, 1953.

The Book of the Crime. New York: Rinehart, 1951; London: Hammond, 1954.

CRITICAL BIBLIOGRAPHY

Butler, Gwendoline. "Henry Gamadge." In *100 Great Detectives*, ed. Maxim Jak-
    ubowski. London: Xanadu; New York: Carroll and Graf, 1991, pp. 231–
    32.
Dudley, Barbara C. M. "Murder Most Rare: Death Strikes the Well-to-Do in Eliz-
    abeth Daly's Mysteries." *The Armchair Detective*, 20 (1987): 240–50.
Waldron, Ann. "The Golden Years of Elizabeth Daly." *The Armchair Detective*, 7
    (1973/74): 25–28.

SUSAN BAKER

BARBARA D'AMATO (1938–   )

Barbara D'Amato was born on April 10, 1938, in Grand Rapids, Michigan.
She attended Cornell University (1956–58) and received her B.A. (1972)
and M.A. (1973) from Northwestern University. Her varied work experience—as surgical orderly, carpenter for stage magic illusions, psychological
and legal researcher, and writing teacher for the Chicago police—often
provides realistic background and details for her novels. She is also a writer
of nonfiction: *The Doctor, the Murder, the Mystery* is based on her extensive investigation of the case of physician John Branion, an African-
American civil rights activist who was wrongfully convicted of murder.

D'Amato has been on the board of Mystery Writers of America and
served several years as national regional vice-president. She was national
secretary of Sisters in Crime and writes a regular column for their newsletter and for *Mystery Scene Magazine*. She was nominated for an Anthony
Award in 1990 for her novel *On My Honor*.

D'Amato's first mystery series features Dr. Gerritt DeGraaf, a Chicago
trauma surgeon and consulting forensic pathologist who solves an ingenious locked-room murder in *The Hands of Healing Murder*. DeGraaf later
continues his investigations, traveling to Arizona in the *The Eyes on Utopia
Murders* to solve a murderous conflict between the senior members of a
retirement community and a small group of children living in their midst.

D'Amato's best-known work is her series on Catherine "Cat" Marsala,
a free-lance investigative reporter frequently on assignment from a popular
newspaper, *Chicago Today*. The city of Chicago features centrally in
D'Amato's work; she engagingly evokes its diversity, corruption, and excitement through the specifics of its streets, lake, restaurants, and neighborhoods.

Cat's investigative journalism provides numerous opportunities to ask
provocative questions that eventually enable her to solve the murders on
which she stumbles in the course of her work. The three novels that take

place in the city itself open with Cat at the scene of a violent crime that immediately draws her—and the reader—into the mystery. In *Hardball*, her debut, she is arranging an interview with the leader of a movement to legalize drugs when her potential interviewee becomes the target of a bomb. The reader of *Hardball* finishes the novel feeling relief that Cat has escaped personal danger and caught the killer, but also remembering the arguments in the drug legalization debate.

Hard Tack is very different from the other novels in the series; it is set on a yacht that leaves Chicago behind. In many ways it resembles the traditional cozy. In *Hard Luck*, the opening scene features a body that falls from a skyscraper just as Cat and her mother are passing by—a body that turns out to have been Cat's morning appointment. Cat's assignment concerns the workings of the Illinois lottery, and the responses to her informed and persistent questioning provide a rich portrait of the manipulative and often destructive nature of the lottery system.

The suspense, humor, and informative research that characterize the series continue in *Hard Women*, in which Cat is preparing a televised report on prostitution, allowing the prostitutes to speak in their own voices. The murder of a young woman who has agreed to appear in Cat's documentary immediately brings the reader into the world of the novel. D'Amato's sensitivity to the societal treatment of women appears in the details of the prostitution business and of Cat's struggle to understand and help others to appreciate the ways in which prostitutes transcend their pejorative label.

D'Amato's writings treat a large number of social issues in a sympathetic fashion: homelessness, poverty, prostitution, drug and alcohol abuse, child abuse, and incest. She archly describes the economically and politically powerful individuals and institutions that are responsible for, and profit from, social inequities.

One of the strongest reflections of D'Amato's commitment to women's issues is her portrayal of Cat as strong and autonomous, yet concerned about family, friends, and vulnerable strangers. Cat shows no interest in possessions, and her free-lancing requires organization, hardfield work, and hours of writing and revising for meager pay. Although two men pursue her, they struggle less against one another than against Cat's desire to retain her independence. Like Sara Paretsky's V. I. Warshawski and Sue Grafton's Kinsey Milhone, Cat uses her humor to upset power relations, making fun of her captors and zinging sarcastic quips at arrogant bureaucrats.

D'Amato's tight writing and attention to detail create a "can't put it down" tension. This series thrives on careful research, a vibrant portrayal of Chicago, exciting plots, and an appealing protagonist.

The Cat series is best read chronologically in order to enjoy her personal growth and changing relationships. City lovers should try Linda Barnes's Boston P.I. novels and Julie Smith's New Orleans police detective series. Readers will also enjoy the Meg O'Brien series featuring Rochester news reporter Jessie James and the British reporter series of Val McDermid, Annette Roome, and Lesley Grant-Adamson.

MYSTERY FICTION

Writing as Barbara D'Amato

Dr. Gerritt DeGraaf Series

The Hands of Healing Murder. New York: Charter Communications, 1980.
The Eyes on Utopia Murders. New York: Charter Communications, 1981.

Catherine "Cat" Marsala Series

Hardball. New York: Scribner's, 1990.
Hard Tack. New York: Scribner's, 1991.
Hard Luck. New York: Scribner's, 1992.
Hard Women. New York: Scribner's, 1993.
Hard Case. Scribner's, 1994.

Writing as Malacai Black

On My Honor. New York: Windsor Publishing, 1989.

NATALIE HEVENER KAUFMAN

DOROTHY SALISBURY DAVIS (1916–   )

Dorothy Salisbury Davis was born in Chicago in 1916 and was educated in area Catholic schools through her A.B. degree in 1938 from Barat College. She was married to actor Harry Davis in 1946 and published her first mystery novel in 1957. From the very beginning of her career she has been consistently the recipient of high praise from her critics and fellow professionals. She is a past president of Mystery Writers of America and received the Grand Master award in 1984 and the Bouchercon Lifetime Achievement Award in 1989. In 1986 she was made an honorary member of the board of directors of the Rockland Center of the Arts, New York. She lives with her husband in Palisades, New York.

Her crime novels number eighteen and reflect in their diversity Davis's large interest in all human affairs. Her skill in writing is manifest in her lively narrative line, her vivid (even poetic) powers of description, and above all her power of creating credible human characters from very different walks of life. The secret of her overall success lies in her primary interest in the fictional creatures—their predicaments and the outcomes of their struggles.

In three of her first four novels (*The Judas Cat, The Clay Hand* and *A Town of Masks*), she depicts three separate small-town communities. The power struggles and the common mean-spiritedness of life as it is often lived are realistically drawn—the shady dealings and the assorted types of good and evil are there, yet there is also a compassionate rendering of the characters' lives.

In *The Judas Cat*, a young journalist (a returned veteran) teams with the sheriff. The two persist in uncovering what many of the townspeople would leave covered—the death of a ninety-two-year-old citizen. In *The Clay Hand*, an interesting love affair develops between another young journalist and the widow of a friend who died under suspicious circumstances. The setting is a coal-mining town in West Virginia, and the reader is drawn into the town's upheaval very compellingly. *A Town of Masks* uses another small town, this time on the Lake Michigan shores. A spinster in her fifties conceives a jealous passion for a young poet and her scheming weaves finally her own death and disgrace.

A Gentle Murderer is one of the author's own favorites among her writings, which is easy to understand. There is a turning in this story toward an in-depth characterization of Tim Brandon, a young man of deep religious feelings, whose pattern of loneliness and habits of judging others provides excitement and tension. From its opening scene of Brandon's confession to Father Duffy to the end, where Sergeant Goldsmith must bring down the "gentle murderer" with his gun, there is intense concern by both priest and policemen—and by the readers themselves—to find the answers. A Catholic ambience often plays a part in Davis's mystery novels, but certainly not in any exclusive fashion. In *A Gentle Murderer* she uses, for the first time, a large city setting.

Dorothy Davis's next three stories exhibit a strikingly different tone than the earlier ones. There is a shift to a more comic note in characterization along with a decision to stay with basically the same set of characters. In *Death of an Old Sinner*, the title character is seventy-two-year-old Gerald Ransom Jarvis, a feisty, adventurous old soldier who does not mind stirring up trouble for his lawyer son, Jim. His valiant Scots housekeeper, Mrs. Norris (a widow), also loves to get into the act of sleuthing. General Jarvis forges some scandalous entries in an old diary which belonged to a long-dead relative (a U.S. president, no less). Trying to raise some money for his own pleasure (his new Jaguar and his many girlfriends), the general becomes involved with the New York underworld, which leads to his death. Mrs. Norris, the housekeeper, joins forces with Jasper Tully, a slim, quiet, young Irish investigator and, with the aid of the general's son, Jimmy, they bring the crooks to justice. Tully has a growing fondness for Mrs. Norris.

The General's rascality, added to the brusque Scots gallantry and the saturnine character of Tully, provide good comic moments.

Davis continued in this vein in *A Gentleman Called*, with Mrs. Norris herself becoming the target of a serial criminal's attacks. Luckily, Jasper Tully and Jim Jarvis are again there to help.

In *Old Sinners Never Die* the author reverts to the humor begun in *The Death of an Old Sinner*. She returns General Jarvis to (fictional) life at the time of his retirement. Washington, D.C., is the scene for this novel, and the general is acting very lively. He is invited, with eleven other celebrities, to be honored at a party. The party proves to be a scam, brought about by a Senator Joe McCarthy type and intended to smear and disgrace all who come to it. The comedy here is broad, and all three of the Jarvis family tales could be faulted for serving humor rather than having humor assist the narrative. There are, however, some good satirical thrusts made on Washington politics and society. Davis is able to suggest realistically the historical qualities of the period she is writing about.

Dorothy Davis made some interesting comments for a piece written about her in *Twentieth Century Crime and Mystery Writers*. In calling herself a "restless and sometimes troubled writer," she went on to challenge her own style of writing mystery stories. Specifically, she faulted herself for not having been able to create a "running character" such as Simenon's Maigret. However, Davis's later novels successfully do develop a single protagonist—a detective.

This young, modern heroine—an ex-actress and friend of the afflicted—first appears in *A Death in the Life*. Julie Hayes's compassion for the lowly and the afflicted is a hallmark of all Davis's later novels. Hayes is a streetsmart woman who mingles with prostitutes, criminals, and the misfits of life. She herself came from an unstable home life—a broken marriage from which she was given her mother's name rather than confront the confusing birth records that her Irish father left behind (which she tries to unscramble). Julie's marriage is also on shaky ground. Her husband, Jeffrey Hayes, is a kindly, successful journalist with an international reputation and many times, he is not as near as she would like him to be. In four novels Julie pursues the truth of her own past as well as that of others, for whose lives she seems drawn to risk her own.

Dorothy Davis can be linked clearly with the tradition of P. D. James and Ruth Rendell in their accent on the psychological aspects of both the pursuer and the pursued. A good novel with which to start is *A Death in the Life*.

MYSTERY FICTION

The Clay Hand. New York: Scribner, 1950; London: Corgi, 1952.
A Gentle Murderer. New York: Scribner, 1951; London: Corgi, 1953.

The Judas Cat. New York: Scribner; London: Corgi, 1952.

A Town of Masks. New York: Scribner, 1952.

Black Sheep, White Lamb. New York: Scribner, 1963; London: Boardman, 1964.

The Pale Betrayer. New York: Scribner, 1965; London: Hodder and Stoughton, 1967.

Enemy and Brother. New York: Scribner, 1966; London: Hodder and Stoughton, 1967.

God Speed the Night. Coauthored with Jerome Ross. New York: Scribner, 1968; London: Hodder and Stoughton, 1969.

Where the Dark Streets Go. New York: Scribner, 1969; London: Hodder and Stoughton, 1970.

Shock Wave. New York: Scribner, 1972; London: Hodder and Stoughton, 1974.

The Little Brothers. New York: Scribner, 1973; London: Barker, 1974.

Tales of a Stormy Night: The Collected Crime Stories. Woodstock, Vt.: One Countryman Press, 1984.

Norris-Tully Series

Death of an Old Sinner. New York: Scribner, 1957; London: Secker and Walburg, 1958.

A Gentleman Called. New York: Scribner; London: Secker and Walburg, 1958.

Old Sinners Never Die. New York: Scribner, 1959; London: Secker and Walburg, 1960.

Julie Hayes Series

A Death in the Life. New York: Scribner, 1976; London: Gallancy, 1927.

Scarlet Night. New York: Scribner, 1980; London: Gallancy, 1981.

Lullaby of Murder. New York: Scribner; London: Gallancy, 1984.

The Habit of Fear.

New York: Scribner, 1987; London: Chivers, 1989.

CRITICAL BIBLIOGRAPHY

Davis, Dorothy Salisbury. "Some of the Truth." In *Colloquium on Crime*, ed. Robin W. Winks. New York: Scribner, 1986.

Freeman, Lucy. "Gently into the Darkness: An Interview with Dorothy Salisbury Davis." *The Armchair Detective*, 20, no. 3 (1987): 266–78.

Hoch, Edward D. "Davis, Dorothy Salisbury," in *Twentieth Century Crime and Mystery Writers*, ed. Lesley Henderson. 3rd ed. Chicago and London: St. James, 1991. pp. 294–96.

JOSEPH P. LOVERING

DORIS MILES DISNEY (1907–1976)

Doris Miles Disney was born in Glastonbury, Connecticut, on December 22, 1907. She worked in an insurance office in Hartford prior to her marriage, in June 1936, to George J. Disney. They had one daughter. Disney's writing career, begun during her marriage, enabled her to support herself and her daughter during many subsequent years of widowhood. Many of her novels make effective use of her New England background, although the late works also employ the Virginia locale of her final years. She died on March 9, 1976, having published a total of forty-seven crime novels.

Jefferson DiMarco, her detective in eight books, is a claims adjuster who investigates frauds and suspicious deaths for his company. Unusual in the genre for his profession, Jeff is typical in other ways: he is an outsider with no family ties who values his independence. His characterization enlarges and deepens as the series progresses; a good introductory novel might be *Trick or Treat*, which depicts him particularly well, or *The Chandler Policy*, which reveals a mellowing trend in his character.

Disney's other detectives are less well known but at least equally interesting. David Madden follows an occupation even more unusual in mystery fiction than that of Jeff DiMarco: he is a U.S. postal inspector. His investigations thus are limited to such crimes as blackmail, poison pen letters, and using the mails to defraud. Disney employed him in only three novels, which are primarily procedurals and contain much information about the work of the postal service and postal law. Like DiMarco, Madden is a loner. He is a widower who fears entanglements but who befriends others during the course of his investigations. The three absorbing novels about this admirable and self-effacing detective may be read in any order.

Disney's other series detective was the first created (in her first published novel) and first discarded; in some respects, he is also her most interesting. Jim O'Neill, a county detective, is the most traditional of the three in profession; unlike the other two men, he is fully developed and grows and changes from novel to novel. A bachelor who meets his future wife in *A Compound for Death*, he progresses into marriage and fatherhood, and in *The Last Straw*, his happy family life is fully developed and balanced against the greed and self-centeredness of the criminal he must apprehend. Because his novels follow his personal growth, they are best read in order.

Although Disney began with conventional mysteries, she gradually moved toward the freer suspense and thriller forms. Her fourth novel, *Who Rides a Tiger*, was her first of that type, which eventually came to predominate in her published fiction. Her victims or potential victims are quite varied, but empathy is often ensured by her use of children or elderly people in these roles or, conversely, as those who are responsible for the resolution of the crime plots. In *The Departure of Mr. Gaudette*, a seven-year-old boy triggers an investigation by insisting that his elderly friend would not have left without a farewell; the characterization of the child is charming and believable. In *The Hospitality of the House*, a teenaged girl sets off to visit the pen pal she has never seen and finds herself entrapped; her effectively depicted wit and courage enable her to outwit her captors. By contrast, *The Day Miss Bessie Lewis Disappeared* is a comic tour de force centering on the foibles and irascibility of elderly characters.

Disney often made use of historical elements, and two novels are set entirely in the past. *Testimony by Silence* is Disney's imaginative recreation of the Bravo murder case in England in 1876, as reset in Disney's Connecticut, and *At Some Forgotten Door* is a Gothic suspense story with penetrating social commentary on the social caste system of a century ago. Equally interesting are her books in which past and present events are paralleled.

Disney's vision darkened as her career drew toward its end. Early on she had been notable for her consistent creation of likable characters. Many of her late novels, however, are studies in the presence of evil in ordinary people. *Money for the Taking*, for example, follows the experiences of a young woman, a bank teller, whose obsessive love leads her into violent crime, while *Winifred* examines a young woman's self-destructive—even psychotic—possessiveness.

Disney's fiction is marked by careful plotting, believable characterizations, and a readable, self-effacing style. She refused to be controlled by the conventions of her genre, a practice that sometimes confused readers and irritated reviewers but that added to the interest of her work. Her experimentation with subgenres, with ways of telling her stories, and with types of crimes and characters brings variety to her work and makes it difficult to suggest similar writers. However, readers who enjoy Disney might also wish to try Charlotte Armstrong or Rae Foley.

MYSTERY FICTION

Who Rides a Tiger. New York: Doubleday, 1946; as *Sow the Wind*. London: Nimmo, 1948.

Enduring Old Charms. New York: Doubleday, 1947; as *Death for My Beloved*. New York: Spivak, 1949.

Testimony by Silence. New York: Doubleday, 1948.

That Which Is Crooked. New York: Doubleday, 1948.

Count the Ways. New York: Doubleday, 1949.

Look Back on Murder. New York: Doubleday, 1951.

Heavy, Heavy Hangs. New York: Doubleday, 1952.

Do unto Others. New York: Doubleday, 1953.

Prescription: Murder. New York: Doubleday, 1953.

Room for Murder. New York: Doubleday, 1955; London: Foulsham, 1959.

My Neighbor's Wife. New York: Doubleday, 1957; London: Foulsham, 1958.

No Next of Kin. New York: Doubleday, 1959; London: Foulsham, 1961.

Dark Lady. New York: Doubleday, 1960; as *Sinister Lady*. London: Hale, 1962.

Should Auld Acquaintance. New York: Doubleday, 1962; London: Hale, 1963.

Here Lies . . . New York: Doubleday, 1963; London: Hale, 1964.

The Departure of Mr. Gaudette. New York: Doubleday, 1964; as *Fateful Departure*. London: Hale, 1965.

The Hospitality of the House. New York: Doubleday, 1964; as *Unsuspected Evil*. London: Hale, 1965.

Shadow of a Man. New York: Doubleday, 1965; London: Hale, 1966.

At Some Forgotten Door. New York: Doubleday, 1966; London: Hale, 1967.

The Magic Grandfather. New York: Doubleday, 1966; as *Mask of Evil*. London: Hale, 1967.

Night of Clear Choice. New York: Doubleday, 1967; as *Flame of Evil*. London: Hale, 1968.

Money for the Taking. New York: Doubleday; London: Hale, 1968.

Voice from the Grave. New York: Doubleday, 1968; London: Hale, 1969.

Two Little Children and How They Grew. New York: Doubleday, 1969; as *Fatal Choice*. London: Hale, 1970.

Do Not Fold, Spindle or Mutilate. New York: Doubleday, 1970; as *Death by Computer*. London: Hale, 1971.

Three's a Crowd. New York: Doubleday, 1971; London: Hale, 1972.

The Day Miss Bessie Lewis Disappeared. New York: Doubleday, 1972; London: Hale, 1973.

Only Couples Need Apply. New York: Doubleday, 1973; London: Hale, 1974.

Don't Go into the Woods Today. New York: Doubleday, 1974.

Cry for Help. New York: Doubleday, 1975; London: Hale, 1976.

Winifred. New York: Doubleday, 1976.

Jim O'Neill Series

A Compound for Death. New York: Doubleday, 1943.

Murder on a Tangent. New York: Doubleday, 1945.

Appointment at Nine. New York: Doubleday, 1947.

Fire at Will. New York: Doubleday, 1950.

The Last Straw. New York: Doubleday, 1954; as *Driven to Kill*. London: Foulsham, 1957.

Jefferson DiMarco Series

Dark Road. New York: Doubleday, 1946; and London: Nimmo, 1947; as *Dead Stop*. New York: Dell, 1956.

Family Skeleton. New York: Doubleday, 1949.

Straw Man. New York: Doubleday, 1951; as *The Case of the Straw Man*. London: Foulsham, 1958.

Trick or Treat. New York: Doubleday, 1955; as *The Halloween Murder*. London: Foulsham, 1957.

Did She Fall or Was She Pushed? New York: Doubleday, 1959; London: Hale, 1962.

Method in Madness. New York: Doubleday, 1957; as *Quiet Violence*. London: Foulsham, 1959. Also, apparently, as *Too Innocent to Kill*. New York: Avon, [1957 or 1959].

Find the Woman. New York: Doubleday, 1962; London: Hale, 1964.

The Chandler Policy. New York: Putnam, 1971; London: Hale, 1973.

David Madden Series

Unappointed Rounds. New York: Doubleday, 1956; as *The Post Office Case*. London: Foulsham, 1957.

Black Mail. New York: Doubleday, 1958; London: Foulsham, 1960.

Mrs. Meeker's Money. New York: Doubleday, 1961; London: Hale, 1963.

CRITICAL BIBLIOGRAPHY

DeMarr, Mary Jean. "Doris Miles Disney and the Historical Mystery." *Clues*, 7, no. 1 (1986): 111–25.
Lachman, Marvin. "Disney, Doris Miles." In *Twentieth Century Crime and Mystery Writers*, ed. Lesley Henderson. 3rd ed. Chicago and London: St. James, 1991, pp. 322–24.

MARY JEAN DeMARR

SUSAN DUNLAP (1943–   )

Susan Dunlap was born in Kew Gardens, N.Y. on June 20, 1943. She received her B.A. degree in English from Bucknell University in June 1965, and her M.A.T. in English from the University of North Carolina in 1966. She worked as a social worker in the Department of Social Services in Baltimore, Maryland, from 1966 to 1967 and in New York City briefly in 1967. She moved to Contra Costa County, California, in 1968 where she resumed work as a social worker in 1968 and remained in that position until 1984, when she became a full-time writer. In 1970 she married editor Newell Dunlap. Dunlap was a founding member of Sisters in Crime and served as president in 1990–91. Her book *Rogue Wave* was nominated for an Anthony award in 1992.

Sue Dunlap is a mystery writer who has utilized all three of the major categories of detective fiction: the amateur detective, the police procedural, and the private investigator. Each one of her series features a strong woman character who exhibits sharp analytical skills and a degree of vulnerability.

Her amateur detective is Veejay Haskell, a former public relations person and divorcee. She moved to the Russian River area of northern California from San Francisco, accepting a job as a meter reader for Pacific Gas and Electric (PG&E). She becomes an amateur detective to clear herself as a suspect in the death of a bar owner in *An Equal Opportunity Death*, much to the chagrin of the local sheriff. In each of the novels, her job as a meter reader is critical in helping her solve the mysteries. Dunlap has commented that now Veejay is retired and living on the beach in Mexico.

The police procedural series features Jill Smith, a Berkeley, California, police officer who has worked her way up from a beat officer to homicide and felony detective. The novels follow the traditional formula of the police procedural involving several different cases interwoven within the main case. Other police personnel help Jill solve the mystery and two play significant roles: Seth Howard, her office mate and a vice and substance officer, and Connie Pereira, a beat officer and financial expert. She is pestered by her boss, Detective Inspector Frederick Doyle, who is suspicious of her promotion at first but comes to accept her as a competent officer, although after her serious accident in *Too Close to the Edge*, he starts to worry about her physical and mental condition. Jill does have her sources, and one particular character plays a significant role in several novels, a rather shady private investigator named Herman Ott.

There is a great deal of similarity between the two characters of Veejay Haskell and Jill Smith. Both are women who have gotten away from unhappy marriages and taken nontraditional female jobs. Neither is seeking romantic involvement but rather deliberately avoiding it. Their eating habits are similarly unorthodox: Veejay enjoys eggs, chorizo, kraut, and black bread, while Jill thrives on jelly doughnuts.

Setting is especially important for both series: the changing nature of Berkeley from student radical to Yuppie in the Jill Smith books and the Russian River environment in the Veejay Haskell stories. Their place of employment is also important; working for PG&E provides Haskell with a means of gaining information and entering into places where most people might not be able to go, and the Berkeley police department is described as being "more Berkeley than police" in *Too Close to the Edge*. Tongue-in-cheek humor plays a significant role in several stories. Furthermore, both women are beset with problems from their male bosses, Mr. Bobs of the PG&E and Lieutenant Davis of the Berkeley Police Department.

The third series features Kiernan O'Shaughnessy, a former medical examiner who resigned under a cloud from the San Francisco coroner's office and went to San Diego, where she began a new career as a private investigator. Along with a former San Diego Charger football player as her housekeeper and a golden retriever, she has been featured in two novels, *Pious Deception* and *Rogue Wave*.

Sue Dunlap is an author who moves skillfully from one form of the detective novel format to another. She is very adept in each form, be it the amateur detective, Veejay Haskell, the police procedural of Jill Smith, or the private investigator, Kiernan O'Shaughnessy. Readers of the Veejay Haskell series might want to investigate the Nancy Pickard books about Jennie Cain; those who enjoy Jill Smith should look into the Sigrid Harald series of Margaret Maron; and the Kiernan O'Shaughnessy devotees should consider the Patricia D. Cornwell books featuring Kay Scarpetta. My favorite Dunlap titles are: Veejay Haskell—*The Last Annual Slugfest*; Jill Smith—*Diamond in the Buff*; and Kiernan O'Shaughnessy—*Rogue Wave*.

MYSTERY FICTION

Jill Smith Series

Karma. New York: PaperJacks, 1984; London: Severn House, 1992.

As a Favor. New York: St. Martin's, 1984; London: Robert Hale, 1985.

Not Exactly a Brahmin. New York: St. Martin's, 1985.

Too Close to the Edge. New York: St. Martin's, 1987.

A Dinner to Die For. New York: St. Martin's, 1987.

Diamond in the Buff. New York: St. Martin's, 1990.

Death and Taxes. New York: Delacorte, 1992.

Time Expired. New York: Delacorte, 1993.

Veejay Haskell Series

An Equal Opportunity Death. New York: St. Martin's; London: Robert Hale 1984.

The Bohemian Connection. New York: St. Martin's, 1985; London: Robert Hale, 1986.

The Last Annual Slugfest. New York: St. Martin's, 1986.

Kiernan O'Shaughnessy Series

Pious Deception. New York: Villard, 1989.

Rogue Wave. New York: Villard, 1991.

High Fall. New York: Delacorte, 1994.

CRITICAL BIBLIOGRAPHY

Harper, Carol. "Dunlap, Susan." In *Twentieth Century Crime and Mystery Writers*, ed. Lesley Henderson. 3rd ed. Chicago and London: St. James, 1991, pp. 337–38.

Nichols, Victoria, and Susan Thompson, "Jill Smith." In *Silk Stalkings*. Berkeley, Calif.: Black Lizard, 1988, pp. 32–34.

———. "Veejay Haskell." In *Silk Stalkings*. Berkeley, Calif.: Black Lizard, 1988, pp. 269–71.

MILES CLOWERS

❧ F ❧

TONY FENNELLY (1945–   )

Born in Orange, New Jersey, on November 25, 1945, Tony Fennelly has made the French Quarter subculture of New Orleans her literary province. She knows it intimately: from an early career that included stints as a barmaid, topless dancer, and stripper, she proceeded to graduate from the University of New Orleans. She worked for the Welfare Department subsequently, to support the studies of her husband, Richard Catoire; this provided the material for her novel *Cherry*.

Her first published novel, *The Glory Hole Murders*, was nominated for an Edgar, and, like its successor, *The Closet Hanging*, it has been more popular in Europe than in the United States. These novels best represent Fennelly's oeuvre, and concern Matthew ("Matty") Sinclair, the scion of an old, aristocratic New Orleans family. Sinclair is a mid-thirtyish graduate of Tulane Law School, a former prosecutor with the district attorney's office, who now owns a pricey furniture shop in the Vieux Carre section of New Orleans. Sinclair is gay, and for some time he has been living with his young lover, Robin Fearing. As a Sinclair, he has an entrée to the highest levels of society; his "in" shop attracts the next upcoming noveau riche; as a former prosecutor, he retains connections to the New Orleans Police Department (notably homicide detective Frank Washington), and as an unabashedly gay male, he is part of a community that has achieved rather more acceptance in New Orleans than in other cities. Attractive to prospective male lovers, he is equally attractive to women and is often drawn into physical relationships with them, hoping that one will be the "right" woman, for the sake of the Sinclair line as well as for his human fulfillment.

Sinclair's homosexuality draws him into a dangerous investigation in *The Glory Hole Murders*. When a politically ambitious entrepeneur is murdered and mutilated in a known gay bar, Frank Washington enlists Matty as a special investigator. The case involves Matty with the mob, and he almost becomes the victim of a charming, gay hit man. He also has an affair with the dead man's secretary (and former mistress). His lover, Robin, tolerates this liaison, finding that he has much in common with the woman.

Matty's first-person narration sustains the reader's interest. He is mercurial: by turns, witty, catty, sophisticated, snobbish, sensitive, courageous, and shocking. In all but one respect he fills Chandler's edict that the detective is "the hero. He is everything." That one discrepancy is a big one. In a city that annually countenances a gay Mardi Gras Ball and Krewe, he is a full participant in the gay society. One of that society's characteristics is its preoccupation with its own sexuality. Matty's milieu is AIDS-aware; perhaps the most poignant moment in *The Closet Hanging* is a garish party at which various "types" gather to raise money for a dying friend. Fennelly's fine ear for sexual banter provides a veneer for deeper characterizations. Matty is fundamentally lonely, like most private eyes. He fears a future without companionship, honor, or progeny, and marked by desperation and a loss of attractiveness. Robin is vacuous, but faithful—for the present.

The Closet Hanging develops Matty's insecurity further. In the course of another murder case, he becomes involved with longtime friend Edwina Devon, and marriage, perhaps even with "an understanding" about his preference, is possible. Other issues are pressing: a struggle against casino gambling in the Quarter, preservation of family rights to land coveted by gambling interests (title rights are confused by old statutes regarding race and property), and an insidious plot against him. Matty is an epileptic and someone has meddled with his medication; as a result, he has lost all memory of a quarrel with the victim shortly before the crime.

Strong points of Fennelly's novels are the complexity of Matty's characterization and her sympathetic portrayal of a wide range of New Orleaneans—wider than that of Julie Smith's Skip Langdon novels or the New Orleans mysteries of John William and Joyce H. Corrington. It is instructive to compare Matty to another gay detective, Joseph Hansen's Dave Brandstetter. Brandstetter represents the proposition that a gay male can be a responsible human and a hero, but he lacks the audacity of Fennelly's protagonist. Matty is a responsible hero, but he also remains an outrageous—and sometimes raunchy—commentator on his world.

MYSTERY FICTION

Cherry. Germany: Rotbuch Krimi, 1993.
The Hippie in the Wall. New York: St. Martin's, 1994.

Matthew Sinclair Series

The Glory Hole Murders. New York: Carroll and Graf, 1985.
The Closet Hanging. New York: Carroll and Graf, 1987.

Murder with a Twist. New York: Carroll and Graf, 1991. (Reprint of *The Glory Hole Murders* and *The Closet Hanging.*)

Kiss Yourself Goodbye. London: Arlington, 1991.

HERBERT V. FACKLER

E. X. FERRARS (1907–)

Born Morna Doris MacTaggart on September 6, 1907, in Rangoon, Burma (then a British protectorate), E. X. Ferrars, also known as Elizabeth Ferrars, is the prolific author of close to sixty-five mysteries, most with amateur sleuths and most in the cozy tradition of the English village mystery, with an occasional spy story or foreign setting for variety amid mainly domestic malice.

Attending Bedales School in Hampshire and University College, London, she received a diploma in journalism in 1928. Her marriage to Robert Brown, a Scottish botanist, in 1940, began a life set primarily in Edinburgh, Scotland, and characterized by travels to scientific conferences of the sort regularly mentioned in her mysteries. It also marked the beginning of a detective fiction writing career that has lasted well over fifty years.

Ferrars writes stories of family and friends who are changed by scandal, blackmail, and sudden death. Though often classified as "traditional," her novels are, in fact, far grimmer in their depiction of human nature than those of Agatha Christie or Dorothy L. Sayers and reveal humankind as basically deceitful, secretive, and capable of any evil. Ferrars explains that she marvels "at the depth of misunderstanding at which nearly all human intercourse is conducted," as she studies the masks of social discourse.

Often Ferrars's novels, like those of Ruth Rendall, are set in a quiet English village, where the countryside, the manicured gardens, and the peaceful life-styles make murder seem unexpected. Gradually, however, the conflicts and hatreds, desires, and disappointments seething beneath the benign surface are revealed. It is "as if an animal out of the jungle had got loose," says a character in *Drowned Rat*. In other words, Ferrars's murders are mainly domestic, intimate, and personal, the unexpected and horrifying product of "a little shut-in world of violent feelings," as a character in *The Small World of Murder* remarks.

Despite their number, Ferrars's works are diverse and rarely predictable. Nonetheless, the mysteries depend on careful characterization, with their solution deriving from ordinary conversations rather than action. Often, a person central to solving the crime has a nagging suspicion about some minor point that has been forgotten—a comment or discrepancy—which could shed light on the mystery—and which, when remembered, does. Ferrars's technique is to move from rumor to possibility, as characters gossip and exchange information, guesses, and sudden insights and formulate theories and interpretations. These are then tested against reality, to be discarded or kept in mind until more details at last reveal a plausible solution. A favorite Ferrars pattern depends on hypothetical speculation to uncover flaws in an argument or to test its truth: "Suppose . . . suppose . . . suppose. . . ." Ferrars has an excellent sense of the give-and-take of ordinary life, the eccentricities and boredom tolerated, the differences in perceptions and interpretations of character, and the deep-seated loyalties and obligations. Due to her husband's career, a number of Ferrars characters are scientists of one sort or another and are given to conventioneering, esoteric monographs, and odd experiments.

Ferrars has three key amateur detective series: the Toby Dykes and George set, the Felix and Virginia Freer set, and the Professor Andrew Basnett set. She also has a few novels set on the island of Madeira with Police Chief Raposo and in the village of Royden Saint Agnes with Inspector Ditteridge. These detectives investigate mainly by moving into a situation as both observer and participant, gossiping and chatting, and receiving the impressions and observations of those around them, often with each conversation adding a different interpretation of character and event until finally, a pattern emerges from which the amateur detective can draw pointed conclusions. Readers are provided with clear-cut clues along the way, but these are frequently merged with the background so that they still prove surprising at the end.

Toby Dyke, an indolent man of leisure, makes witty quips and gets the glory for his investigations, while the more pedestrian George solves the crimes. The long-separated but not divorced couple of Virginia and Felix Freer are also played off against each other: a no-nonsense, down-to-earth, upright physiotherapist is put together with a charming, mischievous, and imaginative kleptomaniac. Virginia provides gossip and background information while Felix solves the crime through intuition, not evidence. The Freer series explores the little misunderstandings that make for marital strife, as old jealousies and conflicts come to the forefront and family scandal is exposed. Andrew Basnett, in turn, is intelligent, detached, and aged seventy; a retired botanist and professor from London University, he finds himself caught up in the troubles of his friends and colleagues. The Basnett series usually involves university personnel—particularly those in the sciences. Often, these amateur detectives are more willing than the police to let the suspects free and may even feel a certain sympathy for them.

Ferrars's main interest is in careful plotting that depends on casually dropped clues that seem trivial and natural in one context but revealing in another and in psychologically sensitive characterization of distinctly English personalities. Ferrars is not a feminist, but in her own quiet way, she deals with questions of women's education and family and social functions, the conflict between personal desires and goals and the expectations of parents and siblings, and the complicated interaction of the sexes, as shaped by jealousies and sexual competition. Many of her female characters are strongly independent: writers, artists, actresses. Her female murderers are cool, collected, devious, unscrupulous and very clever.

Overall, E. X. Ferrars combines a sharp wit, a cynical edge, and an understanding of the complexities of the commonplace with closely observed details, careful character studies, and well-reasoned plots to make each work a special delight. Her sense of human relationships is as subtle as that of Pat Flower, her interest in the exotic and in colonial relationships is like that of Elspeth Huxley, her occasionally upper-class figures are reminiscent of those of Michael Innes, her grim sense of human duality is almost as bleak as Graham Greene, and her lively sense of the fun of a mystery puzzle and of clues is like that of Agatha Christie. *Swaying Pillars, The Pretty Pink Shroud,* and *The Small World of Murder* are particularly good fun. Those readers who enjoy Ferrars's novels should try those of Doris Miles Disney and Margaret Yorke as well.

MYSTERY FICTION

Turn Single. London: Nicholson and Watson, 1932.

Broken Music. London: Nicholson and Watson; New York: Dutton, 1934.

I, Said the Fly. London: Hodder and Stoughton, 1945.

Murder among Friends. London: Collins, 1946; as *Cheat the Hangman.* New York: Doubleday, 1946.

With Murder in Mind. London: Collins, 1948.

The March Hare Murders. London: Collins; New York: Doubleday, 1949.

Hunt the Tortoise. London: Collins; New York: Doubleday, 1950.

Milk of Human Kindness. London: Collins, 1950.

Alibi for a Witch. London: Collins; New York: Doubleday, 1952.

The Clock That Wouldn't Stop. London: Collins; New York: Doubleday, 1952.

Murder in Time. London: Collins, 1953.

The Lying Voices. London: Collins, 1954.

Enough to Kill a Horse. London: Collins; New York: Doubleday, 1955.

Always Say Die. London: Collins, 1956; as *We Haven't Seen Her Lately.* New York: Doubleday, 1956.

Furnished for Murder. New York: Doubleday, 1956.

Murder Moves In. London: Collins, 1956; as *Kill or Cure.* Garden City, N.Y.: Doubleday, 1956.

Count the Cost. London: Collins, 1957; as *Unreasonable Doubt.* New York: Doubleday, 1958.

Depart This Life. Garden City, N.Y.: Doubleday, 1958; as *A Tale of Two Murders.* London: Collins, 1959.

Fear the Light. London: Collins; Garden City, N.Y.: Doubleday, 1960.

Sleeping Dogs. London: Collins; Garden City, N.Y.: Doubleday, 1960.

The Busy Body. London: Collins, 1962; as *Seeing Double.* Garden City, N.Y.: Doubleday, 1962.

The Wandering Widows. London: Collins; Garden City, N.Y.: Doubleday, 1962.

The Decayed Gentlewoman. Garden City, N.Y.: Doubleday, 1963; as *A Legal Fiction*. London: Collins, 1964.

The Doubly Dead. London: Collins; Garden City, N.Y.: Doubleday, 1963.

Ninth Life. London: Collins, 1965.

No Peace for the Wicked. London: Collins; New York: Harper and Row, 1966.

Zero at the Bone. London: Collins, 1967; New York: Walker, 1968.

The Swaying Pillars. London: Collins, 1968; New York: Walker, 1969.

The Seven Sleepers. London: Collins; New York: Walker, 1970.

The Small World of Murder. London: Collins; Garden City, N.Y.: Doubleday, 1973.

Hanged Man's House. London: Collins; Garden City, N.Y.: Doubleday, 1974.

The Cup and the Lip. London: Collins, 1975; Garden City, N.Y.: Doubleday, 1976.

Drowned Rat. London: Collins; Garden City, N.Y.: Doubleday, 1975.

The Pretty Pink Shroud. London: Collins; Garden City, N.Y.: Doubleday, 1977.

In at the Kill. London: Collins, 1978; New York: Doubleday, 1979.

Murders Anonymous. New York: Doubleday, 1978.

Designs of Life. London: Collins; New York: Doubleday, 1980.

Experiment with Death. London: Collins; New York: Doubleday, 1981.

Skeleton in Search of a Cupboard. London: Collins, 1982; as *Skeleton in Search of a Closet*. New York: Doubleday, 1982.

Come to be Killed. London: Collins; New York: Doubleday, 1987.

Trial by Fury. London: Collins; New York: Doubleday, 1991.

Danger from the Dead. London: Collins; New York: Doubleday, 1992.

Thy Brother's Death. New York: Doubleday, 1993.

Toby Dyke and George Series

Give a Corpse a Bad Name. London: Hodder and Stoughton, 1940.

Remove the Bodies. London: Hodder and Stoughton, 1940; as *Rehearsals for Murder*. New York: Doubleday, Doran, 1941.

Death in Botanist's Bay. London: Hodder and Stoughton, 1941; as *A Murder of a Suicide*. New York: Doubleday, Doran, 1941.

Don't Monkey with Murder. London: Hodder and Stoughton, 1941; as *The Shape of a Stain*. New York: Doubleday, Doran, 1942.

Your Neck in a Noose. London: Hodder and Stoughton, 1942; as *Neck in a Noose*. New York: Doubleday, Doran, 1943.

Police Chief Raposo Series

Skeleton Staff. London: Collins; New York: Walker, 1969.

Breath of Suspicion. London: Collins; New York: Doubleday, 1972.

Witness Before the Fact. London: Collins, 1979; New York: Doubleday, 1980.

Root of All Evil. London: Collins; New York: Doubleday, 1984.

Inspector Ditteridge Series

A Stranger and Afraid. London: Collins; New York: Walker, 1971.

Foot in the Grave. Garden City, N.Y.: Doubleday, 1972; London: Collins, 1973.

Alive and Dead. London: Collins, 1974; Garden City, N.Y.: Doubleday, 1975.

Blood Flies Upward. London: Collins, 1976; Garden City, N.Y.: Doubleday, 1977.

Felix and Virginia Freer Series

Last Will and Testament. London: Collins; New York: Doubleday, 1978.

Frog in the Throat. London: Collins; New York: Doubleday, 1980.

Thinner than Water. London: Collins, 1981; New York: Doubleday, 1982.

Death of a Minor Character. London: Collins; New York: Doubleday, 1983.

I Met Murder. London: Collins, 1985; New York: Doubleday, 1986.

Sleep of the Unjust. London: Collins, 1990; New York: Doubleday, 1991.

Beware of the Dog. London: Collins; New York: Doubleday, 1992.

Andrew Basnett Series

Something Wicked. London: Collins, 1983; New York: Doubleday, 1984.

The Crime and the Crystal. London: Collins; New York: Doubleday, 1985.

The Other Devil's Name. London: Collins, 1986; New York: Doubleday, 1987.

A Murder Too Many. London: Collins, 1988; New York: Doubleday, 1989.

Smoke without Fire. London: Collins, 1989; New York: Doubleday, 1991.

Answer Came There None. London: Collins; New York: Doubleday, 1993.

CRITICAL BIBLIOGRAPHY

Baker, Susan. "E. X. Ferrars." In *And Then There Were Nine: More Women of Mystery*, ed. June S. Bakerman. Bowling Green, Ohio: Bowling Green University Popular Press, 1985, pp. 146–57.

Herbert, Rosemary. "The Cosy Side of Murder: Ten Noted British Mystery Writers." *Publishers Weekly*, 15 October 1985, pp. 20–32.

Lachman, Marvin. "It's about Crime." *Mystery FAN-cier*, January-February 1984, p. 17.

Rahn, B. J. "Pardon Me . . . It's Murder!" *The Armchair Detective*, 23, no. 4 (Fall 1990): 408.

GINA MACDONALD

LESLIE FORD (1898–1983)

Born December 8, 1898, in Smith River, California, Zenith Jones was one of eleven children of an Episcopal minister's family. She received her B.A. from the University of Washington in 1921, three years after her marriage to Ford K. Brown. Their daughter, Janet, became a New York attorney.

Accompanying her husband to England in 1928 for study under a Guggenheim Fellowship, Brown began publishing. Returning to the United States in 1931, Brown settled in Annapolis, Maryland, where her husband was professor of English at St. John's College. She lived there until her death in 1983, publishing under the pseudonym Leslie Ford. A short-lived series features Detective Joseph Kelly, while her best-known series features widow and mother Grace Latham and Colonel John Primrose, 92nd Engineers, U.S. Army (retired), assisted by Sergeant Phineas T. Buck.

The protagonist of the Pinkerton series is gray, rabbitlike Welsh widower Evan Pinkerton. Previously a schoolmaster who was bullied by his students, he has escaped into marriage to a tyrannical lodging-house owner, for whom he performs servants' tasks such as shining the boots of lodger Humphrey J. Bull, later of Scotland Yard's CID. After inheriting a fortune on his wife's death, Pinkerton has no notion of how to live and only two interests—films, which he mistakes for reality, and Inspector Bull's work. Pinkerton interferes in Bull's cases and blunders into solutions that endanger him, necessitating his rescue by the inspector.

The characters are well drawn and plots intricate, but a modern reader will question the stereotypical portrayal of Pinkerton's wife as an unpleasant virago and may be distracted by the unexplored emotional bonding between Bull and Pinkerton, the latter of whom more often seems pathetic than comic. The suggestions of an unconscious homosexual love are disconcerting since they are neither negated nor developed. Certainly, the effeminate Pinkerton plays a role traditionally assigned to helpless women, and this reversal of sex roles cannot be accidental. Despite these questions, the novels retain humor and charm, especially in their vivid pictures of 1930s England.

Ford's eye for detail is also evident in the Latham/Primrose stories, few of which fit into the "had-I-but-known" category to which Brown's work is usually relegated. This series should be read in order of publication and accompanied by a good social history of the period. The books give a painstakingly accurate depiction of life among the upper-middle classes before, during, and after World War II. Writing at a time when the war's outcome was still unknown, Ford reveals the fears, prejudices, and anxieties of U.S. citizens coping for the first time with threats of air raids, rationing, and espionage. Many of the novels are set in Washington, D.C., where

Latham and Primrose maintain residences in fashionable Georgetown and where Primrose, called back into intelligence work, provides a pipeline into the workings of law and government.

Her characterization is complex. Latham is a wise woman, a patroness of young lovers whose future is threatened either by their own quixotic impulses or by the wrongheadedness of their elders. In this respect, she closely resembles Elliot Roosevelt's detective Eleanor Roosevelt. Latham restores order so that the young might have their chance at life, even though her own widowhood reminds her that there are no ultimately happy endings.

As a middle-class woman of her time, Latham has no access to power; Primrose provides information and gives credibility to her investigation, only sometimes adding muscle. He is courtly and chivalric in ways Ford often undercuts. Latham is attracted to him, but she is solvent and independent, and frequently, at the novels' end, she sidesteps his attentions with the earnest collaboration of Sergeant Buck. Buck, who is convinced that every marriageable woman is in pursuit of the colonel, is not always aware that he and Latham are on the same side. Latham allows the men to think what they wish as she goes about her business. The feminism is the middle-class feminism of an earlier age, but it is there.

More ambiguous is the patrician's attitude to class and race. Ford's working-class and black dialects are an embarrassment. At the same time, she presents the ambivalences that prevailed among those of her class at that time. Buck, who is awkward and loutish, nevertheless is shrewder and even wealthier, thanks to his investments, than the colonel. (Inherited and leisured wealth is occasionally satirized and often shown as villainous.) Blacks are portrayed stereotypically yet possess more wisdom than do whites and, in *Simple Way of Poison*, the heroine risks her life for her servants.

Old Lover's Ghost is a good starting point for Ford's Latham/Primrose series; although set during World War II, its national park scenery is more important to the plot of the story than is the history of the time. The novels written between 1939 and 1945, for example, can be fully appreciated if read in conjunction with a good social history such as Roy Hoopes's *Americans Remember the Home Front* (New York: Hawthorn, 1977). *Mr. Pinkerton Finds a Body* provides a sound introduction to the Evan Pinkerton series, as does *Date with Death* for the nonseries suspense stories.

Readers who like Ford's nonseries "had-I-but-known" suspense stories will also like the writings of Mary Roberts Rinehart and Mignon Eberhart, among many others. Evan Pinkerton fans will also enjoy the Asey Mayo series by Phoebe Atwood Taylor, a similarly wry series set in New England. Few other writers, however, have equaled the subtle, but deft, handling of history and romance that characterizes the Latham/Primrose series. Perhaps most comparable is the Amelia Peabody series of Elizabeth Peters; Peters

is, however, a far wittier writer and, as is typical of 1990s authors, a better
prose stylist.

MYSTERY FICTION

Writing as Leslie Ford

In at the Death. London: Skeffington, 1929; New York: Longmans, 1930.

The Sound of Footsteps. New York: Doubleday, 1931; as *Footsteps on the Stairs.*
London: Gollancz, 1931.

By the Watchman's Clock. New York: Farrar, 1932.

Burn Forever. New York: Farrar, 1935; as *Mountain Madness.* London: Hutchinson, 1935.

The Town Cried Murder. New York: Scribner; London: Collins, 1939.

The Road to Folly. New York: Scribner, 1940; London: Collins, 1941.

Murder with Southern Hospitality. New York: Scribner, 1942; as *Murder Down
South.* London: Collins, 1943.

Date with Death. New York: Scribner, 1949; as *Shot in the Dark.* London: Collins,
1949.

Murder Is the Pay-Off. New York: Scribner; London: Collins, 1951.

Invitation to Murder. New York: Scribner, 1954; London: Collins, 1955.

Murder Comes to Eden. New York: Scribner, 1955; London: Collins, 1956.

The Girl from the Mimosa Club. New York: Scribner; London: Collins, 1957.

Trial by Ambush. New York: Scribner, 1962; as *Trial from Ambush.* London:
Collins, 1962.

Joseph Kelly Series

Murder in Maryland. New York: Farrar, 1932; London: Hutchinson, 1933.

The Clue of the Judas Tree. New York: Farrar, 1933.

Grace Latham and Colonel Primrose Series

The Strangled Witness. New York: Farrar, 1934.

Ill-Met by Moonlight. New York: Farrar; London: Collins, 1937.

The Simple Way of Poison. New York: Farrar, 1937; London: Collins, 1938.

Three Bright Pebbles. New York: Farrar; London: Collins, 1938.

False to Any Man. New York: Scribner, 1939; as *Snow-White Murder.* London:
Collins, 1940.

Reno Rendezvous. New York: Farrar, 1939; as *Mr. Cromwell Is Dead.* London:
Collins, 1939.

Old Lover's Ghost. New York: Scribner, 1940.

The Murder of the Fifth Columnist. New York: Scribner, 1941; as *The Capital
Crime.* London: Collins, 1941.

Murder in the O.P.M. New York: Scribner's, 1942; as *Priority Murder*. London: Collins, 1943.

Siren in the Night. New York: Scribner's, 1943; London: Collins, 1944.

All for the Love of a Lady. New York: Scribner's, 1944; as *Crack of Dawn*. London: Collins, 1945.

The Philadelphia Murder Story. New York: Scribner's; London: Collins, 1945.

Honolulu Story. New York: Scribner's, 1946; as *Honolulu Murder Story*. London: Collins, 1947.

The Woman in Black. New York: Scribner's, 1947; London: Collins, 1948.

The Devil's Stronghold. New York: Scribner's; London: Collins, 1948.

The Bahamas Murder Case. New York: Scribner's; London: Collins, 1952.

Washington Whispers Murder. New York: Scribner's, 1953; as *The Lying Jade*. London: Collins, 1953.

Writing as David Frome

Major Gregory Lewis Series

The Murder of an Old Man. London: Methuen, 1929.

The Strange Death of Martin Green. New York: Doubleday, 1931; as *The Murder on the Sixth Hole*. London: Methuen, 1931.

Evan Pinkerton Series

The Hammersmith Murders. New York: Doubleday; London: Methuen, 1930.

Two against Scotland Yard. New York: Farrar, 1931; as *The By-Pass Murder*. London: Longmans, 1932.

The Man from Scotland Yard. New York: Farrar, 1932; as *Mr. Simpson Finds a Body*. London: Longmans, 1933.

The Eel Pie Murders. New York: Farrar, 1933; as *The Eel Pie Mystery*. London: Longmans, 1933.

Scotland Yard Can Wait! New York: Farrar, 1933; as *That's Your Man, Inspector!* London: Longmans, 1934.

Mr. Pinkerton Finds a Body. New York: Farrar, 1934; as *The Body in the Turl*. London: Longmans, 1935.

Mr. Pinkerton Goes to Scotland Yard. New York: Farrar, 1935; as *Arsenic in Richmond*. London: Longmans, 1934.

Mr. Pinkerton Grows a Beard. New York: Farrar, 1935; as *The Body in Bedford Square*. London: Longmans, 1935.

Mr. Pinkerton Has the Clue. New York: Farrar and London: Longmans, 1936.

The Black Envelope: Mr. Pinkerton Again! New York: Farrar, 1937; as *The Guilt is Plain: Mr. Pinkerton's Adventures at Brighton*. London: Longmans, 1938.

Mr. Pinkerton at the Old Angel. New York: Farrar, 1939; as *Mr. Pinkerton and the Old Angel.* London: Longmans, 1939.

Homicide House: Mr. Pinkerton Returns. New York: Rinehart, 1950; as *Murder on the Square: Mr. Pinkerton Returns.* London: Hale, 1951.

CRITICAL BIBLIOGRAPHY

Cleary, Maryell. "Money Makes the World Go Around." *The Armchair Detective,* 22, no. 2 (1989): 158.
Dueren, Fred. "Evan Pinkerton." *The Armchair Detective,* 7, no. 3 (1974): 193–94.
Nichols, Victoria, and Susan Thompson. "Grace Latham and John Primrose." In *Silk Stalkings: When Women Write of Murder.* Berkeley, Calif.: Black Lizard, 1988, pp. 223–24.
———. "Evan Pinkerton." In *Silk Stalkings: When Women Write of Murder.* Berkeley, Calif.: Black Lizard, 1988, pp. 264–65.
Waldron, Ann. "An Interview with Leslie Ford." *The Armchair Detective,* 4, no. 1 (1971): 33–36.

BETTY RICHARDSON

KATHERINE V. FORREST (1939–   )

Katherine Virginia Forrest was born April 20, 1939, in Windsor, Ontario, Canada. She was an adopted daughter, and the parents who raised her died when she was in high school. In 1957 she moved to the United States to attend Wayne State University and later the University of California, Los Angeles. After several years in the business world, she began writing full time in 1979, encouraged and supported by her companion, Sheila, the woman to whom many of her books are dedicated. Now a U.S. citizen, Forrest lives in Los Angeles. She is a member of International P.E.N.

Forrest is the senior fiction editor for Naiad Press and its best selling author, publishing romances, science fiction, utopian stories, and other works as well as the lesbian-feminist detective series featuring Los Angeles Police Department Detective Kate Delafield. The first in this solid detective series, *Amateur City,* was chosen as the premier women's offering of Century Book Club (Los Angeles), the first book club specifically for the gay and lesbian reader. *Murder at the Nightwood Bar* is being produced as a feature film. *The Beverly Malibu* won the Lambda Literary Award and also has the distinction of being Naiad's first hardcover publication; and as a result Forrest's mysteries are now more readily reviewed by major newspapers and journals.

Forrest says all her work is directed primarily to a lesbian audience and that she prefers to publish with Naiad (who publishes the most lesbian titles in the U.S.) rather than with a mainstream house. Forrest has a large and loyal readership among lesbians and an increasingly wider audience as well. As the *Library Journal* review of *Murder by Tradition* puts it, this "sizzling" courtroom drama "should quash any doubts concerning Forrest's abilities as a mystery writer, mainstream or otherwise."

From the beginning of the series, Kate Delafield's sexual identity is a vital component of her sense of self. Rather than a "coming out" novel, *Amateur City* (and those that follow) shows Kate as a fully realized character who joyfully accepts herself as a lesbian. An honest and caring person herself, she finds friendship and meaning in her emotional and physical relationships with other women. The seemingly obligatory sex scenes reflect the general inclusion of sex in contemporary detective fiction and join the attempts of other women writers to find words and ways to describe sexual intimacy.

Although Kate consciously separates her personal life from the homophobic atmosphere of her job, as the series develops she is threatened with exposure in various ways and becomes increasingly impatient with homophobic attitudes. In *Murder by Tradition*, for example, after the gory murder of Teddie Crawford, who was "unashamedly gay," the slick lawyer for the defense claims his client was appalled by Teddie's homosexual advances and stabbed Teddie in self defense. This lawyer knows Kate from years before, through Kate's lover at the time, and Kate fears he will expose her in the courtroom to discredit her testimony. In this novel Kate begins to denounce the anti-gay/lesbian remarks of her police partner Ed Taylor. One wonders why or how she endured this through the first books, except to realize that her career was jeopardized; these novels reflect the reality of homophobia as well as attempt to change it.

The social and political problems addressed in the novels are carefully interwoven with plot, character, and themes. *Murder at the Nightwood Bar*, to cite one example, deals overtly with child abuse and family relationships. Because of her sexual orientation, young Dory Quillin is kicked out of her house by her parents, right-wing religious fanatics. When she is later found murdered, the parents show no remorse. Although each novel in the series has its particular appeal and focus—such as the long term effects of the 1950s McCarthy era in *The Beverly Malibu*—*Murder at the Nightwood Bar* has been especially well received in detective fiction classes and courses on women writers. Forrest's portrayal of Dory Quillin's brief and difficult life is unforgettable, as is Kate Delafield's determined search for justice. The action also gives Kate the chance to befriend the local clientele of the Nightwood Bar, a space for women that Kate returns to in subsequent cases. Throughout the series, homicide detective Delafield, a former Marine, is strong and positive, a respected professional, and a very likeable character.

Forrest covers many other issues in her novels: sexual harassment, social ethics and prejudices, the imperfections of the legal system, the abuse of power in its many forms, the need for gay and lesbian community and political action. Yet the books entertain rather than read like polemic tracts. In a 1989 conversation with interviewer Laurie Sosna, Forrest said of her readers, "[I hope they come away with] pleasure, enjoyment, satisfaction. Time well spent. I don't think a writer has any right to ask more than that." Her readers would grant her at least that, and probably more.

Although Kate Delafield is virtually everyone's favorite lesbian detective, there are now many other writers of lesbian detective fiction, including Barbara Wilson, Sandra Scoppettone, Sarah Dreher, Claire McNab, Vickie P. McConnell, Pat Welch, Dorothy Tell, Rita Mae Brown, Karen Saum, and Lauren W. Douglas. It is a rapidly expanding field for women writers.

MYSTERY FICTION

Kate Delafield Series

Amateur City. Tallahassee, Fla.: Naiad Press, 1984.

Murder at the Nightwood Bar. Tallahassee, Fla.: Naiad Press, 1987.

The Beverly Malibu. Tallahassee, Fla.: Naiad Press; London: Pandora, 1990.

Murder by Tradition. Tallahassee, Fla.: Naiad Press, 1991.

CRITICAL BIBLIOGRAPHY

Danni. "Garden-Side Chats: Interview with Katherine V. Forrest." *Book Garden* (Denver, Colo.), March 1992.

Decure, Nicole. "From the Closet to the Bleachers—Kate Delafield: Portrait of a Lesbian as a Lady Cop." *Women's Studies International Forum*, 15 (1992): 267–69.

McDonald, Sharon. "Katherine Forrest: A Passionate, Gutsy Storyteller." *Advocate*, 2 Oct. 1984, pp. 44–45.

Mumford, Laura Stempel. "A Sleuth of One's Own." *Culture* (Madison, Wisc.), 20 April 1990, p. 34.

Lois A. Marchino

ANTONIA FRASER (1932–   )

Antonia Pakenham Fraser was born in 1932 into a political and literary family known as "the literary Longfords." Antonia Pakenham attended schools in Oxford including a convent school which figures as the setting for her first Jemima Shore *Quiet as a Nun*, and later took her B.A. in history from Oxford University. She made her literary reputation with the

1969 biography of Mary Queen of Scots in which she altered the writing of history with details of culture and personality to reconstruct the historical as a living person. Praised for that lively personal voice in her extensively researched work, she is an outspoken social activist whose book *The Weaker Vessel* is a study of women's oppression in the seventeenth century. Her detective Jemima Shore investigates contemporary social and cultural issues on her television series, "Jemima Shore, Investigator."

A strong advocate of freedom of expression and a member of the English PEN, Fraser served both as chair of the Prison Committee and later as the English PEN President. She began writing mysteries in the mid-seventies because "there was something in myself that history didn't express." In 1986, Fraser served as President of the Crime Writers' Association. She is married to playwright Harold Pinter and lives in Kensington.

For her series Antonia Fraser created Megalith television personality and detective Jemima Shore who investigates social issues and specializes in the effects of politics on the lives of her ordinary viewers, particularly women. Jemima's expertise is uncovering secret links between the public sector and the private motive. In seven novels and two short story collections, Jemima Shore is positioned so that she has access to information crucial to exposing those secrets—in Megalith's files, through newspaper archives, and from frequent interaction with Detective Chief Inspector John Portsmouth (Pompey) of the Bloomsbury Police.

Fraser's creation is unusual because she has real professional power, a permanent research assistant, and a production crew at her command. Jemima Shore is not paired with a well-connected male because she has her own significant and wide contacts. Shore is a single, working, "nearly forty" woman who has garnered her connections and her power through hard work, intelligence, shrewd common sense, and a career "carved, sometimes clawed out." Her work on Megalith television pays for her indulgences—white wine, flowers, stylish clothes, her cat, a Porsche she drives inordinately fast, and a small though expensive London flat; and it provides her with income to support her extracurricular investigations.

Like other such sleuths, travel and mobility are prime attributes of "Jemima Shore, Investigator." Unlike many women detectives, she has real clout in the real world; not only does she research and develop much of hers own programming, but cuts deals with her employers. Control over the final edit of her programs frequently engages her in power struggles with the Megalith hierarchy, and her boss, Cy Fredericks. In the Shore mysteries Jemima's decision is generally final. Rarely does she capitulate; more often she devises a clever compromise or coup. Fraser's television commentator began her existence "when no such woman existed in England." Shore's public notoriety and her television forum propel her into more than investigative journalism. Viewers of Shore's program deliberately or unconsciously confound the public persona with a private reality. Shore's fictional debut "case," *Quiet as a Nun*, is a result of this blending of personas. When a schoolmate is found dead at her old convent school, the headmistress calls on Jemima to help out "in a certain very delicate matter," relying on both her loyalty as an old girl and a note from the dead nun claiming that Jemima knows.

Shore's damnable curiosity and her underlying passions, political and ethical, compel her to accept the private consequences of her public persona. The connection between the job and the sleuthing is direct, but subtle. In a twist of the P.I. pattern in which the private turns public, Shore discovers the private dimension of her public self. Often a program of hers triggers a plea for help as in *Quiet as a Nun*, or the information for a program provides her with background to solve the crime as in *A Splash of Red* or *The Cavalier Case*, or her journalism places her on the scene as in *Cool Repentance* or *Your Royal Hostage*. Fraser's mysteries are notable for their interlacing of personal, political, and cultural contexts.

Fraser's Jemima wrestles with personal dilemmas and ethical choices *after* she has achieved many of her goals. Like many professionals, Jemima Shore has made difficult choices to be successful. The mysteries are reminiscent in setting and atmosphere of Gothics; but for Fraser and Shore, reality is preferable; Shore is consistently superior at what she does, and does not spend her time or her job searching for male partners. Sexually liberated Jemima regularly chooses and thoroughly enjoys her liaisons. Serious and proud of the work she does, this career woman appreciates solitude, vacations alone, and as early as *The Wild Island* decides that "Paradise was not for her. She would not seek it again." Jemima Shore prefers the messy reality of career and friends to any illusory cultural romance.

I recommend beginning with *Quiet as a Nun*. It introduces many of the motifs, and provides extensive background on Jemima. It also illuminates Jemima's thought processes and personal issues.

Readers who enjoy Jemima Shore might be interested in works by Nancy Pickard, Sarah Caudwell, Margot Arnold and Carolyn Hart.

MYSTERY FICTION

Jemima Shore Series

Quiet as a Nun. New York: Viking; London: Weidenfeld and Nicolson, 1977.

The Wild Island. New York: Norton; London: Weidenfeld and Nicolson, 1978.

A Splash of Red. New York: Norton; London: Weidenfeld and Nicolson, 1981.

Cool Repentance. London: Weidenfeld and Nicolson, 1982; New York: Norton, 1985.

Oxford Blood. New York: Norton; London: Weidenfeld and Nicolson, 1985.

Jemima Shore's First Case, and Other Stories. New York: Norton; London: Weidenfeld and Nicolson, 1987.

Your Royal Hostage. New York: Atheneum; London: Mandarin, 1988.

The Cavalier Case. New York: Bantam; London: Mandarin, 1991.

Jemima Shore at the Sunny Grave, and Other Stories. London: Bloomsbury Press, 1991; New York: Bantam, 1993.

TELEVISION CREDITS

Quiet as a Nun. Boston: WGBH/"Mystery," 1982.
Jemima Shore Investigates. Thames, 1983. (Patricia Hodge as Jemima Shore.)

CRITICAL BIBLIOGRAPHY

Angelo, Bonnie. "Not Quite Your Usual Historian." *Time*, 135 (15 January 1990): 66–68.
Gussow, Mel. "Antonia Fraser: The Lady Is a Writer." *New York Times Magazine*, 9 September 1984, pp. 60–61.
Herbert, Rosemary. "PW Interviews: Lady Antonia Fraser." *Publishers Weekly*, 231 (19 June 1987): 104–5.

DENISE M. MARSHALL

FRANCES FYFIELD (1948–   )

Born in Derbyshire, England, on November 18, 1948, Frances Fyfield, the pseudonym of Frances Hegarty, earned her B.A. degree from the University of Newcastle-upon-Tyne and then qualified as a solicitor in English law. In 1975, she joined the Crown Prosecution Service in London, England, and currently serves as a practicing solicitor specializing in criminal law.

Fyfield's critically acclaimed crime thrillers have garnered Edgar nominations in the United States and literary prizes in Britain. A recipient of the Rumpole Award from the Crime Writers' Association, Fyfield also won the Association's 1991 Silver Dagger award for *Deep Sleep*.

Like P. D. James and Ruth Rendell, the authors with whom she is most frequently compared, Fyfield writes crime novels characterized by their deep psychological insight and sensitive detectives, yet in her choice of investigative team, she stakes out territory that is distinctly her own. In *A Question of Guilt*, the first of four novels that feature Crown Prosecutor Helen West, an independent professional woman in her thirties, and Detective Superintendent Geoffrey Bailey, a widower in his forties, the lawyer and the policeman form an unlikely alliance since members of their respective professions generally look with skepticism on the efforts of the other. Yet little about Helen and Geoffrey is conventional.

Although their jobs demand that they investigate and prosecute criminals, neither has been hardened by constant contact with the underside of humanity for both know their own dark sides, their own pathological loneliness and self-sufficiency. Nevertheless, they still abhor the criminal acts that inflict such pain upon innocent people who suffer already their own private torments. Their shared compassion for all the victims of crime provides a basis for mutual trust, understanding, and respect that the equivalency of their professional positions only enhances. The combination leads to that rarity in detective fiction—an effective professional alliance, and thus Fyfield challenges the paradigmatic inequality of detective partnerships, especially male-female partnerships.

Their professional relationship leads Helen and Geoffrey almost inevitably to a personal relationship that creates much of the interest of all of the novels in the series. Fyfield's mature lovers are utterly convincing in their mutual need and fear of a relationship that promises to sustain them both emotionally and intellectually but also threatens the seemingly impenetrable armor of self-sufficiency that each has donned to protect against the pain of love. The mystery of their relationship is at least as compelling and as finely drawn as the crimes they must investigate.

The psychological landscape of Fyfield's novels is detailed not only in the relationships of her detectives but also in her cast of secondary characters. Generally, her criminals are themselves victims of loss, neglect, betrayal, and abuse. Poisoned by a lifetime of love withheld, Eileen Cartwright, for instance, the cunning and evil villain of *A Question of Guilt*, orchestrates murder even from her prison cell. Similarly, Pip Carlton, the unctuous pharmacist of *Deep Sleep*, murders and molests without compunction because he was himself a victim of child sexual abuse. Like wounded animals, Fyfield's criminals strike back in perverse self-defense, destroying any possibility of attaining that for which they most desperately seek—the love that affirms their being, and herein lies the pathos of Fyfield's world.

The need for love is ultimately the recurrent theme that unifies all four novels in the West-Bailey series and that links them as well to Fyfield's second novel, *Shadows on the Mirror*. Like Helen West, Sarah Fortune, the novel's lawyer protagonist, lives on the fringes of life, an outsider by choice. Clearsighted but not disillusioned, she has a "subtle capacity for mending lives." She cannot, however, repair her own. Betrayed by love, she now believes herself unworthy of it and begins a downward spiral that leads her to Charles Tysall, a man whose psychopathic need to humiliate and dominate women forces Sarah to reaffirm her being. A hybrid creation, *Shadows* is both a psychological crime thriller and a quirky romance, and in it, Fyfield clearly pushes to the limit the latent tendencies of her series heroine and explores her dominant theme with a sympathetic character.

Like Ruth Rendell, who writes a different type of mystery under another name, Frances Fyfield writes psychological thrillers as well as crime novels, but under her legal name, Frances Hegarty. In *The Playroom* and *Half Light*, Hegarty is free of the conventions of the crime novel. Nevertheless, she continues to explore some of the same themes that predominate in her Fyfield novels, and thus these works provide an interesting counterpoint to the other series.

Fyfield's West-Bailey crime novels certainly gain impact when they are read in order, especially given the importance of the detectives' personal relationship to the series' concerns and to her revision of traditional detective partnerships. Each, however, stands easily alone on its own merits.

Readers who enjoy Fyfield's crime novels should find the works of P. D. James and Ruth Rendell equally satisfying.

MYSTERY FICTION

Writing as Frances Fyfield

Sarah Fortune Series

Shadows on the Mirror. London: Heinemann, 1989; New York: Pocket Books, 1991.

Perfectly Pure and Good. New York: Pantheon, 1994.

Helen West and Geoffrey Bailey Series

A Question of Guilt. London: Heinemann, 1988; New York: Pocket Books, 1989.

Trial by Fire. London: Heinemann, 1990; as *Not That Kind of Place*. New York: Pocket Books, 1990.

Deep Sleep. London: Heinemann, 1991; New York: Pocket Books, 1992.

Shadow Play. London: Heinemann, 1992; New York: Pantheon, 1993.

Writing as Frances Hegarty

The Playroom. London: Hamish Hamilton, 1990; New York: Pocket Books, 1991.

Half Light. London: Hamish Hamilton, 1992.

LINDA C. PELZER

❧ G ❧

ELIZABETH GEORGE (1949–   )

With a daring that is typically American, Elizabeth George has chosen not only to set her novels in Britain, but also, through her series characters, to probe the conflicts and values of British class structure. Born in Ohio in 1949, George's background is all-American. She earned bachelor's and master's degrees in the California university system, and has taught in various Southern California institutions. Married to Ira Toibin in 1971, she currently lives in Huntington Beach, California, and produces a novel a year, each of which is so immersed in British atmosphere, character, and custom that, were it not for the biographical information provided by the publisher, few readers would suspect her true origins.

Her first novel, *A Great Deliverance*, was nominated for the Edgar and won the Agatha, Anthony, and French *Le Grande prix de Littérature Policière* awards. *Well-Schooled in Murder* won the German MIMI for international mystery fiction. Thus, from her earliest efforts, Elizabeth George has achieved enormous popular and critical success, and each new novel in the series (thus far all her novels have been in one series) confirms and enlarges her reputation.

She has frequently been compared to P. D. James and Ruth Rendell as a mystery writer whose focus is psychological as well as criminous, but the association which pleases her most is with Dorothy L. Sayers. George, like Sayers, has a keen interest in her major characters aside from their involvement in the mystery plot, and she places great emphasis on elements such as setting, style, and atmosphere. In each novel there are subplots which resonate with the main one; there are social, psychological, and romantic tensions between and within the characters; there are symbols and themes which reverberate both on the mystery level and in the lives of the continuing characters.

In all the novels George's plots are multilayered, the group of suspects

large and varied, and the relationships between the characters extraordinarily complex. The crimes are violent and the depiction of them realistic,
so that, while George's milieux are often reminiscent of the English "cozy"
tradition, her subjects and her sexual, social, and psychological concerns
put her work in a much more modern, more intense subgenre. She is skilled
in shifting suspicion from one character to another, but, in the end, those
who turn out not to be the chief villain are nevertheless guilty of secondary
offenses so that their earlier positions as potential candidates for the role
of major criminal do not seem artificially contrived.

Without George's command of the mystery plot and all that that implies,
her work would doubtless not receive the respect and popularity that it
does; but, actually, the cast of continuing characters, the relationships between and among them, and the ways in which their lives and problems
are interwoven with the main plot, may well be an equally strong element
in her appeal.

Thomas Lynley, eighth earl of Asherton, is George's aristocratic, New
Scotland Yard detective. A handsome bon-vivant, he has an apparently
earned reputation as a loner and a womanizer. Charming but aloof, he is
assigned as his partner Barbara Havers, a frumpy, working class, chip-on-
the-shoulder Detective Sergeant who believes that "life's central problems—
from the crisis in the economy to the rise of sexual diseases—all sprang
from the class system." This pairing generates enormous friction in *A Great
Deliverance* and to a lesser extent thereafter. Initially Havers is torn between her contempt for Lynley and his values and her need to impress him
professionally lest she be sent back to permanent street patrol. By the time
of *Payment in Blood* she has grown out of her prejudice to the extent that
she is able to sacrifice what would be to her personal advantage in order
to save Lynley from making a fatal misjudgment as the result of his class
loyalties and personal animosity to one of the suspects.

Lynley and Havers must be one of the oddest of odd-couple detectives
in mystery fiction, yet they are individuals not stereotypes. Their fractious
and humorous antagonism is, of course, a subplot that makes a comment
on the conflicts in British social structure. In the later novels that antagonism diminishes as both have matured and learned somewhat grudging
respect for each other. If, however, an amusing tension has been tempered
by this mellowing, something even more important has been gained. By
allowing her characters to grow and change, George avoids the formulaic
molds so many series characters fall into. Havers's need to deal with her
aging, senile parents not only gives her a life aside from her professional
one, but also introduces the issue of care for the elderly. Lynley's tempes-
tuous relationship with his mother and younger brother (which is not fully
explained until the fourth novel, *A Suitable Vengeance*) adds a dimension
to the reader's perception of his already complicated emotional make-up.

While the dynamic pairing of Lynley and Havers is at the center of most of the novels, three other continuing characters, whom George sees as vital to the fabric of them, play important roles. Simon Allcourt-St. James is at once Lynley's best friend, a man permanently disabled by Lynley's negligence, the husband of his former lover, and the foremost forensic expert in Britain. His wife Deborah Cotter, the daughter of St. James's valet-nurse-friend, is a professional photographer, whose earlier affair with Lynley causes lingering problems for all three. Finally, there is Lady Helen Clyde, St. James's assistant in forensics, formerly his fiancée, and currently the elusive object of Lynley's passion. Only a writer with George's self-assurance and firm control could present a cast like this and make them credible human beings rather than soap opera caricatures. She succeeds so well in this that the reader awaits each new novel as much to find out what has happened to the continuing characters as to explore the new mystery.

George has called these four characters, plus Barbara Havers, an ensemble, a close-knit group of friends, each of whom figures more or less prominently in a given novel, depending on its potential for developing the individual. This shifting and evolving of the five players allows George to avoid one-note characters and requisite scenes in which they reaffirm their personalities. This, in turn, makes all five of them three-dimensional in a way that not many other authors' series characters are.

In addition to everything else, Elizabeth George is a consummate, highly literate stylist. The books are rich in vocabulary and allusion; description and dialogue are handled masterfully. What is perhaps most impressive throughout the series is the way in which, with symbols and multiple variations, themes emerge that grow out of, but are more universal than, the plot itself. Thus, George's books are far more than mere solve-the-mystery whodunits; they are literary works of a very high caliber. They are rich in humor, in their probing of human nature, and in their superb capturing of the British landscape.

Because the continuing characters do grow and their relationships evolve, it is probably best to read the series in order of publication.P. D. James, Ruth Rendell, and Dorothy L. Sayers are established writers whose work Elizabeth George readers may find interesting and enjoyable. S. T. Haymon and Caroline Graham are younger authors whose characters, plots, and settings bear similarity to George's.

MYSTERY FICTION

Lynley and Havers Series

A Great Deliverance. New York: Bantam, 1988; London: Bantam Press, 1989.

Payment in Blood. New York: Bantam; London: Bantam Press, 1989.

Well-Schooled in Murder. New York: Bantam; London: Bantam Press, 1990.

A Suitable Vengeance. New York: Bantam; London: Bantam Press, 1991.

For the Sake of Elena. New York: Bantam; London: Bantam Press, 1992.

Missing Joseph. New York: Bantam; London: Bantam Press, 1993.

Playing for the Ashes. New York: Bantam, 1994.

CRITICAL BIBLIOGRAPHY

Stone, Nancy-Stephanie. "Well-Schooled in Murder" [Interview]. *The Armchair Detective,* 25 (1992): 260–69.

Wertheimer, Linda. "Elizabeth George" [Interview]. *All Things Considered* (radio program transcript), 3 August 1992, pp. 32–33.

LANDON C. BURNS

B. M. GILL (1921–   )

B. M. Gill is a pseudonym—actually the maiden name—of Barbara Margaret Trimble who was born in Holyhead, Anglesey, Wales, on February 15, 1921. Encouraged to write from an early age by her father, she was educated at Le Bon Sauveur Convent in Holyhead (although she attended the local Presbyterian Church) and Redland College in Bristol. As Margaret Blake she wrote short stories for the BBC and Irish radio, romances for women's magazines, and eight romance novels. She has worked as a clerk-typist in Holyhead, taught infants in Gloucestershire, and worked as a chiropodist in Bristol. Gill, who is divorced, now lives and writes full-time in her native Holyhead, spending much time helping new writers.

Gill was first used in 1977 as the author's name for the little-known mystery, *Target Westminster.* The eight additional Gill novels in the genre have been widely praised by reviewers, and two have been adapted for radio and television. *The Twelfth Juror* won the Crime Writers' Association Gold Dagger; *The Fifth Rapunzel* was shortlisted for the same award, and Gill has been nominated four times for the Mystery Writers of America Edgar Awards, an unusual tribute for a British author.

Reviewers find unequal achievement in the very diverse Gill crime novels, although all are praised. Gill does not develop an individual formula, and she creates one of the most understated of policemen, Detective Inspector Tom Maybridge, who appears in only three novels, *Victims, Seminar for Murder,* and the *The Fifth Rapunzel.* Moving easily among psychological thriller, suspense novel, inverted mystery, and black comic crime novels, Gill creates a voice and focus of her own, often on disturbed or victimized children, without confining herself to one type of crime novel. Consequently, her work is as difficult to summarize as her novels are to label. Despite this diversity, there are recurring motifs in character and situation and consistently powerful writing. Readers can expect a shock, or at least a surprise, at the conclusion of each novel.

Most readers and reviewers find *Death Drop, Victims*, and *The Twelfth Juror* particularly successful. *Death Drop* is a good choice to read first. The focus is on John Fleming, a widower whose son, aged twelve, is reported to have died in an accident at his boarding school. Seldom have readers of detective fiction been asked so deeply to feel the death of the person sacrificed for their amusement, but, as Gill has observed, her crime stories are concerned with people and their reactions to horrifying situations. A favored plot element is the intense involvement of a sometime absent father for an only child. Fleming's ordeal concludes with a ritual testing which heightens the reader's respect for him and pleasure in the novel. *Victims* is a novel whose synopsis suggests police procedure and the serial sex killer. In fact, it is a novel whose American title, *Suspect*, better fits its focus on the family and person of George Webber, the increasingly solitary suspect. Like Fleming, Webber is in personal crisis, caused in his case by a paralyzed wife, domestic chaos, and physical frustration. This denouement features no heroism, however, displaying instead the violent consequences of naive emotional attachment and thwarted sexual and emotional desire. In the courtroom drama *The Twelfth Juror*, the defendant and the juror protagonist exercise a typical genre prerogative, playing god and incidentally breaking the law. Their combined arrogance leads to a less typical and chilling conclusion.

The next two novels, *Seminar for Murder* and *Nursery Crimes*, are less intense, contain more obvious humor and general satire, and are less successful in the creation of suspense. *Seminar* is the only novel to focus consistently on Maybridge, and the awkwardness of his unofficial standing emphasizes his less-than-heroic status and lack of success in solving the crime. *Nursery Crimes* bears resemblance to the farcical and donnish novel typical of Michael Innes and Edmund Crispin, although the comedy is darker.

By most measures, *Dying to Meet You* is Gill's least successful work. The novel is not tragic, despite elements of tragedy. Like that in *Nursery Crimes*, the ending to the action is more farcical than suspenseful. In a departure, Gill creates in Lowell Marshall, the crippled former pianist, a relatively unattractive character whose circumstances should elicit sympathy but whose reactions to them frustrate reader identification. More successful is *Time and Time Again* which also examines a character who has lost her former way of life and is regarded with growing impatience by friends and family. In this novel Gill makes her only use of first person narration and thereby achieves greater reader investment in Maeve Barclay's odyssey from comfort to prison and only part-way back. That experience serves finally to underscore bald differences between British life lived near the top and that lived close to the bottom, despite Maeve's attempts to link them.

The Fifth Rapunzel is somewhat more conventional and less satisfying, but Gill here creates her most fully delineated adolescent in Simon Bradshaw, reveals more tragedy and weakness in the concerned father, and resorts to hidden crimes and multiple solutions to achieve surprise in the conclusion.

Hallmarks of Gill's fiction include the portrayal of protagonists and antagonists in emotional crisis, an unromantic depiction of urgent sexuality, and skilled delineation of the egocentric world view of the adolescent and the intensity of parental responsibility. Most important, her books bring new possibilities to the genre. Gill's best novels should be read first, and readers who enjoy her works should try those of Josephine Tey, Ruth Rendell, P. D. James, and Elizabeth George.

MYSTERY FICTION

Target Westminster. London: Hale, 1977.
Death Drop. London: Hodder and Stoughton, 1979; New York: Scribner's, 1980.
The Twelfth Juror. London: Hodder and Stoughton; New York: Scribner's, 1984.
Nursery Crimes. London: Hodder and Stoughton, 1986; New York: Scribner's, 1987.
Dying to Meet You. London: Hodder and Stoughton, 1988; New York: Bantam, 1990.
Time and Time Again. London: Hodder and Stoughton, 1989; New York: Scribner's, 1990.

Tom Maybridge Series

Victims. London: Hodder and Stoughton, 1981; as *Suspect*. New York: Scribner's, 1981.

Seminar for Murder. London: Hodder and Stoughton, 1985; New York: Scribner's, 1986.

The Fifth Rapunzel. London: Hodder and Stoughton, 1991; New York: Scribner's, 1992.

CRITICAL BIBLIOGRAPHY

Edwards, Martin. "Gill, B. M." In *Twentieth Century Crime and Mystery Writers*, ed. Lesley Henderson. 3rd ed. Chicago and London: St. James, 1991, pp. 439–40.

NANCY ELLEN TALBURT

DOROTHY GILMAN (1923–   )

Dorothy Gilman was born in New Brunswick, New Jersey on June 25, 1923. She was educated as an artist, but after her marriage in 1945, she wrote fiction for children under the name of Dorothy Gilman Butters. She raised two sons, Christopher and Jonathan. Just after her divorce in 1965, she began to publish adult fiction and introduced Mrs. Pollifax in 1966. She has written other mystery and adventure stories and won the Catholic Book Award for *A Nun in the Closet* in 1975, but the nine books featuring Mrs. Pollifax are her most popular. She now divides her time between Connecticut and New Mexico.

When she first appeared in *The Unexpected Mrs. Pollifax*, Emily Pollifax was sixty-six and depressed, a widowed grandmother with time on her hands. She felt that she had outlived her usefulness, despite her volunteer activities and garden club. To combat her depression she decided to take up an activity she had always longed to try but for which she had never had time. She applied for work at the CIA.

She was unexpectedly in the right place at the right time. Mr. Carstairs of the CIA, mistaking her for an established agent, was charmed by her absurd hat, fly-away white hair, and obvious enthusiasm. She looked the perfect tourist and he asked her to go to Mexico as a courier. Even after he discovered his mistake, his intuition that she was right for the job led him to order an immediate security check and to put her on the payroll. Although captured by spies and flown to Albania, Mrs. Pollifax befriended her Albanian jailer and used her amazing resourcefulness to free herself, a fellow agent, and an imprisoned English scientist as well. A most improbable story, but entertaining and nearly believable as Dorothy Gilman tells it.

Each subsequent book in the series takes Mrs. Pollifax to a new and exotic location. She battles communists in Bulgaria and international plutonium thieves in Switzerland. On safari in Zambia, wrapped in a dust veil and wearing a lapel-pin camera, she attempts to identify an assassin who is also disguised as a tourist. Readers want to hold their breath with her as the Land Rover stops beside a pair of napping lions and they wake and stretch in the sun.

The series is full of charming supporting characters. Mrs. Pollifax has a talent for making friends and for enlisting their help. She often picks up young accomplices; young people naturally gravitate to her and she treats them with respect. Their assistance often proves invaluable. A boy named Ahmad, driving a truck for the first time, crashes through her prison wall and allows her to escape with a fellow agent and the "Whirling Dervish." Debby, a college student, uses her skills at rope climbing to assist in a daring scheme to free a fellow student from a Turkish prison.

Like other spies, this heroine can drop off walls, climb down sheer cliffs, be cuffed and kicked, and still appear all in one piece to be debriefed when her assignment is over. Unlike other spies, she returns home to her geraniums and bakes blueberry muffins for Bishop, her primary CIA contact. She even falls in love and marries partway through the series. Although her husband sometimes accompanies her and offers help, he conveniently goes off visiting when necessary and never overshadows her central role.

Energetic and self-reliant, she seldom loses her cheerful outlook on life. She is inventive, tenacious, and flexible. She trusts her own judgment and has a knack for getting help from the ordinary people around her. In short, she is an exceedingly unique spy. As her employer says in *Mrs. Pollifax on the China Station*, while dealing with dangerous assignments and unforeseen obstacles, she has "shown a remarkable ability to sustain the role of Aggrieved and Misunderstood Tourist."

Dorothy Gilman's other books are equally absorbing. Full of gentle humor and beautifully constructed, her tales are unusual and entertaining. Her heroines have a way of bringing out the best in the people around them. Although they are traditional in many ways and always return to an everyday life when their adventures are over, they enjoy an ability to be untraditional during their adventures. Her protagonists demonstrate, not only how a woman can learn to rely on her own resources, but how she can use them to her advantage. Her books contain plenty of suspense, but not much explicit violence. For readers who like to travel and enjoy meeting real people and experiencing real life in the countries they visit, Dorothy Gilman's protagonists are wonderful companions.

The Mrs. Pollifax series is most enjoyable when read in order. Most of them are also available on audio tape. Readers who like her adventures and want more should try Evelyn Smith's Susan Melville, freelance assassin and socialite artist. For other strong, older protagonists, read the Sheila Travis series set in the South by Patricia Houck Sprinkle or the retirement community murders created by Corrine Holt Sawyer.

MYSTERY FICTION

Uncertain Voyage. New York: Doubleday, 1967; London: Hale, 1968.
The Clairvoyant Countess. New York: Doubleday, 1975; London: Prior, 1976.
A Nun in the Closet. New York: Doubleday, 1975; as *A Nun in the Cupboard*. London: Hale, 1976.
The Tightrope Walker. New York: Doubleday, 1979; London: Hale, 1980.
Incident at Badamya. New York: Doubleday, 1988.
Caravan. New York: Doubleday, 1992.

Mrs. Pollifax Series

The Unexpected Mrs. Pollifax. New York: Doubleday, 1966; London: Hale, 1967; as *Mrs. Pollifax, Spy*. London: Tandem, 1971.

The Amazing Mrs. Pollifax. New York: Doubleday, 1970; London: Hale, 1971.

The Elusive Mrs. Pollifax. New York: Doubleday, 1971; London: Hale, 1973.

A Palm for Mrs. Pollifax. New York: Doubleday, 1973; London: Hale, 1974.

Mrs. Pollifax on Safari. New York: Doubleday; London: Hale, 1977.

Mrs. Pollifax on the China Station. New York: Doubleday, 1983; London: Hale, 1984.

Mrs. Pollifax and the Hong Kong Buddha. New York: Doubleday, 1985; London: Hale, 1986.

Mrs. Pollifax and the Golden Triangle. New York: Doubleday, 1988; London: Piatkus, 1989.

Mrs. Pollifax and the Whirling Dervish. New York: Doubleday, 1990.

Mrs. Pollifax and the Second Thief. New York: Doubleday, 1993.

CRITICAL BIBLIOGRAPHY

Becker, Mary Helen. "Gilman, Dorothy." In *Twentieth Century Crime and Mystery Writers*, ed. Lesley Henderson. 3rd ed. Chicago and London: St. James, 1991, pp. 441–43.
Nichols, Victoria, and Susan Thompson. "Mrs. Emily Pollifax." In *Silk Stalkings*. Berkeley, Calif.: Black Lizard, 1988, pp. 227–29.

ANN SANDERS CARGILL

E. X. GIROUX (1924–   )

Doris Shannon, who writes under her own name and also as E. X. Giroux, was born Doris Giroux on August 7, 1924, in Elmira, New York, of Canadian parents. She grew up in Napanee, Ontario, Canada, graduating from the Napanee Collegiate Institute in 1942. In 1947, she married Frank Shannon and moved to British Columbia, where she has lived since then, raising her two daughters and turning to writing in her forties. She won a *Writer's Digest* creative writing award in 1969 for a short story; her first book was published in 1972, when she was forty-eight years old. A lifelong reader ("I can't remember when I couldn't read"), Shannon has turned her love of reading fiction to writing it, publishing twenty-one novels to date (seven of them nonmystery novels), with another book in progress. Her early novels, written as Doris Shannon, include three mysteries: *The Whispering Runes, The Lodestar Legacy*, and *Little Girls Lost*.

As E. X. Giroux, she writes a mystery series featuring an English barrister named Robert Forsythe and his secretary, Abigail Sanderson, as the detective team. Giroux generates a special interest in her sleuths' activities through the relationship she details between Robbie, the thirtyish barrister, and his secretary, who was his father's secretary before him and began to serve as his substitute mother when Robbie's mother died. Abigail, or Sandy, as only he calls her, appears to be in her early fifties. She is a feisty, independent woman who is warmly fond of Robert Forsythe. Still, she has a mind of her own; she quibbles and argues, and every once in a while, she questions her Watson-like role in his detective investigations. In some adventures, such as *Death for a Dietician*, she takes center stage in another variation on the "spinster sleuth" category. No fluttering female, she takes a bullet in the shoulder in a confrontation with a killer.

In the first book in the series, *A Death for Adonis*, the reader is swept into Robert Forsythe's elegant office at his estate in Sussex. He is interviewing an intent, powerful woman who is determined to engage his help with a profoundly disturbing problem—a murder that took place twenty-five years ago, for which her father was confined to an insane asylum. Forsythe is reluctant, having given up his law practice six years earlier during a scandal that probably would have caused his disbarment. He will not speak of it because of a promise given to a woman in trouble. There's a very heartwarming code of old-fashioned decency, chivalry, and honor at work here, but it is charmingly coupled with a modern tone: much whisky-and-soda drinking by Abigail and Forsythe; much loving, if bewildered, acceptance of the younger generation; and many comic incidents engendered by Abigail's penchant for "giving as good as she gets," as when she returns "a rude gesture" to a leather-jacketed motorcyclist, who almost drives off the road in his surprise. The novels deal with very modern dilemmas—such as the beautiful young homosexual found dead in his aging lover's arms (*Adonis*) and the extremely successful romance writer, complete with white poodles, white furs, and white Cadillac, who writes out of her dream of a lost love (*Dietician*).

All the series novels take place in England, on country estates or in nursing homes (one is set on an island), with a few excursions to and from London. Giroux is able to gather a cast of interesting and unusual characters in the English cozy style, with a closed circle of suspects at a house party or in a rural setting. She is especially accurate and subtle in adjusting and readjusting the reader's perceptions and sympathies about the characters involved, mirroring through Abigail's consciousness the uncertainties of trying to understand what makes people tick. It is probably best to start reading Giroux with *A Death for Adonis*, in which Forsythe gives up playing the wounded knight in retreat (bound by a promise given to a perfidious woman) and actively resumes his practice of law. Readers of Agatha Christie and Sara Woods would enjoy Giroux's novels.

MYSTERY FICTION

Writing as E. X. Giroux

The Dying Room. New York: St. Martin's Press, November, 1993.

Robert Forsythe and Abigail Sanderson Series

A Death for Adonis. New York: St. Martin's Press, 1984.

A Death for a Darling. New York: St. Martin's Press, 1985; London: Hale, 1987.

A Death for a Dancer. New York: St. Martin's Press, 1985; as by Doris Shannon. London: Severn House, 1987.

A Death for a Doctor. New York: St. Martin's Press, 1986; as by Doris Shannon. London: Severn House, 1987.

A Death for a Dilettante. New York: St. Martin's Press, 1987.

A Death for a Dietician. New York: St. Martin's Press, 1988.

A Death for a Dreamer. New York: St. Martin's Press, 1989; as by Doris Shannon. London: Severn House, 1991.

A Death for a Double. New York: St. Martin's Press, 1990; as by Doris Shannon. London: Severn House, 1992.

A Death for a Dancing Doll. New York: St. Martin's Press, 1991.

A Death for a Dodo. New York: St. Martin's Press, 1993.

A Death for a Duchessa. Forthcoming.

Writing as Doris Shannon

The Whispering Runes. New York: Lenox, 1972.
The Lodestar Legacy. New York: Popular Library, 1976.
Little Girls Lost. New York: St. Martin's Press, 1981; London: Sphere, 1983.

CRITICAL BIBLIOGRAPHY

Harper, Carol. "Giroux, E. X." In *Twentieth Century Crime and Mystery Writers*, ed. Lesley Henderson. 3rd ed. Chicago and London: St. James, 1991, pp. 443–44.

Nichols, Victoria, and Susan Thompson. "Robert Forsythe." In *Silk Stalkings*. Berkeley, Calif.: Black Lizard, 1988, pp. 143–44.

JOAN WARTHLING ROBERTS

PAULA GOSLING (1939–   )

Paula Gosling was born in 1939 in Detroit, Michigan, where she attended local grade and high schools and went to Wayne State University. After receiving a B.A. in English in 1962, she trained as a copywriter for Campbell-Ewald Advertising, also in Detroit. In 1964 she moved to London where, for the next six years, she worked as a copywriter for a number of British advertising agencies. In 1968 she married Christopher Gosling, with whom she has two daughters, Abigail and Emily. In 1978 the marriage was dissolved, and she married John Hare in 1981. She currently lives and writes in Bath, England.

Paula Gosling first attempted to write a novel during her lunch hours. A photo of musician Paul McCartney inspired her to draft a book about a poor boy growing up in Liverpool, which she never finished. She went on with her life, married, and had children. Then, one night, she dreamed about the English Department at Wayne State University where she had worked while an undergraduate student. One of the windows in the office where she worked would flop shut, and the handle would drop and lock itself. It was a great plot device for a "closed-room" mystery story. With her daughters in school, she had two hours free each morning, and she once again began to write. The finished product was the size of the Manhattan phone book and was rejected. In short order, however, she wrote another which was accepted and published as *A Running Duck* (and later, in a revised version, as *Fair Game*). That launched her career. Her first novel later appeared, in a much slimmer version, as *Monkey Puzzle* and was the first Jack Stryker book.

Gosling describes herself as more of a writer of suspense fiction than of mystery novels. "My 'detectives' are ordinary people caught up in extraordinary situations, doing the best to survive and make sense of their various dilemmas." She believes that most people have heroic qualities that would surface if they were thrust into circumstances similar to those in her books. In her action-thrillers she creates characters who, when under stress (as one critic has noted), redefine themselves. Starting as passive victims, such figures struggle to gain control over their lives, often warring with conflicts within, as well as with criminals from without. This is especially true of the male protagonists of the early books, who must be drawn out by their growing love for a woman before they can become motivated to take action in their own behalf.

Although she has steadfastly avoided producing a series, over the past few years one has slowly emerged. *Monkey Puzzle*, which was set in the mythical city of Grantham (described as "a foggily remembered Detroit"), featured Lieutenant Jack Stryker and Kate Trevorne, an instructor in the English Department of the local university, where a murder had just been committed. In the novel, they begin their odd-couple relationship. In *Backlash*, a second book set in Grantham, Kate flies off to Great Britain to do research and must confront her feeling about Stryker when she is wooed by an English professor. In the meantime, Stryker is wounded while tracking down the killer of a police officer back in the states. In *The Body in Blackwater Bay*, Kate takes Stryker to stay with her aunt, who lives on Blackwater Bay, a small resort community. During their vacation, the unlikely duo reluctantly investigates a murder. The location of Blackwater Bay is to become the setting for more novels in the future.

Paula Gosling is a versatile writer: She has written American soft-boiled crime novels, Continental thrillers, and traditional British mysteries, all with equal verve. Action and dialogue, seasoned with a marvelous wit, dominate her fiction, which tends to minimize what she once described as the "pretties." Paula Gosling combines skillful plotting, exotic settings, solid action, and a romantic interest that have made her novels among the very best whatever the genre.

MYSTERY FICTION

Writing as Paula Gosling

A Running Duck. London: Macmillan, 1978; as Fair Game (rev. ver.). New York: Coward McCann, 1978.
The Zero Trap. London: Macmillan, 1979; New York: Coward McCann, 1980.
Loser's Blues. London: Macmillan, 1981; as Solo Blues. New York: Coward McCann, 1981.
The Woman in Red. London: Macmillan, 1983; New York: Doubleday, 1984.
The Wychford Murders. London: Macmillan, 1985; New York: Doubleday, 1986.

Lieutenant Jack Stryker and Kate Trevorne Series

Monkey Puzzle. London: Macmillan, 1984; New York: Doubleday, 1985.

Backlash. London: Macmillan, 1988; New York: Doubleday, 1989.

The Body in Blackwater Bay. New York: Mysterious Press; London: Scribners, 1992.

Luke Abbott Series

Death Penalties. New York: Mysterious Press; London: Scribners, 1991.

Writing as Ainslie Skinner

Mind's Eye. London: Secker and Warburg, 1980; as The Harrowing. New York: Rawson Mead, 1981.

CRITICAL BIBLIOGRAPHY

Bakerman, Jane S. "Paula Gosling." In Twentieth Century Crime and Mystery Writers, ed. John M. Reilly. 2nd ed. New York: St. Martin's Press, 1985, pp. 388–89.
———. "Paula Gosling's Thrillers." Clues: A Journal of Detection, 10, no. 1 (Spring/Summer 1989): 89–101.
Decure, Nicole. "A Whole Lotta Grinnin's Goin On . . . and Some Killin' Too: Romance in Paula Gosling's Crime Fiction." Clues: A Journal of Detection, 12, no. 2 (Fall/Winter 1991): 17–33.

Silet, Charles L. P. "Paula Gosling Interview." *Clues: A Journal of Detection*, 13, no. 2 (Fall/Winter 1992): 1–16.

CHARLES L. P. SILET

SUE GRAFTON (1940–   )

Sue Grafton began her writing career as a screenwriter and novelist. Among the programs for which she wrote were "Rhoda" and "Nurses." With Steven Humphrey, she wrote an award-winning pilot for the show, "Seven Brides for Seven Brothers." She also wrote teleplays, including some adaptations of Agatha Christie stories. Her first two books (*Keziah Dane*, 1967, and *The Lolly-Madonna Wars*, 1969) were not mysteries. She also wrote the screenplay for a movie version of *Wars*. Like her female detective protagonist, Kinsey Millhone, Sue Grafton runs every morning and is twice divorced. She lives in Santa Barbara, California, the prototype for the mythical Santa Teresa, where Kinsey Millhone operates. Unlike the resolutely single and child-free Kinsey, Grafton remains married to Steven F. Humphrey (a professor of philosophy, whom she married in 1978) and has three children (from her first two marriages). Her murderous rage at her second husband during a child custody battle turned into her first detective novel, *"A" Is for Alibi*, instead of, she explained, an actual attempt on her ex-husband's life. *Alibi* won the Mysterious Stranger Award from the Cloak and Clue Society. Writing a novel a year, Grafton, who was born in Louisville, Kentucky in 1940, will be age sixty-eight when she reaches the letter "Z." Her mother, Vivian Harnsberger, was a high school chemistry teacher. Her father, Chip W. Grafton, was a lawyer who also wrote a few mystery novels. Her B.A. is from the University of Louisville (1961). *"B" Is for Burglar* won the Bouchercon Award and the Private Eye Writers of America Award (an Anthony and a Shamus, respectively). *"C" Is for Corpse* won an Anthony Award. Her 1986 short story, "The Parker Shotgun" (published in the collection *Mean Streets*, by Mysterious Press) won a Macavity Award for best short story and an Anthony Award.

Grafton's first few novels begin with an abrupt business report as the detective introduces her case and herself. An epilogue ending with, "Respectfully submitted, Kinsey Millhone" usually closes the novels. In *Alibi*, Kinsey's reportage covers for the emotions she experiences after having to kill a man who was briefly her lover. As Kinsey indicates in her opening paragraph, the narrative she writes shows the material that a police or professional P.I. report excludes, and the simple sentence structure and narrative quickly develop in complexity. Like the best of the new female hard-boiled writers, Grafton has her character doubt her motives and methods only to reconfirm most of them, but not without a struggle. Kinsey avoids unnecessary violence, but the criminals she pursues do not.

Following the formula of the hard-boiled detective genre, Grafton creates a detective who is single and lives a stripped-down life—no pets or even plants. She does have an attractive landlord who is in his eighties and who often meets her with the fresh baked goods he makes in swap for meals at a corner restaurant run by Rosie, Kinsey's other friend. Henry Pitts is a former baker who rents a converted garage to Kinsey. In *"E" Is for Evidence*, a bomb destroys the garage, which Henry then rebuilds without Kinsey's input but with respect for the compact, tidy way in which she lives. She prides herself on having few possessions. Her car is an ancient beige Volkswagen "bug" that has seen better days. One friend close to her own age is Vera, who works in the insurance company where Kinsey has an office in exchange for investigating claims. Vera often coaches Kinsey in fashion, a female avocation that Kinsey takes pride in not developing, although at times she feels hampered by her ignorance. In *"I" Is for Innocent*, Kinsey loses her contract with the insurance company because of a change in management. She remains friends with Vera, and she vindicates herself in *"J" Is for Judgment* when she solves a fraud case for her former employer. Her new office situation suits her well, however, and she has no regrets about the break in relations with California Fidelity Insurance. Grafton shows Kinsey developing from a complete rejection of bourgeois comforts to a cautious acceptance of pleasant surroundings as though she fears her toughness and independence will weaken if she relaxes her spartan standards.

Orphaned at five years of age, Kinsey received a supportive, albeit at times unconventional, upbringing by her maiden aunt. Until *Judgment*, Kinsey has been depicted without living relatives. This latest case forces Kinsey to face more about herself and her past than has any other case to date, and Grafton gradually forces Kinsey to recognize the weaknesses that have also protected her.

The crimes that Kinsey Millhone solves often are old murders that were inaccurately detected and prosecuted by the judicial system. Generally, an innocent person has been punished or accused of a crime that he or she did not commit. Kinsey finds the real killer and the real reason for the murder, but not all the novels finish conclusively. Justice is not always left to the patriarchal judicial process, although Kinsey still believes in the system despite its failures. She is a former police officer who quit because of the restrictions on her ability to solve crimes and see them prosecuted. She has enough self-awareness to realize that she cannot tolerate taking orders from others and must be her own boss.

A strong female detective who has no patience with male chauvinism and who appreciates women (except for the spoiled wives of wealthy men), Kinsey can evaluate a woman's appearance without viewing her as competition. Self-reliance is an essential character trait in Kinsey and the people she likes. Kinsey runs regularly to compensate for all the junk food she consumes. She must stay fit to protect herself and do her job. She is regularly attacked, bruised, and patched together, with appropriate rest for a reasonable recovery before continuing her pursuit. However, she will force herself out of her sick bed whenever the chase is imperative. Her choice in men is flawed, although one male has appeared in the series who seems compatible. He, of course, has become unreachable by the novel's end, but Kinsey has some hope in her chances of a relationship.

Kinsey Millhone ranks among the best of the 1980s series detectives and promises to continue as an interesting and always entertaining character (she wisecracks steadily). Those who are unfamiliar with the series should start at *Alibi*. All the novels are good, but my favorites are *"H" Is for Homicide* and *"J" Is for Judgment*. In both, Kinsey deals more directly than in the other novels with the oppression of women of different classes because in these novels, patriarchal attitudes form the destruction of women's lives. I also recommend *Homicide* because it recognizes and portrays Hispanic women, who are an important part of the California population and heretofore virtually ignored by Grafton and many other writers. Grafton's novels usually involve rich, white, middle-class people struggling with lower-middle-class characters, just like the classic male hard-boiled detective novel. Those who like hard-boiled detective fiction will like the Grafton novels and will also like novels by Sara Paretsky, Susan Dunlap, and Marcia Muller.

MYSTERY FICTION

Kinsey Millhone Series

"A" Is for Alibi. New York: Holt, 1982; London: Macmillan, 1986.

"B" Is for Burglar. New York: Holt, 1985; London: Macmillan, 1986.

"C" Is for Corpse. New York: Holt, 1986; London: Macmillan, 1987.

"D" Is for Deadbeat. New York: Holt, 1988; London: Macmillan, 1987.

"E" Is for Evidence. New York: Holt; London: Macmillan, 1988.

"F" Is for Fugitive. New York: Holt; London: Macmillan, 1989.

"G" Is for Gumshoe. New York: Holt; London: Macmillan, 1990.

"H" Is for Homicide. New York: Holt; London: Macmillan, 1991.

"I" Is for Innocent. New York: Holt; London: Macmillan, 1992.

"J" Is for Judgment. New York: Holt; London: Macmillan, 1993.

"K" Is for Killer. New York: Holt, 1994.

NONFICTION

Grafton, Sue, ed. *Writing Mysteries: A Handbook by the Mystery Writers of America.* Cincinnati, Ohio: Writers Digest Books, 1992.

CRITICAL BIBLIOGRAPHY

Geherin, David. "Grafton, Sue." In *Twentieth Century Crime and Mystery Writers,* ed. Lesley Henderson. 3rd ed. Chicago and London: St. James Press, 1991, pp. 459–60.

Irons, Glenwood. "New Women Detectives: G Is for Gender-Bending." In *Gender, Language, and Myth: Essays on Popular Narrative,* ed. Glenwood Irons. Toronto: University of Toronto Press, 1992.

Rabinowitz, Peter J. " 'Reader, I Blew Him Away': Convention and Transgression in Sue Grafton." *Famous Last Words: Women against Novelistic Endings,* ed. Alison Booth. Charlottesville: University of Virginia Press, forthcoming.

Taylor, Bruce. "G is for (Sue) Grafton: An Interview with the Creator of the Kinsey Millhone Private Eye Series Who Delights Mystery Fans as She Writes Her Way through the Alphabet." *The Armchair Detective,* 22, no. 1 (1989): 4–13.

CATHERINE ELIZABETH HOYSER

LINDA GRANT (1942–   )

Linda V. Williams ("Grant" was her paternal grandmother's maiden name) was born in New York City in 1942. She received her B.A. in English from Stanford in 1964 and an M.A. in education there in 1965. She lives in Berkeley with her husband and two daughters. Grant was elected president of Sisters in Crime for 1993–94.

Catherine Sayler, the daughter of a Denver policeman, is a San Francisco private investigator with a small firm specializing in corporate security. Crime is better mannered, she says, and less likely to turn violent, but no safer than police work, and indeed, she is often exposed to danger.

Keith Stone, her employer, mentor, and second father, had taught her to act legally, ethically, and morally, but she discovers that these attitudes may conflict. She is not above allowing a murderer to escape if she believes his or her actions were morally justified, and she uses force as necessary to protect herself and those for whom she cares.

Sayler studies aikido and adopts its physical and spiritual teachings as a touchstone—the strongest foes do not block an attack but rather get out of its way and let it turn on itself. Such a philosophy is suited to a woman in what has been traditionally a man's world, and Sayler is often confronted with gender-based obstructions. Her ex-husband Dan Walker, a San Francisco Police Department homicide detective, displays frustrated anger and boyish hurt when Catherine rejects his smothering protection. Her current lover, private investigator Peter Harman (a grown child of the 1960s), usually provides Catherine with sufficient room to maneuver as a professional.

Women can be invisible among men, Sayler realizes, and people keep an eye on those who are more powerful, while ignoring the powerless. Evil often takes the form of abuse of power, especially when men with position, money, and power exert pressure on women, children, and men who are lower on the social and corporate ladder. Sayler is cynical about her business and reflects that she catches little criminals so that bigger criminals (e.g., corporate executives) can get away with murder. Treachery and betrayal of trust figure as metaphors throughout the novels. In *Random Access Murder*, Peter is hired by a wife whose husband is having an affair. After one of the "other" women is brutally beaten and murdered and Harman is framed, Catherine's usual business proves useful when a theft of intellectual property provides a motive for murder. In *Blind Trust*, Catherine looks for a missing bank employee suspected in an embezzlement scheme, but he is a Mexican-American with a strong family, a pregnant wife, and friends from a military unit that fought in Vietnam, and she is suspicious of the source of the danger. In both books, disloyalty and abuse of power are the evils from which violence flows.

In *Love nor Money*, Catherine has been double-crossed by a client and a young man has committed suicide. To distract herself from the part she feels she has played in this betrayal, she takes a case investigating the murder of a man who had been about to disclose his sexual abuse perpetrated on him years ago by a noted judge. The judge is murdered, her client is suspected of the crime, and Catherine sets out to clear him by finding the murderer, in the process uncovering a child pornography ring. A fourteen-year-old niece, Molly, runs away from home and moves in with Catherine and Peter, and her presence underscores the need for loyalty and the risks of betrayal.

Readers who enjoy the Catherine Sayler mysteries might also like the works of Linda Barnes, Marcia Muller, and Karen Kijewski.

MYSTERY FICTION

Catherine Sayler Series

Random Access Murder. New York: Avon Books, 1988.
Blind Trust. New York: Scribner's, 1990.
Love nor Money. New York: Scribner's, 1991.
A Woman's Place. New York: Scribner's, 1994.

KATHY PHILLIPS

LESLEY GRANT-ADAMSON (1942–   )

Born in London on November 26, 1942, Lesley Heycock attended schools in London and Wales and began work as a journalist in the early 1960s. A series of jobs with magazines and then newspapers ended in 1980 when she left her position as a feature writer with the *Guardian* to become a highly successful free-lance writer. In recent years she has written television documentaries and poetry and published short stories and magazine features, in addition to her seven, highly regarded novels.

Grant-Adamson executes her purposes with notable skill. Her short and focused sentences ensure that the action is well paced. The characters are memorable—idiosyncratic and often delightful. The settings are richly evocative, drawn into sharp focus by an eye that is attentive to detail. In fact, an ability to realize place as an element of theme in many of the books lends special significance to this aspect of her work.

Grant-Adamson situates her series character in the middle of London's Fleet Street. Rain Morgan is the gossip columnist for the *Daily Post*. She is, therefore, a widely recognized figure, for her photograph accompanies her regular column. Rain's editorial assistant—and thus, a version of the detective's side-kick—is Holly Chase, a young, vivacious, black woman with a practical turn of mind. Newspaper cartoonist Oliver West, who is unreliable and self-absorbed, is Rain's on-again, off-again housemate.

In *Death on Widow's Walk*, Rain Morgan takes a country holiday. Arriving just as a fox hunt is about to begin, she enters the world of labyrinthine country paths and evenings of bridge with the lord of the manor. Then, a body is unearthed. Village suspects pass by Rain's cottage each day on their way to gather the post—and red herrings appear. In this fashion, all the familiar elements are nicely put in place, and Grant-Adamson is able to disport with her form all the while she is spinning her tale. (This light touch of a novelistic self-consciousness is also evident elsewhere: *Guilty Knowledge* opens with the dramatically vivid first sentence, "Blood.") The plot of *Death on Widow's Walk* moves quickly on to a thrilling chase scene wherein Rain finds no sanctuary inside the village church.

Moving from the country into the suburbs of London, Grant-Adamson then ventured into the realm of the psychological thriller. In *The Face of Death* she makes use of the eerie anonymity of a new (and soon to be shabby) housing development to plot a nasty tale. The plight of a victim of amnesia is publicized in a television news report, and a man, named Peter Dutton, whose wife is missing steps forward to identify the "mystery woman." Is the woman really Dutton's wife? Rain Morgan is a peripheral character here, while Holly Chase, who lives on Dutton's street, is closer to the action.

Guilty Knowledge and *Wild Justice*, the third and fourth books in the Morgan series, are puzzle mysteries wherein Rain finds herself assisting (more or less) the police to sort out murder. In *Wild Justice* the owner and editor of the newspaper for which Rain works is stabbed in the back and a series of butcher knives begins to turn up. The book offers an insider's look at the bustle and flurry of Fleet Street. In *Guilty Knowledge*, Rain travels on assignment to the French Riviera. She hopes to interview the reclusive mistress of a famous painter, but the subject of her feature piece is found shot and floating in the water. What with nests of thieves, surly drug dealers, unscrupulous art merchants, a missing English heir, and a bumbling gendarmerie, complications abound.

The final work in the Morgan series, *Curse the Darkness*, is also a suspense mystery but presents an altogether new twist: in it, Grant-Adamson interestingly weaves together two quite distinct plots. Perhaps the most experimental of her books, it is unquestionably her most ambitious.

In her last novel to date, Grant-Adamson provides her readers with yet one more surprise. *Too Many Questions* brings a new hard-boiled detective onto the London scene. In creating her fresh character, Grant-Adamson made her first use of a first-person narrator; the wonderfully successful result is the London-Irish Laura Flynn, a feminist and private eye.

Viewed as a whole, Grant-Adamson's collection of novels presents a number of unusual variations within the possibilities of the mystery form. Perhaps most significantly, she is interested in the blurring of the boundaries that mark her characters' understandings of their private and public selves. When characters become one-dimensional in this way, they become enmeshed in circumstances that they find difficult to control.

Because they are all so different from one another, the novels need not be read in any particular order. Fans of Rain Morgan might enjoy Lilian Jackson Braun's early fiction. Readers who like Laura Flynn should seek out Sue Grafton's books. Readers with a taste for a thriller might choose Ruth Rendell or Margaret Millar.

MYSTERY FICTION

Threatening Eye. London: Faber, 1988; New York: St. Martin's Press, 1989.
Flynn. London: Faber, 1991; as *Too Many Questions*. New York: St. Martin's Press, 1991.

Rain Morgan Series

The Face of Death. London: Faber, 1985; New York: Scribner's, 1986.
Patterns in the Dust. London: Faber, 1985; as *Death on Widow's Walk*. New York: Scribner's, 1985.

Guilty Knowledge. London: Faber, 1986; New York: St. Martin's Press, 1988.

Wild Justice. London: Faber, 1987; New York: St. Martin's Press, 1988.

Curse the Darkness. London: Faber; New York: St. Martin's Press, 1990.

CRITICAL BIBLIOGRAPHY

Edwards, Martin. "Grant-Adamson, Lesley." In *Twentieth Century Crime and Mystery Writers*, ed. Lesley Henderson. 3rd ed. Chicago and London: St. James, 1991, pp. 464–65.

Nichols, Victoria, and Susan Thompson. "Rain Morgan." In *Silk Stalkings*. Berkeley, Calif.: Black Lizard, 1988, pp. 175–76.

LORENA STOOKEY

ANNA KATHARINE GREEN (1846–1935)

Born in Brooklyn, New York, on November 11, 1846, Anna Katharine Green died on April 11, 1935, in Buffalo, New York, where she spent most of her adult life. She graduated from the Ripley Female Academy in Vermont, and in 1884 she married Charles Rohlfs, an actor who later turned to the design of furniture and iron stoves. Throughout their marriage, Green's writings provided their major source of income. Although Green served as the family breadwinner, she also bore two sons and a daughter.

Her phenomenally successful first novel, *The Leavenworth Case*, was published in 1878 and sold over a million copies. *The Leavenworth Case* was the first detective novel written by a woman who published under her own name. Finding the concept of a female detective novelist incredible, members of the Pennsylvania State Legislature spent time in session debating whether a woman could even have penned such a work. The Yale Law School faculty, however, who were more interested in the way the author proved the fallacy of relying on circumstantial evidence, made *The Leavenworth Case* a required text.

Her contemporary critics consistently ranked her with Edgar Allan Poe, Émile Gaboriau, and Sir Arthur Conan Doyle as the premier writers of nineteenth-century detective fiction. Green was known for ingenious touches that made her books interesting and inventive: for example, plots hinge on bullets made of ice which melt and leave no trace or retractable wrecking balls which can be lowered with the press of a button in order to kill a victim who had been lured to sit in a certain chair.

Along with inventive plots, Green also created well-rounded characters, four of whom served as series detectives. The first of these was Inspector

Ebenezer Gryce of the Metropolitan Police. Making his debut in *The Leavenworth Case*, Gryce appears in over a dozen more novels, aging from around sixty to ninety. Sometimes he is paired with Caleb Sweetwater, another series detective, who is young and eager to learn from the celebrated Gryce.

With the publication of *That Affair Next Door*, Green extended the boundaries of the genre by transforming the convention of the amateur detective. Invariably, the amateur detective has been male—until Green created a female detective, Amelia Butterworth, who also appears in *Lost Man's Lane* and *The Circular Study*. Butterworth, who is fiftyish, upper-middle class, and most respectable, is the first woman detective in American literature to challenge the accepted role of women. To be sure, other women detectives preceded Miss Butterworth, but they were creations of male authors and, by the end of the novel, these women not only came to find detective work unsuitable for a woman but also were married off by their creators. Totally unlike the previous women detectives, Butterworth is, instead, a precursor of Agatha Christie's Jane Marple, who is probably the best-known example of the amateur, unmarried, woman detective.

Early in *That Affair Next Door*, Amelia Butterworth announces that she changed her first name from "Araminta" because she is "sensible" and "not the piece of antiquated sentimentality" that her given name suggests. Dignity, intelligence, integrity, and curiosity mark the strength of her self-image. In her dealings with Gryce, Butterworth firmly intends to make him her rival and compel him to acknowledge her as his equal. By the end of their first case, she has not only proven herself his equal, she has shown him up. *Lost Man's Lane* builds on their characters, as established by the end of *That Affair Next Door*. No longer is her detecting talent only grudgingly admitted by Inspector Gryce. Butterworth is clearly the central character, with Gryce acting as her assistant. Their last dual appearance occurs in *The Circular Study*, which diverges sharply from Green's previous books. Experimental forms of presentation and characterization occur in this novel; here, Butterworth has lost a little of her independence and self-confidence. Her intelligence, however, is still as strong, and she plays a major part in solving the murder of Felix Adams.

Fifteen years after the last appearance of Amelia Butterworth, Green created another series detective, the debutante Violet Strange. This character is featured only in the collection of nine short stories, *The Golden Slipper and Other Problems for Violet Strange*. She and Amelia Butterworth share some characteristics: intelligence, skill at detection, an upper-class background, and a penchant for doing work considered by society to be unsuitable for a woman. Butterworth involves herself in crime because of her inquisitive nature and because she wants to test her abilities against those of Inspector Gryce. She is clearly an amateur, neither needing nor desiring to be paid for her work.

In contrast, Violet Strange is a full-fledged conception of a woman who sees detective work only as a remunerative activity. Her sole reason for involving herself in such work is to earn enough money to send her widowed sister, whom their father has disowned, to Europe for voice lessons. Strange is young, beautiful, and wealthy, but she cannot use her money to help her sister since her father holds the purse strings. She chooses detective work because she has a talent for it and because her aristocratic background ensures a better welcome in upper-class society than an ordinary police agent would have. In consequence, she makes sure that the contract with her employer contains a secrecy clause. She lives in constant fear that her father will learn of her work and disown her, too. In addition, she puts stringent limitations on what type of tasks she will perform and insists that her employer spare her from involvement in any crimes which are sordid or gory.

Butterworth, on the other hand, believes that her late father would have approved of her work. Most nineteenth-century fathers held out high hopes for their sons but not their daughters; evidently, however, Mr. Butterworth was an anomaly in that respect. His faith in his daughter's intelligence and ability was manifested in his frequent comment that she "would live to make her mark" in the world. Willing to undertake any task, she displays none of Violet Strange's squeamishness. For instance, in *That Affair Next Door*, Butterworth discovers the body of Louise Van Burnam, who has been crushed under a heavy cabinet. While the maid faints and the police officer has an attack of nerves, Butterworth takes charge. In *Lost Man's Lane*, Butterworth puts herself at risk on numerous occasions, including surreptitiously witnessing the burial of a body in the cellar of the house where she is staying and investigating an attic where she expects to find a corpse.

All but three of Green's detective novels are out of print, but because of their immense popularity during her lifetime, many can be found at public libraries and second-hand book shops. Modern readers will enjoy these works, particularly if they keep in mind that many of the conventions that they now take for granted in detective fiction found their first expression in Green's novels. For that, she is universally honored as "The Mother of Detective Fiction."

MYSTERY FICTION

XYZ. New York: Putnam's, 1883.
The Mill Mystery. New York: Putnam's, 1886.

7 to 12. New York: Putnam's, 1887.

The Forsaken Inn. New York: R. Bonner's Sons, 1890. Rpt. Freeport, N.Y.: Books
    for Libraries Press, 1971.

The Old Stone House and Other Stories. New York: Putnam's, 1891.

Cynthia Wakeham's Money. New York: Putnam's, 1892.

Marked "Personal." New York: Putnam's, 1893.

Miss Hurd—An Enigma. New York: Putnam's, 1894.

Dr. Izard. New York: Putnam's, 1895.

A Difficult Problem and Other Stories. New York: F. P. Lupton, 1900. Rpt. New
    York: Garrett, 1969.

One of My Sons. New York: Putnam's, 1901.

The Filigree Ball. Indianapolis, Ind.: Bobbs-Merrill, 1903. Rpt. New York: Arno
    Press, 1976.

The Amethyst Box. Indianapolis, Ind.: Bobbs-Merrill, 1905.

The House in the Mist. Indianapolis, Ind.: Bobbs-Merrill, 1905.

The Millionaire Baby. Indianapolis, Ind.: Bobbs-Merrill, 1905.

The Chief Legatee. New York: Authors and Newspapers Association, 1907.

The Mayor's Wife. Indianapolis, Ind.: Bobbs-Merrill, 1907.

Three Thousand Dollars. Boston: R. G. Badger, 1910.

Initials Only. New York: Dodd, Mead, 1911.

Masterpieces of Mystery. New York: Dodd, Mead, 1912.

Dark Hollow. New York: Dodd, Mead, 1914.

To the Minute, and *Scarlet and Black.* New York: Putnam's, 1916.

The Step on the Stair. New York: Dodd, Mead, 1923.

Ebenezer Gryce Series

The Leavenworth Case. New York: Putnam's, 1878. Rpt. Upper Saddle River, N.J.:
  Literature House, 1970.

A Strange Disappearance. New York: Putnam's, 1880.

Hand and Ring. New York: Putnam's, 1883.

Behind Closed Doors. New York: Putnam's Sons, 1888.

A Matter of Millions. New York: R. Bonner's Sons, 1891.

The Doctor, His Wife and the Clock. New York: Putnam's, 1895.

The Sword of Damocles. New York: Putnam's, 1909.

Mystery of the Hasty Arrow. New York: Dodd, Mead, 1917.

Amelia Butterworth and Ebenezer Gryce Series

That Affair Next Door. New York: Putnam's, 1897.

Lost Man's Lane. New York: Putnam's, 1898.

The Circular Study. New York: McClure, Phillips, 1900. Rpt. New York: Garland,
  1976.

Caleb Sweetwater Series

Agatha Webb. New York: Putnam's, 1899.

The Woman in the Alcove. Indianapolis, Ind.: Bobbs-Merrill, 1906.

The House of Whispering Pines. New York: Putnam's, 1910.

Violet Strange Series

The Golden Slipper and Other Problems for Violet Strange. New York: Putnam's, 1915.

CRITICAL BIBLIOGRAPHY

Cornillon, John. "A Case for Violet Strange." In *Images of Women in Fiction: Feminist Perspectives*, ed. Susan Koppelman Cornillon. Bowling Green, Ohio: Bowling Green University Popular Press, 1972, pp. 206–15.

Hayne, Barrie. "Anna Katharine Green." In *Ten Women of Mystery*, ed. Earl F. Bargainnier. Bowling Green, Ohio: Bowling Green University Popular Press, 1981, pp. 152–78.

Maida, Patricia D. "*Legacy* Profile: Anna Katharine Green (1846–1935)." *Legacy*, 3, no. 2 (1986): 53–59.

———. *Mother of Detective Fiction: The Life and Works of Anna Katharine Green*. Bowling Green, Ohio: Bowling Green University Popular Press, 1989.

Ross, Cheri L. "The First Feminist Detective: Anna Katharine Green's Amelia Butterworth." *Journal of Popular Culture*, 25, no. 2 (Fall 1991): 77–86.

Welter, Barbara. "Murder Most Genteel: The Mystery Novels of Anna Katharine Green." In *Dimity Convictions: The American Woman in the Nineteenth Century*. Athens, Ohio: Ohio University Press, 1976, pp. 130–44.

CHERI LOUISE ROSS

MARTHA GRIMES (1931–   )

Martha Grimes was born in Pittsburgh, Pennsylvania, on May 2, 1931. She grew up in Maryland. Grimes's father died when she was a child and she was raised by her mother, who supported Grimes and her brother by running a hotel at a summer resort. After earning her B.A. and M.A. from the University of Maryland, Grimes studied poetry at the University of Iowa Writers' Workshop. She has taught English at the University of Iowa, Frostburg State College, and Montgomery College. She has also taught a seminar on detective fiction at Johns Hopkins University. Grimes is divorced and has one son, Kent Van Holland. She lives in Washington, D.C., and spends much of her time in England, where she sets her Richard Jury mysteries.

Each novel in the series is named after an English pub, and each features

the same core group of characters. At the center of this group is Richard
Jury, Grimes's Scotland Yard detective. In his early forties and unmarried,
Jury is a melancholy man who likes winter, rain, and mist. He loves Virgil
and from time to time quotes Latin tag lines. He is "over six feet, [with]
chestnut hair, dark grey eyes, good teeth and a ravishing smile." Orphaned
at age seven during the London blitz, Jury is a compassionate man who
shows great kindness to the emotional cripples of the world. For many of
Grimes's readers, he is the quintessential romantic hero: tall, dark, handsome, and a rescuer of the innocent.

Jury is cursed with an inept superior, Chief Superintendent Racer, a fine
comic character who loathes Jury. Racer is a very poor detective. He is
noted for his immaculate desk, which is kept clean by the fact that he is
quick to pass work on to others. He has a running feud with a sly cat
named Cyril, and in each of the novels, Racer's secretary Fiona colludes
with Jury to evade Racer's attempts to evict the cat from the office.

Another person in Grimes's repertory group is Jury's assistant, Sergeant
Wiggins. "A young man made old through hypochondria," Wiggins is a
dear character, "always on the verge of keeling over." He and Jury are
clearly fond of one another, and readers are led to understand that Wiggins
performs as well as he does because Jury takes his multitude of illnesses
seriously, that is, because Jury accepts him as he is.

Divisional Commander Brian Macalvie, with whom Jury works on specific cases, appears in only some of the Jury novels, but readers will look
forward to each appearance, wondering if Macalvie still has a staff (he is
a perfectionist whose subordinates are always in the process of seeking
transfers), if he has managed to quit smoking, and if his contentious relationship with Gilly Thwaite has blossomed into romance.

This group of "official" characters is rounded off by the tenants in Jury's
apartment house: beautiful nineteen-year-old Carole-Anne Palutski, and the
sensitively drawn Mrs. Wasserman, the survivor of a World War II concentration camp.

Grimes also has a second group of characters, centered around amateur
detective Melrose Plant. The scion of a noble British family who has given
up his title of Lord Ardry (but not his ancestral home, Ardry End), Plant
meets Jury in Grimes's first novel, *The Man with a Load of Mischief*, and
a close friendship develops which, somewhat improbably, provides the ra-
tionale for Plant to assist Jury with subsequent cases. Like Jury, the unmarried Plant is in his forties and has no family, although he is encumbered
by Agatha, his American aunt-by-marriage, who dotes on all things British
and longs to take over the ancestral manor, complete with furnishings.

In addition to Aunt Agatha, Plant's extended family includes his long-
suffering butler, Ruthven; a mystery writer, Polly Praed; a beautiful heiress
and poet, Vivian Rivington; an equally beautiful and elusive widow, Jenny

Kennington; an antiques dealer, Marshall Trueblood; and the regulars in Dick Scroggs's pub, the "Jack and Hammer."

Besides her continuing characters, Grimes also includes in her works children who have been abandoned, either intentionally or unintentionally, by the adults who are responsible for them. Such children are heart-breakingly brave and self-reliant. Grimes said, "Children see things we adults have been taught to ignore, and because they are unpredictable, they make perfect characters in fiction."

Grimes is a fine wordsmith, with an excellent ear for the precise word or phrase that will freeze the reader with dread, a skill she uses in her gripping openings. *The Old Fox Deceiv'd* begins with this image of the victim: "She came out of the fog, her face painted half-white, half-black." *The Five Bells and Bladebone* opens by asking, "What else could you think of but getting your throat slit?" and *Jerusalem Inn* starts by teasing the reader with the ambiguous phrase, "A meeting in a graveyard."

Grimes is classified as a writer of classic British mysteries, or "cozies"; since her first mysteries are set in picturesque villages, they deal with murder among the upper classes and have a closed circle of suspects; her two detectives are reminiscent of such Golden Age detectives as Roderick Allyn, Albert Campion, and Lord Peter Wimsey; and the overall focus is on puzzles whose solutions are carefully crafted. However, beginning with *The Anodyne Necklace* (winner of the 1983 Nero Wolfe Award for best mystery of the year), Grimes's later work moves away from the pure form, combining urban with rural settings and opening up the closed circle. These mysteries focus on character rather than plot. Their solutions are often difficult to follow, and their resolutions are ambiguous.

Typically, Grimes's fans are initially drawn to her work because it reminds them of Golden Age classics. Because her characters are at the heart of Grimes's popularity, it is important to read her books in chronological order: in many cases, she provides full background information on people only once, in the novel in which they make their first appearance. When they appear in subsequent works, Grimes assumes that her readers already know who they are. Readers who lack this knowledge will miss much of what makes Grimes a favorite with mystery fans.

In addition to the Jury series, Grimes has written *The End of the Pier*, a mystery with the American setting of Key West, Florida, and a very American detective, Sheriff Sam DeGheyn. This book's strength also lies in its characters rather than in the puzzle it poses, which resolves itself without the aid of the sheriff.

MYSTERY FICTION

The End of the Pier. New York: Knopf, 1992; London: Headline, 1993.

Richard Jury Series

The Man with a Load of Mischief. Boston: Little, Brown, 1981.

The Old Fox Deceiv'd. Boston: Little, Brown, 1982.

The Anodyne Necklace. Boston: Little, Brown, 1983; London: O'Mara, 1989.

The Dirty Duck. Boston: Little, Brown, 1984; London: O'Mara, 1986.

Jerusalem Inn. Boston: Little, Brown, 1984; London: O'Mara, 1987.

The Deer Leap. Boston: Little, Brown, 1985; London: Headline, 1989.

Help the Poor Struggler. Boston: Little, Brown, 1985; London: O'Mara, 1988.

I Am the Only Running Footman. Boston: Little, Brown; London: O'Mara, 1986.

The Five Bells and Bladebone. Boston: Little, Brown, 1987; London: O'Mara, 1988.

The Old Silent. Boston: Little, Brown, 1989; London: Headline, 1990.

The Old Contemptibles. Boston: Little, Brown; London: Headline, 1991.

The Horse You Came In On. New York: Knopf, 1993.

CRITICAL BIBLIOGRAPHY

Butler, Rebecca R. "Martha Grimes." In *Critical Survey of Mystery and Detective Fiction*, ed. Frank N. Magill. Pasadena, Calif.: Salem, 1988.

Carpenter, Richard C. "Martha Grimes." In *Twentieth Century Crime and Mystery Writers*, ed. Lesley Henderson. 3rd ed. Chicago and London: St. James, 1991, pp. 479–81.

Chambers, Andrea. "The Terribly English Mysteries of Martha Grimes Are a Welcome Addition to the Public Domain." *People Weekly*, 2 Feb. 1987, p. 64.

Grimes, Martha. "Necessary Lies." *Writer's Digest*, May 1983, pp. 70–72.

———. "Seeing around Curves." *Writer*, Sept. 1987, pp. 11–13.

Radice, Lisanne. "Ye Quainte Olde English Murder." *London Times* (overseas ed.), 10 Jan. 1991, p. 18.

JOAN G. KOTKER

❦ H ❦

CAROLYN G. HART (1936–   )

Carolyn G. Hart (née Gimpel) was born in Oklahoma City on August 25, 1936. She received a B.A. degree in journalism from the University of Oklahoma in 1958 and married in the same year. She worked as a reporter briefly before becoming an editor on an alumni newspaper. From 1961 to 1982 Hart was a free-lance writer; she joined the University of Oklahoma as an assistant professor of journalism in 1982, but in 1986 she returned to writing full time. She has a son and a daughter.

Carolyn Hart published her first book in 1964 (a children's book), and her first mystery novel in 1975. She published a total of nine novels before writing and publishing her first Annie Laurance and Max Darling mystery, in 1987; this is the series for which she is known. Set on Broward's Rock Island, a resort off the coast of South Carolina, the series follows Annie Laurance, the owner of Death on Demand Bookstore, in her encounters with murder; Max Darling, whom she eventually marries; and her mother-in-law, along with other friends and customers. The bookstore detailed in the first novel, *Death on Demand*, is at the heart of each subsequent book, and any reader would do well to begin here. The bookstore shelters Annie's black cat, Agatha, coffee mugs painted with the names and titles of classic mysteries, and a monthly series of paintings depicting an unnamed mystery novel, the identification of which entitles the winner to a prize.

An admirer of Agatha Christie, Mary Roberts Rinehart, and Phoebe Atwood Taylor, Hart stays close to the cozy tradition and places her murders in the traditional settings of the genre: a nearby historical society, a local college, a conference at a posh hotel, and a swank housing estate. The characters are also the traditional ones: the rich residents of the estate, including aging actors and business executives, Max Darling's rich and flaky mother, acerbic writers and critics, and thwarted young lovers. The plots are well worked out, with a good distribution of clues to challenge the reader, but these are not the qualities for which Hart is known.

Since Arthur Conan Doyle's Sherlock Holmes first referred to his predecessors, Edgar Allan Poe's C. Auguste Dupin and Émile Gaboriau's Lecoq, mystery writers have included a subcommentary on the genre, debating its conventions, parodying another writer's series character, and sometimes addressing the reader directly. Hart has taken love of the genre to an extreme by building into each novel a series of quizzes and puzzles about mysteries. The most obvious puzzle is the series of paintings described in each book, but sprinkled throughout are also tantalizing questions about other novels, references to secondary sources, and scenes alluding to earlier works.

The most highly developed example is *The Christie Caper*, in which Annie cosponsors a conference on Agatha Christie at the Palmetto House on Broward's Rock Island. Someone is trying to murder Neil C. Bledsoe, an outrageously offensive critic and lover of the hard-boiled school of fiction, and nearly everyone in the story has a motive. In addition to the plot, which reaches a clever and satisfying ending (as do all Hart's books in this series), readers can tackle a treasure hunt (with answers included at the end of the book for the less well-read) and numerous references to Christie's work. In *Something Wicked*, in addition to exploring the sadness behind a failed career in the performing arts, Hart compares butterflies and the flowers to which they are attracted with mystery readers and their preferred subgenres.

Hart's books are known for their humor, which arises from her dialogue, hilarious situations, and careful development of minor characters over several books. For example, Max Darling's much-married mother, Laurel, is forever advising Annie that a wife must "cleave" to her husband. She enrolls in Annie's course, in *A Little Class on Murder*, in order to offer moral support, and winds up as a chief suspect in *Deadly Valentine*. Mrs. Henny Brawley follows a similar trajectory, appearing in *Death on Demand* as Annie's most demanding, but devoted, customer and as someone who is determined to assist Annie in her investigations in *A Little Class on Murder*. Hart comments on the genre in other, more subtle ways; for example, by carrying on a dialogue with contemporary writers in the same genre through allusions to their series characters and stories. The most recent novel in the series, *Southern Ghost*, plays with the conventions and cliches of the "had-I-but-known" school. In her overall approach to genre, Hart never forgets that she is a fan.

Hart's work is not without its serious side. For example, she comments on the state of education, and journalism education in particular; the pathetic underside to so-called glamorous careers; and the neediness behind flamboyant behavior.

Hart's recent work signals a change in direction. In "Henrie O's Holiday," she introduces Mrs. Henrietta Collins, who was dubbed Henrie O by her late husband because she "packed more surprises into a single day than O. Henry ever did into a short story." Henrie O is over sixty, has an occasional lover in Jimmy Lennox, a widower and author of investigative books, and herself engages in investigations whenever she gets the chance. She has a reputation in her hometown of Derry Hills, Missouri, but it fails to follow her to the Crystal Lagoon resort in the Caribbean. There she becomes suspicious of Frank Hamilton, who is married to a woman at least twice his age. The story is told with a lighthearted tone reminiscent of the Annie Laurance and Max Darling books, but there is no genre commentary at all.

In addition to the classic authors mentioned previously, readers who enjoy Hart's lightness of touch might enjoy the works of Joan Hess and Stefanie Matteson.

MYSTERY FICTION

Flee from the Past. New York: Bantam, 1975.

A Settling of Accounts. New York: Doubleday, 1976; London: Hale, 1978.

Castle Rock. London: Hale, 1983.

Death by Surprise. London: Hale, 1983.

The Rich Die Young. London: Hale, 1983.

Skullduggery. London: Hale, 1984.

Annie Laurance and Max Darling Series

Death on Demand. New York: Bantam, 1987.

Design for Murder. New York: Bantam, 1988.

Something Wicked. New York: Bantam, 1988.

Honeymoon with Murder. New York: Bantam, 1989.

A Little Class on Murder. New York: Doubleday, 1989.

Deadly Valentine. New York: Doubleday, 1990.

Christie Caper. New York: Bantam, 1991.

Southern Ghost. New York: Bantam, 1992.

Henrie O. Series

Dead Man's Island. New York: Bantam, 1993.

Scandal in Fair Haven. New York: Bantam, 1994.

CRITICAL BIBLIOGRAPHY

Harper, Carol. "Hart, Carolyn." In *Twentieth Century Crime and Mystery Writers*, ed. Lesley Henderson. 3rd ed. Chicago and London: St. James, 1991, pp. 511–12.
Oleksiw, Susan. "Dossier: Carolyn G. Hart." *Drood Review of Mystery*, 11, no. 9 (September 1991): 20.
Silet, Charles L. P. "A Little Class on Murder." *The Armchair Detective*, 26, no. 4 (1993): 46.

SUSAN OLEKSIW

S. T. HAYMON (1918–   )

Sylvia Haymon was born in 1918, in Norwich, Norfolk. She has worked in journalism, public relations, and broadcasting. In addition to her six detective novels under the name S. T. Haymon, she has published two memoirs of her childhood, *Opposite the Cross Keys* (1988) and *The Quivering Tree* (1990). Married, with two daughters, she presently lives in London. Her second detective novel, *Ritual Murder*, received the Crime Writers Association Silver Dagger Award.

Haymon's six novels, all featuring Detective-Inspector Benjamin Jurnet, are complex, literate, and rich in character and thematic interest. Jurnet is an appealing hero whose character becomes more textured as the series progresses. Each novel's murderer or murderers rival Jurnet in complexity and subtlety. Moreover, each novel boasts a multiplicity of subplots that refract and comment on the murder investigation that drives the action. Finally, each novel's thematic concerns are shaped as an extended meditation on religious faith—hard-won and ambiguous.

Ben Jurnet is the "still center" of all six of Haymon's detective novels, and he becomes more interesting and intriguing as the series progresses. Cursed by an exotic handsomeness that is at odds with his English stolidity, Jurnet is nicknamed "Valentino" by his colleagues. His looks, which resemble portraits of George Bullen, the brother of Queen Anne Boleyn, bring him nothing but embarrassment, and he is almost relieved when he learns that he may well be the descendent of Jurnet of Norwich, a medieval Jew. He is in love with Miriam, who will not consider marriage unless—and until—he converts to Judaism. The novels chart Jurnet's unenthusiastic attempts at conversion while his cases confront him with possible miracles—sometimes religious, and never entirely subject to rational proof—such as a pregnant virgin. Absolutely devoted to the elusive Miriam, Jurnet becomes increasingly uncertain about the wisdom of marrying her, and is, once, unfaithful (and unrepentant). He suffers from a ferocious inferiority complex; moreover, he is uneasy with class differences, troubled by the wickedness that surrounds him, self-conscious, and shy.

Jurnet, who is a lapsed Unitarian, is surrounded by religious concerns, both Anglican and Judaic. Haymon provides deft social comedy by placing this intrinsically nonreligious man in conflict with ardent believers of many dogmas.

All six Jurnet novels are grounded in the standard plot of the British police procedural, but Haymon's use of formulaic material is lively, erudite, and amusing. An example is the way in which Haymon deals with the inevitable confession, when the murderer is revealed and all is explained. In each novel, Haymon's murderer confesses at length; sometimes, the confession takes up an entire chapter. The confession is always an essay in self-justification and self-delusion; these murderers are not abject cowards cringing before Her Majesty's justice. They are eager to explain what happened and, more important, why it happened—and why they are not to blame. The confessions take interesting forms in the novels: one is a love letter to Jurnet, another is a letter addressed to God and hidden in the Wailing Wall in Jerusalem, and a third is a private conversation with Jurnet about a murder about which no one knows and that cannot be brought to justice.

Each of the novels provides a variety of subplots and atmospheric textures that comment on the primary plot. In *Stately Homicide*, for example, the mystery begins with the discovery of the love letters, undoubtedly genuine, of Anne Boleyn, queen of England, and her brother, George. This astonishing news seems to prove that Henry VIII had legitimate grounds for the execution of his second wife. Before the night is over, the letters are taken and the man who planned to edit them is violently murdered. As Jurnet unravels the mystery, the investigation is surrounded by ancillary actions that refract on this historical story of incest. The novel's young lovers turn out to be siblings; even more daringly, Haymond has Jurnet (after the investigation is concluded and the murderer caught) solve another murder which involves incest and betrayal. One of the most striking plot elements common to all six novels is the immense damage done to the innocent—not so much by the murderer, but by the fact of murder itself. The focus on the violence done to the social fabric becomes an important thematic concern.

All the novels focus on themes dealing with religion and the difficulty of maintaining religious faith in the secular world. Jurnet's reluctant journey toward conversion to Judaism is a consistent motif; he is not religious, and so has little to give up, yet the acquisition of faith seems at times impossible for him. Jurnet's difficulty is brought into sharp relief by the transcendent belief of Miriam, as well as that of characters in the various books (very often either the murderer or the victim).

Haymon is at her best and most harrowing when she considers the costs of faith, the possibility of the miraculous, and the tension between the modern arrogance of scientific rationalism and traditional religious belief. She looks clear-sightedly at the grotesqueries that result—the woman who finds salvation in her love for a retarded, HIV-positive boy, whom she tries to murder (*Death of a Warrior Queen*); the boy who, torn between his scientist father and minister stepfather, resolves his dilemma in a horrific recreation of the story of Salome and John the Baptist (*A Very Particular Murder*).

Haymon's novels will appeal to all devotees of the traditional English detective novel. She is particularly strong in presenting rich and varied backgrounds in archaeology, history, rock music and, most prominently, the closed society of the Anglican church. Readers of Agatha Christie, Margery Allingham, and Ngaio Marsh will welcome Haymon's sure touch in delineating the English class system and English society as a whole.

Although the series is best read in sequence, either *Stately Homicide* or *Ritual Murder* is a good choice for the reader who wishes to read only one.

MYSTERY FICTION

Ben Jurnet Series

Death and the Pregnant Virgin. London: Constable; New York: St. Martin's Press, 1980.

Ritual Murder. London: Constable; New York: St. Martin's Press, 1982.

Stately Homicide. London: Constable; New York: St. Martin's Press, 1984.

Death of a God. London: Constable; New York: St. Martin's Press, 1987.

A Very Particular Murder. London: Constable; New York: St. Martin's Press, 1989.

Death of a Warrior Queen. London: Constable; New York: St. Martin's Press, 1991.

A Beautiful Death. New York: St. Martin's Press, 1994.

CRITICAL BIBLIOGRAPHY

Harper, Carol. "Haymon, S. T." In *Twentieth Century Crime and Mystery Writers*, ed. Lesley Henderson. 3rd ed. Chicago and London: St. James, 1991, pp. 516–17.

ELIZABETH BUCKMASTER

JOAN HESS (1949–   )

Joan Hess was born January 6, 1949, in Fayetteville, Arkansas, where she currently lives. She received her B.A. from the University of Arkansas in 1972 and an M.S. from Long Island University in 1974. Hess has had a variety of jobs, working in real estate, insurance, and education. Divorced, she has two children.

Her awards include an Anthony Award nomination for *Strangled Prose*, an Agatha Award nomination for *Mischief in Maggody*, the American Mystery Award for *A Diet to Die For*, and the Agatha Award for best short story for "Too Much to Bare."

In her two series as Joan Hess and her additional series as Joan Hadley, Hess has taken the traditional mystery of crimes committed and perpetrators unmasked to new comic levels while presenting varied aspects of late twentieth-century American culture.

The chief setting for the Claire Malloy series is Farberville, Arkansas, a medium-sized college town. Claire, who is a widow, supports herself and her adolescent daughter Caron by operating a bookstore. The mother-daughter relationship is an ongoing theme in this series. Like all parents with a resident adolescent, Claire is beset with minor rebellions, dramatic moods, and messy rooms, all of which she views with love, dismay, resignation, and humor.

Although she is an independent woman and not interested in a second marriage, Claire meets Lt. Peter Rosen of the Farberville police department in *Strangled Prose*, and their developing relationship continues in the following books, sparked by a competitive spirit: Peter, the professional detective, tries his best to keep the meddling amateur from interfering. However, Claire goes her own way, sometimes because of partisanship for a suspect—as when she is positive that Miss Parchester did not put cyanide in the peach compote (*Dear Miss Demeanor*). Often, her actions, reactions, and deductions lead her to the correct solution before anyone else. Moreover, she progresses from needing Peter to rescue her, in *Strangled Prose*, to saving herself, in *Poisoned Pins*.

Since the books are told from Claire's point of view, the reader can follow her unraveling of the puzzle and her feelings about events and issues. From the lighthearted—the description of the Homecoming game in *Dear Miss Demeanor* is wonderfully comic—to the more serious, the events and activities in the Claire Malloy series are many and varied. Beauty pageants, political ambition, diet programs, drugs, sexual misconduct between faculty and students, sororities, animal rights, and even attitudes toward racial questions come briefly, yet pointedly, into Claire's life.

Arly Hanks, the chief of police in Maggody, Arkansas (population 755), must confront many similar problems, but it is the atmosphere of Maggody and its residents that bemuse this independent woman. After several years in Manhattan and the end of a disastrous marriage, Arly goes home again and becomes police chief when there are no other applicants. Her mother, Ruby Bee, is a meddlesome amateur when she is not occupied worrying about Arly's love life and fixing pork chops with okra at Ruby Bee's Bar & Grill. Ruby Bee's cohort, Estelle Oppers of Estelle's Hair Fantasies, assists her to thwart—and help—Arly's efforts to solve Maggody's sporadic crime waves.

Hess writes along a fine line between caricature and character in her portrayal of Maggody's inhabitants, and the humor verges on the raunchy. Nonetheless, most readers will return to Maggody for the ongoing saga of the efforts of Brother Verber and Mrs. Jim Bob to purify the town, the adventures of Kevin Buchanan and his 300-pound sweetheart, and the lives and times of Raz Buchanan and his prize sow, Marjorie.

Arly more than holds her own in police work, yet compassion and outrage are also part of her persona. Her detached amusement at the antics of her fellow citizens vanishes when she realizes that the townspeople were too busy repeating gossip to help—or even hear—a sexually abused child (*Madness in Maggody*).

The point of view is varied in the Maggody series, shifting from Arly's first-person narrative to the third-person perspective of other characters, which enables the reader to understand more completely the actions and interactions.

The third series features a male detective, Theo Bloomer, who is a retired florist. In the two mysteries featuring Theo, he is coerced by his snobbish sister to come to the rescue of his niece, a Wellesley College student who is seemingly concerned only with clothes, hair, makeup, and knowing the right people.

In all three series Hess mixes humor, well-designed plots, and a variety of people and approaches to create entertaining mysteries that are just perfect to lessen stress and elicit chuckles and even guffaws. Beginning with the first book in each series does help keep the ongoing characters straight, but is not necessary for enjoying the mysteries. Readers who like Joan Hess and appreciate humor might enjoy books by Dorothy Cannell, Mary Daheim, Carolyn G. Hart, and Charlotte MacLeod.

MYSTERY FICTION

Writing as Joan Hess

Claire Malloy Series

The Murder at the Murder at the Mimosa Inn. New York: St. Martin's Press, 1986.

Strangled Prose. New York: St. Martin's Press, 1986.

Dear Miss Demeanor. New York: St. Martin's Press, 1987.

A Really Cute Corpse. New York: St. Martin's Press, 1988.

A Diet to Die For. New York: St. Martin's Press, 1989.

Roll Over and Play Dead. New York: St. Martin's Press, 1991.

Death by the Light of the Moon. New York: St. Martin's Press, 1992.

Poisoned Pins. New York: Dutton, 1993.

Tickled to Death. New York: Dutton, 1994.

Arly Hanks Series

Malice in Maggody. New York: St. Martin's Press, 1987.

Mischief in Maggody. New York: St. Martin's Press, 1988.

Much Ado in Maggody. New York: St. Martin's Press, 1989.

Madness in Maggody. New York: St. Martin's Press, 1991.

Mortal Remains in Maggody. New York: Dutton, 1991.

Maggody in Manhattan. New York: Dutton, 1992.

O Little Town of Maggody. New York: Dutton, 1993.

Writing as Joan Hadley

Theo Bloomer Series

The Night-Blooming Cereus. New York: St. Martin's Press, 1986.

The Deadly Ackee. New York: St. Martin's Press, 1988.

CRITICAL BIBLIOGRAPHY

Browne, Ray B. "Joan Hess's Humanistic Silk-Stockinged Sleuths." *Clues*, 9, no. 2 (1982): 29–36.

De Marr, Mary Jean. "Hess, Joan." In *Twentieth Century Crime and Mystery Writers*, ed. Lesley Henderson. 3rd ed. Chicago and London: St. James, 1991, pp. 525–26.

MARILYN SPARKS SEVERSON

GEORGETTE HEYER (1902–1974)

Georgette Heyer, the granddaughter of a Russian fur merchant who immigrated to England in the nineteenth century, was born August 16, 1902, in Wimbledon. After her father, a schoolmaster, gave up teaching for charitable fund-raising, the Heyers moved frequently, returning from Paris after the outbreak of World War I to Wimbledon, where Heyer completed her schooling.

Heyer's intelligence endeared her to her teachers, but her acerbic wit made her less popular with her classmates. Attractive, unusually tall, intellectually arrogant, and caustic, she was particularly close to her father, who stimulated and encouraged her intellectual and creative interests. Throughout her life she preferred the company of men to that of women, and

although she believed middle-class English society to be fundamentally unfair to women, she was not a feminist. Nevertheless, her heroines tend to
be, like herself, resourceful women who shoulder burdens without com-
plaint.

At nineteen she became a major contributor to her family's income following the successful publication of her first novel, *The Black Moth*. Like
most of her fifty-six novels, this was a historical romance with vivid characterization, witty dialogue, and accurate period detail. The ironic wit and
antisentimental love interest of her Regency romances (a genre Heyer virtually invented and perfected) also distinguish the twelve detective novels
she published between 1912 and 1953, and although her detective novels
never sold as well as her immensely popular historical romances, Heyer
was a significant contributor to the Golden Age of English detective fiction,
wedding comic romance (and occasionally, melodrama) to classic detection.
She died in 1974.

Her barrister husband encouraged her to write detective novels. When
they married in 1925, George Ronald Rougier was an engineer. After a
brief stay in Africa, Heyer settled into a comfortable, productive writing
life, first in a series of country homes and later in their London flat, where,
as Mrs. Rougier, Heyer guarded her privacy. Her writing helped support
not only her widowed mother and brothers but also her husband, for Rougier, who hated engineering, was reading for the Bar throughout the 1930s.

Heyer's first detective novel, *Footsteps in the Dark*, was published in
1932 on the day her son Richard was born. Both events were the result of
collaboration: for each of her detective novels, Rougier provided a plot;
Heyer then fleshed out the characters, added atmosphere, and garnished
the story with sprightly dialogue. Not surprisingly, she sometimes had difficulty fitting her characters into the technical demands of her husband's
plots, once confessing that she did not completely understand *Why Shoot
a Butler?*

Footsteps in the Dark was a conventional haunted-priory thriller in the
Hound of the Baskervilles tradition, but in her next two novels, *Why Shoot
a Butler?* and *The Unfinished Clue*, Heyer established her own formula.
Frank Amberley, the hero of *Why Shoot a Butler?*, is a prototype for Heyer's amateur detectives: an elegant, sardonic barrister who courts an independent, unconventional heroine through verbal sparring. *The Unfinished
Clue* introduced a theme that was to be repeated in *Behold, Here's Poison*,
Envious Casca, and *Penhallow*: a rich, tyrannical husband (or uncle) bullies
his wimpy wife or relations (on whom Heyer, incidentally, wastes no sympathy). *Why Shoot a Butler?* and *The Unfinished Clue* also feature a favorite Heyer device of a secret heir or relation, which she used again in
They Found Him Dead, *No Wind of Blame*, and *Penhallow*. The lovers in
Why Shoot a Butler?, *Behold, Here's Poison*, *A Blunt Instrument*, and *No*

Wind of Blame (like those in her Regency romances) owe more to Shake-speare's Beatrice and Benedick than Romeo and Juliet, preferring frank insult to romantic sentiment, while beautiful, superficial young women like Violet Williams in *Death in the Stocks*, Valerie Dean in *Envious Casca*, or Cynthia Haddington in *Duplicate Death* prove venal or worse.

While Heyer essentially deploys the conventions of Golden Age detective fiction—her characters live in large houses with servants and would rather inherit money than earn it—her point-of-view characters tend to share her distaste for social hypocrisy. Nevertheless, Heyer is not above snobbery, and her writing reflects the prejudices of her time and class. Her servants are an inferior species. Similarly, her ethnic characters are caricatures: an egotistical Mexican cabaret dancer, a specious White Russian prince, a Gaelic-spouting Scottish policeman. Police detectives are usually clever tradesmen outwitted by barrister-heroes. Granted, in *The Unfinished Clue*, Heyer does employ a policeman hero, but Inspector Harding of Scotland Yard is a gentleman who read law at Oxford before the war, and when he falls in love with Dinah Fawcett, one of Heyer's frank, managing heroines, he decides to quit the force.

In her fourth novel, *Death in the Stocks*, Heyer introduced her series detectives Inspector (later Superintendent) Hannasyde and Sergeant (later Chief Inspector) Hemingway of Scotland Yard, who are featured in seven of her remaining eight detective novels. This is also the first of her "What Fun!" novels, including *Behold, Here's Poison, No Wind of Blame, A Blunt Instrument, Envious Casca*, and *Detection Unlimited*, in which bright young suspects defy social conventions, frankly enjoying the murder inves-tigation while Hannasyde gamely soldiers on and Hemingway prattles about "décor," "flair," and "psychology."

Heyer departed from this formula only once, in *Penhallow*, a brutal tale of a semifeudal Cornish family worthy of Heathcliff. While a few Penhal-low scions indulge in the campy wit of Heyer at her best, this is stock melodrama with little detection, and repetitive to boot.

Heyer's novels remain in print. *Death in the Stocks* makes an amusing entry point from which to follow the limited character development of Hannasyde and Hemingway, while *Behold, Here's Poison, Envious Casca*, and *A Blunt Instrument* are particularly clever.

Readers who enjoy Heyer's wit should try Agatha Christie's "Tommy and Tuppence" series or Dorothy L. Sayers's earlier novels.

MYSTERY FICTION

Footsteps in the Dark. London: Longmans, 1932. Rpt. Cutchague, N.Y.: Buccaneer, 1976.

Why Shoot a Butler? London: Longmans, 1933; New York: Doubleday, 1936.

The Unfinished Clue. London: Longmans; New York: Doubleday, 1937.

Penhallow. London: Heinemann, 1942; New York: Doubleday, 1943.

Inspector Hannasyde and Sergeant Hemingway Series

Death in the Stocks. London: Longmans, 1935; as *Merely Murder*. New York: Doubleday, 1938.

Behold, Here's Poison. London: Hodder; New York: Doubleday, 1936.

They Found Him Dead. London: Hodder; New York: Doubleday, 1937.

A Blunt Instrument. London: Hodder; New York: Doubleday, 1938.

Inspector Hemingway Series

No Wind of Blame. London: Hodder; New York: Doubleday, 1939.

Envious Casca. London: Hodder; New York: Doubleday, 1941.

Duplicate Death. London: Heinemann, 1951; New York: Dutton, 1969.

Detection Unlimited. London: Heinemann, 1952; New York: Dutton, 1969.

CRITICAL BIBLIOGRAPHY

Bander, Elaine. " 'What Fun!': Detection as Diversion." In *Comic Crime*, ed. Earl F. Bargainnier. Bowling Green, Ohio: Popular Press, 1987.

Bargainnier, Earl F. "The Dozen Mysteries of Georgette Heyer." *Clues: A Journal of Detection*, 3, no. 2 (Fall/Winter 1982): 30–39.

Devlin, James P. "A Janeite's Life of Crime: The Mysteries of Georgette Heyer." *The Armchair Detective*, 17, no. 3 (Summer 1984): 300–315.

Hodge, Jane Aiken. *The Private World of Georgette Heyer*. London: Bodley Head, 1984.

ELAINE BANDER

PATRICIA HIGHSMITH (1921–   )

Patricia Highsmith was born in Fort Worth, Texas, on January 19, 1921. Highsmith graduated from Barnard College and has lived in Europe since 1963. Among her many awards, she has received the Grand Prix de Littérature Policière, the Silver Dagger from the Crime Writers' Association of Great Britain, and the O. Henry Memorial Award. *The Talented Mr. Ripley* won the Edgar Allan Poe Scroll from the Mystery Writers of America. Highsmith is one of those authors whose work expands the definitions usually assigned a genre. In Europe she is categorized as a modern novelist rather than a suspense or mystery writer. American editions of many of her books have become available only in recent years, however. *Strangers on a Train* is unique among her works in becoming an English-language film— and it was directed by British film director, Alfred Hitchcock.

Strangers on a Train, her first and, until recently, her most popular novel in the United States, fully explores many of the thematic and stylistic elements that are further developed in Highsmith's later works. The exchange of murders and the sharing of guilt that form the plot of this novel force the reader into an examination of the nature of crime, criminals, punishment, and innocence. Two men meet on a train, talk, share a meal—innocent activities involving situations that most readers have experienced. However, Highsmith uses her meticulous presentation of the ordinary as a means of drawing the reader into a situation that becomes increasingly complex. Form and content are united; character and reader are drawn into inescapable relationships without realizing they are caught until it is too late to escape. Small events and little details begin to intrude. The characters and situations, which seem so familiar, subtly shift. One of the men, Charles Anthony Bruno (the one who has initiated the contact), introduces the idea of murder as he talks about his father. Both Guy Haines, the other man, and the reader realize that Bruno has crossed an invisible boundary from the ordinary to the uncomfortable, and continuing on to the illegal, when he suggests trading murders to avoid detection. Readers realize too late that identification with the central character means sharing the thoughts of a murderer. Not only have they crossed the line from innocence to guilt with Guy, but never saw the line when they stepped over it. While Highsmith explores the exchange of identities suggested by the corresponding exchange of murders, readers must alter their traditional views of crime and punishment when experiencing Guy's point of view.

Other Highsmith heroes may seem even more innocent than Guy. The central character in *The Tremor of Forgery*, which many consider her best novel, travels to Tunisia to write a film script. Any situation that removes a character even slightly from a normal routine is dangerous in Highsmith's world. Howard Ingham becomes isolated from his world in New York City. Telephones do not work, and letters take many days. He cannot communicate with most of the people he encounters, and he has difficulty understanding their customs. Gradually, his life shifts. When it occurs, the actual death is less troubling than its consequences. Again, the reader is pulled into this world through the stream of details that Highsmith provides. No single event is heightened in her even presentation: The reader must decide what is important, just as Ingham must make choices based on his own resources and what little he can understand about his surroundings. In the end, readers are also left to make their own judgments about Ingham and the other characters.

While all Highsmith's novels engage readers in a personal examination of their own morals, they are most directly challenged in the Ripley series. Tom Ripley is never innocent. From the opening sentences of the first novel, *The Talented Mr. Ripley*, he is a man on the run. In this case, the man who is following him is Dickie Greenleaf's father, who wants Tom to get Dickie to come home from Italy, where he has lived for two years. Mr.

Greenleaf is not a good judge of character: Tom will ultimately get Dickie home, but not in the way Mr. Greenleaf had wanted. As in the rest of the series, most of the novel is narrated from Tom's point of view. Readers are forced to identify with someone who commits crimes they believe are wrong, yet they find themselves wanting the perpetrator to succeed.

A sense of place is very important in this series. Tom is not the American innocent corrupted by Europe. Rather, he is the image of the new American who will win against the sophistication of inherited or earned wealth and Old World education. In subsequent novels, Ripley lives outside Paris. He is able to set down roots, marry a French woman, and tend his garden while continuing a life of crime. It is his very adaptability that makes his life-style possible. In the Ripley novels, those characters who must rigidly hang on to either their Old World or New World morality are doomed. Ripley's accommodation to change is closely allied with Highsmith's interest in the exchange of identities between characters. Ripley actually becomes Dickie Greenleaf, while in another novel, he impersonates a dead painter. It may be Tom's ability to flourish in a fluid world, to value both the peace of his home and the challenge of the chase, that allows readers to enjoy his character at the same time that his amorality may shock them.

If Highsmith's male characters must either adapt to an immoral universe, die, or go mad, Highsmith's female characters do not often face such choices. Many of the women in her novels have already learned to live within the limited parameters that society has allocated for them. Ripley's wife, Heloise, has abandoned the stifling world of her conservative parents by marrying Tom. She does not know the full extent of his criminal activities, but it is her choice to remain ignorant. Heloise spends much of her time traveling, an indication of her love of change. Other wives or lovers survive in their relationships when they accept the conflicts experienced by their mates. A few become tragically caught in the destructive situations generated by men. Highsmith's women are as much reflections of her view of society as are her male characters. They are all caught in plots where chance and choice pull both character and reader into situations with little hope for happy resolutions. Highsmith's novels may not present a hopeful view of the world; anyone who acts is at risk. However, the reader who enters her world will be drawn into a complex relationship with her characters that can prove not only fascinating but also revealing of one's own attitude toward a personal moral universe. The Ripley series should be read in chronological order. *The Tremor of Forgery* is a good nonseries entry to Highsmith. She has also written several books of short stories: *Mermaids on the Golf Course* and *The Animal-Lover's Book of Beastly Murder* are two of my favorites. Highsmith's style is so unique that it is difficult to suggest other authors whose work is similar.

MYSTERY FICTION

Strangers on a Train. New York: Harper; London: Cresset, 1950.

The Blunderer. New York: Coward McCann, 1954; London: Cresset, 1956.

Deep Water. New York: Harper, 1957; London: Heinemann, 1958.

A Game for the Living. New York: Harper, 1958; London: Heinemann, 1959.

This Sweet Sickness. New York: Harper, 1960; London: Heinemann, 1961.

The Cry of the Owl. New York: Harper, 1962; London: Heinemann, 1963.

The Two Faces of January. New York: Doubleday; London: Heinemann, 1964.

The Glass Cell. New York: Doubleday, 1964; London: Heinemann, 1965.

The Story-Teller. New York: Doubleday, 1965; as *A Suspension of Mercy*. London: Heinemann, 1965.

Those Who Walk Away. New York: Doubleday; London: Heinemann, 1967.

The Tremor of Forgery. New York: Doubleday; London: Heinemann, 1969.

The Snail-Watcher and Other Stories. New York: Doubleday; as *Eleven*. London: Heinemann, 1970.

A Dog's Ransom. New York: Knopf; London: Heinemann, 1972.

The Animal-Lover's Book of Beastly Murder. London: Heinemann, 1975; New York: Mysterious, 1986.

Edith's Diary. New York: Simon and Schuster; London: Heinemann, 1977.

Little Tales of Misogyny. London: Heinemann, 1977; New York: Mysterious, 1986.

Slowly, Slowly in the Wind. London: Heinemann, 1979; New York: Mysterious, 1987.

The Black House. London: Heinemann, 1981.

People Who Knock on the Door. London: Heinemann, 1983; New York: Mysterious, 1985.

Mermaids on the Golf Course. London: Heinemann, 1985; New York: Mysterious, 1988.

Found in the Street. London: Heinemann, 1986; New York: Atlantic Monthly, 1987.

Tales of Natural and Unnatural Catastrophes. London: Bloomsbury, 1987; New York: Atlantic Monthly, 1989.

Tom Ripley Series

The Talented Mr. Ripley. New York: Coward McCann, 1955; London: Cresset, 1957.

Ripley Underground. New York: Doubleday, 1970; London: Heinemann, 1971.

Ripley's Game. New York: Knopf; London: Heinemann, 1974.

The Boy Who Followed Ripley. New York: Lippincott; London: Heinemann, 1980.

Ripley under Water. London: Bloomsbury, 1991; New York: Knopf, 1992.

CRITICAL BIBLIOGRAPHY

Cooper-Clark, Diana. "Patricia Highsmith: Interview." *The Armchair Detective*, 14, no. 4 (Spring 1981): 313–20.

Evans, Odette L'Henry. "A Feminist Approach to Patricia Highsmith's Fiction." In
    American Horror Fiction: From Brockden Brown to Stephen King, ed. Brian
    Docherty. New York: St. Martin's, 1990, pp. 107–19.
Hilfer, Anthony Channell. "Not Really Such a Monster: Highsmith's Ripley as
    Thriller Protagonist and Protean Man." *Midwest Quarterly*, 25, no. 4 (Sum-
    mer 1984): 361–74.
Hubly, Erlene. "A Portrait of the Artist: The Novels of Patricia Highsmith." *Clues*,
    5, no. 1 (Spring-Summer 1984): 115–30.
Klein, Kathleen Gregory. "Patricia Highsmith." In *And Then There Were Nine:
    More Women of Mystery*, ed. Jane Bakerman. Bowling Green, Ohio: Popular
    Press, 1985, pp. 170–97.

SHARON A. RUSSELL

DOROTHY B. HUGHES (1904–1993)

Upon her death at age eighty-eight on May 13, 1993, Dorothy B. Hughes
was eulogized by Dorothy Salisbury Davis in the *Third Degree*: "Except
for a few nineteenth century foundation blocks, the life of the mystery is
encompassed in her lifetime, and once she found a place of her own within
it, her commitment was as durable as herself."

Hughes's fifteen novels are haunting and disturbing, conveying an excellent sense of character and place, particularly her beloved Southwest.
The novels include wartime espionage tales as well as postwar stories that
deal with social problems. She was a historian of mystery fiction, receiving
a Mystery Writers of America nomination for her critical biography of Erle
Stanley Gardner in 1978, the same year she was honored with their prestigious Grand Master Award.

She was born Dorothy Belle Flanagan on August 10, 1904, in Kansas
City, Missouri, the daughter of Frank Sylvester and Calla Haley Flanagan.
Educated at the University of Missouri, along with additional studies at
Columbia University, she worked on newspapers and wrote poetry, winning the Yale University Press award in 1931 for her book of poems, *Dark
Certainty*. While doing graduate work at the University of New Mexico,
she met her future husband, Levi Allen Hughes, Jr., and discovered the
beauties and mysteries of the Southwest which would become the settings
for several of her best books.

The So Blue Marble received accolades about which first-time mystery
writers usually only dream. This domestic thriller, in which a fashion designer discovers herself being used by a set of European twins to secure a
priceless treasure, established Hughes's principal approach to her protagonists. Usually they were intelligent professionals (designers, doctors, writers) who, like Hitchcock heroes, become innocently involved in an

intriguing set of circumstances that force them to deal with a nether world they had not realized existed. Her fourth novel, *The Fallen Sparrow*, is the story of a disillusioned American back from the Spanish Civil War and pursued by fascists. It brought her to further national prominence in 1943 when R-K-O Studios made a compact, pre-noir film version starring John Garfield, Maureen O'Hara, and Walter Slezak. Two subsequent wartime espionage thrillers, *The Blackbirder* and *The Delicate Ape*, were singled out by mystery historian James Sandoe in his 1946 Modern Arts Series lecture as "superbly skillful tales of pursuit and escape."

When World War II ended, Hughes turned her attention to postwar social problems. *Dread Journey* contains, within this suspense novel of a movie star's terror-filled cross-country ride, the secondary character of a highly intelligent and thoughtful black pullman-car porter, a depiction that would set the stage for the character of her last and best novel, *The Expendable Man*, eighteen years later. She was also becoming adept at descriptions of minor characters, summarizing in as little as three sentences everything a reader needs to know about them. Her sense of locale would reach its zenith in her next novel, *Ride the Pink Horse*, which is set during Fiesta Week in Santa Fe, New Mexico. A revenge tale dealing with a high-placed political double cross, it is memorable for its examination of the interaction of American, Indian, and Mexican cultures in the immediate postwar years. It would later become a classic film noir directed by, and starring, Robert Montgomery.

Moving to Los Angeles in the late 1940s, Hughes then wrote her most well-received and probably most famous book, *In a Lonely Place*. Her protagonist, a failed and insecure Los Angeles writer named Dix Steele, is so possessive and jealous of his current love, a fledgling actress named Laurel, that his irrational reactions to her imagined betrayals parallel a series of murders of young women. A superb film version directed by Nicholas Ray (though considerably altered in plot) was made in 1950, starring Humphrey Bogart and Gloria Grahame. Then in 1963 came her last and best work, *The Expendable Man*. Critic Anthony Boucher praised its "unrelenting suspense, deft trickery, firmly penetrating treatment of individual and social problems." The book centers on Hugh Densmore, a University of California at Los Angeles graduate student en route to his parents' middle-class home in Phoenix. Reluctantly—and foolishly—he picks up a female hitchhiker and thereupon encounters a succession of terrifying events. It is not until the reader is one-third through the engrossing tale that it is discovered that the hero is black, a discovery that forces readers to reexamine all their previous reactions, mental images, and assumptions. It is a remarkable, and disturbing, achievement.

Dorothy Salisbury Davis described her admiration of, and indebtedness to, her favorite author: "In the late 1940's, when I started, the writer who was doing what I hoped I could one day do was Dorothy B. Hughes. Her social awareness, the urgency of her theme, always integral to the plot, pointed the way I wanted to go. I admired all those Golden Age people . . . [and] above all, Dorothy B. Hughes."

MYSTERY FICTION

The Bamboo Blonde. New York: Duell, 1941.
The Blackbirder. New York: Duell, 1943; London: Nicholson and Watson, 1948.
The Delicate Ape. New York: Duell, 1944.
Johnnie. New York: Duell, 1944; London: Nicholson and Watson, 1946.
Dread Journey. New York: Duell, 1945; London: Nicholson and Watson, 1948.
Ride the Pink Horse. New York: Duell, 1946; London: Bantam, 1979.
The Scarlet Imperial. New York: Mystery Book Club, 1946; as *Kiss for a Killer.* New York: Spivak, 1954.
In a Lonely Place. New York: Duell, 1947; London: Nicholson and Watson, 1950.
The Big Barbecue. New York: Random House, 1949.
The Candy Kid. New York: Duell, 1950.
The Davidian Report. New York: Duell, 1952; as *The Body on the Bench.* New York: Dell, 1955.
The Expendable Man. New York: Random House, 1963; London: Deutsch, 1964.

Inspector Tobin Series

The Cross-Eyed Bear. New York: Duell, 1940; London: Nicholson and Watson, 1943.

The So Blue Marble. New York: Duell, 1940; London: Bantam, 1979.

The Fallen Sparrow. New York: Duell, 1942; London: Nicholson and Watson, 1943.

CRITICAL BIBLIOGRAPHY

Oliver, Lawrence J. "The Dark-Skinned 'Angels' of Dorothy B. Hughes's Thrillers." *Melus*, 11, no. 3, 27–39.

CHRISTOPHER J. WARREN

❦ J ❦

P. D. JAMES (1920–   )

P. D. James (Phyllis Dorothy James White, Baroness James of Holland Park) was born in Oxford, England, on August 3, 1920. After completing her education at the Cambridge Girls' High School at age sixteen, James went to work rather than college since she could not afford the education she desired and her father did not support education for women. She worked at a tax office and later at the Cambridge Festival Theatre until her marriage in 1941 to Ernest Connor Bantry White, a medical student. During World War II, James worked as a Red Cross nurse. After demobilization, her husband was institutionalized for schizophrenia until his death in 1964. To support herself and her two daughters, Jane and Clare, James went to work in the Civil Service in the National Health Service, where she attained the rank of principal administrative assistant. After 1968, she worked at the Home Office in the Police and Criminal Policy Departments until her retirement in 1979. Although she had always wanted to be a writer, James only began her first novel at age thirty-eight, writing in the early morning hours before going to her job. Since retirement, James has been active in public life. She belongs to the Church of England, but to no political party.

James won Crime Writers' Association (CWA) awards in 1967, 1971, 1975, and 1986, as well as the CWA Diamond Dagger Award in 1987 and the American Edgar Allan Poe Scroll Award twice. She was accepted into the Royal Society of Authors in 1987. James is an associate fellow, Downing College, Cambridge; a governor at the British Broadcasting Corporation; and chairman of the Literature Panel, British Council of the Arts. She received the Order of the British Empire (OBE) in 1983 and a life barony in 1991.

A reigning author of mystery fiction, James writes in the British tradition of Agatha Christie, Dorothy L. Sayers, and Margery Allingham. James herself rejects classification with Christie but acknowledges admiration for Sayers's attention to detail and Allingham's ability to evoke settings. James uses, but deemphasizes, the traditional elements developed by Christie, such as a carefully worked-out puzzle, a limited number of equally possible suspects, and sudden twists of the plot at a novel's end. Like Sayers, James looks back to nineteenth-century literature in the tradition of Wilkie Collins's *The Moonstone* in her creation of complex characters and detailed portraits of social relationships. Her novels, which are more complex than those of her immediate predecessors, are lengthy, slow-paced, and detailed in their analyses of the backgrounds that explain her characters' psychological and sociological motivations. The portraits of individual lives form a composite view of a troubled contemporary society. Thus, James moved the mystery toward realism by subordinating the formulaic elements, abandoning the detective structure completely in *Innocent Blood*.

Critics also relate James's fiction to a nineteenth-century literary tradition because of anticlimactic and lengthy endings in which the guilty are always punished, even if they escape legal justice. Although her resolutions convey James's sense of a basic moral order underlying the universe, they do not dispel a lingering sense of evil and contamination. Evil exists on a metaphysical level, but the act of murder makes this evil present in daily life. As her detective, Adam Dalgliesh, remarks in *Devices and Desires*, "No one even remotely touched by murder goes unscathed." James makes it clear that the effects of evil are not undone, whether that evil takes the form of murder or more hidden, psychological damage. In many novels, James traces the effects of the collapse of moral values and social structures on children who become innocent victims, and then, psychologically damaged adults and potential criminals.

James again follows established tradition in limiting descriptions of physical violence. Although the actual murders occur off-stage, James never hesitates to present the reader with all the graphic details of death. Death has a palpable presence in her novels, made real by descriptions of dead victims and police autopsies. She frequently draws on her civil service experience for detailed descriptions of hospital and police settings which present death in a realistic context.

Although James's two detectives are very different types of characters, both are agents of justice who live according to a strict moral code. Like James herself, Adam Dalgliesh, James's earliest and most frequently appearing detective, is a civil servant and a writer, a policeman by profession and a poet by necessity. The roses on his desk at Scotland Yard recall Collins's Sergeant Cuff. Dalgliesh is the complete professional, and is almost totally absorbed by his work. He appears in James's first novel, *Cover Her Face*, as a fully realized character with a complete history. He is a sensitive, intelligent, and extremely private person who has remained a widower after the loss of his wife and son. His work at Scotland Yard has earned him a reputation for solving the most difficult crimes with great speed. Dalgliesh proceeds on the assumption that the reason for murder stems from the victim's life, which he investigates in great detail. James's use of a shifting point of view in the Dalgliesh series reveals a crime as a point of intersection in the lives of individuals from different social strata.

Taken in chronological order, the novels trace Dalgliesh's advancement and his growing disillusionment but do not alter the outlines of his character. The first novel hints at his developing romantic interest in one of its characters, Deborah Riscoe. They meet again briefly at the beginning of *A Mind to Murder*, the subsequent novel. In *Unnatural Causes*, James's third novel, Deborah ends the relationship because she realizes Dalgliesh will never give up his solitary life.

Cordelia Gray, James's female detective, appears in only two novels and develops along very different lines. She is a young and innocent woman who stumbles on the occupation of private eye almost by chance. In *An Unsuitable Job for a Woman*, Cordelia inherits an agency from an ex-CID fired by Dalgliesh. Her partner imparts all Dalgliesh's maxims to Cordelia. Later on, Cordelia meets Dalgliesh in person, first as an adversary and later as a friend. The first novel initiates Cordelia into her profession and establishes her as a survivor, a detective in the making, an independent young woman, and a feminist like her creator. Cordelia makes her second appearance in *The Skull beneath the Skin*. Both novels' narratives stick closely to Cordelia's point of view, and her style of detective work emphasizes her concern, compassion, and senses of personal responsibility. Although an orphan, Cordelia identifies closely with the victims and is a slightly less solitary figure than Dalgliesh.

James's criminals are a diverse lot who usually have complicated psychological motivations for their crimes, even when the ostensible reasons are money, power, hatred, or concealment. Criminals are often professionals who do not live up to the ethics of their professions, putting personal desires first. Arrogant doctors and unprincipled sensualists are among James's most unpleasant characters.

While reading the novels in order traces the careers of her two detectives, readers might enjoy beginning with novels that represent James at her best. I recommend *Shroud for a Nightingale* and *An Unsuitable Job for a Woman*. Those who enjoy James's novels may like to read works by her predecessors, Dorothy L. Sayers and Margery Allingham, or works by a contemporary, Elizabeth George.

MYSTERY FICTION

Innocent Blood. London: Faber; New York: Scribner's, 1980.

Adam Dalgliesh Series

Cover Her Face. London: Faber, 1962; New York: Scribner's, 1966.

A Mind to Murder. London: Faber, 1963; New York: Scribner's, 1967.

Unnatural Causes. London: Faber; New York: Scribner's, 1967.

Shroud for a Nightingale. London: Faber; New York: Scribner's, 1971.

The Black Tower. London: Faber; New York: Scribner's, 1975.

Death of an Expert Witness. London: Faber; New York: Scribner's, 1977.

A Taste for Death. London: Faber; New York: Knopf, 1986.

Devices and Desires. London: Faber, 1989; New York: Knopf, 1990.

Cordelia Gray Series

An Unsuitable Job for a Woman. London: Faber, 1972; New York: Scribner's, 1973.

The Skull beneath the Skin. London: Faber and Faber; New York: Scribner's, 1982.

CRITICAL BIBLIOGRAPHY

Bakerman, Jane S. "Cordelia Gray: Apprentice and Archetype." *Clues: A Journal of Mystery and Detection*, 5 (1984): 101–4.

————. "Interview with P. D. James." *The Armchair Detective*, 10 (1977): 55–57, 92.

Benstock, Bernard. "The Clinical World of P. D. James." In *Twentieth-Century Women Novelists*, ed. Thomas S. Staley. Totowa, N.J.: Barnes and Noble, 1982, pp. 104–29.

Budd, Elaine. "P. D. James." In *13 Mistresses of Murder*. New York: Ungar, 1986, pp. 65–74.

Campbell, Sue Ellen. "The Detective Heroine and the Death of the Hero: Dorothy Sayers to P. D. James." *Modern Fiction Studies*, 29 (1983): 497–510.

Cooper-Clark, Diana. *Designs of Darkness: Interview with Detective Novelists*. Bowling Green, Ohio: Bowling Green Press, 1983.

de la Torre, Lillian. "Cordelia Gray: The Thinking Man's Heroine." In *Murderess Ink*, ed. Dilys Wynn. New York: Workman, 1977, pp. 113–16.

Gidez, Richard B. *P. D. James*. Boston: Twayne, 1986.

Hubley, Erlene. "Adam Dalgliesh: Byronic Hero." *Clues: A Journal of Mystery and Detection*, 3 (1982): 40–46.

————. "The Formula Challenged." *Modern Fiction Studies*, 29 (1983): 511–21.

Joyner, Nancy Carol. "P. D. James." In *Ten Women of Mystery*, ed. Earl F. Bargainnier. Bowling Green, Ohio: Bowling Green State University Popular Press, 1981, pp. 106–23.

Maxfield, J. F. "The Unfinished Detective: The Work of P. D. James." *Critique*, 28 (1987): 211–23.

Siebenheller, Norma. *P. D. James*. New York: Ungar, 1981.

Symons, Julian. "The Queen of Crime: P. D. James." *New York Times Magazine*, 5 Oct. 1986, pp. 48, 60.

MARILYN RYE

❦ K ❦

LUCILLE KALLEN (1926–   )

Although born in Los Angeles in 1926 and educated at Harbord Collegiate in Toronto, Lucille Kallen has spent her working life in New York. The daughter of Samuel and Esther Kallen Chernos took her mother's maiden name when she became a professional. She moved from creating revues in the Pocono Mountains of Pennsylvania to writing for television in New York and, in 1949, became a member of the original team of comedy writers for the NBC network's hit program, "Your Show of Shows." In a November 1992 *New York Times* article, she recalled with amusement the difficulties of being the only woman on the program's creative staff, yet she remained until 1954. Thereafter, she wrote for the theater and for other television programs until the latter industry moved to California.

In 1952 she married a businessman, Herbert W. Engel. Attempts to balance her writing career and the care of their two children, Paul and Lise, may have inspired her first novel, which she published in 1964. Its English title, *Gentlemen Prefer Slaves*, is more suggestive of its feminist import than the American title, *Outside There, Somewhere*.

In 1979, *Introducing C. B. Greenfield* introduced Kallen to the world of mystery readers. It is the first of five novels about the urbane publisher of the *Sloan's Ford Reporter* and his part-time reporter, Maggie Rome. After twenty-five years with NBC news, the widowed Greenfield, his children grown, purchased the suburban weekly to become his version of a knight-errant, tilting at the local windmills of graft, skulduggery, and incompetence. Maggie has had her years as full-time wife and mother, but now, with her sons in college and her husband frequently out of town, she has developed her own life, much of which includes Greenfield.

Theirs is a relationship that develops throughout the novels. In addition to their newspaper work, they share Wednesday night dinner after sending the paper to press; they play chamber music with a friend on Fridays; and eventually, they do their sleuthing together. In *The Tanglewood Murders*, Maggie has no qualms about driving Greenfield to the summer home of the Boston Symphony when his car breaks down and then letting him pay for her stay there as compensation. She knows that neither one would do anything to disturb the comfortable, if contentious, camaraderie they enjoy. Each obviously admires the taste and intelligence of the other, and Maggie has earned Greenfield's respect because she will not allow him to put her down in the way he puts down so many other people. In the last novel, *A Little Madness*, the relationship changes somewhat, but the mutual regard remains.

Notable in the novels are Kallen's portraits of women. Pictured in various stages of liberation, they range from those who have recoiled and sought refuge in traditional roles to those who are in the vanguard of change. In the third novel, *No Lady in the House*, the murder of a shared cleaning woman ties together the portraits. Kallen seems concerned with showing how women balance contemporary roles with marriage and family. Not all succeed, and there are several portraits of divorcees trying to define life anew. The reader sees all the women through the eyes of Maggie, who narrates the novels. Her vision seems trustworthy because she seems to know who she is, at least until the last novel, when even Maggie embraces a little madness.

While the mysteries can be enjoyed at any level, it is obvious that Lucille Kallen writes for an audience familiar with the arts. Kallen's parents were both musicians, and she herself studied to be a concert pianist. She makes allusions to drama, literature, and painting, but it is to music that she directs most of her attention. In *The Piano Bird*, when Greenfield uses his acquaintance with the composer Gustav Mahler to unmask an imposter, the astute musical student recognizes the trap. Musical knowledge on the part of the reader can thus enhance an appreciation of Kallen's work.

These are classic mysteries with elements of the cozy, at least in those novels centered in the town of Sloan's Ford. Greenfield assigns Maggie the footwork and gives credit to his own logic for finding solutions. However, the reader knows that Greenfield's information would have been incomplete without Maggie's observations. An expected ingredient of all the novels is humor. The situations are often funny, though not improbable, while the dialogue sparkles and gives as much pleasure as the chase.

Because there is some reference in late novels to previous ones, the reader may find it agreeable, if not necessary, to read them in order. Those who enjoy Charlotte MacLeod's Sarah Kelling books should give Kallen a try.

MYSTERY FICTION

C. B. Greenfield and Maggie Rome Series

Introducing C. B. Greenfield. New York: Crown; London: Collins, 1979.
The Tanglewood Murder. New York: Wyndham; London: Collins, 1980.

No Lady in the House. New York: Wyndham; London: Collins, 1982.

The Piano Bird. New York: Random; London: Collins, 1984.

A Little Madness. New York: Random; London: Collins, 1986.

CRITICAL BIBLIOGRAPHY

Nichols, Victoria, and Susan Thompson. "C. B. Greenfield." In *Silk Stalkings*, Berkeley, Calif.: Black Lizard Press, 1988, pp. 163–64.
Stasio, Marilyn. "Interview." *Publishers Weekly* 14 March 1986, pp. 88–89.

MARCIA J. SONGER

FAYE KELLERMAN (1952–   )

Faye Marder Kellerman was born in St. Louis, Missouri, in 1952. She is married to novelist Jonathan Kellerman, and they have three children. She is a real estate investor, dentist, and luthier as well as a writer. Her detective series includes six novels featuring Police Sergeant Pete Decker and his romantic interest, Rina Lazarus, an Orthodox Jew. Kellerman received the Mystery Readers of America Macavity Award for best first novel (*The Ritual Bath*) in 1986.

Kellerman's series combines elements of the police procedural set in the violent world of Los Angeles and a delicate romantic and spiritual progress toward marriage and conversion. This odd fusion succeeds because of the attractiveness and believability of the characters and the series' thematic sophistication. The books' greatest appeal is their honest spirituality, which is striking and exotic in this secular genre.

All the books focus on Sgt. Pete Decker, and it is through his perspective that most of the action is seen. Decker is approaching job burnout; police work has hardened and coarsened him. He is still carrying a load of guilt from military service in Vietnam, and the past and present combine to make him a cynical, unsentimental, and psychically and spiritually damaged hero. At work, he is surrounded by police colleagues who are just as damaged as he is—racist, sexist, homophobic, and casually callous. Decker and his partner, Marge Dunn, are superb cops, in part because they are almost beyond feeling.

Decker meets Rina Lazarus in *The Ritual Bath*, and courts and marries her as the series progresses. Rina is the source of much of the interest in the series; she lives the cloistered life of a widow in an isolated yeshiva, surrounded by ancient religious ritual which defines her existence and that of her two young sons.

In a way, this sounds clichéd: a cynical, world-weary cop meets a beautiful, sheltered woman. However, Kellerman manages to give new life and interest to the cliché by creating rich, complex characters who, through their differences, present opposed value systems and beliefs. Rina Lazarus is especially interesting, initially because her life is as exotic to the reader as it is to Decker.

Kellerman's accomplishment is to make the two lovers believable as they learn from each other and begin to love and accept each other. Decker is aware of Rina's delicacy and wishes to preserve it so, while he himself does not become more open and trusting, he acknowledges her choices, respecting and trying to honor them. Rina is shown to have a similar capacity for growth without fundamental change. She is not coarsened by her exposure to the violence of Decker's world, but she accommodates it and responds with a strength and toughness on her own terms.

In addition to the violent and convoluted plots and the growing complexity of the relationship between the two central characters, each book in the series is an extended meditation on a theme. For example, *Milk and Honey*, the third book in the series, examines familial destructiveness, and particularly the damage done to children by parents. The novel begins with Decker's discovery of a two-year-old girl dressed in blood-soaked pajamas and wandering the streets of a housing development in the middle of the night. Kellerman surrounds the scenes of horrific, graphic violence and detection with a number of motifs that deal with families. Rina is in New York staying with her late husband's family and dealing with an amorous uncle; there is a forlorn mother and a private investigator searching for an abducted child; and Decker is overwhelmed by lost and damaged children and their fragmented families, including his hostile ex-wife and their teen-aged daughter.

The murderer is revealed—as a family member. All but one of the victims are the adult sons and daughters of the murderer, who attempts to persuade the single surviving child, a retarded boy, to confess to the police. As the murder plot unravels, the familial costs continue to mount higher. Another subplot finds Decker trying to help an old Vietnam War buddy to answer an accusation of rape and assault. His friend is innocent, and Decker knows it. However, his belief in his friend's innocence does not stop him from treating the man as if he were guilty when the man innocently flirts with Rina, who is visiting from New York. After losing an old friendship, Decker solves this case, and the answer again is parental violence. Rina finds a photograph of a teenaged Decker in Vietnam and mourns the damage done to the child, while Decker cannot even bear to view the image of himself—looking happy, confident, and young. Underpinning the theme is the fact that Decker and Rina are planning to form their own new family unit through marriage, gathering together Rina's two sons and Decker's daughter—children already hurt by death and divorce.

Each novel, then, is rich in thematic interest. *The Ritual Bath* explores the nature of exclusion—the Orthodox Jews who try to live a spiritual life within the secular world, only to find that the outside world cannot bear their separateness and tries to destroy it. *Sacred and Profane* examines the place of religious belief in a world that is hostile to it, while *Day of Atonement* examines the idea of guilt and its expiation.

All six novels in the series are, however, most notable for their examination of religion. Kellerman's great accomplishment is to make a religious life not only believable, but attractive. Rina and Peter both want to live religious lives. When Rina tells him that she could not consider marrying a non-Jew, Peter, who is Jewish by birth but was raised as a Baptist, embraces Judaism with a fervor quite different from the usual marriage-driven conversion. Never as religious as Rina would like him to be, he is, nevertheless, religious enough to welcome the religious ritual and restrictions, even as they make his life in the secular police world more difficult. One of the most attractive of the continuing characters is Rav Schulman, the rabbi in charge of Decker's religious education. The novels' religious seriousness is irresistible; it makes up for at times unbelievable plots and the occasional overly graphic scenes of violent death.

The novels are best read in sequence. The earlier novels are stronger than the later ones: Kellerman has, perhaps, written her characters into a box. In the next-to-last novel, *False Prophet*, Rina, who is adjusting to marriage and pregnancy, is less visible and less of a good sport. In *Grievous Sin*, the birth of a daughter further limits Rina's mobility. Nevertheless, the novels will appeal to fans of realistic action and romantic drama. Readers of the British novelist S. T. Haymon will particularly enjoy the differences between this romantic couple and her own Ben Juret and his love, Miriam.

MYSTERY FICTION

Pete Decker and Rina Lazarus Series

The Ritual Bath. New York: Arbor House, 1985; London: Collins, 1987.

Sacred and Profane. New York: Arbor House, 1987; London: Coronet, 1989.

Milk and Honey. New York: Morrow; London: Headline, 1990.

Day of Atonement. New York: Morrow; London: Headline, 1991.

False Prophet. New York: Morrow; London: Headline, 1992.

Grievous Sin. New York: Morrow, 1993.

CRITICAL BIBLIOGRAPHY

Rodgerson, Gillian. "Kellerman, Faye." In *Twentieth Century Crime and Mystery Writers*, ed. Lesley Henderson. 3rd ed. Chicago and London: St. James, 1991, pp. 620–21.

Uffen, Ellen. "The Orthodox Novels of Faye Kellerman." *Studies in Jewish Literature*, 11, no. 2 (1987): 195–203.

ELIZABETH BUCKMASTER

SUSAN KELLY (1949–   )

Like the protagonist of her novels, Susan Kelly left her birthplace in New York City to reside in New England. Born April 10, 1949, she spent her early college years in Massachusetts, earning B.A. and M.A. degrees in English. After an interlude at the University of Edinburgh, where she received a Ph.D. in medieval literature, she returned to the United States to settle in Cambridge, Massachusetts, the city that also serves as the locale for her six mystery novels.

Kelly began her career as a college instructor. Focusing on writing courses, she taught management communication at the Harvard University Graduate School of Business and crime-report writing at the Cambridge Police Academy. These early experiences and her later service as a consultant to the Massachusetts Criminal Justice Training Council stood her in good stead when she turned her attention to writing fiction. Her novels clearly draw on a valuable body of insider information that she has garnered through her varied professional associations.

The Gemini Man, Kelly's first novel, immediately claimed the attention of mystery readers. The book was named one of the top ten in the National Mystery Readers Poll of 1985 and was also nominated in that year for an Anthony Award for best first novel. Moreover, it was in *The Gemini Man* that readers were initially afforded the pleasure of meeting Liz Connors, the flamboyantly red-haired narrator of Kelly's suspense series.

The pivotal voice in Kelly's fictional world, Liz Connors hails from the baby-boom generation of young working professionals. A sometime English professor who is struggling to establish her reputation as a free-lance writer, she is willing to take on the occasional freshman English class to earn her rent. Nevertheless, she is strong-minded and inquisitive enough to prefer the life of an independent contractor to that of a salaried employee. Liz's special interest is in writing true crime feature articles. For this reason she also finds occasion to call on the Cambridge Police Department.

All Kelly's novels to date offer her own characteristic mixture of suspense, humor, and romance. Throughout the first five books of the series, Liz Connors's romantic interest is homicide detective Jack Lingemann. While Liz pursues the background inquiries required for her articles, Lieutenant Lingemann conducts his criminal investigations. Naturally, the interests of this pair often intersect, and the resulting collaboration offers Kelly an opportunity to introduce highly realistic elements of the police procedural into her suspense fiction. The couple's relationship also provides engaging moments of humor, for Connors and Lingemann are wry and witty indeed. (The endearing charm of their banter can bring to mind Nick and Nora Charles.)

Kelly's suspense mysteries are essentially whodunits, but they also reflect an interest—often a psychologically insightful interest—in the further question of "whydunnit." This feature is particularly striking in the most haunting of the novels, *The Summertime Soldiers*. Here, a cell of student revolutionaries who had moved underground in the 1970s reappears fifteen years later to target for murder research scientists working on military defense projects. The group claims responsibility for its actions, so in one sense, its members are known. In another sense, though, a much deeper question of identity arises: who, really, are people for whom the "summertime era" of the 1970s never truly ended? The book invites speculation about the ruthless dedication and abstract principles of political radicals who form secret societies.

Although "why" is not a matter that can always be addressed with a useful certainty, it is one that ineluctably arises in the kinds of plots that interest Kelly. In *And Soon I'll Come to Kill You*, for instance, she focuses on a heedless will for vengeance. Here, someone from Liz Connors's past nurtures a private and deadly grudge against her. In *Until Proven Innocent* and *Trail of the Dragon*, she explores the wanton irresponsibility of people who are inordinately greedy or ambitious. Moreover, as might well be expected, she shares with other suspense writers a fascination for the ultimately incomprehensible obsessions of the serial killer. Figures of this sort appear in both *The Gemini Man* and *Out of the Darkness*.

What is particularly interesting in Kelly's books is that while she well understands that element of a "motiveless malignity" on which the successful suspense novel often depends, she nevertheless insists, usually through the sympathetic persona of her protagonist, on searching out some reason why. Liz Connors is, after all, a writer, and even when her understanding is only partial or provisional, she is determined to make sense of the world.

Susan Kelly's readers will want to sample from her first five novels before turning to *Out of the Darkness*, in which Liz Connors's long-standing relationship with Jack Lingemann appears to come to an end. Novels by Susan Conant, Barbara D'Amato, or Dorothy Bryant may interest Kelly's readers. Holly Winter, Susan Conant's series protagonist, is also a freelance writer who lives in Cambridge.

MYSTERY FICTION

Liz Connors Series

The Gemini Man. New York: Walker, 1985.
The Summertime Soldiers. New York: Walker, 1986.

Trail of the Dragon. New York: Walker, 1988.

Until Proven Innocent. New York: Villard Books, 1990.

And Soon I'll Come to Kill You. New York: Villard Books, 1991.

Out of the Darkness. New York: Villard Books, 1992.

CRITICAL BIBLIOGRAPHY

Nichols, Victoria, and Susan Thompson. "Liz Connors." In *Silk Stalkings*. Berkeley, Calif.: Black Lizard, 1988, pp. 177–79.

LORENA STOOKEY

SUSAN KENNEY (1941–   )

Born in Summit, New Jersey, on April 28, 1941, Susan Kenney earned her B.A. at Northwestern University and her M.A. and Ph.D. at Cornell University. In 1968, she began teaching at Colby College in Waterville, Maine, where she is currently professor of English and director of the Creative Writing Program. In addition to her mystery fiction, Kenney writes critically acclaimed literary novels.

Kenney's intricately plotted whodunits in the classic English style all feature a college professor-turned-amateur-sleuth, named Rosamund ("Roz") Howard, whose probing intelligence, indefatigable curiosity, and underdeveloped sense of danger lead her inevitably to the truth. In the first of the series, *Garden of Malice*, Howard travels to England to edit the personal documents of a poet (who bears a strong resemblance to Vita Sackville-West), only to confront instead the cruelty and deception of a cast of characters determined to prevent her efforts. A series of deadly accidents at Canterbury College leads Roz into her second foray into detection, in *Graves in Academe*. On this idyllic Maine campus, Roz must discover who is using her course syllabus as a program for murder before she herself becomes a Desdemona-like victim. *One Fell Sloop*, the third in the series, finds Roz attempting to solve what is essentially a locked-room mystery on a deserted island.

Despite their divergent settings and plots, a recurrent theme unifies Kenney's series: the inhumanity of those who selfishly wield power and authority to control the will of others. While the theme itself is certainly linked to gender issues—and Kenney does, indeed, tackle sexism and sexual discrimination head-on in *Graves*—her mysteries are not stridently political, nor do they challenge generic conventions.

Nevertheless, Kenney's puzzles provide their readers with a great deal of pleasure, and her sleuth, with plenty of opportunities to exercise her wit and derring-do—and Roz, who is a specialist in medieval and women's studies, proves equal to the task. She is not, however, without her failings, chief of which is a naive belief in the goodness of others. The most troubling consequence of this weakness is Roz's tendency to become the victim. Roz may be a feminist who values her independence and prides herself on her self-sufficiency, but far too often, others must save her from poor judgment and foolish bravado, all of which undermine her feminism, as, too, does her relationship with Alan Stewart, her erudite Scottish lover.

The relationship itself is not the source of the problem, for Alan is, in many respects, a perfect match for Roz. An intellectual equal who respects and values the very qualities in Roz that she herself cultivates, Alan gives Roz the space to be independent, and as the "white knight" he aspires to be, Alan is little more than a parody, generally arriving too late to save his fair lady. Nevertheless, Roz spends far too much time whining and pining about Alan: she can't live with him or without him. This romantic cliché is worthy of neither party nor their relationship, and it becomes especially irritating in *One Fell Sloop*, where issues of gender such as power and control nearly overwhelm the mystery (unnecessarily so).

Ultimately, Roz Howard is not so much a feminist as an independent professional woman, and the pleasure of Kenney's mysteries lies not in an innovation and reformulation of the genre, but in the puzzle itself. Readers who enjoy classic English mysteries will not want to miss *Garden of Malice*, and those who favor the academic sleuths of Amanda Cross, Joan Smith, and Valerie Miner will want to read *Graves in Academe*, my favorite in the series.

MYSTERY FICTION

Garden of Malice. New York: Scribner's, 1983.
Graves in Academe. New York: Viking, 1985.
One Fell Sloop. New York: Viking, 1990.

CRITICAL BIBLIOGRAPHY

Pearlman, Mickey. "Susan Kenney." In *Listen to Their Voices: Twenty Interviews with Women Who Write*, ed. Mickey Pearlman. New York: Norton, 1993, pp. 183–91.

LINDA C. PELZER

KAREN KIJEWSKI (1943–   )

Karen Kijewski (pronounced "Key-*ev*-ski") was born in 1943 in Berkeley, California, where she attended school through graduate school at the University of California. While raising two daughters, she taught high school

English for ten years. From 1980 to 1991 she supported herself and her family by tending bar at night while writing novels during the day. She moved to Sacramento in 1982, where she lives and works today. *Katwalk* was awarded the prize for the best first private eye novel by the Private Eye Writers of America, the Shamus Award for best first mystery, and the Anthony Award for best first novel. She is the former president of the Northern California chapter of the Mystery Writers of America.

Kijewski's bartending experience undoubtedly gave her the background for Kat Colorado, a fast-talking, wise-cracking private investigator who, like her creator, worked as a bartender before becoming a full-time private eye. From her former profession, Kat has developed skills that serve her well in her new profession. Talking is what Kat does best, whether interviewing a client, consoling her best friend, or challenging a bad guy. Her wit, which is sometimes loaded with sarcasm, gets her into trouble on numerous occasions, but also gets her out of some very tight spots. Kat's first-person narrative is terse, funny, and fast-paced. Her humorous one-liners usually provide accurate, concise assessments of characters and events that keep the action moving right along.

Kijewski's series gives the traditional hard-boiled detective genre a twist. Like Philip Marlowe and Sam Spade, Kat Colorado is independent, tough, and committed to her own sense of justice. She does not always obey the law during the course of her investigation. Out of a sense of personal responsibility (and insatiable curiosity), she often continues to work on cases long after she has been warned or threatened to quit (sometimes by her own clients). She walks (or drives) the mean streets of Sacramento and Las Vegas to investigate murders, sometimes carrying a gun, and not afraid to use it if she has to. Like Mickey Spillane, she doles out her own punishment to unredeemable criminals, sometimes skirting the law to act as judge and jury (although rarely executioner).

Unlike her male predecessors, however, Kat is no loner. An orphan with a traumatic childhood, Kat was raised by a woman she calls "Alma" and considers her grandmother. Instead of shunning family ties, Kat's dysfunctional background seems to draw her to lonely and troubled people, and her concern for family and friendship is a continuing theme throughout the novels. In the first book in the series, *Katwalk*, Kat tracks her best friend's husband to Las Vegas, where she uncovers corruption and greed in the real estate market, in which both the husband and Kat's old schoolmate are involved. In the second novel, *Katapult*, she solves the murder of her cousin and virtually adopts a lonely teenaged hooker. In the third novel, *Kat's Cradle*, Kat involves herself in another family mystery, this time involving a missing mother and a vindictive grandmother. With *Copy Kat*, the fourth novel in the series, Kat goes undercover as a bartender to investigate the murder of a young wife and mother, to whose husband and child she becomes emotionally attached.

Although she is unmarried and eschews a permanent commitment to her on-again, off-again cop boyfriend Hank, Kat is no radical feminist. Hank often shows up at convenient moments in the novels to help Kat, either by saving her from threatening male bullies or by solving the crime. Hank's insistence that she quit her job and settle down is a continual source of friction between them and leads to several short-term breakups. To her credit, Kat sticks by her career choice and her ideals, but she expresses continual self-doubt about her abilities, most notably (and dangerously) when her usually astute judgment of character fails in *Kat's Cradle*. While self-questioning and a willingness to admit mistakes are traits she shares with several of the new female private eyes, this vulnerability in the traditionally tough veneer of the hard-boiled detective sometimes undermines and weakens the character's credibility. Nevertheless, Kat's conviction, humor, persistence, and hard work almost make up for what she lacks in skill and confidence, and they establish her firmly alongside Sara Paretsky's V. I. Warshawski and Sue Grafton's Kinsey Millhone in the new tradition of the hard-boiled female private eye.

Both the novels, and Kat as a character, seem to improve and become more complex as the series develops, so it is not necessary to read them in order. The best book in the series is *Copy Kat*, which I would suggest as a good introduction. Readers who like the Kat Colorado novels might also enjoy works by Sue Grafton, Sara Paretsky, Susan Dunlap, and Linda Barnes.

MYSTERY FICTION

Kat Colorado Series

Katwalk. New York: St. Martin's Press, 1989.

Katapult. New York: St. Martin's Press, 1990.

Kat's Cradle. New York: Doubleday, 1991.

Copy Kat. New York: Doubleday, 1992.

Wild Kat. New York: Doubleday, 1994.

KATHLEEN OSER

❧ L ❧

JANE LANGTON (1922–   )

Born December 30, 1922, in Boston, Massachusetts, Jane Gillson Langton currently lives in Lincoln, MA. She attended Wellesley College and the University of Michigan, where she earned a B.S. degree, Phi Beta Kappa, in 1944 and an M.A. in 1945. Returning to New England, she studied at Radcliffe College and received another M.A. in 1948. Langton married William Langton in 1943; they are the parents of three sons. She received the Nero Wolfe Award (1984) and an Edgar Award nomination from the Mystery Writers of America (1985), both for *Emily Dickinson Is Dead*.

In her mystery fiction Jane Langton has broadened the tradition of an erudite sleuth restoring order by combining wide-ranging interests, an acute sense of place, intriguing characters, and often, a concern for social issues. Her main continuing character and chief detective, Homer Kelly, is a former police detective with a law degree, turned scholar and teacher of literature. A description in *The Dante Game* summarizes clearly this "exaggerated person, somewhere at one end of the curve of human possibility. . . . Given to various forms of hyperbole[,] . . . he was noisy and gregarious, indulging in spasms of euphoria that alternated with fits of gloom. . . . He was nosy and inquisitive and apt to spring to conclusions by leaps of intuition rather than logical reasoning. Lastly Homer Kelly was rapacious of experience, wallowing in the present moment, greeting the morning with savage appetite."

The well-developed characters who work and interact with Kelly keep his exuberance from overwhelming the story. For example, in the first novel, *The Transcendental Murder*, Mary Morgan (who will later become Mary Kelly) assists in the murder investigation, and the story is told chiefly from her point of view. Furthermore, it is Mary's young nephew, John Hand, whose knowledge of natural history helps unravel the complexities of villainous Buddy Whipple's plot in *Natural Enemy*.

Indeed, the complex plots have many characters—over fifty names are listed at the beginning of *Good and Dead*—and the subplots may give the impression of a clever juggling act. However, Langton is skilled in combining actions, people, and information about topics as diverse as music, spiders, poets, Thoreau, and Dante. Even when the reader knows the identity of the principal perpetrator, the puzzle of "whydunit" and the interwoven subplots keep interest alive. The puzzles unfold within a broader context, and Langton gives the reader credit for having an interest in such subjects as American culture, literature, art, natural history, Florence and its heritage, and many social issues.

The use and preservation of land is a recurring consideration. The choice between establishing a conservation trust or permitting extensive commercial development of Nantucket are treated in *Dark Nantucket Moon*. A family acreage is under siege in *Natural Enemy*, while commercial development, waste disposal, and the homeless are issues in Langton's latest book, *God in Concord*. Langton is a realist and her solutions to these problems are pragmatic: landfills and developers will always be a fact of life, even if the immediate battles are won.

Another social—and moral—issue, the right of the terminally ill to die in dignity, is the focal point of *Good and Dead*. When an inordinate number of funerals take place in the Old West Church during a brief time span, questions arise. The reader knows who is helping the terminally ill, and Homer figures it out but decides to say nothing. An unexpected car accident presents one moral answer to what might happen when an individual provides the means to an end.

It is interesting to note that many of the guilty in Langton's books die before facing justice. Some of her criminals are obviously going to be judged by the legal system, but others die in "natural occurrences." No regular pattern is evident, but the moral question of what should happen to the guilty is raised.

The sense of place draws the reader into Langton's books. The Concord of Ralph Waldo Emerson and Henry David Thoreau and the Amherst of Emily Dickinson come alive. The heritage of Dante's Florence engrosses tourists and students. All Langton's settings are important to the mysteries, serving to create atmosphere, develop clues or red herrings, and embellish subplots.

Langton's wit also enhances her books. *Murder at the Gardner* illustrates human greed with a comic tone—zany characters, bizarre happenings in Boston's Gardner Museum, a picture-perfect wedding interrupted at the right moment—it is all great fun. Fun, erudition, mayhem, disruption, restoration of essential order, intricate puzzles—these qualities characterize the mystery fiction of Jane Langton, making her a readable and entertaining author.

It is not necessary to read Langton in chronological order; a book such as *Emily Dickinson Is Dead* introduces a new reader to her finely drawn settings, sense of humor, and use of interesting characters and subplots. Readers who appreciate Jane Langton's mysteries might consider books by Lucille Kallen and Jane Haddam.

MYSTERY FICTION

Homer Kelly Series

The Transcendental Murder. New York: Harper and Row, 1964; as *The Minute-man Murder*. New York: Dell, 1976.

Dark Nantucket Moon. New York: Harper and Row, 1975.

The Memorial Hall Murder. New York: Harper and Row, 1978; London: Gollancz, 1990.

Natural Enemy. New Haven, Conn.: Ticknor and Fields, 1982.

Emily Dickinson Is Dead. New York: St. Martin's Press, 1984; London: Gollancz, 1989.

Good and Dead. New York: St. Martin's Press, 1986.

Murder at the Gardner. New York: St. Martin's Press, 1988.

The Dante Game. New York: Viking; London: Gollancz, 1991.

God in Concord. New York: Viking, 1992.

Divine Inspiration. New York: Viking, 1993.

CRITICAL BIBLIOGRAPHY

Bakerman, Jane S. "Langton, Jane." In *Twentieth Century Crime and Mystery Writers*, ed. Lesley Henderson. 3rd ed. Chicago and London: St. James, 1991, pp. 650–52.

Carr, John C. "Interview." In *The Craft of Crime*. New York: Houghton, 1983.

MARILYN SPARKS SEVERSON

EMMA LATHEN

Emma Lathen is the pseudonym for Mary Jane Latsis (b. 1927) and Martha Henissart (b. 1929). Latsis, an economist, and Henissart, a lawyer, met as graduate students at Harvard and began collaborating on detective novels. They also write novels under the pseudonym of R. B. Dominic.

Lathen's work is topical. To enjoy it, one must necessarily suspend all political convictions, *especially* if one is a liberal. Although she does not pontificate in her novels, and is in fact humorous in her presentation of overt political themes, Lathen is consistently conservative in her vision— even, on occasion, reactionary. Her hero, John Thatcher, is executive vice-president of Sloan Guaranty Trust. Thatcher neatly inhabits a world defined by the boundaries of rational self-interest: he has an eighteenth-century worldview in which the market, if left to itself, will inevitably propel all human beings toward mutual enrichment. A modern-day Ben Franklin, Thatcher knows his world and does not waste time dreaming of a different, better one.

To be sure, his world is vulnerable to crime, but this occurs mainly when human beings hubristically attempt to wrest control of the free market—when, in the words of one novel, they ignore "the claims of honesty or decency or compassion" that the market embodies. The typical villain in Lathen's work is the anti-Libertarian: the person who steps outside the marketplace, ignoring the "Invisible Hand" that rules the market. For Lathen, social injustice, racial inequity, class conflicts, and environmental concerns are merely illusions besotting the liberal utopian dreamer.

To imply that Lathen's true criminal is the liberal interventionist would be too crude. She never, for example, chooses as her criminal a character with explicit liberal credentials. Her most flagrant novel is (to my liberal mind) *Death Shall Overcome*, which satirizes the civil rights movement of the 1960s by shifting the basis of the struggle to an incident on Wall Street: a brokerage firm transfers a seat on the exchange to one Edward Parry, an African-American. The novel's red herring—a rabid group of racists who wish to thwart Parry's ascension to a seat—provides Lathen the opportunity for her political commentary.

The novel's commentary expresses the absurdity of political protest for social change. The racists are "balanced" by Lathen's depiction of blacks who claim that Wall Street, and the Establishment in general, is dominated by white economic interests that are hostile to improving conditions for blacks and the poor (for Lathen, a ludicrous claim). Specifically, Lathen ridicules the African-American spokesman Richard Simpson (in a parody of Malcolm X), whose foolish diatribes include the phrase, "using whatever means [necessary]." Sharing Lathen's invective is the gullible liberal press of New York City (a frequent target of her satire).

Thatcher's equanimity in the face of this onslaught of liberalism is predictably salutary. Thatcher is in favor of Parry's seating on the exchange; nevertheless, he is continually disturbed by those who believe that social change should occur precipitously. Both Thatcher and Parry do their best to ignore the furor swirling around them, for they understand that social change must come gradually, even if infinitesimally slowly.

Lathen satirizes foreign governments also, and with a similar lack of sensitivity. In *When in Greece*, for example, she takes as her subject the then-ruling military junta, but the novel, which is intended as a comedy, cannot take seriously the repressively brutal nature of the fascist regime. She also pokes some ill-advised fun at the Greek working class and peasantry. Inevitably, Thatcher and his business executive allies get things done; he protects Sloan's interest and makes the world safer for capitalism.

Even though these two novels are perhaps her most egregiously offensive, Lathen's work is almost always entertaining. She writes with wit and intelligence, and her phrasing is amusing, even when her satiric targets are not. Additionally, she generally provides the reader with an economic education. In *Murder against the Grain*, Lathen chooses international finance and trade with the former Soviet Union as her subject; the novel involves the first American grain sales to the USSR in the 1960s. In *East Is East*, Lathen's narrative centers on Japanese-American cooperation in commerce and comments on the necessity for international competition. Lathen's novels, then, are intended for a *disinterested* reader who enjoys discovering a new subject, even if the author herself is clearly biased in her presentation.

The R. B. Dominic series is less well known than the Thatcher novels, though these novels, too, are focused on political issues—though not unaccountably, since they detail the investigations of Congressman Ben Safford (Dem., Ohio). Among the issues interrogated are the following: environmentalism and nuclear power (*Murder Out of Commission*), medical care and federal assistance (*The Attending Physician*), and governmental scandal (*Epitaph for a Lobbyist*).

The reader coming to Lathen for the first time should be guided by his or her own interests in current events, since Lathen's work is stringently topical. Her titles—and the year of publication—usually provide a reliable index for her subjects. Her puzzle novels are somewhat reminiscent of Agatha Christie.

MYSTERY FICTION

Writing as Emma Lathen

John Putnam Thatcher Series

Banking on Death. New York: Macmillan, 1961; London: Gollancz, 1977.

A Place for Murder. New York: Macmillan, 1963; London: Gollancz, 1978.

Accounting for Murder. New York: Macmillan, 1964; London: Gollancz, 1978.

Death Shall Overcome. New York: Macmillan, 1966; London: Gollancz, 1978.

Murder Against the Grain. New York: Macmillan, 1967; London: Gollancz, 1967.

Come to Dust. New York: Simon and Schuster, 1968.

A Stitch in Time. New York: Macmillan, 1968.

Murder to Go. New York: Simon and Schuster, 1969.

When in Greece. New York: Simon and Schuster, 1969; London: G. K. Hall, 1972.

Pick Up Sticks. New York: Simon and Schuster, 1970; London: Gollancz, 1970.

Ashes to Ashes. New York: Simon and Schuster, 1971; London: Gollancz, 1978.

The Longer the Thread. New York: Simon and Schuster, 1971; London: Gollancz, 1972.

Murder without Icing. New York: Simon and Schuster, 1972; London: Gollancz, 1972.

Sweet and Low. New York: Simon and Schuster, 1974; London: Gollancz, 1974.

By Hook or by Crook. New York: Simon and Schuster, 1975; London: Gollancz, 1975.

Double, Double, Oil and Trouble. New York: Simon and Schuster, 1978; London: Gollancz, 1978.

Going for the Gold. New York: Simon and Schuster, 1981.

Green Grow the Dollars. New York: Simon and Schuster, 1982.

Banking on Murder: Three by Emma Lathen. New York: Macmillan, 1984.

Something in the Air. Thorndike, Me. Thorndike Press, 1989.

East Is East. New York: Simon and Schuster, 1991.

Right on the Money. New York: Simon and Schuster, 1993.

Writing as R. B. Dominic

Congressman Ben Safford Series

Murder Sunny Side Up. New York: Abelard-Schuman, 1968.

Murder in a High Place. New York: Doubleday, 1970.

Murder Out of Court. New York: Macmillan, 1971.

There Is No Justice. New York: Doubleday, 1971.

Epitaph for a Lobbyist. New York: Doubleday, 1974.

Murder Out of Commission. New York: Doubleday, 1976.

The Attending Physician. New York: Harper and Row, 1980.

Unexpected Developments. New York: St. Martin's Press, 1984.

CRITICAL BIBLIOGRAPHY

Bakerman, Jane S. "A View from Wall Street: Social Criticism in the Mystery Novels of Emma Lathen." *The Armchair Detective*, 9, no. 3 (1976): 213–17.
———. "Women and Wall Street: Portraits of Women in Novels by Emma Lathen." *The Armchair Detective*, 8, no. 1 (1975): 36–41.
Bedell, Jeanne F. "Emma Lathen." In *Ten Women of Mystery*, ed. Earl F. Bargainnier. Bowling Green, Ohio: Popular Press, 1981, pp. 250–70.
Brownell, David. "Comic Construction in the Novels of Emma Lathen and R. B. Dominic." *The Armchair Detective*, 9, no. 2 (1976): 91–92.

Lawrence, Barbara. "Emma Lathen: The Art of Escapist Crime Fiction." *Clues*, 3, no. 2 (1982): 78–82.

Sarjeant, William. "Crime on Wall Street." *The Armchair Detective*, 21, no. 2 (1988): 128–45.

GARY STORHOFF

ELIZABETH LEMARCHAND (1906–   )

Born in 1906, in Barnstaple, England, Elizabeth Lemarchand only became a novelist in her sixties. When she was sixteen, the sudden death of her father, a country doctor, altered her educational plans. Of necessity she studied at a provincial school, where she received a London University External Degree. Teaching had always been her goal, she wrote me (Sept. 27, 1992). On obtaining her degree she "was fortunate in walking into a really good post [Clifton High School, Bristol], and going on to other equally good schools." In time, "unwillingly," she became headmistress of a girls' public school. An illness led to her retirement, and soon afterwards, she began to create mystery fiction. Her letter states she had had "about 20 odd [detective novels] published," but a list provided to *Contemporary Authors* contains seventeen titles of novels dating from 1967 to 1988. No longer writing, Lemarchand is "revelling in reading" at home in that "very pleasant place" that is Devon.

"Pleasant" also describes the novels; another good term is "traditional." Lemarchand clearly was influenced by predecessors of the Golden Age period. Similarities exist in casts of characters, maps of areas, and diagrams of police activities. Like mystery fiction of the twenties and thirties, her novels generally have country settings, featuring lovely, undisturbed villages with pubs, estates and manor houses, boarding schools, and churches. Although Lemarchand is a contemporary novelist who utilizes professional detectives, the world she describes is more like that of Agatha Christie's Miss Marple than Ruth Rendell's Inspector Wexford or P. D. James's Adam Dalgleish. Settings and evident class distinctions recall the fiction of Christie, Margery Allingham, and most of all, Dorothy L. Sayers. However, events of World War II—bombings, losses, and disappearances—frequently influence the course of the plot.

Like other traditionalists, Lemarchand features a central detective figure, Thomas (Tom) Pollard, and his sidekick, Gregory (Greg) Toye. However, she does not follow the earlier pattern in which sleuths were often amateurs, dilettantes, or eccentrics. Pollard and Toye, who are employed by New Scotland Yard, move up in the ranks from book to book. Initially, Pollard, whose early title is chief detective-inspector, is ambitious and concerned about making a good impression, both on his superiors and on his beautiful, talented, art historian wife, Jane. He wants a promotion, recognition, money, and status. In time, he achieves those things, maturing into a confident leader in his department, a proud and confident husband, and a loving father of twins.

In *Death of an Old Girl*, the first, and one of her best, novels, Pollard is more individualized than in later books. Almost nothing about his personality is developed as the years go on; thus, a reader randomly selecting a book would have little sense of his uniqueness. Pollard and others age, but after an attractive beginning, he appears a static, predictable character. Language, tastes, attitudes, and methodology all fail to change. Toye is more idiosyncratic than his chief, although Pollard describes him as a "human chameleon with a remarkable facility for blending into the environment." Where Pollard has no religious convictions, Toye is dogmatic. He seems anti-Catholic, "a staunch evangelical." Toye likes movies, maps, driving, and hazardous roads. The two men characteristically discuss cases while driving or eating pub meals. Pollard, who is the unflagging leader, ignores the clock, yet they work harmoniously, with Toye's role sometimes reminiscent of Sayers's Bunter.

All the novels have similarities. The detectives are brought in when the local police are unable or too busy to solve a crime, and Pollard always gets those cases involving individuals higher up on the social ladder. Throughout the series, class distinctions matter. The status of people may be discerned through speech patterns: dropped *h*s and endings, mispronounced words, mixed tenses, and cockney accents. Speaking in public school English is an identifying mark. Plots focus on the wealthy and well educated.

Women generally work at hobbies rather than jobs. The wives tend to be superb cooks. Even when there are housekeepers, wives are often shown preparing or offering food to their husbands, while tea, as a great medicinal restorative, is recommended by everyone; attitudes and activities often resemble the leisurely Victorian milieu of Anne Perry's novels. Relationships between the sexes are patterned after romantic fiction, and every Lemarchand novel includes romance of some kind. The romance element is the weakest part of the novel, and is often wooden or saccharin, with cardboard figures for lovers. The love affairs come from another age or type of fiction, where dainty little wives sit on the knees of kind, strong husbands. Lemarchand's eccentrics and villains are more inspired.

All the novels engage the reader's attention immediately with their strong openings, detailed descriptions of settings, and air of suspense. Local color and history are important. A cast of characters and a map precede the story, and at least once, as the plot unfolds, Pollard summarizes the major points. Generally, Lemarchand plays fair with the reader. The pace of most of the novels is unhurried, but the solution is sometimes abrupt. Typically, all ends are tied and everyone is accounted for. Some Lemarchand books have been reissued in large-print editions. Her readers should enjoy novels by Catherine Aird, Ngaio Marsh, and Sheila Radley.

MYSTERY FICTION

Tom Pollard and Greg Toye Series

Death of an Old Girl. London: Hart-Davis, 1967; New York: Walker and Co., 1986.

The Affacombe Affair. London: Hart-Davis, 1968; London: State Mutual Books, 1985.

Alibi for a Corpse. London: Hart-Davis, 1969; New York: Walker and Co., 1986.

Death on Doomsday. London: MacGibbon and Kee, 1971; New York: Walker and Co., 1975.

Cyanide with Compliments. London: MacGibbon and Kee, 1972; New York: Walker and Co., 1973.

Buried in the Past. London: Hart-Davis, 1973; New York: Walker and Co., 1976.

Let or Hindrance. London: Hart-Davis, 1973; as *No Vacation from Murder.* New York: Walker and Co., 1974.

Step in the Dark. London: Hart-Davis, 1976.

Unhappy Returns. London: Hart-Davis, 1977; New York: Walker and Co., 1978.

Suddenly While Gardening. London: Hart-Davis, 1978; New York: Walker and Co., 1979.

Change for the Worse. New York: Walker and Co., 1980.

Nothing to Do with the Case. New York: Walker and Co., 1981.

Troubled Waters. New York: Walker and Co., 1982. Rev. ed., 1985.

The Wheel Turns. London: Piatkus, 1983; New York: Walker and Co., 1984.

Light through Glass. London: Piatkus, 1984; New York: Walker and Co., 1986.

Who Goes Home? London: Piatkus, 1986; New York: Walker and Co., 1987.

The Glade Manor Murder. London: Piatkus, 1988; New York: Walker, 1989.

CRITICAL BIBLIOGRAPHY

Becker, Mary Helen. "Lemarchand, Elizabeth." In *Twentieth Century Crime and Mystery Writers*, ed. Lesley Henderson. 3rd ed. Chicago and London: St. James, 1991, pp. 661–62.
Nichols, Victoria, and Susan Thompson. "Tom Pollard." In *Silk Stalkings*. Berkeley, Calif.: Black Lizard, 1988, pp. 42–43.

HELEN S. GARSON

ELIZABETH LININGTON (1921–1988)

Born in Aurora, Illinois, on March 11, 1921, Linington was an adopted Californian. Her education began in Aurora, but her B.A. was completed in Hollywood (Glendale College). She was an activist in political causes, primarily for the John Birch Society. A prolific writer (generally producing three crime novels a year), she used several pseudonyms as well as her own name. She died on April 5, 1988, having published approximately eighty novels. Almost all were police procedurals, the genre in which she made her major contribution.

Linington consistently followed a particular method—or formula—which endeared her to many readers. This calls for two basic plot strands that parallel each other. In terms of the genre, the primary strand is the group of crimes, some relatively minor or easily solved, and one or more that present greater challenges. Of greater interest for many readers, however, is the secondary strand: the personal lives of her series characters. It is these continuing characters and their settings that are the principal differentiation between the series. In her best work, contrasts or parallels are drawn between the sane world of the off-duty police and their families and pets and the insane and chaotic world into which their work draws the police officers.

The first of the series to be initiated is also the most numerous and the best known. Published as written by Dell Shannon, these novels center around Luis Mendoza of the Los Angeles Police Department. The series was published over a period of more than twenty-five years. The novels in the series were produced at a rate of one or two a year, but their action, being almost continuous from novel to novel, compresses the apparent time of occurrence. Mendoza is followed from his beginnings as a womanizing cardsharp of Mexican-American origins (he is bilingual and regularly shifts back and forth between Spanish and English) and great personal wealth (inherited from a gambling grandfather, about whom he feels deep ambivalence). From the first novel he has a reputation among his peers for his detecting skills and intuition which enable him to solve particularly difficult cases. A detached loner at first, he takes greatest pleasure in his cat (an Abyssinian) and his car (throughout the series he continues to collect exotic sports cars).

In the early novels, Mendoza's personality is established and the running story of his reluctant infatuation with Allison, the red-headed woman he eventually marries is begun. At the same time, a number of his colleagues in police work are introduced. Gradually, as the series proceeds, the cast is enlarged: additional policemen and an occasional policewoman enter, and their lives are also examined. Occasionally, in fact, one of the police officers is killed in the line of duty, to be replaced by a new character. Verisimilitude is strengthened by this realistic treatment of the hazards of police work.

No matter how large and complex the cast of continuing characters becomes, Mendoza and Allison remain the center. Their courtship and marriage, the births of their children and the accumulation of their menagerie of pets, the building of one home and the later acquisition of an estate create the structure of the series. Around them circle, first, other courting couples, and then other growing families. Always, these mostly very ordinary lives create a pattern of sanity, of normality, against which the brutality of the world of the streets and the criminal mind are set.

Other series follow similar patterns. Those written under Linington's own name center around Ivor Maddox and Sue Carstairs (later Maddox) and are set in Hollywood rather than Los Angeles. The formula is the same, however. As a working wife (she continues with the police force after her marriage), Sue realistically depicts the situation of many employed women. Despite its more believable protagonists, this series never achieved the popularity of the Mendoza novels, which may explain why it includes fewer books.

As Lesley Egan, Linington wrote a pair of interconnecting series. Central in one is Jesse Falkenstein, an attorney who often calls on Andrew Clock, a policeman, for help with his cases. Vic Varallo, a policeman, anchors a separate series which occasionally intersects with the Falkenstein stories. These novels are set in Glendale, Linington's home for many years, and like the better-known series, they contrast warm and loving personal lives with sordid crime and suffering.

A notable characteristic of Linington's work is its careful presentation of the ethnic diversity of its California setting. Mendoza, a Mexican-American, is only the most obvious example; other police officers represent other ethnic groups, most notably, perhaps, Jason Grace, an African-American who is introduced in *Death by Inches*. The son of a wealthy and cultivated family, he is clearly not an "affirmative action" employee, and Linington often uses him to convey her notion of equal opportunity. Criminals, as well, represent various ethnic groups, though teenagers and homosexuals seem particularly heavily represented. Of all the groups represented in these novels, homosexuals are most unfavorably treated; police officers refer to them with impunity as "fags," and the suspicion of being gay is frequently an indication that the character in question will turn out to be a perpetrator.

Linington's politics have been controversial, and her commitment to right-wing causes is mirrored in her fiction. Comments denigrating intellectuals, people on welfare, liberal politicians, homosexuals, and others are frequent; however, since these remarks are generally put into the mouths of characters who might well hold these opinions, they are not as obtrusive as they might otherwise be. The mockery by Jason Grace, a privileged African-American, of the speech and attitudes of his less-favored ghetto brothers, however, is sometimes grating. Similarly, female characters tend to make antifeminist remarks; neither Allison Mendoza nor Sue Carstairs Maddox sympathizes with the women's movement.

Early in her career, Linington was praised for her accuracy as a writer of police procedurals. She took pains to inform herself about police work and, particularly, about the structure and policies of the Los Angeles Police Department. Her police officers doubtless speak for law enforcers everywhere in their sense of the job as "keeping the wild animals in the jungle at bay on behalf of the citizenry." If there is any serious flaw in her portrayal of the police, it is in her idealization of them; corruption is absent, and what police brutality is shown is portrayed as justified.

In her later years, Linington's work continued to be eagerly sought out by fans caught up in the life stories of her police families. However, she was increasingly ignored by reviewers and critics. Her political views were not popular, and she doubtless wrote too much and too hastily, perhaps even carelessly. Her style became increasingly cliché-ridden, though many of those clichés were of her own making: her officers regularly refer to "the thankless job," for instance.

Because a major interest in Linington's work lies in the continuing stories of her police characters, a new reader would be well advised to read each series in chronological order. A number of the early books in the Mendoza series have been republished by Mysterious Press and should be readily available.

MYSTERY FICTION

Writing as Anne Blaisdell

Nightmare. New York: Harper, 1961; London: Gollancz, 1962.

Writing as Dell Shannon

Luis Mendoza Series

Case Pending. New York: Harper; London: Gollancz, 1960.
The Ace of Spades. New York: Morrow, 1961; London: Oldbourne, 1963.
Extra Kill. New York: Morrow; London: Oldbourne, 1962.
Death of a Busybody. New York: Morrow; London: Oldbourne, 1963.
Knave of Hearts. New York: Morrow, 1962; London: Oldbourne, 1963.

Double Bluff. New York: Morrow, 1963; London: Oldbourne, 1964.

Mark of Murder. New York: Morrow, 1964; London: Oldbourne, 1965.

Root of All Evil. New York: Morrow, 1964; London: Gollancz, 1966.

The Death-Bringers. New York: Morrow, 1965; London: Gollancz, 1966.

Death by Inches. New York: Morrow, 1965; London: Gollancz, 1967.

Coffin Corner. New York: Morrow, 1966; London: Gollancz, 1967.

With a Vengeance. New York: Morrow, 1966; London: Gollancz, 1968.

Chance to Kill. New York: Morrow, 1967; London: Gollancz, 1968.

Rain with Violence. New York: Morrow, 1967; London: Gollancz, 1969.

Kill with Kindness. New York: Morrow, 1968; London: Gollancz, 1969.

Crime on Their Hands. New York: Morrow, 1969; London: Gollancz, 1970.

Schooled to Kill. New York: Morrow, 1969; London: Gollancz, 1970.

Unexpected Death. New York: Morrow, 1970; London: Gollancz, 1971.

The Ringer. New York: Morrow, 1971; London: Gollancz, 1972.

Whim to Kill. New York: Morrow; London: Gollancz, 1971.

Murder with Love. New York: Morrow; London: Gollancz, 1972.

With Intent to Kill. New York: Morrow, 1972; London: Gollancz, 1973.

No Holiday for Crime. New York: Morrow, 1973; London: Gollancz, 1974.

Spring of Violence. New York: Morrow, 1973; London: Gollancz, 1974.

Crime File. New York: Morrow, 1974; London: Gollancz, 1975.

Deuces Wild. New York: Morrow; London: Gollancz, 1975.

Streets of Death. New York: Morrow, 1976; London: Gollancz, 1977.

Appearances of Death. New York: Morrow, 1977; London: Gollancz, 1978.

Cold Trail. New York: Morrow, 1978; London: Gollancz, 1979.

Felony at Random. New York: Morrow; London: Gollancz, 1979.

Felony File. New York: Morrow; London: Gollancz, 1980.

Murder Most Strange. New York: Morrow; London: Gollancz, 1981.

The Motive on Record. New York: Morrow; London: Gollancz, 1982.

Exploits of Death. New York: Morrow; London: Gollancz, 1983.

Destiny of Death. New York: Morrow, 1984.

Chaos of Crime. New York: Morrow, 1985; London: Gollancz, 1986.

Blood Count. New York: Morrow, 1986; London: Gollancz, 1987.

Murder by the Tale. New York: Morrow, 1987.

  Writing as Elizabeth Linington

Alter Ego. New York: Doubleday, 1988.

Ivor Maddox and Sue Carstairs Maddox Series

Greenmask! New York: Harper, 1964; London: Gollancz, 1965.

No Evil Angel. New York: Harper; London: Gollancz, 1965.

Date with Death. New York: Harper; London: Gollancz, 1966.

Something Wrong. New York: Harper, 1967; London: Gollancz, 1968.

Policeman's Lot. New York: Harper, 1968; London: Gollancz, 1969.

Practice to Deceive. New York: Harper; London: Gollancz, 1971.

Crime by Chance. Philadelphia: Lippincott, 1973; London: Gollancz, 1974.

Perchance of Death. New York: Doubleday, 1977; London: Gollancz, 1978.

No Villain Need Be. New York: Doubleday; London: Gollancz, 1979.

Consequence of Crime. New York: Doubleday, 1980; London: Gollancz, 1981.

Skeletons in the Closet. New York: Doubleday, 1982; London: Gollancz, 1983.

Felony Report. New York: Doubleday, 1984; London: Gollancz, 1985.

Strange Felony. New York: Doubleday; London: Gollancz, 1986.

Writing as Lesley Egan

Jesse Falkenstein and Andrew Clock Series

A Case for Appeal. New York: Harper; London: Gollancz, 1961.

Against the Evidence. New York: Harper, 1962; London: Gollancz, 1963.

My Name Is Death. New York: Harper; London: Gollancz, 1965.

Some Avenger, Rise! New York: Harper, 1966; London: Gollancz, 1967.

A Serious Investigation. New York: Harper, 1968; London: Gollancz, 1969.

In the Death of a Man. New York: Harper; London: Gollancz, 1970.

Paper Chase. New York: Harper, 1972; London: Gollancz, 1973.

The Blind Search. New York: Doubleday; London: Gollancz, 1977.

Look Back on Death. New York: Doubleday, 1978; London: Gollancz, 1979.

Motive in Shadow. New York: Doubleday; London: Gollancz, 1980.

The Miser. New York: Doubleday, 1981; London: Gollancz, 1982.

Little Boy Lost. New York: Doubleday, 1983; London: Gollancz, 1984.

The Wine of Life. New York: Doubleday, 1985; London: Gollancz, 1986.

Vic Varallo Series

The Borrowed Alibi. New York: Harper; London: Gollancz, 1962.

Run to Evil. New York: Harper; London: Gollancz, 1963.

Detective's Due. New York: Harper, 1965; London: Gollancz, 1966.

The Nameless Ones. New York: Harper, 1967; London: Gollancz, 1968.

The Wine of Violence. New York: Harper, 1969; London: Gollancz, 1970.

Malicious Mischief. New York: Harper, 1971; London: Gollancz, 1972.

Scenes of Crime. New York: Doubleday; London: Gollancz, 1976.

A Dream Apart. New York: Doubleday; London: Gollancz, 1978.

The Hunters and the Hunted. New York: Doubleday, 1979; London: Gollancz, 1980.

A Choice of Crimes. New York: Doubleday, 1980; London: Gollancz, 1981.

Random Death. New York: Doubleday; London: Gollancz, 1982.

Crime for Christmas. New York: Doubleday; London: Gollancz, 1984.

Chain of Violence. New York: Doubleday; London: Gollancz, 1985.

CRITICAL BIBLIOGRAPHY

Duke, Elizabeth F. "Linington, Elizabeth." In *Twentieth Century Crime and Mystery Writers*, ed. Lesley Henderson. 3rd ed. Chicago and London: St. James, 1991, pp. 671–73.
King, Rufus. "Interview with Elizabeth Linington." *The Armchair Detective*, 13, no. 4 (1980): 299–307.
Nichols, Victoria, and Susan Thompson. "Luis Mendoza, LAPD." In *Silk Stalkings*. Berkeley, Calif.: Black Lizard, 1988, pp. 26–28.
Potts, Rinehart. "Elizabeth Linington (Dell Shannon) 1921–1988." *The Armchair Detective*, 22, no. 1 (1989): 79.

MARY JEAN DeMARR

MARIE BELLOC LOWNDES (1868–1947)

"Little Marie Belloc lunched with me the other day and bristled with the fruits of ubiquity and omniscience in a manner even remarkable for her." So wrote Henry James in 1914 with characteristic felinity; but the idea expressed is not inaccurate. Marie Belloc Lowndes had a wide circle of friends and acquaintances—wider even than James, who did not mingle with royalty—and she wrote on a wide variety of subjects. Her crime or mystery novels number just short of fifty, and many of them, most notably *The Lodger* and *Lizzie Borden*, are based in fact and research. She wrote four volumes of personal reminiscence, and she analyzed the royal family from Edward VII to Edward VIII, reserving special praise for King George and Queen Mary (whom James had called "the wretched little Yorks"). Her family connections were remarkable: she was descended from the chemist Joseph Priestley and from the French translator of *Uncle Tom's Cabin*; Hillaire Belloc was her brother.

About the same time that James was patronizing her, the *Bookman* was reviewing her latest novel as "Mrs. Belloc Lowndes's sort of thing—an odd blend of sensational incident and the ladylike manner." She is a superior Mignon G. Eberhart or a Mary Roberts Rinehart, though more distinctively English than either. However, whereas their heroines—had they but known it—are in perpetual peril, Lowndes's female protagonists are frequently the instigators of the peril. One of her best novels, *The Chink in the Armour*, which no less a writer than Ernest Hemingway called "that uncanny masterpiece of dread and suspense," follows the Rinehart pattern, with a young, rich widow stalked by a murderously predatory couple at a European gambling center, and the story ends with the helpless girl's rescue by her two suitors, with one of whom she finds happiness. However, most of Lowndes's women are more resourceful: in at least ten of her novels, the pattern is repeated of a young woman, usually of an inferior class, who is married to an older man but loves another (or, more usually, has designs on another man's money), who murders her husband. In almost all these cases the formula is repeated even to the minor details; Lowndes is very fond of arsenic as the murderess's panacea.

She is also very fond of the occult, and it is her frequent suggestion of the supernatural that places her work in the genre of sensational or crime fiction rather than the more conventionally rational world of detective fiction. In several of her novels a dream predicts the future, and more than once her central character consults a fortune-teller, whose predictions are equally accurate. *The Chink in the Armour* provides several examples of the operations of the other world, including the hero sensing the ghost of the murdered woman in his hotel room, a presence that is never rationally explained (heroes are invariably more sensible than heroines for Lowndes). She even wrote her own version of one of the most chilling of mystery archetypes, though explicable in rational terms: a couple registers at a hotel. The husband disappears in the night, and the management, which has altered the very structure of the lodgings, professes utter ignorance of his existence next day. This old story, realized widely in film as well as in novel (such as *The Lady Vanishes, So Long at the Fair,* and *Bunny Lake Is Missing*) is based in fact: the actual disappearance of a young Englishman at the Paris Exposition of 1889. Much of Lowndes's fiction *is* based in fact, which brings us to her two best, and best-known, works, *The Lodger* and *The Story of Ivy*. Both were made into successful pictures, the first by Alfred Hitchcock in 1926. There were also three later versions, the most successful, and faithful, being that of 1944 starring Laird Cregar, while the second featured Joan Fontaine turning from her usual victim's role to that of murderess. Both these novels do what Lowndes does most successfully—create a convincing point of view, a feat not undeserving of Jamesian praise, had he read her.

Many of her novels contain convincing trial sequences, grounding the airy mystery in the pedestrian legal system. The most successful such novel (and one of her very best) is *What Really Happened*. Here, as the judge sums up, we are told, in parallel narrative, the story of the events leading up to the murder, mainly from the point of view of the woman who, for good reason, actually did the killing. Her own plausible testimony, with the help of the invincible advocate Sir Joseph Molloy, the only recurring character in Lowndes's novels, acquits the defendant and the murderess escapes the operation of the law. There *is* a recurrent character in several short stories: a Hercules Popeau, late of the Paris Sureté. However, even he, in such stories as "A Race for Life" and "Popeau Intervenes," is hardly a detective. He is a big man, we may note, has a head of hair, and speaks impeccable English—and he is French, not Belgian.

Marie Belloc Lowndes's ultimate theme, which is acted out again and again, is the very Victorian one of outward respectability and hidden vice. One can be transformed by some psychic quirk from a respectable wife to a murderess, and who can tell the difference? Society works on certain assumptions, and the reversal of such assumptions, undetected, is the chink in the armour.

MYSTERY FICTION

When No Man Pursueth. London: Heinemann, 1910; New York: Kennerley, 1911.
Jane Oglander. London: Heinemann; New York: Scribner, 1911.
The Chink in the Armour. London: Methuen; New York: Scribner, 1912; as *The House of Peril*. London: Readers Library, 1935.
The End of Her Honeymoon. New York: Scribner, 1913; London: Methuen, 1914.
The Lodger. London: Methuen; New York: Scribner, 1913.
Studies in Love and Terror. London: Methuen; New York: Scribner, 1913.
Good Old Anna. London: Hutchinson, 1915; New York: Doran, 1916.
The Price of Admiralty. London: Newnes, 1915.
Love and Hatred. London: Chapman and Hall; New York: Doran, 1917.
Out of the War? London: Chapman and Hall, 1918; as *The Gentleman Anonymous*. London: Philip Allan, 1934.
The Lonely House. London: Hutchinson; New York: Doran, 1920.
The Reason Why. London: Benn, 1921.
What Timmy Did. London: Hutchinson, 1921; New York: Doran, 1922.
Why They Married. London: Heinemann, 1923.
The Terriford Mystery. London: Hutchinson; New York: Doubleday, 1924.
Bread of Deceit. London: Hutchinson, 1925; as *Afterwards*. New York: Doubleday, 1925.
Some Men and Women. London: Hutchinson, 1935; New York: Doubleday, 1928.
What Really Happened. London: Hutchinson; New York: Doubleday, 1926.
The Story of Ivy. London: Heinemann, 1927; New York: Doubleday, 1928.
Thou Shalt Not Kill. London: Hutchinson, 1927.
Cressida: No Mystery. London: Heinemann, 1928; New York: Knopf, 1930.
Love's Revenge. London: Readers Library, 1929.
One of Those Ways. London: Heinemann; New York: Knopf, 1929.

Letty Lynion. London: Heinemann; New York: Cape and Smith, 1931.

Vanderlyn's Adventure. New York: Cape and Smith, 1931; as *The House by the Sea.* London: Heinemann, 1937.

Jenny Newstead. London: Heinemann; New York: Putnam, 1932.

Love Is a Flame. London: Benn, 1932.

Another Man's Wife. London: Heinemann; New York: Longman, 1934.

The Chianti Flask. New York: Longman, 1934; London: Heinemann, 1935.

Who Rides on a Tiger. New York: Longman, 1935; London: Heinemann, 1936.

And Call It Accident. New York: Longman, 1936; London: Hutchinson, 1939.

The Second Key. New York: Longman, 1936; as *The Injured Lover.* London: Hutchinson, 1939.

The Marriage-Broker. London: Heinemann, 1937; as *The Fortune of Bridget Malone.* New York: Longman, 1937.

Motive. London: Hutchinson, 1938; as *Why It Happened.* New York: Longman, 1938.

Lizzie Borden: A Study in Conjecture. New York: Longman, 1939; London: Hutchinson, 1940.

Reckless Angel. New York: Longman, 1939.

The Christine Diamond. London: Hutchinson; New York: Longman, 1940.

Before the Storm. New York: Longman, 1941.

A Labour of Hercules. London: Todd, 1943.

CRITICAL BIBLIOGRAPHY

Macdonald, Gina. "Lowndes, Marie." In *Twentieth Century Crime and Mystery Writers*, ed. Lesley Henderson. 3rd ed. Chicago and London: St. James Press, 1991, pp. 682–84.

BARRIE HAYNE

❧ M ❧

SHARYN McCRUMB (1948–   )

Sharyn Arwood McCrumb was born February 26, 1948, in Wilmington, North Carolina, and lives in Shawsville, Virginia, with her husband and three children. She received her B.A. in 1970 from the University of North Carolina, Chapel Hill, and her M.A. in 1985 from Virginia Tech. She won the 1983 Sherwood Anderson Short Story Competition for "Precious Jewel." *Lovely in Her Bones* was named Best Appalachian Novel of 1985 by the Appalachian Writers Association, and *Bimbos of the Death Sun* won the 1988 Edgar Award for best original paperback mystery. *If Ever I Return Pretty Peggy-O* was named a *New York Times* Notable Book, won the Macavity Award, and was a finalist for the Anthony and Nero awards.

McCrumb's early comic novels often raise important concerns, but her most recent Ballad series deals directly with larger themes which reverberate beyond resolutions provided by personally motivated evil. *If Ever I Return Pretty Peggy-O*, the first, opens on Memorial Day as a sheriff visits the grave of his brother who died in the Vietnam War. Spencer has to deal with the conflict between image and reality in the world's view of his older brother, but his deputy, Joe LeDonne, is a Vietnam veteran who still cannot master the simple act of sleeping. Thus, personal pasts merge with the history of the United States. In this series McCrumb returns to the setting she seems to prefer, Appalachia. Her Appalachia is not, however, filled with lovable comic characters or gothics from *Deliverance*. The people who live in Hamelin, Tennessee, are different because they have remained connected with their past, their history, but are not reconciled with it. By making their problems real, McCrumb does not allow a reader to become nostalgic about small-town America, about our collective past. The second novel in this series, *The Hangman's Beautiful Daughter*, continues to explore McCrumb's broader concerns as she examines the impact of industry on the environment through one set of characters. Mystery is subordinated to a presentation of the region and its concerns, and the main plot blends Appalachian myths with personal pain to develop a unique vision of this part of the United States.

While McCrumb rightly considers her Ballad series her most important work, her comic series are the largest part of her mystery production. Her first mystery, *Sick of Shadows*, introduces the comic adventures of Elizabeth MacPherson and her extended family. The series, which now includes seven novels, features Elizabeth, but she is assisted by relatives and love interests. Investigations are joint male-female efforts in most of McCrumb's work. Women are not usually successful detectives in her comic worlds, but they are always central to the plot. During her investigations, Elizabeth discovers her career as a forensic anthropologist, completes her Ph.D., and marries. McCrumb balances her development of the personal lives of her characters with interesting puzzles in a variety of locations. Her first novel is most traditional in its presentation of motive and solution. By her second, McCrumb begins to expand her concerns. Evil is connected to larger societal problems, and McCrumb's attachment to place is integrated directly into the plot.

As the MacPherson series continues, Elizabeth explores connections between past and present and differences between the various cultures she encounters. Mysteries often deal with the influence of past crimes on the present and those who must live with their personal histories. In her recent MacPherson novels, McCrumb expands the personal into the greater concerns of a historical past. As she investigates the broader concerns of her characters, murder no longer becomes as central to her novels.

McCrumb's second series contains many of the comic elements of her first but with a decided twist. The two novels in this series use the world of science fiction as both their setting and source of humor. Dr. James Owens, an engineering professor, has written a science fiction novel under the pen name, Jay Omega. He is assisted in his investigations by his friend, Dr. Marion Farley, who teaches science fiction in the English Department at the same university. The progress of their relationship is tempered by the perils of the tenure process: they cannot commit to each other until the university commits to them. *Bimbos of the Death Sun* is the name of both Jay Omega's and McCrumb's novel. Hers is set at Rubicon, a science fiction convention where Jay is an invited author. McCrumb deftly and lovingly depicts the "con" experience. In the second, *Zombies of the Gene Pool*, Jay and Marion interact with science fiction greats, near-greats, and has-beens from the 1950s during the retrieval of the group's time capsule. It comes to be retrieved because the lake which covered the farm is drained for repairs to its dam. The draining of the lake connects the mystery plot to larger themes. The dam can be repaired, but the characters whose lives are simultaneously revealed are drained of a vitality that cannot be as easily repaired or restored. Humans change the natural world, and the alterations may occur for a good cause, but the drained lake is as ephemeral as the attempt to appreciate the past captured in the time capsule (a pickle jar).

Readers should start the Elizabeth MacPherson series in chronological order. *Bimbos of the Death Sun* is a great introduction to her comic style. My personal favorite is *If Ever I Return Pretty Peggy-O*. Readers who enjoy McCrumb's comic novels should try those by Carolyn G. Hart, Joan Hess, and Charlotte MacLeod. The use of setting in her Ballad series is similar to other authors' use of the Southwest.

MYSTERY FICTION

Elizabeth MacPherson Series

Sick of Shadows. New York: Avon Books, 1984; London: Severn House, 1992.

Lovely in Her Bones. New York: Avon Books, 1985; London: Severn House, 1993.

Highland Laddie Gone. New York: Avon Books, 1986; London: Severn House, 1993.

Paying the Piper. New York: Ballantine Books, 1988; London: Severn House, 1991.

The Windsor Knot. New York: Ballantine Books, 1990.

Missing Susan. New York: Ballantine Books, 1991.

MacPherson's Lament. New York: Ballantine Books, 1992.

Jay Omega Series

Bimbos of the Death Sun. New York and London: TSR, 1988.

Zombies of the Gene Pool. New York: Simon and Schuster, 1992.

Ballad Series

If Ever I Return Pretty Peggy-O. New York: Scribners, 1990.

The Hangman's Beautiful Daughter. New York: Scribners, 1992.

She Walks these Hills. New York: Scribners, 1994.

CRITICAL BIBLIOGRAPHY

Sexton, Rebecca. "The Art of Writing Intelligent Fiction: An Interview with Sharyn McCrumb." *Clues*, 11, no. 2 (1990): 95–101.

SHARON A. RUSSELL

VAL McDERMID (1955–   )

Val McDermid was born June 4, 1955, in Kirkcaldy, Scotland, and received a B.A. in English language and literature from St. Hilda's College, Oxford, in 1975. She began a career as a journalist that same year with the *Plymouth and South Devon Times* and *Sunday Independent*. She was National Trainee Journalist of the Year in 1977 and has held several posts in the National Union of Journalists, including chair of the Equality Council. She has written for many publications, among them the *Scottish Daily Record*, the *Tatler*, and the *People* (Manchester). McDermid has had two stage plays performed: *Like a Happy Ending* (adapted for broadcast by BBC radio) and *Battle beyond the Black Hole*, a children's science fiction extravaganza. She resides in Bolton.

McDermid's first mystery novel, *Report for Murder*, introduces the series character, Lindsay Gordon, who mockingly describes herself as "a cynical socialist lesbian feminist journalist." Lindsay is free-lancing a feature on a gala fund-raising event at a girls' public school when a famous cellist is strangled. Paddy Callaghan, a housemistress and friend of Lindsay, is arrested, and Lindsay comes to her rescue. In *Common Murder*, a call comes in to the news desk of Lindsay's London office about a protester arrested for murder near the missile base at Brownlow Common. Lindsay is dispatched to the scene only to discover the woman in custody is her former lover, Deborah Patterson.

One reason why Lindsay is the sleuth of choice for friends facing police inquiries is her reporter's skills at successfully following leads and pitching stories to newspaper editors. Another reason is that Lindsay is gay. In *Final Edition*, Claire Ogilvie's former lover has been convicted (in Claire's opinion, unjustly) of murder. When Lindsay asks why she did not enlist the services of a professional private detective, Claire replies, "I have to say that in my experience professionally with the breed, I wouldn't expect to find one who was sympathetic to a gay woman."

McDermid is on familiar turf in *Union Jack* when she brings her amateur detective back to Sheffield, England, after three years in San Francisco. Lindsay attends an Amalgamated Media Workers' conference to conduct research for her dissertation on women in the trade union movement. Her old colleague, Tom "Union" Jack, plunges to his death from Lindsay's tenth-floor window, and Lindsay becomes the prime suspect.

In this first series of novels, gay subculture is openly portrayed. McDermid's works are consistent with popular fiction in the 1970s for their positive portrayal of homosexual characters engaged in a wide range of professions and with relationships and problems common to heterosexual characters. Readers new to this series should read the books in order of publication as Lindsay undergoes dramatic changes throughout. Readers who enjoy this series might consider books by Claire McNab and Lauren Wright Douglas.

McDermid's second series character debuts in *Dead Beat*, a novel about Kate Brannigan, a conventional British private detective. Kate is the female and junior half of the Manchester firm of Mortensen and Brannigan, which usually investigates computer fraud and security systems. Through her lover, rock journalist Richard Barclay, Kate is drawn into a hunt for a rock star's missing friend and a subsequent murder investigation. In the second novel, *Kick Back*, Kate investigates a bizarre case of real estate fraud for a contractor whose installed conservatories are vanishing, and she finds a scam going sour, resulting in murder.

In a 1993 article for the *Scotsman*, McDermid wrote, "The challenge I face is to create situations that allow my characters to develop. Unlike Miss Marple and Hercule Poirot, the modern series detective is not a creature who remains fixed in amber like a strand of dinosaur DNA." Readers who appreciate Kate Brannigan would also enjoy English investigator Anna Lee in the series by Liza Cody.

MYSTERY FICTION

Lindsay Gordon Series

Report for Murder. London: Women's Press; New York: St. Martin's Press, 1987.

Common Murder. London: Women's Press, 1989.

Final Edition. London: Women's Press, 1991; as *Open and Shut*. New York: St. Martin's Press, 1991.

Union Jack. London: Women's Press, 1993.

Kate Brannigan Series

Dead Beat. London: Gollancz, 1992; New York: St. Martin's Press, 1993.

Kick Back. London: Gollancz, 1993; as *Kickback*. New York: St. Martin's Press, 1993.

Crack Down. Forthcoming.

JUANA R. YOUNG

JILL McGOWN (1947–)

Jill McGown of Colby, England, is the author of five mystery novels featuring the professional and personal partnership of Inspector Lloyd (whose first name has yet to be revealed) and Inspector Judy Hill, as well as four other nonseries detective novels.

Although the five Lloyd-Hill novels are entertainingly baffling and pleasantly readable as police procedurals, the deepening relationship between Judy Hill and Lloyd commands at least as much interest as do the criminal investigations in which they are involved. In addition to solving murders, the two are forced to resolve a number of issues: their love and Lloyd's desire to marry Judy; Judy's paralysis about her marriage; Judy's ambition and the overt sexism she must confront when she is promoted; and most important, the meshing of their private lives with their professional careers. McGown portrays their increasing emotional and physical entanglement, as well as their frequent rows and subsequent reconciliations, in the context of their developing careers and the failing Hill marriage.

Inspectors Lloyd and Hill are introduced in *A Perfect Match* as colleagues in the Stansfield CID—Lloyd, a detective inspector, and Judy Hill, a detective sergeant. Theirs is a longtime friendship initiated in London sixteen years earlier when their mutual attraction was halted by Judy's refusal to engage in an affair with the married Lloyd. Since then, much has happened to the two of them: Judy has married a computer salesman and moved to Nottingham with him, and thence to Stansfield, when her husband was transferred to that town; Lloyd has divorced and returned to Stansfield where he grew up and where his career began. Now Judy's marriage—which was never much of a relationship—is unraveling, and as she and Lloyd study the events leading to the murder of merry widow Julia Mitchell, the two detectives, after much thought and discussion—and a few false starts—at last become lovers.

Murder at the Old Vicarage combines the investigation of the Christmas Eve murder of an abusive husband with Judy's slow journey toward a decision to abandon her emotionless marriage. The emerging details of the victim's manipulative treatment of his wife force Judy to admit that her own marriage is turning her into a pawn—of her husband and his parents—and when she is injured in the violent conclusion of the investigation, her brush with mortality propels her at last toward a decision to leave her husband, Michael.

In *Gone to Her Death*, Judy and Lloyd pursue the murderer of the beautiful—and promiscuous—wife of the headmaster of a nearby school, even as they struggle with guilt about their illicit relationship. Lloyd has been promoted to chief inspector, while Judy's own promotion to detective inspector is in the works, and the two must deal, not only with career success, but with Judy's continuing inability to leave Michael, who has begged her to remain with him until her transfer to another town. Once again, there are connections between the detectives' professional and personal lives. Judy's unwillingness to think badly of Michael parallels her misreading of facts she has collected about the murder, and in both cases, Lloyd forces her to face reality, interpret the signs correctly, and draw the right conclusions.

With the Hill marriage no longer a problem, and with Judy and Lloyd sharing Lloyd's flat, they are faced with a new set of personal dilemmas in *The Murders of Mrs. Austin and Mrs. Beale*. Judy has earned her promotion; furthermore, she is temporarily in command at Malworth, and there are rumblings that should a proposed rape squad become a reality, she might first rise to Lloyd's rank and then, finally, outrank him. Lloyd is torn. Meanwhile, a double murder with ties to both Stansfield and Malworth throws Judy and Lloyd into partnership on the job again.

The Other Woman finds Judy Hill settled into a flat in Malworth at the order of her superior officer, who believes that police detectives should live in the towns in which they work. Although she is unhappy with her colleagues at Malworth, she enjoys having her own flat for the first time in her life, and when Lloyd manages to get her transferred back to Stansfield, she refuses to return to his flat. As they sort out the changing dynamics of their relationship, they must also discover who is responsible for the deaths of two women involved with the same man.

Of Jill McGown's other crime novels, one—*Murder Movie*—is also a police procedural with romance (this time between suspects) thrown in for spice. *The Stalking Horse* features amateur detective Bill Holt, who is working to clear his name of a murder charge, while *An Evil Hour* follows the work of private investigator Harry Lambert.

Readers who enjoy the Lloyd–Judy Hill series for its engaging pair of sleuths might also consider the novels of Frances Fyfield, Elizabeth George, Carolyn G. Hart, Lucille Kallen, Susan Kelly, Anne Perry, Elizabeth Peters, and Audrey Peterson.

MYSTERY FICTION

Writing as Jill McGown

Record of Sin. London: Macmillan, 1985.

An Evil Hour. London: Macmillan, 1986; New York: St. Martin's Press, 1987.

The Stalking Horse. London: Macmillan, 1987; New York: St. Martin's Press, 1988.

Murder Movie. New York: St. Martin's Press; London: Macmillan, 1990.

Judy Hill and Lloyd Series

A Perfect Match. New York: St. Martin's Press; London: Macmillan, 1983.

Murder at the Old Vicarage. New York: St. Martin's Press, 1988; as *Redemption*. London: Macmillan, 1988.

Gone to Her Death. New York: St. Martin's Press, 1989; as *Death of a Dancer*. London: Macmillan, 1989.

The Murders of Mrs. Austin and Mrs. Beale. New York: St. Martin's Press; London: Macmillan, 1991.

The Other Woman. London: Macmillan, 1992; New York: St. Martin's Press, 1993.

Murder—Now and Then. New York: St. Martin's Press, 1993.

Writing as Elizabeth Chaplin

Hostage to Fortune. London: Scribners, 1992; New York: Mysterious Press, 1993.

CRITICAL BIBLIOGRAPHY

Pike, B. A. "McGown, Jill." In *Twentieth Century Crime and Mystery Writers*, ed. Lesley Henderson. 3rd ed. Chicago and London: St. James, 1991, pp. 748–49.

EDELMA HUNTLEY

CHARLOTTE MacLEOD (1922–   )

Charlotte MacLeod was born on November 12, 1922, in Bath, New Brunswick, Canada; in her author's note to *A Pint of Murder*, she comments, "Canada is a vast land of endless variety and frequent mystery. To a Canadian child growing up in another country, it was always the place where the stories came from." MacLeod's first two mystery novels, *Mystery of the White Knight* and *Next Door to Danger*, were aimed at a young-adult audience. She is best known for her four series of adult mysteries: two set in Massachusetts and two, written under the name Alisa Craig, set in Canada. MacLeod is a cofounder and president of the American Crime Writers League. She has won a variety of awards: five American Mystery Awards (two of them as Alisa Craig), a Nero Wolfe Award, two Edgar nominations, and a lifetime achievement award at the twenty-third Bouchercon convention.

MacLeod's first mystery novel, *Rest You Merry*, has an honored place in detective fiction as arguably the most hilarious Christmas detective novel ever written. In that novel, series protagonist Peter Shandy is under siege due to the Christmastime-decorating obsessions of his neighbors; he plots an absurdly wonderful revenge, which backfires.

Like all the characters in MacLeod's novels, Shandy comes surrounded by an extensive web of relationships, objects, rituals, and places. Balaclava Agricultural College, where Shandy teaches as an agronomist, is presented complete with philosophy, customs, a president of mythic proportions, and an elaborate history which continues to appear in a variety of different forms, including selected chunks from the doggerel archives of Balaclava's own poet laureate, Corydon Buggins.

The opening novel of MacLeod's second Massachusetts series are even more dominated by the past. Set in the historic old Beacon Hill area, *The Family Vault* features the thicket of family entanglements surrounding Sarah Kelling Kelling (the repetitive-sounding name caused by her marriage to an older first cousin, who also served as her trustee when she was orphaned). Over the course of the novels, Sarah moves some distance away from the claustrophobic presence of the past, acquiring a second husband and a new last name, but she never relinquishes—nor is relinquished by—her clan of eccentric, bizarre, and generally demented relatives.

MacLeod's two Canadian detective series, written under the name Alisa Craig, are equally dense with unlikely past relationships and past histories. In the Madoc Rhys and Janet Wadman series, family relationships are prominent. In the Grub-and-Stakers series, as in the Peter Shandy novels, MacLeod creates an entire town complete with founders, a history, a favored sport, and an endangered species of plant. The wild inventiveness and extravagance seen in the other series are even more spectacular in the Grub-and-Stakers series.

MacLeod's novels are particularly notable for the exuberance of detail, the vivid eccentricity of her characters, and the sweeping force of her humor. In a MacLeod novel, anything is possible. For new readers, going chronologically through each series is probably the easiest. MacLeod's novels are difficult to compare with anything in the known universe. Ngaio Marsh's novel *Death of a Peer*, with its charming and eccentric Lamprey family, is one possibility for readers looking for MacLeod-like material. A writer whose humor is more sophisticated than MacLeod's but similar in its extravagance of detail is Sarah Caudwell. Some of the humorously eccentric characters in Emma Lathen's John Putnam Thatcher series may also appeal to MacLeod fans.

MYSTERY FICTION

Writing as Charlotte MacLeod

Grab Bag. New York: Avon, 1987.

Peter Shandy Series

Rest You Merry. New York: Doubleday, 1978; London: Collins, 1979.

The Luck Runs Out. New York: Doubleday, 1979; London: Collins, 1981.

Wrack and Rune. New York: Doubleday; London: Collins, 1982.

Something the Cat Dragged In. New York: Doubleday, 1983; London: Collins, 1984.

The Curse of the Giant Hogweed. New York: Doubleday, 1985.

The Corpse in Oozak's Pond. London: Collins, 1986; New York: Mysterious Press, 1987.

Vane Pursuit. New York: Mysterious Press; London: Collins, 1989.

An Owl Too Many. New York: Mysterious Press, 1991.

Something in the Water. New York: Mysterious Press/ Warner, 1994.

Sarah Kelling and Max Bittersohn Series

The Family Vault. New York: Doubleday, 1979; London: Collins, 1980.

The Withdrawing Room. New York: Doubleday, 1980; London: Collins, 1981.

The Palace Guard. New York: Doubleday, 1981; London: Collins, 1982.

The Bilbao Looking Glass. New York: Doubleday; London: Collins, 1983.

The Convivial Codfish. New York: Doubleday; London: Collins, 1984.

The Plain Old Man. New York: Doubleday; London: Collins, 1985.

The Recycled Citizen. London: Collins, 1987; New York: Mysterious Press, 1988.

The Silver Ghost. London: Collins, 1987; New York: Mysterious Press, 1988.

The Gladstone Bag. London: Collins, 1989; New York: Mysterious Press, 1990.

The Resurrection Man. New York: Mysterious Press, 1993.

Writing as Alisa Craig

The Terrible Tide. New York: Doubleday, 1983; London: Hale, 1985.

Janet Wadman and Madoc Rhys Series

A Pint of Murder. New York: Doubleday, 1980.

Murder Goes Mumming. New York: Doubleday, 1981.

A Dismal Thing to Do. New York: Doubleday, 1986.

Trouble in the Brasses. New York: Avon, 1989.

The Wrong Rite. New York: William Morrow, 1992.

The Grub-and-Stakers Series

The Grub-and-Stakers Move a Mountain. New York: Doubleday, 1981.

The Grub-and-Stakers Quilt a Bee. New York: Doubleday, 1985.

The Grub-and-Stakers Pinch a Poke. New York: Doubleday, 1988.

The Grub-and-Stakers Spin a Yarn. New York: Avon, 1990.

The Grub-and-Stakers House a Haunt. New York: William Morrow, 1993.

CRITICAL BIBLIOGRAPHY

Bakerman, Jane S. "Bloody Balaclava: Charlotte MacLeod's Campus Comedy Mysteries." *Mystery Fancier*, 7 (Jan./Feb. 1983): 23–29.
———. "MacLeod, Charlotte." In *Twentieth Century Crime and Mystery Writers*, ed. Lesley Henderson. 3rd ed. Chicago: St. James Press, 1991, pp. 703–5.
Chouteau, Neysa. "Hanky-Panky in the Middle Ages—and Older: Charlotte MacLeod's Use of Romance as Subplot." *Clues: A Journal of Detection*, 6 (Fall/Winter 1985): 53–59.
Marks, Jeffrey. "Murder Most Cozy: An Interview with Charlotte MacLeod." *The Armchair Detective*, 26 (Summer 1993): 6–11.

Nichols, Victoria, and Susan Thompson. "Behind the Badge: Madoc Rhys." In *Silk Stalkings*. Berkeley, Calif.: Black Lizard Books, 1988, pp. 65–66.

————. "The Blood Runs Blue: Sarah Kelling." In *Silk Stalkings*. Berkeley, Calif.: Black Lizard Books, 1988, p. 75.

————. "A Blot in the Copybook: Peter Shandy." In *Silk Stalkings*. Berkeley, Calif.: Black Lizard Books, 1988, pp. 6–7.

————. "Museum Pieces: Max Bittersohn." In *Silk Stalkings*. Berkeley, Calif.: Black Lizard Books, 1988, pp. 187–88.

————. "Unexpected Detectives: The Grub-and-Stakers." In *Silk Stalkings*. Berkeley, Calif.: Black Lizard Books, 1988, pp. 187–88.

MaryKay Mahoney

CLAIRE McNAB (1940–)

Claire McNab was born August 4, 1940, in Melbourne, Australia. Although she recently moved to Los Angeles, she spent most of her life in Sydney, the seaport capital of New South Wales—and the setting for her detective novels featuring Detective Inspector Carol Ashton of the Sydney Police.

McNab's father made an avocation of collecting documentation on British crimes and trials, and McNab has said she was "a lover of whodunnits from an early age." All McNab's early jobs, from television production to teaching school, involved writing and language. Money that she earned from writing textbooks enabled her to devote herself full time to fiction writing. Although McNab says she did not know at the time that *Lessons in Murder* would be the first of a series, additional volumes continued to appear, one each year, through the fifth novel, *Dead Certain*.

The Australian setting adds interest to the novels; the reader will enjoy McNab's descriptive landscapes, the place names, and the flora and fauna—eucalyptus; gumtrees; jacaranda trees, with their purple mists of flowers; kookaburras; magpies; rainbow lorikeets; and the elusive koel birds. It is ironic that while McNab is the first Australian writer to be published by Naiad Press, the largest publisher of lesbian titles in the United States, her books were only later printed in Australia (starting in 1990). Naiad has been influential in shaping McNab's works. All her mysteries are edited by Katherine V. Forrest, herself the author of several lesbian detective novels.

Carol Ashton is first introduced to readers early in *Lessons in Murder*: "Inspector Carol Ashton's spectacular career had not been hindered by her cool blonde good looks[:] . . . the tanned skin, sleek hair, firm mouth, and direct green eyes so familiar from television newscasts. . . . Her presence [at the murder scene] was a testament to the power of political influence." Each novel opens with the discovery of a murder victim. The high-ranking

Ashton investigates particularly complex cases or those involving socially prominent individuals.

Ashton's exceptional good looks and her "usual smooth efficiency" make her an ideal media spokesperson, a role that McNab uses to examine such issues as the media's relentless invasion of personal privacy and their power to shape the public agenda. Throughout the five novels in the series, a dramatic conflict persists between Carol's identities as the media darling, the police officer exposing secrets to solve crimes, and the closeted lesbian trying to come to terms with her own secret life.

Early in the first novel, Carol meets Sybil Quade, a schoolteacher, and throughout the next four books their relationship continues and develops, though not always smoothly. In *Fatal Reunion*, Carol's ex-lover is accused of murdering her husband, the man she had left Carol to return to, and her call for Carol's help creates problems for Sybil and even greater ones for Carol. In *Death Down Under*, Carol is drawn to a television news-woman who is, like Carol, a circumspect lesbian afraid of the effect that exposure will have on her career. The murder victim in *Cop Out* is married but is a closeted bisexual, and Carol must examine her own attitudes as she deals with his homophobic family.

In *Dead Certain*, Sybil increasingly rejects homosexual invisibility and urges Carol to join her in this new openness and civil rights activism. Their relationship also allows McNab to explore her character's sexual pursuits. Her sex scenes, however, seem more like a marketing strategy than anything else. The books are clearly meant to appeal to a lesbian audience, although McNab says, "I'm writing for anyone who will read the book" (Murrie interview, 1991). Readers who enjoy McNab's mysteries might also try those by Katherine V. Forrest, Mary Wings, Barbara Wilson, and Karen Saum.

MYSTERY FICTION

Lessons in Murder. Tallahassee, Fla.: Naiad Press, 1988; St. Leonard's, NSW, Australia: Allen and Unwin, 1990.

Fatal Reunion. Tallahassee, Fla.: Naiad Press, 1989; St. Leonard's, NSW, Australia: Allen and Unwin, 1990.

Death Down Under. Tallahassee, Fla.: Naiad Press; St. Leonard's, NSW, Australia: Allen and Unwin, 1990.

Cop Out. Tallahassee, Fla.: Naiad Press; St. Leonard's, NSW, Australia: Allen and Unwin, 1991.

Dead Certain. Tallahassee, Fla.: Naiad Press, 1992; as *Off Key*. St. Leonard's, NSW, Australia: Allen and Unwin, 1992.

Body Guard. Tallahassee, Fa.: Naiad Press, 1994

CRITICAL BIBLIOGRAPHY

Murrie, Jon. [Interview]. *Advertiser* (Adelaide, Australia), 14 Sept. 1991.

LOIS A. MARCHINO

MARGARET MARON (?–   )

Margaret Maron was born in Gainsboro, N.C. She studied at the University of North Carolina in Greensboro and Charlotte. Currently she lives on her family farm, south of Raleigh, N.C. Maron has written ten mystery novels and various short stories, which have won her awards such as an Agatha, two Macavitys, and nominations for every major award within the field of mystery writing. She is past president of Sisters in Crime.

Seven of Maron's novels feature Lieutenant Sigrid Harald of the New York Police Department. Sigrid is a woman in her thirties who is very competent professionally but somewhat awkward in her personal relationships. She takes little interest in either her appearance or the opposite sex until she meets the dynamic artist and professor Oscar Naumann in the course of a murder investigation at a university in the first novel, *One Coffee With*.

In the subsequent novels, Sigrid learns to accept both her vulnerability and her femininity. Professionally she is both admired and feared by her colleagues because of her intelligence and aloofness. Sigrid is well aware of the fact that to some extent, she has been promoted simply because she is a woman, and for that reason she has to prove herself in an environment dominated by men. Outwardly unemotional, she has a severe hairstyle and dresses very plainly, in spite of her southern grandmother's attempts to make her more attractive. Sigrid's outward appearance is deceptive, however, as her few intimate acquaintances discover; underneath her dull clothes, Sigrid wears fine lace lingerie. Her apparent lack of femininity and detachment at work keep her colleagues guessing about her personal life. Off-duty, Sigrid relaxes by solving puzzles, at which she excels. The latter interest may explain her choice of profession as well as her success at it; she thinks logically and is good at seeing connections.

Sigrid's relationship with men is complex. Her superior, McKinnon, was on duty with her father, also a policeman, when the latter (whom Sigrid never really knew) was killed. She is curious about her father, and in the course of the series she comes to find out more about him. Although Sigrid values her independence, she is attracted to the very masculine Oscar Naumann, who makes her aware of her femininity.

As far as justice is concerned, Sigrid's prime concern is to solve murders, of course, and to see that the criminals are punished. If, in the course of her investigation, however, she discovers that one of her suspects may have been involved in something illegal innocently or because of altruistic motives, such as protecting a loved one, she may turn a blind eye to aspects that do not directly affect her ability to bring the real criminal to court.

Sigrid is a feminist who hates being treated condescendingly by anyone because of her sex, but unlike some detectives such as Sara Paretsky's V. I. Warshawski, she does not talk in a tough way, and in this sense she does not fit into the tradition of the female hard-boiled detective of the 1980s.

With *Bloody Kin, Bootlegger's Daughter*, and *Southern Discomfort*, Maron shifts her setting from New York City to her native rural North Carolina, whose atmosphere she evokes very skillfully. In *Bloody Kin*, a minor character in the Sigrid Harald series, Kate Honeycutt, moves from New York to her husband's family farm after her husband is killed there, supposedly in a hunting accident. As in *Bootlegger's Daughter*, there are excellent evocative descriptions of family gatherings and southern hospitality, food, and customs.

Unlike the previous novels, *Bootlegger's Daughter* is narrated in the first person. The title heroine, Deborah Knott, is an emancipated lawyer who becomes involved in solving a murder committed some years ago, when a young woman whom she used to baby-sit asks her to clear up the mystery surrounding her mother's murder. The book also provides an excellent insight into election campaigns in the rural South, with descriptions of Deborah's appearances at church socials and political rallies as she campaigns to be elected a judge, at which she succeeds in the last novel in the series. Unlike Sigrid Harald, whose feminism she shares, Deborah is well aware of her femininity.

mysteries are a delight to read. She deals sympathetically with contemporary social issues such as AIDS, homosexuality, and lesbianism, and she portrays corruption in the police force. She depicts academic and artistic milieus very realistically in the Sigrid Harald series. Her descriptions are evocative and convincing, and her plots have all the hallmarks of the classic detective novel, with lots of red herrings, subplots, likely suspects, and excellent dialogue in the style of Dorothy L. Sayers. The latest novel is as good an introduction to any of her novels as the rest, and I am looking forward to reading the third Deborah Knott novel, which is scheduled for 1994.

MYSTERY FICTION

Bloody Kin. New York: Doubleday, 1985.

Sigrid Harald Series

One Coffee With. New York: Raven House, 1981; Leicester, U.K.: Ulverscroft, 1991.

Death of a Butterfly. New York: Doubleday, 1984; Leicester, U.K.: Ulverscroft, 1991.

Death in Blue Folders. New York: Doubleday, 1985.

The Right Jack. New York: Bantam, 1987.

Baby Doll Games. New York: Bantam, 1988; London: Headline, 1991.

Corpus Christmas. New York: Doubleday, 1989.

Past Imperfect. New York: Doubleday, 1991; London: Severn House, 1993.

Deborah Knott Series

Bootlegger's Daughter. New York: Mysterious Press/Warner, 1992.

Southern Discomfort. New York: Mysterious Press/Warner, 1993.

Shooting at Loons. New York: Mysterious Press/Warner, 1994.

JOHN MICHIELSEN

NGAIO MARSH (1895–1982)

Edith Ngaio Marsh was born in Christchurch, New Zealand, on April 23, 1895. Her parents encouraged her in her early interests in the theater and in reading (her father particularly loved pulp mysteries), and provided her with a strong classical education, culminating in her study of painting at the Canterbury University College School of Art. Marsh then traveled with a Shakespearean acting company throughout New Zealand, not only learning the technical aspects of the theater, which she was later to incorporate very successfully into her mysteries, but also developing her sharp ear for dialogue. In 1928, she traveled to England for the first time, an event she described as a homecoming. This sense of both belonging to England and also of having come to the country as an outsider is reflected in the loving but critical eye with which she views British society in her books set in England, and in the clash of British and colonial cultures in her books set in New Zealand. Still, her mysteries are firmly ensconced in the heart of England's Golden Age: it was in England on a rainy Sunday afternoon in 1931 that she began to write about her detective protagonist, Roderick Alleyn. This start grew into her first book, which was published three years later as *A Man Lay Dead*. During the next fifty years, while living alternately in New Zealand and England, Marsh wrote thirty-one additional mysteries about Alleyn, earning herself a place among the "big four" of the Golden Age mystery writers, with Margery Allingham, Agatha Christie, and Dorothy L. Sayers.

Ironically, it was not for her mysteries that Marsh wished to be remembered, but for her work in the theater as an acting coach, producer, and founder of a New Zealand Shakespeare company. For this work, she won many awards, culminating in 1966 when she was honored as Dame Commander of the Order of the British Empire. Her mysteries also garnered her kudos: in 1977, she received the Grand Master Award from the Mystery Writers of America. She died on February 18, 1982, shortly before publication of her last mystery, *Light Thickens*.

Marsh's strengths as a mystery writer are many, but greatest is her sympathetic understanding of character. No villain is ever simply evil in a Marsh mystery and no hero or heroine is ever unconflicted. Even her walk-on characters are vivid. The harried junk dealer and his harridan mother in *Clutch of Constables* and the miserable antidebutante in *Death in a White Tie* are there only to provide clues; they could be sketched in flatly and still accomplish their purpose (as was usually done in contemporary detective novels), but Marsh's brilliant ear for dialogue and deep understanding of motive makes them as memorable as her center-stage characters.

The most central of all of her characters is, of course, the detective, Roderick Alleyn. Although of noble birth, Alleyn is never supercilious or pompous; in fact, the very sympathetic nature of his character, combined with his inborn sense of authority, leads people to trust and confide in him, earning him his reputation as a great detective. In the characterization of Alleyn, Marsh pulls off a difficult coup: her detective is brilliant, sensitive, sensually handsome, and aristocratic, and yet he is at all times human, believable, and likable. Although he veers close to flippancy in the early books, Alleyn begins to deepen and mature as a character when he meets and falls in love with the gifted artist, Agatha Troy, in *Artists in Crime*. Troy is a complex woman. She is fiercely independent and distrustful of marriage as an institution that might interfere with her art. When she does commit to Alleyn, at the end of *Death in a White Tie*, she does so secure in the knowledge that he recognizes her genius and has sworn to support her art at the expense of his own career, if necessary. Their marriage becomes the firm emotional base on which Alleyn relies throughout the remaining books.

Marsh's permanent supporting cast is equally well drawn and includes the loyal and pragmatic Inspector Fox, Alleyn's assistant at Scotland Yard; the bombastic journalist, Nigel Bathgate; and Alleyn's charming mother, Lady Alleyn, who knows all the right people and says all the right things. However, the best of the supporting players are those who are not continuing characters but rather burst forth in individual books to be suspected and dissected by Alleyn, who is, as always, humane but unwavering in his search for the truth. Although these characters are legion in the March canon, the best must be the portrait of the Lampreys, members of an eccentric, aristocratic family without financial means who suddenly become wealthy after the head of the family gets skewered in their apartment elevator (*Death of a Peer*). Like the Lampreys, most of Marsh's suspects tend to be clustered in various types of families so that the reader can watch them interact before the act of death: groups of people traveling on shipboard, theater companies, and a class of student artists, among others. These closed groups give Marsh the opportunity to display her characters, not only in isolation, but also as they react to, and act on, each other, giving them a depth not usually achieved in the detective fiction of this period. Because Marsh's murders always occur several chapters into her books, her readers know, and sometimes mourn, her victims, creating an emotional involvement that is rare in the Golden Age puzzle plot.

Marsh's mysteries do not rely on character alone, however. Closely plotted and following all Golden Age rules of fair play, her books feature bizarrely clever murderers who bludgeon their victims with jeroboams of champagne, decapitate them with ancient weapons, shoot them by means of booby traps in pianos, and poison them horribly with acid. Marsh's sense of theater is evident, not only in her dramatic murder methods, but also in her careful (and eminently fair) staging of the murders in theaterlike sites and in her vivid, detailed settings which also reveal the painter's eye that she developed in her early art studies.

Although all Marsh's mysteries can be enjoyed for their characterizations alone and can be read in chronological order for a sense of the progression of Alleyn's life, the best of her work is found in her middle years. Most enjoyable among these books is *Death of a Peer*, featuring the hapless Lampreys, and her theater books, especially *Killer Dolphin*. Readers who enjoy Marsh novels may also enjoy mysteries by Margery Allingham, Catherine Aird, Agatha Christie, Martha Grimes, and Dorothy L. Sayers.

MYSTERY FICTION

Roderick Alleyn Series

A Man Lay Dead. London: Bles, 1934; New York: Sheridan, 1942.

Enter a Murderer. London: Bles, 1935; New York: Pocket Books, 1941.

The Nursing Home Murder, with Dr. Henry Jellett. London: Bles, 1935; New York: Sheridan, 1941.

Death in Ecstasy. London: Bles, 1936; New York: Sheridan, 1941.

Vintage Murder. London: Bles, 1937; New York: Sheridan, 1940.

Artists in Crime. London: Bles; New York: Furman, 1938.

Death in a White Tie. London: Bles; New York: Furman, 1938.

Overture to Death. London: Bles; New York: Furman, 1939.

Death at the Bar. London: Collins; Boston: Little, Brown, 1940.

Death of a Peer. Boston: Little, Brown, 1940; as *A Surfeit of Lampreys*. London: Collins, 1941.

Death and the Dancing Footman. Boston: Little, Brown, 1941; London: Collins, 1942.

Colour Scheme. Boston: Little, Brown; London: Collins, 1943.

Died in the Wool. Boston: Little, Brown; London: Collins, 1945.

Final Curtain. Boston: Little, Brown; London: Collins, 1947.

Swing, Brother, Swing. London: Collins; as *A Wreath for Rivera.* Boston: Little, Brown, 1949.

Opening Night. London: Collins; as *Night at the Vulcan.* Boston: Little, Brown, 1951.

Spinsters in Jeopardy. Boston: Little, Brown, 1953; London: Collins, 1954.

Scales of Justice. Boston: Little, Brown; London: Collins, 1955.

Death of a Fool. Boston: Little, Brown, 1956; as *Off with His Head.* London: Collins, 1957.

Singing in the Shrouds. Boston: Little, Brown, 1958; London: Collins, 1959.

False Scent. Boston: Little, Brown, 1959; London: Collins, 1960.

Hand in Glove. Boston: Little, Brown; London: Collins, 1962.

Dead Water. Boston: Little, Brown, 1963; London: Collins, 1964.

Killer Dolphin. Boston: Little, Brown, 1966; as *Death at the Dolphin.* London: Collins, 1967.

Clutch of Constables. London: Collins, 1968; Boston: Little, Brown, 1969.

When in Rome. London: Collins, 1970; Boston: Little, Brown, 1971.

Tied Up in Tinsel. London: Collins; Boston: Little, Brown, 1972.

Black as He's Painted. Boston: Little, Brown; London: Collins, 1974.

Last Ditch. Boston: Little, Brown; London: Collins, 1977.

Grave Mistake. Boston: Little, Brown; London: Collins, 1978.

Photo-Finish. Boston: Little, Brown; London: Collins, 1980.

Light Thickens. Boston: Little, Brown; London: Collins, 1982.

CRITICAL BIBLIOGRAPHY

Acheson, C. "Cultural Ambivalence: Ngaio Marsh's New Zealand Detective Fiction." *Journal of Popular Culture*, 19 (1985): 159–74.

Ball, John. "A Visit with Dame Ngaio Marsh." *Mystery*, 3 July 1981, pp. 23–25.

Bargainnier, E. F. "Ngaio Marsh." In *Ten Women of Mystery*, ed. Earl F. Bargainnier. Bowling Green, Ohio: Bowling Green University Popular Press, pp. 78–105.

———. "Ngaio Marsh's 'Theatrical' Murders." *The Armchair Detective* 10, no. 2 (1977): 175–81.

———. "Roderick Alleyn: Ngaio Marsh's Oxonian Superintendent." *The Armchair Detective* 11, no. 1 (1978): 63–71.

Dooley, Allan C., and Linda J. Dooley. "Rereading Ngaio Marsh." In *Art in Crime Writing*, ed. Bernard Benstock. New York: St. Martin's, 1983, pp. 33–48.

Elsom, J. "At the End of the World." *Contemporary Review* 237 (1980): 78–83.
Mann, Jessica. *Deadlier than the Male*. New York: Macmillan, 1981, pp. 218–33.
Marsh, Ngaio. "Birth of a Sleuth." *Writer*, April 1977, pp. 23–25.
———. *Black Beech and Honeydew*. Boston: Little, Brown, 1965; London: Collins,
    1966. [Autobiography.]
McDorman, Kathryne Slate. *Ngaio Marsh*. Boston: Twayne, 1991.
White, Jean M. "Murder Most Tidy." *New Republic*, 30 July 1977, pp. 36–38.

JENNIFER SMITH

LIA MATERA (?–   )

Since Lia Matera is herself a lawyer, it is not surprising that her two heroines are also lawyers. Matera graduated from Hastings College of Law,
where she served as editor of the *Constitutional Law Review*. She later
served as a teaching fellow at Stanford Law School. Matera and her son
currently live in Santa Cruz, California.

Matera began her mystery writing career with the 1987 publication of
Where Lawyers Fear to Tread (nominated for an Anthony Award), which
introduced her first series character, Willa Jansson. Willa is a law student
in San Francisco who becomes acting editor-in-chief of the law review after
the current editor is murdered. As other students are murdered, Willa becomes an amateur sleuth (à la Nancy Drew, one of Willa's favorite childhood heroines). In *A Radical Departure* (nominated for an Anthony Award
and an Edgar Allan Poe Award) and the subsequent Jansson novels, Willa
is a lawyer who finds herself dragged into other murder investigations.

Willa Jansson's life is filled with problems, some comic and others serious. After an affair in college, Willa suffers from genital herpes (perhaps
the first mystery series character to do so). She also has to deal with the
extremist views of her parents, a pair of dedicated left-wing activists. (Her
mother is a major source of humor in the novels since she inevitably says
the wrong thing at the wrong time.) In addition, Willa faces inner conflicts
as she tries to balance the more liberal beliefs of her upbringing with the
interests of her often-conservative legal associates. Finally, she has an unfulfilling and unconsummated relationship with a homicide lieutenant, Don
Surgelato.

In *The Smart Money*, Matera introduced her second series character
Laura DiPalma, another lawyer who finds herself involved in murders.
However, the three DiPalma novels are more serious in tone and themes.
Laura DiPalma has rejected the smalltown values to which she was exposed
while growing up (bigotry, materialism, and concern for social position),
and she tries to use her legal skills and knowledge to benefit others. Nonetheless, at times she recognizes in herself similar negative values: a yuppie's

pride in possessions and the desire to win cases more for self-gratification than for justice or concern for clients.

Among the serious issues examined in the DiPalma novels is the process by which people become victims. In the series, Laura becomes aware of other characters who are trapped in various ways: some by family expectations, some by their environment, some by physical disabilities, and some by the failure to overcome their own feelings of anger and frustration.

Another recurring issue in the DiPalma novels is that of taking moral responsibility for one's acts. *The Good Fight*, one of Matera's best novels, examines moral responsibility (or the lack thereof) from a number of angles. Laura comes to realize in the course of the novel that even well-intentioned acts can have negative consequences.

Both series have a number of similarities. In each, the main character serves as narrator. In the Jansson novels, Willa provides witty and sarcastic insights; while in the DiPalma novels, Laura can reveal to the reader her fears, doubts, and frustrations. Neither woman is a professional detective; as a result, little violence occurs "on-stage," and neither woman is skilled in self-defense techniques. Finally, both women are modern professionals who struggle to deal with sexist attitudes in the workplace, a world of shifting moral values, and tenuous emotional and sexual relationships.

The Jansson and DiPalma novels differ from the current trend toward hard-boiled women PIs (as seen in Sara Paretsky's V. I. Warshawski or Sue Grafton's Kinsey Millhone). While, like Paretsky and Grafton, Matera examines the role of women in American society and current moral issues, her characters are pulled into becoming investigators by circumstances beyond their control. Her bright amateurs are more like Barbara Wilson's character of Pam Nilsen, who finds herself involved in a crime that she explores out of curiosity and a desire to help and protect those about whom she cares.

Since the later novels in both series often refer to events in the early ones, the books should be read sequentially. For a reader coming to Matera for the first time, I recommend starting with the Laura DiPalma series. Readers who like Matera's novels might also enjoy works by Rita Mae Brown and Barbara Wilson.

MYSTERY FICTION

Willa Jansson Series

Where Lawyers Fear to Tread. New York: Bantam, 1987.

Hidden Agenda. New York: Bantam, 1988.

A Radical Departure. New York: Bantam, 1988.

Prior Convictions. New York: Simon and Schuster, 1991.

Laura DiPalma Series

The Smart Money. New York: Bantam, 1988.
The Good Fight. New York: Simon and Schuster, 1990.
A Hard Bargain. New York: Simon and Schuster, 1992.
Face Value. New York: Simon and Schuster, 1994.

DAVID CONNOR WALLACE, JR.

M.R.D. MEEK (1918–   )

Margaret Reid Duncan Meek was born in 1918 in Greenock, Scotland. She attended a commercial college in Glasgow, worked as a secretary-typist, and after her marriage to a physician, she worked for him as a receptionist. She also spent four years in Germany with her husband when he served there in the British Army. After her husband's death in 1959, Meek articled with a solicitor, passed all examinations, and received a law degree from London University. She practiced as a solicitor in London and Cornwall and married Colin Meek, a retired government physicist. After her own retirement in 1978 in Cornwall, Meek started writing detective fiction (in 1980). Since then she has written a series of ten detective novels featuring Lennox Kemp.

When readers first encounter Kemp, he is working as an operative at very low wages for the tight-fisted owner of Macready's Detective Agency. He has had to take this job because both his marriage and his professional life have fallen apart. In order to pay off his ex-wife's gambling debts, he embezzled his clients' trust funds and consequently was disbarred by the Law Society. In the course of the series he is reinstated as a lawyer and then goes to work for the firm of Gillorns in Newtown, outside London. He finds, however, that his legal work does not prevent him from investigating mysteries in which the police force is not interested or that it seems incapable of solving.

Kemp is an affable, portly man in his forties, who is described as looking like a teddy bear. Because he looks so harmless, many people trust and confide in him. He is not particularly good looking and yet women are attracted to him and he to them; this forms the basis for some interesting subplots in the novels. Kemp's intelligence and talent for remembering details and noticing unusual patterns in people's behavior frequently allow him to see aspects of a case that the police detectives have overlooked, although he does call for police assistance when necessary. Since he himself has been on the wrong side of the law, he is very tolerant of other people's behavior.

One of the reasons why, in *A Mouthful of Sand*, his unadventuresome fiancée, Penelope Marsden, breaks up with Kemp is that she senses that his six years as a detective have given him a certain insight into how people live. She feels that they have provided him with an unorthodox perception that is rare in the legal field, which tends to make him impatient with the statutes. This may be the cause, she reflects, for his sneaking aptitude for the sleazy side of life—his preference for it, even. She also accuses him, quite justifiably, of getting emotionally involved with the women in his cases.

Meek excels at describing locales. Her depictions of rural Scotland and Cornwall, where some of her novels are set, are extremely evocative. Newtown, where Kemp moves after he takes up practicing law again, is typical of some of the towns that have sprung up around London since World War II. Kemp is critical of the utilitarian ugliness of towns such as these, and a recurring theme in the novels is the rape of the English countryside by land developers.

Contrasting with these urban settings are descriptions of great English country manors in which some of the novel's characters live, and many of the plots of Meek's novels revolve around crimes committed to acquire possession of or hold on to them.

Meek's well-drawn characters come from all walks of life, from English aristocrats to the middle and working classes and people trying to eke out an existence while living on welfare. Kemp shows a great deal of sympathy for welfare recipients; quite often they are victims of the system or their circumstances, and he can understand why they try to cheat the system at times, as in *This Blessed Plot*. Meek's fascination with the workings of the human mind is demonstrated by Kemp's attempts to understand the motives of the characters with whom he comes into contact; like most criminals, they are motivated by greed, jealousy, and lust. Human pathological behavior is a common theme in all the novels, and madness, repressed sexual desires, incest, and drug addiction are other common topics. The nature of evil in the universe also interests Meek, as shown by some of her characters who are diabolic in the true sense of the word: they have no sense of morality.

Meek's own experience with the British legal system allows her to give an extremely credible description of Kemp's work as a lawyer. Quite a few of the cases he handles involve unraveling family disputes about family inheritances, insurance scams, and land deals.

Although the novels form a series and certain characters introduced in the earlier ones reappear in the later ones, they may be read in any order. *This Blessed Plot* and *A Mouthful of Sand* provide a good introduction to Meek's work. Those readers who enjoy Nicolas Freeling's detective novels will especially like Meek's mysteries.

MYSTERY FICTION

Lennox Kemp Series

With Flowers That Fell. London: Hale, 1983.

Hang the Consequences. London: Collins, 1984; New York: Scribner's, 1985.

The Sitting Ducks. London: Collins, 1984.

The Split Second. London: Collins, 1985; New York: Scribner's, 1987.

In Remembrance of Rose. London: Collins, 1986; New York: Scribner's, 1987.

A Worm of Doubt. London: Collins, 1987; New York: Scribner's, 1988.

A Mouthful of Sand. London: Collins, 1988; New York: Scribner's, 1989.

A Loose Connection. London: Collins, 1989; New York: Scribner's, 1989.

This Blessed Plot. London: Collins, 1990; New York: Scribner's, 1990.

Touch and Go. London: Crime Club, 1992; New York: Scribner's, 1993.

CRITICAL BIBLIOGRAPHY

Huang, Jim. "Meek, M.R.D." In *Twentieth Century Crime and Mystery Writers*, ed. Lesley Henderson. 3rd ed. Chicago and London: St. James, 1991, pp. 760–61.

JOHN MICHIELSEN

ANNETTE MEYERS (1934–   )

Although she was born in New York City (during the mid-1930s) and spent the first four years of her life living in the Bronx, Annette Meyers, née Brafman, grew up in Toms River, New Jersey, on a chicken ranch, where her father's great-uncle was trying to establish a community of Jewish farmers. After college she taught high school English for five years and wrote stories. In 1960 she took a cut in salary, gave up tenure, and became involved in the "glamorous life" of the theater by going to work for producer Harold Prince. She raised money and collaborated with the creative staff on all his productions through 1976, including *Fiddler on the Roof, Cabaret, Zorba, Company, Follies*, and *Candida*. Between 1976 and 1979 Meyers completed two novels for which she was unable to find an agent or a publisher. She went back to teaching but eventually became a headhunter placing stockbrokers with Wall Street firms, a vocation she still pursues.

One day during an interview, a client disappeared to make a phone call, leaving her sitting in the Four Seasons Restaurant with his attaché case.

After half an hour, she found him huddled in a phone booth. The thought struck her: "What if I open the door and he slides out dead?" At that moment, Annette Meyers became a crime novelist, and since then she has combined her need to write with her insider knowledge of the brokerage business. Amid the sex, greed, and illegal drugs of the financial world, she has been plotting gory death among the cutthroats and white-collar players on Wall Street.

"A good headhunter," Meyers has written, "is by nature an instinctive detective." Similarly, so her central protagonist, Leslie Wetzon, is both a high-quality listener and a nosey parker. To offset Wetzon's basic trust in people (bred of her rural upbringing and theatrical background), she is teamed with the harder-edged Xenia Smith, who is sufficiently streetwise to protect her partner from users who would take advantage of her. It is a marvelous combination.

The Big Killing begins with the death—in a phone booth—of a client who leaves Leslie a briefcase containing illegal drugs, a gun, and a tape cassette full of financially incriminating information. During the ensuing police investigation she meets Sergeant Silvestri, who attracts her with his gentle sexuality and angers her with his paternalism. The Russian émigré community of Brooklyn's Little Odessa draws Leslie out of her familiar haunts and into a billion-dollar scam involving the elderly rich in *Tender Death*. Emboldened by her previous detective experience and knowledge of the workings of the New York Police Department, Wetzon takes greater risks with each novel, often endangering her own life as she searches for those who have taken the lives of others.

The mysterious death of one of Wall Street's legendary figures, Goldie Barnes (who collapses at his retirement party), sets Smith and Wetzon to investigating the inside of the brokerage business. Their tracing of the labyrinthian interconnections of the financial world parallels in complexity the aggressive plotting of the book itself. Smith, an inveterate reader of the Tarot, gives Leslie (as a birthday gift) a visit to a fortune-teller who predicts death and mayhem at the beginning of *Blood on the Street*. In this novel, however, Silvestri is away on a professional training course, leaving Leslie to her own devices for solving the mystery.

It is tempting to see the Smith and Wetzon books as providing *exempla* for the 1980s, little morality plays about the effects of excess, money and power when unchecked by ethics or even common decency. Annette Meyers skillfully weaves together the personal story of her protagonists with the details of life in New York City, counterposed against the values and attitudes of Wall Street. Thus, she creates a convincing fictional world combining exquisite settings and high-energy plotting with a bravura style.

Readers can begin the Smith and Wetzon series with any of the novels; the first, *The Big Killing*, still provides the best introduction. The fifth in the series, *Murder: The Musical*, combines the two worlds in Leslie's life,

Wall Street and Broadway. In addition, Annette Meyers is writing a historical mystery series with her husband, Martin, under the pseudonym of Maan Meyers. All three, to date, are set in seventeenth-century New York and follow the history of the Tonneman family.

MYSTERY FICTION

Writing as Annette Meyers

Smith and Wetzon Series

The Big Killing. New York: Bantam, 1989.
Tender Death. New York: Bantam, 1990.
The Deadliest Option. New York: Bantam, 1991.
Blood on the Street. New York: Bantam, 1992.
Murder: The Musical. New York: Bantam, 1993.
These Bones Were Made for Dancing. New York: Doubleday, 1995.

Writing as Maan Meyers (with Martin Meyers)

Tonneman Series

The Dutchman, An Historical Mystery 1664. New York: Doubleday, 1992.
The Kingsbridge Plot. New York: Doubleday, 1993.
The High Constable. New York: Doubleday, 1994.
The Two-Mile Stone. New York: Bantam, 1995.

CHARLES L. P. SILET

MARGARET MILLAR (1915–   )

Margaret Millar was born in Kitchener, Ontario, Canada, on February 5, 1915. She studied classics at the University of Toronto, but in 1938 left school to marry Kenneth Millar (also known as Ross MacDonald). The Millars took up residence in Santa Barbara, Calif., where she still lives. Both her husband and a daughter, Linda, are deceased. President of the Mystery Writers of America from 1957 to 1958, Millar received two Edgars. She was named 1965 Woman of the Year by the *Los Angeles Times*.

Margaret Millar is a remarkably consistent writer. Always a good read, one wonders why she remains in the second tier of mystery writers. She tackles social issues with relish. While she was safe enough when engaging religious cults in *How Like an Angel*, she may have been ahead of her time in treating pedophilia, in *The Fiend*, or racial animosities, in *A Stranger in*

My Grave and *Beyond This Point Are Monsters*. The audience probably caught up with her in the 1980s when she took on transvestism in *Banshee* and homosexuality and drug addiction in *Spider Webs*. *Banshee* earned her a second Edgar. (*Beast in View* was first.)

Women are at the center of most of Millar's novels. They are often victims of society, circumstances, and brutality, but sometimes villainous, manipulative, and vengeful. Frequently, her women are independent, or want to be but are trapped. Take the women in *Rose's Last Summer*: a faded actress seeking a comeback, her greedy daughter, looking for a quick buck, a wealthy woman trapped by tax laws, and her bright daughter, who is not allowed to run the family business because her two useless brothers have first call by dint of their gender. Many of her women are searching for their identity. In *The Listening Walls* a girl is willing to commit murder to escape her Mexican peasant background. The victim, a spoiled, self-indulgent, and wealthy American, suffers from manic depression, but the story is complicated by the deceased's fragile friend, who threatens to confess because the trauma of witnessing the crime has caused her to assume the guilt. In *Ask for Me Tomorrow* and *The Murder of Miranda*, women suffer agonies to stave off the inevitable march of age, while in *Spider Webs*, the defense attorney's wife is a tragic abuser of prescription medications. In *The Fiend*, painful divorce and repressed maternity fuel bizarre actions. Millar makes the reader attentive to the pain that many women suffer.

Among Millar's best portraits are those of children. In *The Fiend*, ten-year-olds Jessie and Mary Martha are victims of their parents' misbehavior, and the novel hinges on the threat of molestation by an outsider. In *Banshee*, a child disappears, and the eventual discovery of her remains sets up a search through a rogues' gallery of suspects—the too-friendly transvestite neighbor, a witch-like recluse watching the child through her binoculars, and the white-robed fanatic who twice offers a cryptic warning. To the deceased princess is contrasted her down-to-earth engaging cousin, and the surprise ending is a reminder of how precarious a child's life can be. Hardly a victim, spoiled Freddy Quinn in *The Murder of Miranda* is that fiendishly delinquent, overindulged brand of child who invites everyone's wrath while delighting readers.

While Millar did not develop a series around any one figure, she has written as many as three novels featuring a single investigator. Her first three books introduced Parker Prye, a Toronto psychiatrist; Inspector Sands of the Toronto Police was featured in two early novels and a short story; and lawyer Tom Aragon is central to three novels. Prye is a version of the consulting scientist whose ability to solve complex puzzles is coupled with eccentricity and wit. Sands, a loner, is insightful and sympathetic with those who are on the edge. We learn much about Aragon indirectly. He is married, but his wife is a medical intern in San Francisco while he lives in Los Angeles and carries on his connubiality via long distance. He works for an influential lawyer and the firm's secretary, Charity Nelson, runs the office—and Tom.

Millar employs laundry marks, diaries, and poisons—but the real revelations rest in the relationships among characters. In this, she is not unlike her husband of forty-five years, Kenneth Millar. However, while he locates his answers buried in the past, she probes the present, using the past to enrich what she finds but largely shying away from notions of tainted blood or fated families. When an individual's background *is* critical, it is often an issue of race or class.

Millar has a penchant for black comedy. Sometimes it weakens her work, as in *Wall of Eyes*, but in *The Murder of Miranda*, there is a splendid cast of human oddities. Old Mr. Van Eyck spends his days writing poison pen letters; Cordelia and Juliet, thirtyish twins, are both cunning and batty, and Freddy Quinn is the "crown-prince of royal bratdom." Miranda herself, a widow in her fifties, appears first at poolside suffering under a coating of a prescribed ointment intended to dissolve her wrinkles. While mocking, Millar also expresses sympathy for her foolishness.

Because Millar is such a master of surprise endings, readers come to look in dark corners for clues to the unexpected. To catch her at her most skillful, I recommend *How Like an Angel*, *The Fiend*, and *Beast in View*. Readers who enjoy Millar might also like Dorothy Salisbury Davis or Dorothy B. Hughes.

MYSTERY FICTION

Fire Will Freeze. New York: Random House, 1944.

Do Evil in Return. New York: Random House, 1950; London: Museum Press, 1952.

Rose's Last Summer. New York: Random House, 1952; London: Museum Press, 1954; as *The Lively Corpse*. New York: Dell, 1956.

Vanish in an Instant. New York: Random House, 1952; London: Museum Press, 1953.

Beast in View. New York: Random House; London: Gollancz, 1955.

An Air That Kills. New York: Random House, 1957; as *The Soft Talkers*. London: Gollancz, 1957.

The Listening Walls. New York: Random House; London: Gollancz, 1959.

A Stranger in My Grave. New York: Random House; London: Gollancz, 1960.

How Like an Angel. New York: Random House; London: Gollancz, 1962.

The Fiend. New York: Random House; London: Gollancz, 1964.

Beyond This Point Are Monsters. New York: Random House, 1970; London: Gollancz, 1971.

Banshee. New York: Morrow; London: Gollancz, 1983.

Spider Webs. New York: Morrow, 1986; London: Gollancz, 1987.

Parker Prye Series

The Invisible Worm. New York: Doubleday, 1941; London: Long, 1943.

The Devil Loves Me. New York: Doubleday, 1942.

The Weak-Eyed Bat. New York: Doubleday, 1942.

Inspector Sands Series

Wall of Eyes. New York: Random House, 1943.

The Iron Gates. New York: Random House, 1945; as *Taste of Fears*. London: Hale, 1950.

Tom Aragon Series

Ask for Me Tomorrow. New York: Random House, 1976; London: Gollancz, 1977.

The Murder of Miranda. New York: Random House, 1979; London: Gollancz, 1980.

Mermaid. New York: Morrow; London: Gollancz, 1982.

CRITICAL BIBLIOGRAPHY

Hoch, Edward D. "Millar, Margaret." In *Twentieth Century Crime and Mystery Writers*, ed. Lesley Henderson. 3rd ed. Chicago and London: St. James, 1991, pp. 766–77.

Lachman, Marvin. "Margaret Millar: The Checklist of an 'Unknown' Mystery Writer." *The Armchair Detective*, 3, no. 2 (1970): 85–88.

Nichols, Victoria, and Susan Thompson. "Tom Aragon." In *Silk Stalkings*. Berkeley, Calif.: Black Lizard, 1988, pp. 152–54.

Reilly, John M. "Margaret Millar." In *Ten Women of Mystery*, ed. Earl F. Bargainnier. Bowling Green, Ohio: Popular Press, 1981, pp. 225–49.

VIRGINIA S. HALE

GLADYS MITCHELL (1901–1983)

Born April 19, 1901, in the village of Cowley at Oxford, Gladys Maude Winifred Mitchell studied from 1919 to 1921 at Goldsmith's College, London, receiving a history degree from the University of London in 1926. Until her writing finally made her financially independent in 1961, she taught English and history, primarily in girls' boarding schools in the London area. She was a member of the Society of Authors, the Crime Writers' Association, and the Detection Club, and was also a fellow of the Ancient

Monuments Society. In 1976, she received the Crime Writers' Association Silver Dagger Award. In an entry in *Contemporary Authors*, published in 1983, the year of her death, she listed her politics as conservative and her religion as agnostic. Among her interests was English architecture, from Roman times to the eighteenth century, and she had an equally keen eye for English landscape and folklore; critics have noted, for example, her careful use of actual historical sites and of British Ordnance Survey maps.

It is not these devices that set her apart from her contemporaries, however, but her primary series character, Dame Beatrice Adela Lestrange Bradley, who is Mitchell's sole significant contribution to the detective genre, although she also wrote adult novels, under the pseudonym Stephen Hockaby, and children's novels. Mitchell also wrote a relatively unimportant series of detective stories under the pseudonym of Malcolm Torrie. In 1933, she contributed to *Ask a Policeman*, a Detection Club collaborative novel in which writers including Anthony Berkeley and Dorothy L. Sayers attempted to solve a mystery posed by John Rhode. Each writer wrote about a detective created by someone else.

Mitchell's Dame Beatrice is unique and fares poorly in other hands. Mitchell has created a singularly emancipated heroine, acting against a backdrop that distinctively mingles myth, folklore, Freudian theory, compassion, and practical common sense. The almost mythic figure that results has been compared by some of Mitchell's few critics to Sherlock Holmes, while by others it has been seen as a satiric attack on Agatha Christie's Miss Marple or Patricia Wentworth's Maud Silver. Certainly, Dame Beatrice possesses Holmes's erudition, grand manner, and links with the British Establishment. She is unquestionably a stark contrast to the meek, modest, and traditionally feminine heroines of Christie and Wentworth. Dame Beatrice, who, but for her tolerance and sense of humor, would seem to foreshadow the Honor Klein of Irish Murdoch's *The Severed Head*, is a study in female power. If anything, her debt is to the feminism of Virginia Woolf and to Woolf's notion, as restated from Coleridge and the Greeks, that all great minds are androgynous; it is significant that Woolf was repopularizing this idea at the time when Mitchell began her writing career. In Dame Beatrice, Mitchell creates a truly liberated woman with the brains and spirit to laugh at convention, education to produce sufficient wealth to be free of economic intimidation, and the daring to rise above partriarchal laws and rules about female behavior and appearance.

Dame Beatrice is, indeed, candidly and uncompromisingly above the law. In the first novel in the series, *Speedy Death*, she is acquitted of what she believes to be justifiable homicide. Later in the series, when referring back to this and to other deaths in which she has been implicated, she denies any sense of guilt. She stands, not for human laws, but for principles of life and justice that she has discovered through her various studies, especially of psychology. She is candid, as is her author, in taking up matters usually shunned by writers of popular fiction; *Speedy Death*, for example, involves transvestism and the advisability of birth control.

As the series progresses, Mrs. Bradley becomes Dame Beatrice who, as a psychiatrist, is consultant to the British Home Office. She is a Dame of the British Empire, a noted author, and the recipient of many degrees, both earned and honorary. She also is a brilliant player of pub darts, snooker, billiards, and bridge, and she is an expert knife thrower. Her idea of light reading is modern poetry. As do Miss Marple and Miss Silver, she knits, but at this skill she is totally inept. If her talents are not conventionally feminine, neither are her looks, which are repeatedly called "saurian" and "reptilian"; her assistant, among others, affectionately refers to her as "Mrs. Croc." She cackles, leers, and shrieks her way through the series. She is equally impervious to conventional morality. She has been married three times and is the mother of at least two sons, one a prominent attorney—Sir Ferdinand Lestrange—who sometimes assists her, and the other an expert in tropical medicine, whose education she paid for with profits from her writing. Men are, indeed, attracted to her person because of her power, and she takes lovers (sometimes young) when it suits her. Young men, women, children, animals—all gravitate to her strength. Dame Beatrice is a somewhat sardonic comment on what real female strength and autonomy might be if a woman had the resources—economic and intellectual—and daring to possess them.

Dame Beatrice changes little throughout the series, but the characters around her do. Her first Watson figure is Noel Wells, an obtuse and somewhat pompous young curate (he carries a swastika as a watch fob), who first patronizes her and then comes to admire her. Whatever his judgments, her reaction is tolerant affection. In 1942, Wells is replaced by Laura Menzies who, in *Laurels Are Poison*, is a student in a teacher-training college where a crime occurs. She abandons her career to become secretary and companion to Dame Beatrice. Over the course of time, this hearty and beer-drinking young woman acquires a husband (the future Chief Detective-Inspector Robert Gavin of New Scotland Yard) and two children. Dame Beatrice shares her homes with them.

Ideally, the Dame Beatrice Lestrange Bradley series should be read in order of publication because of the development of the style and the supporting cast through time. Realistically, few of the novels are readily available; Dame Beatrice's sexual freedom, her contempt for conventional morality, and her wisdom, age, and homeliness are well within the British tradition of eccentrics but never found Mitchell a regular publisher in the United States. Most often available through British or Canadian presses are such works as *The Saltmarsh Murders, St. Peter's Finger, Watson's Choice*, and *Spotted Hemlock*. These provide good starting points.

Readers who enjoy the Dame Beatrice series will find themselves frustrated by the absence of any similar detective fiction. Readers who enjoy Mitchell's series may also enjoy the series featuring Irene Adler by Carole Nelson Douglas, the series featuring Eleanor Roosevelt by Elliott Roosevelt, the series featuring Miss Lucilla Teatime by Colin Watson, the Susan Melville series by Evelyn E. Smith and D. B. Borton's *One for the Money*. By comparison, however, all are pale shadows of the complexity of Dame Beatrice Lestrange.

MYSTERY FICTION

Writing as Gladys Mitchell

Dame Beatrice Lestrange Bradley Series

Speedy Death. London: Gollancz; New York: Dial, 1929.

The Longer Bodies. London: Gollancz, 1930.

The Mystery of a Butcher's Shop. London: Gollancz; New York: Dial, 1930.

The Saltmarsh Murders. London: Gollancz, 1932; Philadelphia: Macrae, 1933.

Death at the Opera. London: Grayson, 1934; as *Death in the Wet*. Philadelphia: Macrae, 1934.

The Devil at Saxon Wall. London: Grayson, 1935.

Dead Men's Morris. London: Joseph, 1936.

Come Away, Death. London: Joseph, 1937.

St. Peter's Finger. London: Joseph, 1938; New York: St. Martin's, 1987.

Printer's Error. London: Joseph, 1939.

Brazen Tongue. London: Joseph, 1940.

Hangman's Curfew. London: Joseph, 1941.

When Last I Died. London: Joseph, 1941; New York: Knopf, 1942.

Laurels Are Poison. London: Joseph, 1942.

Sunset over Soho. London: Joseph, 1943.

The Worsted Viper. London: Joseph, 1943.

My Father Sleeps. London: Joseph, 1944.

The Rising of the Moon. London: Joseph, 1945; New York: St. Martin's, 1984.

Here Comes a Chopper. London: Joseph, 1946.

Death and the Maiden. London: Joseph, 1947.

The Dancing Druids. London: Joseph, 1948.

Tom Brown's Body. London: Joseph, 1949.

Groaning Spinney. London: Joseph, 1950.

The Devil's Elbow. London: Joseph, 1951.

The Echoing Strangers. London: Joseph, 1952.

Merlin's Furlong. London: Joseph, 1953.

Faintley Speaking. London: Joseph, 1954; New York: St. Martin's, 1986.

Watson's Choice. London: Joseph, 1955; New York: McKay, 1976.

Twelve Horses and the Hangman's Noose. London: Joseph; New York: British Book Centre, 1956.

The Twenty-Third Man. London: Joseph, 1957.

Spotted Hemlock. London: Joseph; New York: British Book Centre, 1958.

The Man Who Grew Tomatoes. London: Joseph; New York: London House, 1959.

Say It with Flowers. London: Joseph, 1960.

The Nodding Canaries. London: Joseph, 1961.

My Bones Will Keep. London: Joseph; New York: British Book Centre, 1962.

Adders on the Heath. London: Joseph; New York: London House, 1963.

Death of a Delft Blue. London: Joseph; New York: London House, 1964.

Pageant of Murder. London: Joseph; New York: London House, 1965.

The Croaking Raven. London: Joseph, 1966.

Skeleton Island. London: Joseph, 1967.

Three Quick and Five Dead. London: Joseph, 1968.

Dance to Your Daddy. London: Joseph, 1969.

Gory Dew. London: Joseph, 1970.

Lament for Leto. London: Joseph, 1971.

A Hearse in May-Day. London: Joseph, 1972.

The Murder of Busy Lizzie. London: Joseph, 1973.

A Javelin for Jonah. London: Joseph, 1974.

Winking at the Brim. London: Joseph, 1974.

Convent on Styx. London: Joseph, 1975.

Late, Late in the Evening. London: Joseph, 1976.

Fault in the Structure. London: Joseph, 1977.

Noonday and Night. London: Joseph, 1977.

Mingled with Venom. London: Joseph, 1978.

Wraiths and Changelings. London: Joseph, 1978.

The Mudflats of the Dead. London: Joseph, 1979.

Nest of Vipers. London: Joseph, 1979.

Uncoffin'd Clay. London: Joseph, 1980; New York: St. Martin's, 1982.

The Whispering Knights. London: Joseph, 1980.

The Death-Cap Dancers. London: Joseph; New York: St. Martin's, 1981.

Lovers, Make Moan. London: Joseph, 1981.

Death of a Burrowing Mole. London: Joseph, 1982.

Here Lies Gloria Mundy. London: Joseph; New York: St. Martin's, 1982.

Cold, Lone, and Still. London: Joseph, 1983.

The Greenstone Griffins. London: Joseph, 1983.

The Crozier Pharaohs. London: Joseph, 1984.

No Winding-Sheet. London: Joseph, 1984.

Writing as Malcolm Torrie

Heavy as Lead. London: Joseph, 1966.
Late and Cold. London: Joseph, 1967.
Your Secret Friend. London: Joseph, 1968.
Churchyard Salad. London: Joseph, 1969.
Shades of Darkness. London: Joseph, 1970.
Bismarck Herrings. London: Joseph, 1971.

CRITICAL BIBLIOGRAPHY

Hutchinson, Mary Ann. "Gladys Mitchell." In *Critical Survey of Mystery and Detective Writers*, ed. Frank N. Magill. Pasadena, Calif.: Salem, 1989, pp. 1231–35.
Nichols, Victoria, and Susan Thompson. "Dame Beatrice Adela Lestrange Bradley." In *100 Great Detectives, or The Detective Directory*, ed. Maxim Jakubowski. New York: Carroll, 1991, pp. 42–44.
———. "Dame Beatrice Adela Lestrange Bradley." In *Silk Stalkings: When Women Write of Murder*. Berkeley, Calif.: Black Lizard, 1988, pp. 120–22.
Pike, B. A. "In Praise of Gladys Mitchell." *The Armchair Detective*, 9, no. 4 (1976): 250–60.
Todd, Janet. "Gladys Mitchell." In *British Women Writers: A Critical Reference Guide*, ed. Janet Todd. New York: Continuum, 1989, pp. 467–68.

BETTY RICHARDSON

GWEN MOFFAT (1924–   )

Gwen Moffat was born in Brighton, Sussex, England on July 3, 1924. She served in the women's branch of the army, the Auxiliary Territorial Service (ATS), from 1943 to 1947. While on leave she did her first rock climbing under the guidance of a free spirit named Tom. She returned to the ATS only to desert and take up a nomadic existence. Though she did eventually turn herself in and serve out her time, these months of freedom were formative for Moffat. She developed a taste for climbing and the bohemian life. The years she spent living in and observing from the margins of existence tell in her novels, as do the variety of occupations she has pursued, including: driver, farmhand, youth hostel warden, journalist, professional climbing guide, and rescue team member. Moffat was the first woman to be certified by the British Mountaineering Council in 1953, and then, by the Association of Scottish Climbing Clubs in 1957.

Moffat combines climbing with crime to produce a distinctive type of fiction. She has lived in the American West as well as the British Isles, and now spends her time writing and traveling, with her home base in Wales.

All but two of Moffat's crime novels feature Miss Melinda Pink, a slightly arthritic, somewhat overweight justice of the peace (retired in the later novels). Miss Pink is a climber, an author of Gothic novels, an amateur detective, and a self-possessed, opinionated, independent, and highly capable woman. Therefore, readers who like Amanda Cross's Kate Fansler will probably enjoy the adventures of Miss Pink. Though the settings are different, both authors integrate a pro-woman perspective into their work. *Miss Pink at the Edge of the World* is a good volume with which to begin. In its pages, the simple life of a remote Highland village confronts the threat of the attention and visitors the community would attract if a film were made there. If an American setting is preferred, *The Raptor Zone* or *Veronica's Sisters* introduces Miss Pink transplanted to the western states.

By the publication of *Rage*, in 1990, Miss Pink is described as having turned sixty and looking her age; she is characterized as a solid, sensible woman with the appearance of affluence and some style. Her gray hair is carefully layered. Although she can easily assume a blank expression, the eyes, rimmed by designer glasses, are sharp. A Miss Marple-like mask of cozy vagueness can be assumed to cover her acumen; she is up to both mental and physical challenges.

The real Miss Pink is emphatically not cozy, asserts Moffat. Though the novels in which she appears have characteristics that might suggest they belong to the tradition of coziness, in fact they undermine the conventions. Domestic malice is as pure an evil as any other. Moffat sabotages the tradition by juxtaposing, as she herself describes: "human cosiness with elemental violence. Initially there is an ambiance where people have learned to live with Nature, however untamed; perhaps some of them preserving only a fragile balance but managing to maintain it somehow. Then an event occurs, a visitor arrives; the cosiness cracks and horror oozes out. First menace, then fear, then, inevitably, murder"—often, multiple murders. As with Miss Pink, coziness, when it appears in human communities, is a mask.

Whether the setting is a remote glen in the Scottish Highlands or the rugged country of the American Southwest, Moffat characteristically explores the dynamics of an isolated small community after a murder occurs within it. The beautiful is transformed into the awful. Tensions that usually form the emotional substructure of the community become apparent. The uneasy members of the community are drawn together in self-protection against the intruders. Not only the secrets of the victim and murderer will be uncovered during the investigation.

Often Miss Pink allows the community to effect its own form of justice, and thus to manage to keep concealed the secrets it has invested so much energy in protecting. Miss Pink usually has a privileged position as an outsider temporarily accepted into the circle, either because of connections she has with one member or because she is perceived as a kindred spirit. It is frequently her climbing ability that gains her acceptance.

Veronica's Sisters is the latest volume in the Miss Pink series. Like many of her contemporaries in crime writing, Moffat brings feminist concerns to her recent novels. Child abuse is central to the plot of *Sisters*. While exploring a cave in New Mexico, Miss Pink finds a decomposing body. After making a report to the authorities, she stays on as participant-observer. Natural forces act as a background to the workings of plot. At the conclusion, nature seems to accede to the resolution and find a new equilibrium.

MYSTERY FICTION

Deviant Death. London: Gollancz, 1973.
The Corpse Road. London: Gollancz, 1974.

Miss Pink Series

Lady with a Cool Eye. London: Gollancz, 1973.

Miss Pink at the Edge of the World. London: Gollancz; New York: Scribner's, 1975.

Over the Sea to Death. London: Gollancz; New York: Scribner's, 1976.

A Short Time to Live. London: Gollancz, 1976.

Persons Unknown. London: Gollancz, 1978.

Die like a Dog. London: Gollancz, 1982.

Last Chance Country. London: Gollancz, 1983.

Grizzly Trail. London: Gollancz, 1984.

Snare. London: Macmillan, 1987; New York: St. Martin's, 1988.

The Stone Hawk. London: Macmillan; New York: St. Martin's, 1989.

Rage. London: Macmillan; New York: St. Martin's, 1990.

The Raptor Zone. London: Macmillan, 1990.

Pit Bull. London: Macmillan, 1991.

Veronica's Sisters. London: Macmillan, 1992.

CRITICAL BIBLIOGRAPHY

Oleksiw, Susan. "Moffat, Gwen." In *Twentieth Century Crime and Mystery Writers*, ed. Lesley Henderson. 3rd ed. Chicago and London: St. James, 1991, pp. 776–77.

BARBARA BOEHNKE

SUSAN MOODY (?–   )

Susan Moody was born in Oxford, England, the daughter of an English don. After a two-year sojourn in France as a personal assistant to one of that country's top orchid growers, she married an American biologist and lived in Tennessee for ten years. With her three sons, she now lives in Bedford, England. She appears frequently on radio and television as an expert on crime writing.

Although the seven novels chronicling the sleuthing exploits of black photographer Penny Wanawake are currently somewhat difficult to find, many readers admire them for their clever, unflappable heroine—one of the very few minority sleuths in detective fiction—as well as for Susan Moody's jaunty, telegraphic prose and quick twists of language.

Penny Wanawake's literary ancestors include any number of aristocratic detectives in that she has a titled parent and moves easily in country house society; moreover, she is possessed both of sophistication and a healthy income. She shares with other amateur investigators an eye for detail, plenty of curiosity, and the ability to cut through deliberate obfuscations. However, Penny's antecedents also include countless street-smart, wise-cracking PIs who take chances and who speak the terse, fragmented lingo of tough neighborhoods. More significantly, Penny Wanawake is both more and less than a female version of Dorothy L. Sayers's Lord Peter Wimsey; she might seem an amalgam of Sara Paretsky's V. I. Warshawski and Antonia Fraser's Jemima Shore, but she is neither. Penny is an original.

The daughter of Lady Helena Hurley of Hurley Court and Dr. Benjamin Wanawake, Senangaland's permanent ambassador to the United Nations, Penelope Wanawake has an English country-estate upbringing and a Swiss finishing-school education, capped by a year at Stanford University in California. She is six feet tall in her bare feet and, weighing in at 126 pounds, she is fashion-model slender and strikingly beautiful. Penny wears only white (she prefers designer labels) and only pearls, and she comes home to a Chelsea flat decorated in white silk, wool, and suede. She shares the flat intermittently with the red-haired, South African-born Barnaby Midas, who was educated at Eton and credentialed in sophisticated burglary by a brief stay in Parkhurst Prison. Penny is an award-winning photographer and Barnaby is a reputable antiques dealer—and secretly, they run a Robin Hood scheme to raise money for African famine relief.

First introduced in *Penny Wise* (all the Wanawake titles are puns on the main character's name), Penny lives an eventful life—both professional and avocational—in the seven novels that feature her detective activities. Her family and friends are not exempt from the mayhem: Monsignor Capet is killed at Hurley Court; a friend's body is found at the Los Angeles airport

(*Penny Black*); a childhood playmate, Kendal Sartain, is murdered (*Penny Post*); a school-friend's lover vanishes (*Penny Royal*); and Penny's own father is kidnapped (*Penny Pinching*). Although Penny does her detective work mainly in her native England and in the United States (where her parents live), one novel is set in Italy and others make frequent references to her trips to Africa and the Middle East on photographic assignments.

Readers in search of a strong female protagonist à la Linda Barnes's Carlotta Carlyle will admire Penny's tough talk and courage, her economy of emotion, her strength of will, her complete self-confidence and chutzpah, and especially, her ability to size up a situation rapidly and act quickly. Penny differs from the new feminist heroine, however, in her obvious indulgence in expensive clothes and jewelry and other luxuries (one meal consists of quail eggs), as well as her many, temporary lovers (one in nearly every book, Barnaby notwithstanding) and her frank admiration of the male body and men in general. Although Penny is black, racism is only peripherally an issue; Moody's focus is on exotic adventure and fantasies of female derring-do in familiar locales. Indeed, Penny Wanawake has quite a bit in common with James Bond's playmates, including such flamboyant heroines as Peter O'Donnell's Modesty Blaise. Penny is larger than life— more beautiful, clever, enterprising, and daring, and, yes, taller, richer, and slimmer than any woman has a right to be. She is a woman's fantasy woman, and in that fact lies her appeal.

In her more recent works, Susan Moody has abandoned (temporarily, I hope) Penny Wanawake and branched out into other subgenres of crime fiction, namely, international intrigue and the psychological thriller.

Readers who enjoy the Penny Wanawake series and wish to encounter other minority sleuths might be interested in the novels of Marcia Muller and in Jean Hager's *Ravenmocker*. Another possibility is Jaqueline Girdner's *Fat-Free and Fatal*, although the Asian Barbara Chu is more a sidekick than a principal. Susan Moody's other novels will appeal to those who enjoy the works of Helen McInnes or Mary Roberts Rinehart.

MYSTERY FICTION

Playing with Fire. London: Macdonald, 1990.
Hush-a-Bye. London: Macdonald, 1991.
Mosaic. New York: Delacorte Press, 1991.

Penny Wanawake Series

Penny Wise. London: Macmillan, 1981.
Penny Black. London: Macmillan, 1984; New York: Fawcett, 1986.
Penny Dreadful. London: Macmillan, 1984; New York: Fawcett, 1986.
Penny Post. London: Macmillan, 1985; New York: Fawcett, 1986.

Penny Royal. London: Macmillan, 1986; New York: Fawcett, 1987.

Penny Pinching. New York: Fawcett, 1989; London: Penguin, 1990.

Penny Saving. London: Joseph, 1991.

Cassandra Swan Bridge Series

Death Takes a Hand. New York: Macmillan, 1994.

CRITICAL BIBLIOGRAPHY

Nichols, Victoria, and Susan Thompson. "Miss Melinda Pink." In *Silk Stalkings.*
     Berkeley, Calif.: Black Lizard, 1988, pp. 257–58.
Rhodes, Judith. "Moody, Susan." In *Twentieth Century Crime and Mystery Writ-
     ers*, ed. Lesley Henderson. 3rd ed. Chicago and London: St. James, 1991,
     pp. 777–78.

EDELMA HUNTLEY

ANNE MORICE (1918–1989)

Anne Morice, who died in 1989, was born Felicity Worthington in 1918
in Kent, England. Educated in schools in London, Paris, and Munich, she
married film director Alexander Shaw in 1939 and became the mother of
three children. All but two of her twenty-four mysteries feature actress
Tessa Crichton, and the theatrical setting that forms the background of
these books arises naturally from her family history: her father was a playwright, and her sister, daughters, and three of her nephews have worked
in theater or film. Similarly, the Oxfordshire countryside where so many
of her characters live was her home for many years and at the time of her
death.

Morice's work is often characterized as English cozy, and certainly, the
setting and the social class of her characters fall under this category. However, her sophisticated tone and acerbic wit make her unique in this genre.
Tessa, whose wide network of friends, colleagues, and family leads her
from mystery to mystery, has been called by Dilys Winn, "one of mystery
fiction's great talkers." Moreover, it is largely through her talk that the
reader is treated to pointed character observations and clever musings on
human foibles and peccadilloes.

Tessa's inveterate curiosity leads her to sniff out crime even when its
presence is not immediately obvious to anyone else, including her policeman husband. Her usual pattern is to ask questions (which are generally
unwelcome); to develop several scenarios with various perpetrators, only
to discard them as they prove unworkable; and finally, to come to the real
solution. Her more imaginative crime reconstructions are kept in check by

comments from her cousin Toby Crichton, a well-known playwright, her legion of friends who take her to task for her snoopiness, and her husband, Robin Price. Robin, a chief inspector for Scotland Yard, can sometimes conveniently provide information about the course of an investigation. Equally important, however, he helps her rein in some of her flights of fancy with such teasing remarks as, "By some fluke you get hold of the glimmerings of the right idea and then your feverish and twisted imagination goes to work and transforms it into something unrecognisable."

Despite some detours, Tessa eventually discovers the perpetrator, and her ironic humor and self-mockery allow her to take friendly criticism with grace. Along with Robin, her other chief companion is Toby, whose fondness for Tessa and gossip equals only his distaste for work and the telephone. Toby frequently provides Tessa with a convenient getaway from London at his house at Roakes Common where, as Tessa notes fondly, he "leads a self-centered and reclusive life . . . pretending to be hard at work writing plays and just occasionally putting a line or two to paper."

Tessa, Robin, and Toby are the only characters who are featured in all the novels in the Tessa series, but other characters appear regularly. Chief among these is Toby's daughter, Ellen, who is some years Tessa's junior. Ellen provides a quiet counterpoint to Tessa's need to know whatever is going on, and Tessa, to her credit, recognizes both her shortcomings and Ellen's strength. For example, she once remarks, upon discovering that Ellen has not pressed a reluctant friend for information, "I sighed, wondering how it would feel to have been born like Ellen and to go through life minding my own business."

One welcomes not only the reappearance of both minor and major characters from book to book, but also Tessa's sharp observations and trenchant descriptions. In *Dead on Cue,* for example, she describes an elderly mystery writer as "large and straight-backed with Grecian features and lots of dyed red hair, and had she been auditioning for the part of Cleopatra's grandmother during a stormy period of her life, she would have got it without opening her mouth." Similarly, in *Publish and be Killed,* she tells of a self-absorbed character whose "words came clattering out and tumbling over each other, practically every one centring on herself."

Morice's two non-Tessa books are equally enjoyable. *Design for Dying* and *Planning for Murder* are set in the world of real estate rather than the theater, but like the Tessa books, they are characterized by deft description, tight and well-developed plots, and delicious wit. It is tempting to quote entire sections of Morice's work and so to share the pleasure of her careful crafting, sharp eye, and sophisticated dialogue, but that would spoil the discovery for those who do not yet know her. For readers who like Agatha Christie, Ngaio Marsh, and Josephine Tey, but with a tang, Morice is certain to please.

MYSTERY FICTION

Writing as Anne Morice

Design for Dying. London: Macmillan; New York: St. Martin's Press, 1988.
Planning for Murder. London: Macmillan, 1990; New York: St. Martin's Press, 1991.

Tessa Crichton Series

Death in the Grand Manor. London: Macmillan, 1970.

Death of a Gay Dog. London: Macmillan, 1971.

Murder in Married Life. London: Macmillan, 1971.

Death and the Dutiful Daughter. London: Macmillan, 1973; New York: St. Martin's Press, 1974.

Death of a Heavenly Twin. London: Macmillan; New York: St. Martin's Press, 1974.

Killing with Kindness. London: Macmillan, 1974; New York: St. Martin's Press, 1975.

Nursery Tea and Poison. London: Macmillan; New York: St. Martin's Press, 1975.

Death of a Wedding Guest. London: Macmillan; New York: St. Martin's Press, 1976.

Murder in Mimicry. London: Macmillan; New York: St. Martin's Press, 1977.

Murder by Proxy. London: Macmillan; New York: St. Martin's Press, 1978.

Scared to Death. London: Macmillan, 1977; New York: St. Martin's Press, 1978.

Murder in Outline. London: Macmillan; New York: St. Martin's Press, 1979.

Death in the Round. London: Macmillan; New York: St. Martin's Press, 1980.

The Men in Her Death. London: Macmillan; New York: St. Martin's Press, 1981.

Hollow Vengeance. London: Macmillan; New York: St. Martin's Press, 1982.

Sleep of Death. London: Macmillan, 1982; New York: St. Martin's Press, 1983.

Getting Away with Murder? London: Macmillan; New York: St. Martin's Press, 1984.

Murder Post-Dated. London: Macmillan, 1983; New York: St. Martin's Press, 1984.

Dead on Cue. London: Macmillan; New York: St. Martin's Press, 1985.

Publish and be Killed. London: Macmillan; New York: St. Martin's Press, 1986.

Fatal Charm. London: Macmillan; New York: St. Martin's Press, 1988.

Treble Exposure. London: Macmillan, 1987; New York: St. Martin's Press, 1988.

Writing as Felicity Shaw

The Happy Exiles. London: Hamish Hamilton; New York: Harper, 1956.
Sun Trap. London: Blond, 1958.

CRITICAL BIBLIOGRAPHY

Alderson, Martha. "Death at the Stage Door: Anne Morice's Theresa Crichton and
    Simon Brett's Charles Paris," *Clues*, 2, no. 4 (1983): 21–29.
Alderson, Martha, and Neysa Chouteau. "Anne Morice." In *And Then There Were
    Nine: More Women of Mystery*, ed. Jane S. Bakerman. Bowling Green, Ohio:
    Popular Press, 1985, pp. 59–79.
Purcell, J. M. "Anne Morice's Latest: An Apologia for A. M." *The Armchair De-
    tective*, 17, no. 4 (1984): 370–74.

THERESA PERRI AMMIRATI

PATRICIA MOYES (1923–   )

Patricia Moyes was born on January 19, 1923, in Bray, County Wicklow, Ireland. Readers of her novels will note that some of her occupations have been reflected in her novels: flight officer in the Women's Auxiliary Air Force (WAAF) during World War II (*Johnny Underground*); company secretary to a film production company (*Falling Star*); assistant editor at a fashion magazine (*Murder à la Mode*). The locales of her novels are also reflections of her own experiences: in addition to England and Ireland, Moyes has lived in Switzerland, Holland, and the United States, and she is currently living in the British Virgin Islands. In 1971, Moyes received the Mystery Writers of America's Edgar Allan Poe Award.

All Moyes's detective novels feature Scotland Yard detective Henry Tibbett and his wife, Emmy. Henry, who begins as a chief inspector but progresses to the rank of chief superintendent, is known for both his highly developed analytical skills and the intuitive quality that he refers to as "my nose."

Henry Tibbett, despite his mental and intuitive prowess, is misleadingly ordinary in demeanor and appearance: both criminals and neutral bystanders often have trouble reconciling his exalted rank with his actual presence. Henry has an ironic sense of humor, a tolerant acceptance of the standards and moral choices of others, and an ability to mix smoothly with characters from a variety of classes, backgrounds, and nationalities.

Henry Tibbett has been described by Don C. Wall as a notable example of the "great policeman" figure in detective fiction. As Wall points out, Tibbett's intuitive streak, his freedom from mundane police procedures, and his habit of acquiring cases in unusual ways and in exotic locales make him representative of that category, as does the degree to which he operates as a lone investigator even though aided by his wife.

Throughout Moyes's novels, Henry is accompanied by his wife, Emmy, who, while clearly secondary as an investigator, takes on a number of information-gathering tasks, both major and minor. Moyes's sixth novel, *Johnny Underground*, is perhaps the most interesting for fans of Emmy, since the mystery arises out of Emmy's past as a WAAF during World War II. In an article entitled, "The Lot of the Policeman's Wife," Moyes describes what she sees as the function of that character in detective fiction: the wife "is the projection of the writer's own personality"; she "provides the detective with a lively and reassuringly normal sex life that can be taken for granted"; she "dispenses with the need for a Dr. Watson or a Captain Hastings—tedious characters by definition"; and she "acts as a leaven to the stodgiest plot" since she is able to "make silly mistakes and get herself into scrapes." Moyes's view of the role of characters like Emmy Tibbett in a detective plot clarifies some of the limitations in Emmy that readers may find frustrating.

Critics have, at times, described Moyes's work as particularly notable in terms of her brilliant puzzles, and her plots are indeed ingeniously constructed. For many readers, however, Moyes's books are equally memorable for their powerful sense of locale or for their perceptively drawn characters, who remain vivid long after the reader has witnessed the solving of the puzzle in the final pages. Moyes's own descriptions of her personal writing process emphasize all three elements. According to Moyes, the ideas for her novels originate with a particular setting and background; the second stage is then the creation of the puzzle plot, which is integrally linked with that setting. It is only after a rigid puzzle structure has been developed that she is able to focus in depth on her characters, who sometimes develop unexpected personalities and behaviors. Moyes commented: "I have always felt that the problem of free will versus predestination has an excellent analogy here. The author is the maker of his [*sic*] book: He creates his people, and he has a pretty good idea of what he intends them to do, but ... unless he respects their personalities and lets them develop in their own way, he defeats his own ends. He is all-powerful, he can *make* them act any way he chooses, but if he does he will find himself maneuvering lifeless puppets instead of real people."

Although the novels are totally independent and can be read in any order, a first-time reader of Moyes might best start chronologically; the first novel, *Dead Men Don't Ski*, is extremely effective in its depiction of a small Alpine ski village, its clever puzzle, and its fascinating characters. Readers can, if they choose, group a number of the novels in terms of repeated locales: *Dead Men Don't Ski* and *Season of Snows and Sins* take place in the Alps; *Death and the Dutch Uncle* and *Night Ferry to Death* focus on the Netherlands; and *Black Widower*, *To Kill a Coconut*, *Angel Death*, and *Black*

Girl, White Girl are set in the Caribbean. Two of the novels are substantially different from the others in their shift away from Moyes's usual third-person narration: *Falling Star* is a first-person narration by Pudge Croombe-Peters, the self-satisfied executive producer of an independent film company; and the narration of *Season of Snows and Sins* is split between sections of a diary and first-person narrations by a sculptor and by Emmy Tibbett.

Readers who enjoy Moyes's work might also enjoy Martha Grimes's Scotland Yard investigator Richard Jury or Anne Perry's Victorian-setting detective fiction. Those who are especially interested in the puzzle element of Moyes's novels might consider the novels of Emma Lathen.

MYSTERY FICTION

Henry and Emmy Tibbett Series

Dead Men Don't Ski. London: Collins, 1959; New York: Rinehart, 1960.

The Sunken Sailor. London: Collins, 1961; as *Down Among the Dead Men.* New York: Holt Rinehart, 1961.

Death on the Agenda. London: Collins; New York: Holt Rinehart, 1962.

Murder à la Mode. London: Collins; New York: Holt Rinehart, 1963.

Falling Star. London: Collins; New York: Holt Rinehart, 1964.

Johnny Underground. London: Collins, 1965; New York: Holt Rinehart, 1966.

Murder Fantastical. London: Collins; New York: Holt Rinehart, 1967.

Death and the Dutch Uncle. London: Collins; New York: Holt Rinehart, 1968.

Who Saw Her Die? London: Collins, 1970; as *Many Deadly Returns.* New York: Holt Rinehart, 1970.

Season of Snows and Sins. London: Collins; New York: Holt Rinehart, 1971.

The Curious Affair of the Third Dog. London: Collins; New York: Holt Rinehart, 1973.

Black Widower. London: Collins; New York: Holt Rinehart, 1975.

To Kill a Coconut. London: Collins, 1977; as *The Coconut Killings.* New York: Holt Rinehart, 1977.

Who Is Simon Warwick? London: Collins, 1978; New York: Holt Rinehart, 1979.

Angel Death. London: Collins, 1980; New York: Holt Rinehart, 1981.

A Six-Letter Word for Death. London: Collins; New York: Holt Rinehart, 1983.

Night Ferry to Death. London: Collins; New York: Holt Rinehart, 1985.

Black Girl, White Girl. New York: Holt Rinehart, 1989; London: Collins, 1990.

Twice in a Blue Moon. Forthcoming.

CRITICAL BIBLIOGRAPHY

Caudwell, Sarah. "Henry and Emmy Tibbett." In *100 Great Detectives*, ed. Maxim
    Jakubowski. New York: Carroll and Graf, 1991, pp. 211–13.
Nichols, Victoria, and Susan Thompson. "Behind the Badge: Henry Tibbett." In
    Silk Stalkings: When Women Write of Murder. Berkeley, Calif.: Black Lizard
    Books, 1988, pp. 41–42.
Shibuk, Charles. "Moyes, Patricia." In *Twentieth Century Crime and Mystery Writ-
    ers*, ed. Lesley Henderson. 3rd ed. Chicago: St. James Press, 1991, pp. 786–
    88.

MARYKAY MAHONEY

MARCIA MULLER (1944–   )

Marcia Muller was born in Detroit, Michigan, on September 28, 1944. Her
college education came from the University of Michigan in Ann Arbor,
where she received a B.A. in English in 1966 and an M.A. in journalism
in 1971. In 1967 she married Frederick T. Gilson, from whom she was
divorced in 1981. In 1992 she married detective writer Bill Pronzini, with
whom she has cowritten and coedited several books. She currently lives in
northern California. From 1967 to 1969, Muller was Merchandising Su-
pervisor for *Sunset* magazine in Menlo Park, Calif.; she worked as an interviewer in San Francisco for the University of Michigan Institute of Social
Research during 1971–73. From that time until 1979 she worked at several
part-time jobs, including secretary, freight forwarder, and proposal writer;
in 1979 she became a partner in Invisible Ink, a consulting firm for writers,
in San Francisco, and in 1983 she herself became a full-time writer.

With the appearance of Sharon McCone in *Edwin of the Iron Shoes*, the
female hard-boiled detective was born in American detective fiction—Marcia Muller was the mother. Muller is one of the most prolific women detective writers working today, and although she has written other series
characters—including Elena Oliverez and Joanna Stark—her most popular
and most influential character is McCone. When Sharon appears in *Edwin*,
she is an independent young woman living on her own in San Francisco,
working as a private detective for the All-Souls Legal Cooperative. College-
educated McCone began her detective career working in department store
security. In the first novel, she claims that her strongest point as a detective
is her ability as an interviewer. The young detective in *Edwin* who, although excited about her first murder case shudders when she discovers
that her friend has been stabbed, becomes a mature, somewhat weary detective in *The Shape of Dread*. Although still concerned about the social
injustice in the world, the more recent McCone fears she might be losing
her empathy and enthusiasm for detective work. The long, black hair that

causes Lt. Marcus in the first novel to call her "papoose," a reference to her Indian ancestry, is touched with gray by the tenth novel.

Muller's McCone differs somewhat from other female hard-boiled detectives who came along in the 1980s. Although aware from the first novel that discrimination against women exists, initially she could not be called a feminist. In *Games to Keep the Dark Away*, the fourth novel, Sharon is pleased when construction workers whistle at her, admitting that "more militant feminists" would take offense at this behavior. However, her feminist awareness, as well as her social consciousness, generally grow as the series progresses. By the thirteenth novel, *Pennies on a Dead Woman's Eyes*, she is troubled by the power the government has over the "largely powerless individual." One of the most negatively drawn characters in *The Shape of Dread* is Kathy Soriano, whom Sharon describes as a woman who does not like other women, a type Sharon "instantly distrusts." In the same novel is Lisa McIntyre, a sympathetic character and a lesbian who was abused by her father. The development of her feminine persona can also be seen in Sharon's love relationships. In the early novels she plays an unexpectedly traditional role in her relationship with Lt. Greg Marcus of the San Francisco police. He often assists Sharon with her cases, and at the end of the novels he comforts her. Although their romantic relationship has ended by the fourth novel, Marcus continues to appear occasionally as a friend. By *Pennies*, he and Sharon are working together on a case with mutual respect and concern.

Muller's detective is different from other hardboiled detectives, both men and women, in that she has a family—parents and siblings, who are often part of the stories. These family connections do not, however, interfere with Sharon's ability to fulfill her role of private eye, at least partially because none of her family members live in San Francisco. Additionally, her co-workers at All-Souls become a local extended family to Sharon. Hank Zahn, her boss; Rae Kelleher, her assistant; Ted Smalley, the secretary; as well as others at the cooperative are recurring characters who provide an important emotional, as well as professional, base for Sharon. In *Pennies*, Sharon calls All-Souls "the closest thing that many of us had to a home and an extended family." This extended family based on professional and emotional ties has been part of the McCone series from the beginning. Later women detective writers, such as Sue Grafton and Sara Paretsky, have also used such personally conceived families for their detectives, but the concept was first seen here in Muller's McCone books.

From the beginning of the McCone series, Muller depicts Sharon as a detective who becomes personally involved with her cases, and in the later books, an awareness of social concerns becomes apparent. The issue of racial injustice and the death penalty dilemma appear in *The Shape of Dread*, while environmental issues are featured in *Where Echoes Live*.

Besides Sharon McCone, Marcia Muller has written about two other series characters: Elena Oliverez and Joanna Stark. Joanna Stark, the head of an art security firm, appears in three interconnected books. Each book involves a separate art-related mystery, with the ongoing story of Stark's past influencing her present to unify the series. Oliverez, an amateur sleuth whose job is as curator of the Museum of Mexican Arts in Santa Barbara, Calif., also appears in three books. In the first, *The Tree of Death*, she is implicated in the murder of her boss and investigates to prove her own innocence. In the second book, Oliverez investigates the death of a Chicano historian and finds that events in the past are involved with the murder. The theme of the power of the past on the present runs through much of Muller's fiction.

The final book in the Oliverez series, *Beyond the Grave*, was written with Bill Pronzini. Besides coediting several collections of short stories, Muller and Pronzini have collaborated on three detective novels. In each, the collaboration works similarly. For example, in the Oliverez book, part of the story is told by Muller's detective and another part by Pronzini's nineteenth-century detective, John Quincannon. *The Lighthouse*, Muller's only nonseries novel, was cowritten with Pronzini and is told from the point of view of two characters. In *Double*, Muller's McCone and Pronzini's nameless detective work on the same case, with the story told in chapters that alternate between McCone's and the nameless detective's points of view.

Since the Sharon McCone character develops significantly through the series, readers will find the detective in the later novels to be a very different character from that in the early books. The entire series is recommended; the later half will probably be more enjoyable to readers accustomed to the 1990s version of the female hard-boiled detective. *The Shape of Dread* is one of the best examples of Muller's work. Readers who like the Sharon McCone novels might also enjoy works of Sara Paretsky or Elisabeth Bowers.

MYSTERY FICTION

The Lighthouse, with Bill Pronzini. New York: St. Martin's, 1987.

Sharon McCone Series

Edwin of the Iron Shoes. New York: McKay, 1977; London: Penguin, 1978.

Ask the Cards a Question. New York: St. Martin's Press, 1982; London: Hale, 1983.

The Cheshire Cat's Eye. New York: St. Martin's Press; London: Hale, 1983.

Double, with Bill Pronzini. New York: St. Martin's Press, 1984.

Games to Keep the Dark Away. New York: St. Martin's Press, 1984; London: Severn, 1985.

Leave a Message for Willie. New York: St. Martin's Press, 1984.

There's Nothing to Be Afraid of. New York: St. Martin's Press, 1985.

Eye of the Storm. New York: Mysterious Press, 1988.

The Shape of Dread. New York: Mysterious Press, 1989; London: Women's Press, 1992.

There's Something in a Sunday. New York: Mysterious Press, 1989; London: Women's Press, 1992.

Trophies and Dead Things. New York: Mysterious Press, 1990; London: Women's Press, 1992.

Pennies on a Dead Woman's Eyes. New York: Mysterious Press, 1992.

Where Echoes Live. New York: Mysterious Press, 1992; London: Women's Press, 1992.

Wolf in the Shadows. New York: Mysterious Press, 1993.

Till the Butchers Cut Him Down. New York: Mysterious Press, 1994.

Elena Oliverez Series

The Tree of Death. New York: Walker, 1983; London: Hale, 1986.

The Legend of the Slain Soldiers. New York: Walker, 1985.

Beyond the Grave, with Bill Pronzini. New York: Walker, 1986.

Joanna Stark Series

The Cavalier in White. New York: St. Martin's, 1986.

There Hangs the Knife. New York: St. Martin's Press, 1988.

Dark Star. New York: St. Martin's Press, 1989.

CRITICAL BIBLIOGRAPHY

Isaac, Frederick. "Situation, Motivation, Resolution: An Afternoon with Marcia Muller." *Clues: A Journal of Detection*, 2 (1984): 20–34.

Pettengell, Michael. "The First Lady of Female Detection: An Interview with Marcia Muller." *Mystery Scene*, 35 (1992): 35–38.

Taylor, Bruce. "The Real McCone." [interview]. *The Armchair Detective*, 23 (1990): 260–69.

Bonnie C. Plummer

❦ N ❦

MAGDALEN NABB (1947–   )

Magdalen Nabb was born in the Lancashire village of Church, England, on January 16, 1947. Trained as a potter, she practiced her art in England before moving to Florence, Italy, in 1975. There she lived for a time in Casa Guidi, the former residence of Robert and Elizabeth Barrett Browning. Now she lives in an apartment on the Oltrarno, Florence's "Left Bank," which is also the setting of several of her novels.

Nabb collaborated with Italian journalist Paolo Vagheggi on a fictionalized treatment of the investigation of the kidnapping and murder of Italian premier Aldo Moro (*The Prosecutor*), contributed nonfiction articles (mostly on Florence) to English newspapers, authored a play, and is writing a series of children's stories.

Nabb's first mystery novel, *Death of an Englishman*, was named best first crime novel of 1982 by the British Crime Writers' Association, and Granada Television filmed a documentary, *Death in Florence*, about Nabb's series of Florentine mystery novels.

To say that Nabb's mystery novels are set in Florence is insufficient, for Florence is more than the place where things happen. Nabb reveals the dark underside of the city, a side that tourists can hardly imagine, which provides the conflicts that erupt into murder. Her themes and crimes are derived from real events that only an intimate of the city would know: the first novel focuses on an antiques scam and involves the separate, but intersecting, worlds of Florentines and resident Britons; the next fuses the formalities of burial (and disinterment) in an Italian cemetery to a volatile international marriage; and the third mingles Sardinian shepherds, an American kidnap victim, and Italian property law. Other novels in the series find motivations and intrigues in animosities smouldering since the partisan-Nazi conflicts of World War II, in a particularly Florentine kind of insanity, in transsexual prostitution, in the violent pageantry of the annual medieval football tournament, and in the crumbling foundations of ancient families and their ancient palazzos. The four seasons (or more) of the city are always in sharp focus, too, whether represented by an unseasonable March snowstorm or by the August shop closings that almost paralyze neighborhoods unfrequented by tourists.

This Florence and these seasons are mediated for the reader by a quasi-outsider, Carabinieri Marshal Salvatore Guarnaccia, a Sicilian, who has been posted to Florence to command the small Carabinieri station at the Palazzo Pitti. In the first novel, the Marshal is suffering from the flu and most of the legwork is done by a young subordinate of two months' experience who has only disdain for Guarnaccia, whom he finds excessively Sicilian, clumsily large and fat, and embarrassingly afflicted (by an allergy to sunlight which causes him to weep copiously). However, even were the Marshal not originally envisioned as the central and continuing character, his intuition makes him perfect to solve the crime. Moreover, the developing story of his family relationships is a significant subcurrent starting in the early novels. As with Georges Simenon's Maigret, to whom he is frequently compared, the Marshal's effectiveness in solving crimes and bringing "criminals" to justice derives not from strict police or judicial procedure (which he sometimes flouts), but from his sympathetic perception of human character and understanding of its social nuances. This kind of emphasis means that exploring relationships and revealing motivations is more important than discovering "whodunnit," and Nabb has asserted that she was happy to move away from the early titles (with "Death" as a key word) to titles focusing on the Marshal.

The novels are probably best read in chronological order so as to follow the Marshal's unfolding family history, which often mirrors the criminal concerns, but there is no absolute need to do so. If a reader wishes to use the novels as an adjunct to the usual guidebook when visiting Florence, as I recently did, the best ones may be *Death of a Dutchman* (it is possible to use a chase scene therein as a guide through the Boboli Gardens) and *The Marshal and the Madwoman* (which begins in the fictionalized version of Nabb's own small piazza and takes the reader backward for a terrifying glimpse of the disastrous flood of 1966).

Readers who like Nabb's novels will certainly like Georges Simenon's Maigret books, and they may also like the Dutch and French settings and characters of Nicolas Freeling and the Swedish settings and characters of Maj Sjowall and Per Wahloo. Those who wish to see more of Italy might try Michael Dibdin's novels featuring policeman Aurelio Zen.

MYSTERY FICTION

Salvatore Guarnaccia Series

Death of an Englishman. London: Collins; New York: Scribner's, 1982.
Death of a Dutchman. London: Collins; New York: Scribner's, 1983.

Death in Springtime. London: Collins; New York: Scribner's, 1984.

Death in Autumn. London: Collins; New York: Scribner's, 1985.

The Marshal and the Murderer. London: Collins; New York: Scribner's, 1987.

The Marshal and the Madwoman. London: Collins; New York: Scribner's, 1988.

The Marshal's Own Case. London: Collins; New York: Scribner's, 1990.

The Marshal Makes His Report. London: HarperCollins, 1991; New York: HarperCollins, 1992.

The Marshal at the Villa Torrini. London: HarperCollins, 1993; New York: HarperCollins, 1994.

CRITICAL BIBLIOGRAPHY

Nichols, Victoria, and Susan Thompson. "Guarnaccia." In *Silk Stalkings*. Berkeley, Calif.: Black Lizard, 1988, pp. 69–72.
Taylor, Anna-Marie. "Nabb, Magdalen." In *Twentieth Century Crime and Mystery Writers*, ed. Lesley Henderson. 3rd ed. Chicago and London: St. James, 1991, p. 794.

MARYBETH WHITE

SHIZUKO NATSUKE (1938–   )

Shizuko Natsuke is commonly referred to as "the Agatha Christie of Japan," a comparison she does not like. In an interview with Mark Schreiber, she observed: "Christie's novels don't go into social problems the way mine do. These days mystery stories have to reflect human problems in a way that readers can relate to, so if people feel that I resemble Christie, except on a superficial level of being a female mystery writer, I must be doing something wrong." However, her sales of over eighty novels and short stories over a twenty-five-year writing career reflect that, on the contrary, she is doing something right.

Although Natsuke is a second-generation adherent of Seicho Matsumoto's social detective school of postwar crime fiction, which emphasized the inherent problems within Japan's postwar changes, her background is very different from that of Masako Togawa, with whom her name is often linked. She was born in 1938 into an affluent Tokyo family and spent the war years in Atama (a seaside resort town). Natsuke attended Keio University, majoring in English literature with an interest in writing that dated from the sixth grade. While at the university, her short story, "Only I Know," was nominated for the Edogawa Rampo Mystery Award. Her writing career was interrupted by her marriage and her husband's insistence that she devote herself to her family. When her two children reached their teens, Natsuke returned to writing, however, winning the 1974 Edogawa

Rampo Award for *The Disappearance* (which remains unavailable in English).

Natsuke's stories of human relationships and social problems are far more accessible to western readers than Togawa's unsavory world of misfits. Unfortunately, however, her first book to appear in English, *Murder at Mount Fuji*, was a bad introduction, as it was burdened by both a poor translation (strong in description but weak in dialogue) by the usually competent Robert B. Rohmer and adaptation for export. In its intended form, it is a story of a wealthy family's New Year's reunion, at which everyone's submerged hatred surfaces to interrupt the unpleasant gathering, which ends in murder. Instead of pursuing this study of Japanese group dynamics and conspiracy by consent, the export version added an unconvincing American character, Jane Prescott. "I thought the change would make the book more appealing to foreign readers, by giving them at least one character they could relate to," Natsuke said. However, the Prescott inserts repeat information and disrupt the story, emphasizing the difficulty of crossing cultural divides. The original *Murder at Mount Fuji* was adapted into a well-received film in Japan.

Another casualty of the cultural divide, which clearly limits Natsuke's accessibility to occidental readers, is *Innocent Journey*, about a woman who is convinced by her lover to join in *seppuku* (double suicide), only to wake up with her hand on a knife sticking out of his back. Written in the *pazuraa* (puzzle) style rather than the "social detective style" (a Japanese label for novels promoting social change), the plot is complex and slow, with ample opportunities for readers unfamiliar with Japanese culture to go astray. Unfortunately, a fair percentage of her eighty books were written for a specific audience and cannot easily be exported.

Unlike most Japanese women of her generation, Natsuke is well traveled and goes abroad annually. Unlike most Japanese crime writers, several of her books are set outside Japan. *The Third Lady* begins in French château country where two Japanese strangers have an un-Japanese, personal conversation on hatred and injustice, concluding with an implied agreement for murder. Within a framework reminiscent of Patricia Highsmith's *Strangers on a Train*, Natsuke then examines the moral consequences of social action in postwar Japan. Aided by Robert B. Rohmer's sympathetic translation, *The Third Lady* is Natsuke at her best.

Natsuke's own exceptional grasp of English is evidenced in her translation of *The Obituary Arrives at Two O'Clock*, which focuses on Japanese business in the aftermath of the oil price slump. Highlighting the influence of the *yakuza* (Japan's crime syndicate) in business and middle-class society, *Obituary* is fine example of the social detective style in contemporary Japanese crime fiction.

Natsuke is skilled in other forms of the genre, as evidenced by her most recent book available in translation, *Portal of the Wind*, which ventures into the supernatural, an area usually associated with Togawa. In an attempt to extend the lives of two successful and respected men, doctors perform unusual surgery. The surgery, as well as a murder and an apparent suicide, are discovered by a young woman determined to find out the time of her father's death.

Like most Japanese crime writers, Natsuke annually turns out a number of stories that span the genre's stylistic spectrum. For example, "Cry from the Cliff" (in *Ellery Queen's Golden Japanese Dozen*) is a predictable story (in the Agatha Christie style) of a sculptor who fakes his wife's death for the insurance money, only to have things go awry. "The Pawnshop Murder" (in *Murder in Japan*) returns to the puzzle style with a tale of a young reporter demolishing a murder alibi by mathematical calculation. "The Sole of the Foot" (found in *Murder in Japan*) is a paragon of the social detective style, with its clash between traditional and modern values, in the tale of ritual suicide intended to highlight corruption within a religious sect.

In spite of Natsuke's evident talents, cultural barriers as well as translation problems effectively limit her access to occidental readers. Consequently, she will remain a sister in crime outside the Western family. Readers might be interested in comparing her work with Togawa's to see the variations possible within the social detective school of writing, but comparisons with Anglo-American women writers are not really appropriate.

MYSTERY FICTION

Books Available in English

Murder at Mt. Fuji. New York: St. Martin's, 1984; as *W no higeki*. Tokyo: Bungeishunju, 1984.

The Third Lady. New York: Ballantine, 1987; Tokyo: Shueisha, 1978.

The Obituary Arrives at Two O'Clock. New York: Ballantine, 1988; as *Fuhu Wa Gogo Niji Ni Todoku*. Tokyo: Bungeishunju, 1983.

Innocent Journey. New York: Ballantine, 1989; as *Kobukyaku No Tabiji*. Tokyo: Kodansha, 1976.

Portal of the Wind. New York: Ballantine, 1990; as *Kaze No Tobira*. Tokyo: Bungeishunju, 1980.

CRITICAL BIBLIOGRAPHY

Apostolou, John L. "Japanese Mystery Fiction Revisited." *The Armchair Detective*, 15, no. 2 (1982).

Hoida, Naomi. "Natsuke, Shizuko." In *Twentieth Century Crime and Mystery Writers*, ed. Lesley Henderson. 3rd ed. Chicago and London: St. James Press, 1991, p. 1135.

Schreiber, Mark. "The Agatha Christie of Japan." *The Armchair Detective*, 20, no. 1 (1987): 54–57.

Stone, Nancy-Stephanie. "Death under the Rising Sun." *Drood Review of Mystery*, 9, no. 5 (May 1989): 1.

NANCY-STEPHANIE STONE

LILLIAN O'DONNELL (1926–   )

Born Lillian Udvardy in Trieste, Italy, in 1926, Lillian O'Donnell was educated in Italy and New York City. O'Donnell worked as an actress on Broadway and in television, activities often reflected in her novels, and was the first woman stage manager of a New York production. She gave up her theatrical career when she married Leonard O'Donnell, and then turned her hand to writing.

Except for a couple of police procedurals, O'Donnell's first ten novels are largely uneven Gothic tales. Heavily laced with romance, they feature women trapped in mysterious circumstances, which they flutter through. While women are the main characters in most of these books, all the sleuths are men. O'Donnell's style, which later develops into a serviceable prose, is clumsy. Her plotting, however, is ingenious; one can never be sure, in any O'Donnell novel, that one has figured out the twists and turns of plot until the last page is turned.

O'Donnell introduced her major series character, Norah Mulcahaney, in 1972 in *The Phone Calls*. O'Donnell took her idea for the crime from some obscene phone calls that her mother had been receiving. She modeled Mulcahaney on a friend, policewoman Peggy Driscoe, whose efficiency and dedication during the New York blackout had impressed her. In her twenties, Mulcahaney has the job of examining the bodies of women victims. Coming under the influences of her future husband, Joe Capretto, and the tutelage of her police rabbi, Jim Felix, she acts as a decoy (a role policewomen fill with some frequency). In the first novel, Norah is transferred to detective, beginning her long climb to lieutenant.

O'Donnell does not consciously choose Norah's cases because they concern women but, since "all good mysteries are rooted within the frame of their own times," her novels show police attitudes toward women on the force and as victims. When Norah joined the Homicide Squad in 1972, it had no women members; seven years later there were six.

O'Donnell's novels are marked by violence, including a decapitation, the slaughter of animals in a children's zoo, and serial killers of various MOs. Murder, when necessary to the novels, is described graphically. Mulcahaney revels in finding serial killers and going underground as a possible victim. She is jealous of Kathryn Webber, a rookie whose youth makes her a more suitable decoy than Mulcahaney, in *Pushover*.

O'Donnell claims that there are few possible variations in mysteries: "You have the crime, and the story is how it's solved and the perpetrator brought to justice. The differences are in the approach, the personalities." O'Donnell feels that her women characters gain from being created by a woman. The series details Norah's biography, from her courtship through her marriage, widowhood, and later courting. One of Norah's greatest desires, to have a child, eludes her. Nonetheless, Norah and Joe have an almost perfect marriage, despite their brief separation in *Leisure Dying*. Norah's social relations, especially with Joe's mother, Emilia, often get in the way of the detection, yet they create a social dimension that adds to the series' depth.

The fourteen Norah Mulcahaney books tell the continuing story of Norah's development as a person and a police officer. While Norah's biography is consistent and has some interest, the personal dimension often gets in the way of the police work. According to O'Donnell, her character "was Norah Mulcahaney right from the beginning—an average, decent young woman, no sexpot, attractive without being glamorous, whose particular ambition led her to be a policewoman."

Among my favorites is *Dial 577–R-A-P-E*, which illustrates Norah's sympathy for the victim. Norah refuses to accept the motivations for rape that might exculpate the rapist, since the crime also involves a victim. Norah is indignant, both as a police officer and as a woman: it is in the acknowledgment of her gender that much of the impetus of the case comes about. However, even Norah makes mistakes. She underestimates Lieutenant Wilburn, head of the Rape Squad, because she is a woman, acknowledging to herself that she would not be as impressed with her savvy if Wilburn had been Lieutenant Felix, whose competence she takes for granted. What deepens the novel's effect is that Gabby Constantine, who is pregnant from the rape and carrying the child, loses her boyfriend and goes back to Puerto Rico in the worst possible condition for a woman, with a child and no husband.

The Children's Zoo is particularly gruesome, beginning with a killing spree in the Children's Zoo in Central Park as part of an initiation. During the spree, three boys kill the night watchman as well. As a subplot to the teenage violence, Norah's niece, Toni, is violated by five girls using a Coke bottle. The perpetrators will not be punished because of their age. Norah figures out which of the boys committed the murders, but both he and Norah know that since he is only fifteen, he will probably go free. It is Norah's frustration that marks the end of the novel.

Pushover shows Norah turning forty and feeling disturbed by Felix's young niece, Kathryn Webber, who is a reflection of herself when she joined the force. Norah is too old to be a decoy to catch Nathaniel Gorin, who has been pushing young women under the wheels of oncoming subway trains. In another disturbing occurrence, although Norah solves the kidnapping of ten-year-old Todd Millard with style, the case increases her desperate need for the love of a child.

O'Donnell has written three novels featuring former dancer Mici (pronounced Mitzi) Anhult, who works for the Crime Victims Compensation Board. O'Donnell's sympathies have always been with the victim, and this series almost seems to be propaganda for the board. Best of the three is the first, *Aftershock*, which intertwines three stories in expert fashion.

O'Donnell's latest series features Gwenn Ramadge, a former model turned private detective who has to find her own way in a man's world. The second Ramadge novel, *Used to Kill*, concerns the beating death of Douglas Trent. O'Donnell nicely peels back layers of her story, revealing one possible murder after another until she comes to the final perpetrator, a person who convinced two young boys to commit the murder.

O'Donnell is at her best in her plotting and her use of police procedures. Readers who want her at her best should turn to the Norah Mulcahaney series. Those who enjoy reading O'Donnell's novels might also enjoy former transit policewoman Dorothy Uhnak's procedurals with Christie Opara and others or Susan Dunlap's Jill Smith series. Mulcahaney fares differently than the women in Ed McBain's 87th Precinct series.

MYSTERY FICTION

Death on the Grass. New York: Arcadia House, 1960.
Death Blanks the Screen. New York: Arcadia House, 1961.
Death Schuss. New York and London: Abelard Schuman, 1963.
Death of a Player. New York and London: Abelard Schuman, 1964.
Murder under the Sun. New York and London: Abelard Schuman, 1964.
Babes in the Woods. New York and London: Abelard Schuman, 1965.
The Sleeping Beauty Murders. New York and London: Abelard Schuman, 1967.
The Face of the Crime. New York and London: Abelard Schuman, 1968.
The Tachi Tree. New York and London: Abelard Schuman, 1968.
Dive into Darkness. New York: Abelard Schuman, 1971; London, Abelard Schuman, 1972.

Norah Mulcahaney Series

The Phone Calls. New York: Putnam; London: Hodder and Stoughton, 1972.
Don't Wear Your Wedding Ring. New York: Putnam, 1973; London: Barker, 1974.

Dial 577–R-A-P-E. New York: Putnam; London: Barker, 1974.

The Baby Merchants. New York: Putnam, 1975; London: Bantam, 1976.

Leisure Dying. New York: Putnam, 1976.

No Business Being a Cop. New York: Putnam, 1979; London: Hale, 1980.

The Children's Zoo. New York: Putnam, 1981; London: Hale, 1992.

Cop without a Shield. New York: Putnam, 1983.

Ladykiller. New York: Putnam, 1984.

Casual Affairs. New York: Putnam, 1985.

The Other Side of the Door. New York: Putnam, 1987.

A Good Night to Kill. New York: Putnam, 1989.

A Private Crime. New York: Putnam, 1991.

Pushover. New York: Putnam, 1992.

Lockout. New York: Putnam, 1994.

Mici Anhult Series

Aftershock. New York: Putnam, 1977; London: Hale, 1979.

Falling Star. New York: Putnam, 1979; London: Hale, 1981.

Wicked Designs. New York: Putnam, 1980; London: Hale, 1983.

Gwenn Ranadge Series

A Wreath for the Bride. New York: Putnam, 1990.

Used to Kill. New York: Putnam, 1993.

CRITICAL BIBLIOGRAPHY

Choteau, Neysa, and Martha Alderson. "Lillian O'Donnell." *And Then There Were Nine: More Women of Mystery*, ed. Jane S. Bakerman. Bowling Green, Ohio: Bowling Green State University Popular Press, 1985, pp. 100–119.

Delatiner, Barbara. "Fans Keep Watch on Prolific Mystery Writer." *New York Times*. July 15, 1990.

Maida, Patricia. "Interview with Lillian O'Donnell." *The Armchair Detective*, (Spring 1981): 164–65.

O'Donnell, Lillian. "Norah Mulcahaney: New York's Finest." In Dilys Winn, ed., *Murderess Ink: The Better Part of the Mystery.* New York: Workman Publishing, 1979, pp. 118–20.

———. "Plot Versus Character in the Mystery." *Writer*, December 1982, pp. 11–13.

———. "Routines and Rules for the Police Procedural." *Writer*, February 1978, pp. 17–19, 46.

SIDNEY POGER

EMMUSKA ORCZY (1865–1947)

Baroness Orczy's background was both aristocratic and cosmopolitan: she inherited her father's title and spent her childhood in the Austro-Hungarian Empire of the Belle Epoque, with schooling in Brussels and Paris, before age fifteen, when the family moved to London. There, she studied art, and she subsequently exhibited at the Royal Academy. Through her father, who was also a distinguished musician, she moved in artistic circles: from Crown Prince Rudolph and Marie Vetsera, the fated couple of Mayerling, to the Winston Churchills, and from Franz Liszt to Henry Irving, she knew everybody who was anybody. Her husband of nearly fifty years was also a painter and reputedly helped with her writing. She lived much of her later life on the Riviera, and died in London in 1947.

In her life is foreshadowed her art: Baroness Orczy's stories embody an aristocratic superiority that brings the lower orders to justice but often allows the upper classes to hush up their crimes; this bias, however, is little different (except that it is honestly come by) from the outlook that is ubiquitous in the detective fiction of the Golden Age. In later life she remembered herself as being "an insignificant, mediocre personage among so many clever people," and in that statement is the ambiguity that governs many of her characters, not least her most famous, the Scarlet Pimpernel, a seemingly insignificant dilettante who is, in truth, a personage helping aristocrats to escape the French Revolutionary terror. Disguise, moreover (at which Lady Molly is also adept), is the pivot of several of Orczy's stories, most notably "The Man in the Inverness Cape," where two people pose as three, working the permutations on the mistaken identity theme.

Orczy's contribution to detective fiction is threefold: in the Old Man in the Corner series, she provided an early example of the disinterested armchair detective; in Lady Molly, a no less early example of the woman detective; and in Skin o'My Tooth she may have initiated the irascible, bullying, none-too-scrupulous lawyer-detective. Almost all her detective fiction belongs to the years before *The Scarlet Pimpernel* (1905), and all of it was first published in magazines; she wrote no book-length detective fiction. In the 1920s she did try to resurrect the Old Man in the Corner, but he had undergone a Reichenbachian fall in the meantime, and these stories are greatly inferior to the earlier ones.

By general consent, the Old Man in the Corner is Orczy's most interesting detective. There he sits, at his table in the A.B.C. (Aerated Bread Company), a London teashop, with his glass of milk and his cheesecake. This "animated scarecrow," a "veritable Jack-in-the-Box," solves mysteries for an audience of one: Miss Polly Burton, who is a reporter for the *Evening Observer* (mostly on "things modistical and fashionable"). The Man in the

Corner is mercurial, almost always on the point of evanescence; at the end of each story, all we see of him is a swinging glass door or a tailcoat disappearing down the street.

Though Orczy insisted on his originality ("That personality must in no way be reminiscent of Sherlock Holmes. . . . And I must 'say it as shouldn't,' that the 'Old Man in the Corner,' as I conceived him, was in no way reminiscent of any other character in detective fiction"), and though presented in the third person, he has many of the Holmesian touches. The Old Man asserts the primacy of common sense in detecting, deriding its lack in both his "Watson" and the police, whose investigations he makes no attempt to help. Though Orczy protested—too much—that her Old Man was not reminiscent of Holmes, many of her plots are derivative: "The Hocussing of Cigarette" has a whinny or two from "Silver Blaze"; "Who Stole the Diamonds?" has the King of Bohemia as a central character; and "The Disappearance of Count Collini" uses the same device as "A Case of Identity."

Whereas the Old Man appeared in three collections, Orczy's second important detective, Lady Molly, appears in only one collection of twelve stories. These stories have attracted more attention in recent years, but what Lady Molly has gained from the general unearthing of female detectives she has commensurately lost through her allegiance to the upper class and her patronization of her cloying auxiliary, Mary Granard, who loves her to the other side idolatry. Lady Molly, the daughter of an earl, is the head of the Female Department at Scotland Yard and is deferred to by all her colleagues, as well as by the chief, who regularly assigns her to those cases "where feminine tact and my lady's marvellous intuition might prove more useful than the more approved methods of the sterner sex." However, pace her critics, she is no flibbertigibbet, and stories such as "The Ninescore Mystery," "The Fordwych Castle Mystery," and "The Bag of Sand" all show a nice balance between her intuitive and her rational powers.

Finally, there is Patrick Mulligan, the slightly unsavory lawyer who earned his nickname, Skin o'My Tooth, from his habit of getting off his clients in that hair's breadth way. He is repulsive in appearance ("Fat and rosy and comfortable as an Irish pig, with a face as stodgy as a boiled currant pudding"), but his unscrupulousness is more a matter of reputation, played up by himself, than an actuality to which the reader can bear witness. As notes his Boswell (his confidential clerk, Muggins), it is his fellow lawyers who regard him as "unprofessional," because he usually settles his cases out of court through a mixture of bluffing and what sometimes looks like blackmail. (The real "professional" gets his client into court in order to collect the fee.)

Baroness Orczy's three detectives, therefore, are all still very much worthy of acquaintance, especially for enthusiasts of Golden Age detective fiction.

MYSTERY FICTION

Lady Molly of Scotland Yard. London: Cassell, 1910; New York: Arno, 1976.
Skin o'My Tooth. London: Hodder and Stoughton; New York: Doubleday, 1928.

The Old Man in the Corner Series

The Case of Miss Elliott. London: Unwin, 1905.

The Old Man in the Corner. London: Greening, 1909; as *The Man in the Corner*. New York: Dodd, Mead, 1909.

Unravelled Knots. London: Hutchinson, 1925; New York: Doran, 1926. Five Old Man in the Corner stories were separately published between 1923 and 1925 by Doran under the title, *The Old Man in the Corner Unravels the Mystery of . . .* and later collected in *Unravelled Knots*.

CRITICAL BIBLIOGRAPHY

Duren, Fred. "Was the Old Man in the Corner an Armchair Detective?" *The Armchair Detective*, 14, no. 3 (1981)): 232–33.

BARRIE HAYNE

❦ P ❦

ORANIA PAPAZOGLOU (1951–)

Orania Papazoglou was born on July 13, 1951, in Bethel, Connecticut; she received a bachelor's degree from Vassar in 1973 and a master's in English from the University of Connecticut in 1975. Abandoning graduate work at Michigan State University for New York City in 1980, she joined the staff of the magazine *Greek Accent* and also began working as a free-lance writer. She married William DeAndrea in 1984 and now lives in Connecticut with her husband and son.

Papazoglou's first mystery series features Pay McKenna, a six-foot, 125-pound, wry, chain-smoking journalist who pays the bills by writing category romances. After the first book, *Sweet, Savage Death*, McKenna becomes decidedly better off and advances her career by writing true crime books about her cases. During her career, McKenna collects a cat, a small child (not her own), a husband, and a reputation as quite a sleuth. In at least two novels, real people appear as themselves: Orania's husband, in *Death's Savage Passion*, and Gail Larson of The Butler Did It Bookstore in Baltimore in *Rich, Radiant Slaughter*.

Similar in tone but far different in depth is her second series, featuring Gregor Demarkian, retired founder and head of the Federal Bureau of Investigation (FBI) Department of Behavioral Science. Demarkian, whom the newspapers insist on labeling the Armenian-American Hercule Poirot, rose to great heights in the bureau as an expert on serial killers, and then chose to retire, during the final months of his beloved wife's illness. Elizabeth dies before the opening of the first novel, when Demarkian is retired, depressed, and recently returned to the now prosperous Armenian neighborhood on Cavanaugh Street in Philadelphia, the site of his early, impoverished childhood. Despite his twenty years with the bureau, Demarkian is not a company man; he despises J. Edgar Hoover for his personal and professional corruption and has equally strong feelings against the Central Intelligence Agency, whose agents lack professionalism, in Gregor's view.

The cast of Cavanaugh Street is part of every novel, with the men and women of the tight-knit ethnic community concerned with life here and their Armenian cousins in less-secure circumstances elsewhere in the world supplying the background to the violence of modern America. The only true outsider in the neighborhood is Bennis Hannaford, a fantasy writer who meets Gregor during his first case as a retired agent, when he investigates the death of her father; she occasionally serves as his Watson. The central figure of the Armenian community is Father Tibor Kasparian, who survived torture and imprisonment in the Soviet Union before escaping to the United States. Educated, compassionate, and dedicated to his faith, Father Tibor has reduced his life to two beliefs: Christianity and constitutional law.

Papazoglou belongs in part to the puzzle school of mystery writing; in every story the victim, murderer, and method are convincing and carefully worked out, with bizarre forms of murder for which ample clues have been presented. The author is equally careful not to repeat herself in the choice of victim, murderer, or motive; men and women, old and young, rich and poor—all are given equal opportunity to reveal their baser natures. Moreover, each novel also has a richly developed setting. Papazoglou never chooses an average family in Anytown, U.S.A.; instead, the settings and characters are precise and fully realized.

The Demarkian books are more than a series of mystery novels, however; instead, Papazoglou uses them to examine and express her views on various issues. One of the most obvious targets of her analytical skills is censorship, with Father Tibor proving the case for its prohibition merely by a brief description of his trials in the Soviet Union. Another favorite topic is feminism. When the bureau decides to accept women as working agents, for example, Demarkian reads the main texts of feminism to prepare himself, casting a practiced eye on the arguments therein; some he finds "outrageous," some "tautological," and some "brilliant," but he cannot accept the theory of women being infantilized by the culture, and he explains his reasoning. In other passages, feminism is presented, not as a liberating force, but as a form of brainwashing that demands unquestioning devotion from its adherents.

Despite the author's outspokenness, it would be a mistake to think she is simply out to smash every sacred image she can find; she is not a complete iconoclast. Demarkian is, after all, a man in the FBI, while the Church, which she knows intimately and depicts vividly, produces its share of villains but retains an inherent strength beyond mortal corruption. Moreover, Papazoglou never attacks anyone for how they have been shaped by birth or misfortune in life; her targets are presumed values that fail to accord with reality.

Each book is set around a holiday, and the volumes take place within a few months of each other. Nevertheless, a reader can read them in any order and still enjoy almost everything that Papazoglou has put in them. *Quoth the Raven* exemplifies the author's goals, attitudes, and skills, and can serve as a good introduction to the rest of the Demarkian series.

Papazoglou is also the author of two nonseries, suspense novels, *Sanctity* and *Charisma*. Readers who enjoy Papazoglou's expert plotting and explicit discussions in the Gregor Demarkian series might also enjoy books by Elizabeth George, Jane Langton, and Ngaio Marsh (although no one has attempted to combine controversial issues with mystery fiction to the same extent as Papazoglou), while those who favor the Pay McKenna series might enjoy books by Julie Smith and Joan Hess.

MYSTERY FICTION

Writing as Orania Papazoglou

Sanctity. New York: Crown, 1986.
Charisma. New York: Crown, 1992; London: Headline, 1992.

Pay McKenna Series

Sweet, Savage Death. New York: Doubleday Crime Club, 1984.

Wicked Loving Murder. New York: Doubleday Crime Club, 1985.

Death's Savage Passion. New York: Doubleday Crime Club, 1986.

Rick, Radiant Slaughter. New York: Doubleday Crime Club, 1988.

Once and Always Murder. New York: Doubleday Crime Club, 1989.

Writing as Jane Haddam

Gregor Demarkian Series

Not a Creature Was Stirring. New York: Bantam, 1990.

Act of Darkness. New York: Bantam, 1991.

Precious Blood. New York: Bantam, 1991.

Quoth the Raven. New York: Bantam, 1991.

Feast of Murder. New York: Bantam, 1992.

A Great Day for the Deadly. New York: Bantam, 1992.

A Stillness in Bethlehem. New York: Bantam, 1992.

Murder Superior. New York: Bantam, 1993.

Bleeding Hearts. New York: Bantam, 1994.

Dear Old Dead. New York: Bantam, 1994.

Festival of Deaths. forthcoming.

And One to Die On. forthcoming.

CRITICAL BIBLIOGRAPHY

Nichols, Victoria, and Susan Thompson. "Patience McKenna." In *Silk Stalkings*.
    Berkeley, Calif.: Black Lizard, 1988, pp. 171–72.

Susan Oleksiw

SARA PARETSKY (1947–   )

Sara Paretsky was born in Ames, Iowa, in 1947 and grew up in Lawrence,
Kansas, the only girl of five children. She paid for her own education at
the University of Kansas and later at the University of Chicago, where she
received an M.B.A. and a Ph.D. in history (in 1977). Only in 1985, after
publishing three novels and agreeing to a lucrative sale of movie rights, did
Paretsky leave the unsatisfying corporate world to pursue her career as a
professional writer. In 1985, the Friends of American Writers honored her
for *Deadlock*. *Ms. Magazine* named her as one of their 1987 Women of
the Year. Paretsky also received a Silver Dagger Award from the Crime
Writers Association in 1988 for *Blood Shot*. She is a member of the Private
Eye Writers of America, the Authors Guild, the Crime Writers Association,
the Chicago Network, and the Mystery Writers of America (serving as vice-
president in 1989).

Paretsky's strong interest in women's issues colors her life and her fiction.
She serves as a longtime member of the Chicago National Abortion Rights
Action League (and has been its director since 1987). Moreover, Paretsky
founded Sisters in Crime, a group dedicated to furthering "the careers of
women in the mystery field and to correcting imbalances in the treatment
of women."

All eight of Paretsky's novels feature professional private investigator
V. I. (for Victoria Iphigenia) Warshawski. Like her creator, V. I. boasts a
University of Chicago degree and an early career in a prestigious corporation. Having found the institutional road to success unfulfilling, V. I.
struck out on her own. Paretsky has endowed her character with many of
her own social concerns, including a healthy suspicion of most of the fundamental institutions of patriarchal society. Though Paretsky insists that
"the quickest way to kill your fiction is to be writing sermons with it," she
proves herself capable of exploring social conditions with an energy and
skill that bring her work into the bestseller marketplace.

Paretsky's thematic concerns develop with her series; the early books
evolved from the author's desire to write a novel in the style of Raymond
Chandler, only with a female protagonist. Paretsky claims that "at first . . .
[the novel] was too much of a parody," but she continued to try to produce
a female protagonist with whom contemporary readers could identify, "a

woman who could solve her own problems . . . [and] who could operate successfully in a tough milieu and not lose her femininity." V. I. Warshawski survives in the vicious world of her work without rescue by a knight in shining armor. She uses her wits and physical skills to stay alive and complete her investigations. However, though able, Warshawski is never brutal. While Paretsky has her character carry a gun for protection, V. I. rarely uses it (and then, generally without much success).

All eight of Paretsky's novels indict patriarchal society by placing traditionally respected, authoritative institutions at the center of whatever evil V. I. probes. *Indemnity Only* uncovers the unsavory traits of insurance companies and labor unions; *Deadlock* exposes the ruthless upper-class magnates who control shipping on the Great Lakes; *Killing Orders* proclaims unethical links between Chicago and big business, the Catholic church, and organized crime; *Bitter Medicine* throws light on the terrors of medical malpractice; *Blood Shot* unmasks corporate responsibility for environmental and health hazards; *Burn Marks* exhibits the progression of urban decay and the destructive aspects of real estate development; and *Guardian Angel* exposes society's ineffective system of care for the elderly through a scenario of pension fraud, junk bond sales, and unethical legal practices. At the heart of every crime lies a patriarchal institution with a history of oppressing the marginal elements of society, including women, the poor, nonwhites, and the elderly.

Paretsky cuts even deeper into the heart of contemporary society when she locks the motive for every murder firmly in the desire of white-collar workers to maintain their status within a patriarchal institution, no matter what the cost to other people. Manufacturers cover up their inadvertent poisoning of workers, businesses hire law firms to hide bankruptcy, families adhere to decades of silence to bury incest, and desperate people murder, rob, libel, blackmail, and terrorize others to hurry their capture of success. Such a critical stance on traditional patriarchal values provides Paretsky's novels with their unique and feminist flavor. With a strong personal code of honor, Paretsky's detective marches into the fray of capitalistic corruption, conducting in each novel what Marilyn Stasio calls "a criminal investigation that is a genuine heroic quest."

During her quest, Warshawski investigates not only the world in which she lives, but also how she operates within that milieu. V. I. remains remarkably self-aware throughout the novels, constantly questioning her own motives and authority in a world where truth and justice do not seem to exist except as relative perceptions. Warshawski does come to realize, however, that higher, less malleable values than truth exist: these she finds in friendship, life, and freedom from oppression.

While Paretsky's feminist viewpoint suggests that perhaps the "sacred" traditional institutions are unworthy of the almost automatic respect they receive, it does offer an alternative—though not an easy one—through friendship and the establishment of a carefully selected surrogate family. With the third novel, *Killing Orders*, Paretsky moves beyond the plotting of convincing crime novels toward the extensive development of her characters. Drawn together by the human need for companionship, V. I. and her family of friends—Lotty Herschel, physician, women's clinic operator, and victim of Nazi concentration camps; Bobby Mallory, a police lieutenant with traditional values and a debt to V. I.'s dead father; Mr. Contreras, a retired union worker appalled by the ethical flimsiness of his own daughter; and Peppy, a golden retriever extraordinaire—struggle to establish relationships that support without confining.

The intensity in Paretsky's novels of characterizations, actions, and themes increases if the books are read in chronological order. In the later works, the mystery plot becomes tightly woven with the central characters and their relationships; since the portraiture in each novel builds on the preceding fiction, the mysteries gain impact when read in the order written.

Readers who enjoy the feminist professional detective that Sara Paretsky creates may also wish to explore the fiction of such authors as Linda Barnes, Marcia Biederman, Mickey Friedman, Sue Grafton, Linda Grant, Marcia Muller, and Barbara Wilson.

MYSTERY FICTION

V. I. Warshawski Series

Indemnity Only. New York: Dial; London: Gollancz, 1982.

Deadlock. New York: Dial; London: Gollancz, 1984.

Killing Orders. New York: Morrow, 1985; London: Gollancz, 1986.

Bitter Medicine. New York: Morrow; London: Gollancz, 1987.

Blood Shot. New York: Delacorte, 1988; as *Toxic Shock*. London: Gollancz, 1988.

Burn Marks. New York: Delacorte; London: Chatto and Windus, 1990.

Guardian Angel. New York: Delacorte, 1991; London: Penguin, 1992.

Tunnel Vision. New York: Delacorte, 1994.

CRITICAL BIBLIOGRAPHY

Bakerman, Jane S. "Living 'Openly and With Dignity': Sara Paretsky's New-Boiled Feminist Fiction." *Midamerica*, (1985): 120–35.

Dudar, Helen. "Queen of the Gumshoes." *Lear's*, August 1991, pp. 72–74, 96–98.

Herbert, Rosemary. "Aiming Higher: Some of Today's Top Crime Writers Are Breaking New Ground in Terms of Setting, Sleuths and Motivations." *Publishers Weekly*, 13 April 1990, pp. 30–32.

Reddy, Maureen T. "The Feminist Counter-Tradition in Crime: Cross, Grafton, Paretsky, and Wilson." In *The Cunning Craft*, ed. Ronald G. Walker and June M. Frazer. Macomb, Ill.: Western Illinois University Press, 1990, pp. 174–87.

Shapiro, Laura. "Sara Paretsky (*Ms. Magazine* Woman of the Year)." *Ms. Magazine*, January 1988, p. 66.

Shepherdson, Nancy. "The Writer behind Warshawski." *Writer's Digest*, September 1992, pp. 38–40.

Stasio, Marilyn. "Lady Gumshoes: Boiled Less Hard." *New York Times Book Review*, 28 April 1985, p. 1.

ELIZABETH A. TREMBLEY

BARBARA PAUL (1931–   )

Barbara Paul was born in Maysville, Kentucky, on June 5, 1931. She received her undergraduate degree at Bowling Green State University in 1953, her M.A. from the University of Redlands in 1957, and her Ph.D. from the University of Pittsburgh in 1969. She has been married, is now divorced, and has one son, Kenneth. She taught at Berry College, Erskine College, and the University of Pittsburgh, teaching speech, writing, and literature (usually drama). She also directed a number of plays. In 1973 she became a full-time writer of science and crime fiction. She is a member of the American Crime Writers League, Science Fiction Writers of America, Sisters in Crime, and Novelists, Inc.

Perhaps the key phrase for Paul's crime fiction is variety. Her novels are best described as psychological thrillers, but not at the expense of tight plotting; rather, character and plot are integral to each other. Paul tends to avoid series detectives. The Enrico Caruso and Geraldine Farrar series is a notable exception, and Marian Larch has appeared in three novels to date; however, she is not the only focal point in these stories. While several of Paul's novels are set in the theater, she by no means limits herself to one setting. While her stories often take a feminist slant, they are never simplistically feminist. Her women, while psychologically stronger and more resilient than her male characters, tend to be severely flawed. They succeed at detection, but may well fail in their personal lives. Thus, while one can discern patterns in Paul's work, one cannot find formulas.

Paul envisions a contaminated society in which people must fight to survive. Her characters live in densely populated urban areas and, while not everyone is corrupt, no one remains untouched by a scrambling-rat kind of mentality. Moreover, no one is quite what he or she appears to be.

Living under the stress of trying to succeed in a competitive society whose ruthlessness is camouflaged by a veneer of politeness, these characters typically react by taking an expedient way out of their dilemmas. The unethical murder or arrange murders, while the ethical find less criminal modes of avoidance that nevertheless follow lines of weakness within the self. The novels then become systematic revelations, not only of the whodunit but of the psyches of one or more of the main characters. *He Huffed and He Puffed* is seen through the eyes of the victim and each of the three suspects, in turn, and then concluded by the police. *The Renewable Virgin* is seen through the eyes of three women, giving three feminist perceptions of the crime, while *First Gravedigger* is narrated by a man who arranges to have his employer murdered in order to marry the victim's wife and succeed to his business.

A more sympathetic examination of personality is found in *In-Laws and Outlaws*, which deals with a societally high echelon of characters who, despite their status, operate on principles not dissimilar from those of the protagonist in *Gravedigger*, and who are, in fact, more violent. The protagonist, however, is a finer individual. Gillian Clifford Decker left her only family, her in-laws, when her husband died. She returned to her first love, the theater, and to personal freedom, finding her niche as curator for a Chicago museum of theatrical history. When her husband's brother dies in an accident, she goes to Boston for the funeral and remains to investigate what she becomes increasingly certain is not an accident but rather one of a series of brutal murders. She is brilliantly successful as a detective. In the process, her own sense of self is stripped away and she is revealed as a fake. First she realizes that not only had she run from the Deckers, she has been running all her life. Second, she has succeeded professionally only because of her husband's money. Third, even her name is false: she is really named Gladys, not Gillian. She responds by trying to run away again, this time on a sailboard. With cosmic irony, the winds blow her back to the shore she had left and into the loving arms of the Deckers, where she will remain, secure, loved, and imprisoned.

Paul can write happier novels containing strong protagonists without lethal flaws. Healthy, vibrant heroines include Kelly Ingram, in *The Renewable Virgin*, and Geraldine Farrar, in *Prima Donna at Large*. They are winners, in control of themselves and of their worlds, and they do not allow men to dominate their emotional lives. Consequently, they are free to enjoy life in all its forms, which includes sex, fame, and material luxuries. Nor are Farrar and Ingram superficial personalities. Paul's vision is not inevitably a dark one: sometimes people *do*—if they have luck, beauty, brains, and ability—escape.

Readers who enjoy Barbara Paul might also enjoy Ruth Rendell, P.D. James, and Sara Paretsky.

MYSTERY FICTION

The Fourth Wall. New York: Doubleday, 1979; London: Women's Press, 1988.
First Gravedigger. New York: Doubleday, 1980; London: Collins, 1982.
Liars and Tyrants and People Who Turn Blue. New York: Doubleday, 1980.
Your Eyelids Are Growing Heavy. New York: Doubleday, 1981; London: Collins, 1982.
Kill Fee. New York: Scribners; and London: Collins, 1985; as *Murder C.O.D.* [movie made for television]. NBC Network, Sept. 21, 1990.

But He Was Already Dead When I Got There. New York: Scribner's; London: Collins, 1986.

Good King Sauerkraut. New York: Scribner's; as *King of Misrule.* London: Piatkus, 1990.

In-Laws and Outlaws. New York: Scribner's, 1990; as *Death Elsewhere.* London: Piatkus, 1991.

The Apostrophe Thief. New York: Scribner's, 1993; London: Macmillan, 1993.

Enrico Caruso and Geraldine Farrar Series

A Cadenza for Caruso. New York: St. Martin's Press, 1984; Bath, U.K.: Chivers, 1986.

Prima Donna at Large. New York: St. Martin's Press, 1985.

A Chorus of Detectives. New York: St. Martin's Press, 1987.

Marian Larch Series

The Renewable Virgin. London: Collins; New York: Scribner's, 1984.

He Huffed and He Puffed. New York: Scribner's; London: Macmillan, 1989.

You Have the Right to Remain Silent. New York: Scribner's; London: Piatkus, 1992.

JUDITH J. KOLLMANN

ANNE PERRY (1938–   )

Anne Perry was born on London, England, on October 28, 1938. She was educated privately and worked as an airline stewardess, an assistant buyer for an English department store, and a property underwriter in California from 1967 to 1972. She currently lives in the tiny seacoast village of Portmahomack, Scotland.

Before turning to murder mysteries, Perry wrote two unpublished historical novels, and when she decided to set a murder mystery in London of the 1800s, she retained her historical novelist's perspective, focusing on "human beings . . . torn apart by [the] fears, horrors, beliefs, and ideals" of that particular period.

Perry's mysteries have a strong feminist perspective, highlighting the restrictions on females in Victorian society—in every area from the paucity of their education to the tightness of their corset stays. In *The Cater Street Hangman*, Perry introduces Charlotte Ellison, the daughter of a family of quality with aspirations to rise socially. She has been taught to paint watercolors, do needlework samplers, make social calls, and dress for dinner.

Her father does not allow her to read the newspaper because he considers her to be too pure and delicate for its vulgarity and too intellectually weak to understand its substantive issues.

However, Charlotte is unsuited to this world, and her unconventional marriage to Thomas Pitt, a policeman socially far beneath her, frees her from stifling social conventions and gives her access to information about social conditions in the world outside the withdrawing room. When her sister Emily marries a lord—as far above their social station as a policeman was beneath it—Charlotte also gains access to the upper reaches of Victorian society.

As a detective team, Charlotte and Pitt are equals. Charlotte does not play the Watson or Hastings role of admirer or dupe to the superior intellect of the detective. She and Pitt have separate areas of expertise and work in similar ways, observing suspects under stress, provoking situations or crises, watching for slight muscle movements or flickers of the eye, and often arriving at the same solution independently. Pitt handles the official police investigation of the slums, the streets, and obligatory interviews with suspects, while Charlotte joins Emily in the carefully restricted, mannered and coded world of high society to search for relationships, fears, and hatreds that might provide the motive or emotional atmosphere for murder. The heart of Perry's vision lies in the connection between these two worlds.

Perry herself cites G. K. Chesterton's *The Man Who Was Thursday* as her favorite book for its message that "we all face the same battles, but to overcome when believing yourself alone, simply because you care so much, is the ultimate victory." Perry's sympathies often lie with the murderer, but she treats harshly those who would use their social or political station to hide a crime or to blame others for it.

The male-female power conflict becomes just one of a series of social issues of suppression and domination that Perry explores. The early books center on the discovery of corruption in high society. The surprise is that the murderer is not an outsider but "one of us," the respectable—even the privileged—struggling with a secret shame or twisted by a pressure too great to bear.

Later books explore social abuses in more detail—including workhouses, brothels, incest, and child prostitution. London slums exist literally in the shadow of elite neighborhoods and, as Pitt tells Charlotte, both ends of society live off each other in a symbiotic relationship. The mansions of the wealthy are built from the profits of brothels. Idealistic reformers find to their horror that to stamp out corruption in the slums, they must first deal with, and even abet, corrupt politicians in Parliament. Through it all runs the theme of the destruction of the weak, particularly women, who are mere pawns of the system, whether sold into prostitution as poor children or whether suffering from the "morally numbing effects of boredom," which lead rich women to prostitution for amusement or escape from their stifling world.

Although *Bethlehem Road*, *Highgate Rise*, and *Belgrave Square* deal with specific nineteenth-century movements of women's suffrage and property rights in divorce, the Fabians, and venture capital, the roots of murder in each lie in individual spiritual corruption and sexual perversion that preys on others. Women particularly are expected to uphold the social order but are ignorant of how the world works and powerless to affect it. They uphold a male order that destroys them for its own greed. Their manners and virtue become the facade behind which men hide sinful deeds.

Inspector Pitt is an uncomplicated detective-hero. Suffused with personal integrity, compassion, and social consciousness, he discovers and defeats the evil in society and emerges unscathed. The hero of Perry's second series, Inspector William Monk, is a more complex man on a more dangerous journey. As the result of a carriage accident, Monk has completely lost his memory. In each of the series books, his search for the truth behind the crime mirrors his search for his own identity. Moreover, this is not simply a matter of recovering his memory and fitting back into the old mold: the accident obliterated his old values and desires as well. Monk is truly a man reborn. As he discovers clues to his old identity, he begins to dislike the man he once was—skillful, courageous, ruthless and cold, and ambitious to climb to the top of his profession at any cost to his colleagues and subordinates. Handsome, mysterious even unto himself, harboring a secret guilt, and equally capable of cruelty and suffering, Monk is a Byronic hero in a Gothic-novel world filled with the terrors of uncertainty and obscurity.

As he pursues his dual investigation in the first book of the series, *The Face of a Stranger*, he encounters Hester Latterly, a stronger and more independent version of Charlotte Pitt. Hester was a nurse with Florence Nightingale in the Crimea at the time of the Charge of the Light Brigade. She returned with hot contempt for the incompetence, confusion, pride, and inefficiency of the army command, which had sent thousands of soldiers to their deaths unnecessarily. Forced to earn her own living, she serves as a nurse in a London hospital where she comes up against the further incompetence and stubborn, patronizing pride of the exclusively male medical profession. Like Charlotte, she has access to high society through family connections.

Monk and Hester do not get along. In fact, their equally strong wills repel each other, and only at the end of the story are they brought to work together to identify the murderer. They move together, but only gradually, through the next two books. Set thirty years earlier than the Pitt series, the Monk books are longer and treat all their characters in more psychological depth, dealing with the even more starkly lurid side of the upper crust of Victorian England.

Both the Pitt and the Monk series are best read in order. Readers who like Anne Perry might also enjoy Elizabeth Peters's Amelia Peabody series.

MYSTERY FICTION

Sins of The Wolf, forthcoming.
Traitors Gate, forthcoming.

Charlotte and Thomas Pitt Series

The Cater Street Hangman. London: Hale; New York: St. Martin's, 1979.

Callander Square. London: Hale; New York: St. Martin's, 1980.

Paragon Walk. New York: St. Martin's, 1981.

Resurrection Row. New York: St. Martin's, 1981.

Rutland Place. New York: St. Martin's, 1983.

Bluegate Fields. New York: St. Martin's, 1984.

Death in the Devil's Acre. New York: St. Martin's, 1985.

Cardington Crescent. New York: St. Martin's, 1987; London: Souvenir Press, 1990.

Silence in Hanover Close. New York: St. Martin's, 1988; London: Souvenir Press, 1989.

Bethlehem Road. New York: St. Martin's, 1990.

Highgate Rise. New York: Fawcett Crest, 1991.

Belgrave Square. New York: Fawcett Columbine, 1992.

Farrier's Lane. New York: Fawcett Columbine, 1993.

The Hyde Park Headsman. New York: Fawcett Columbine, 1994.

Inspector William Monk Series

The Face of a Stranger. New York: Fawcett Columbine, 1990.

A Dangerous Mourning. New York: Fawcett Columbine, 1991.

Defend and Betray. New York: Fawcett Columbine, 1992.

A Sudden, Fearful Death. New York: Fawcett Columbine, 1993.

CRITICAL BIBLIOGRAPHY

Borck, Helga, and GraceAnne A. DeCandido. "Perry, Anne." In *Twentieth Century Crime and Mystery Writers*, ed. Lesley Henderson. 3rd ed. Chicago: St. James Press, 1991, pp. 843–43.

Cooper-Clark, Diana. "Interview with Anne Perry." In *Designs of Darkness: Interviews with Detective Novelists*. Bowling Green, Ohio: Bowling Green State University Popular Press, 1983, pp. 205–23.

Nichols, Victoria, and Susan Thompson. "Charlotte Ellison." In *Silk Stalkings: When Women Write of Murder*. Berkeley, Calif.: Black Lizard Books, 1988, pp. 78–79.

———. "Thomas Pitt." In *Silk Stalkings: When Women Write of Murder*. Berkeley, Calif.: Black Lizard Books, 1988, pp. 34–35.

JOAN WARCHOL ROSSI

ELIZABETH PETERS (1927–   )

Elizabeth Peters, née Barbara Gross, was born in Canton, Illinois, on September 29, 1927. She studied at the Oriental Institute of the University of Chicago, receiving a Ph.B. in 1947, an M.A. in 1950, and her Ph.D. in 1952. She married Richard R. Mertz in 1950 and had two children, Elizabeth and Peter. She was divorced in 1968. She belongs to the American Crime Writers League, Egypt Exploration Society, American Research Council in Egypt, Society for the Study of Egyptian Antiquities, and National Organization for Women, as well as Sisters in Crime. She received the Grandmaster Award, Bouchercon, 1986; Agatha Award for best mystery novel of 1989, Malice Domestic Convention, for *Naked Once More*; and a D.H.L. from Hood College in 1989.

She writes nonfiction under Barbara Mertz, supernatural romantic thrillers under Barbara Michaels, and comedy-suspense romance under Elizabeth Peters.

When Peters first began publishing, she seemed not to have intended to write series, but the novels do manifest certain common tendencies. Not only are they all essentially comic and possess independent heroines and competent heroes, but many deal with archaeological treasures; a number are also set in the Near East. The early 1970s were the years of the spy stories and the spy-spoof tales; this was also the era when feminine liberation was a significant item on the political agenda. Vicky Bliss was made for spy fiction, and Jacqueline Kirby, as she was then conceived, for women's liberation.

Vicky Bliss herself is an intellectual Marilyn Monroe. She has stunning, tall blonde beauty coupled with intellect, verve, and a rich sense of derring-do. Vicky works for the National Museum in Munich. She is, technically speaking, the expert on medieval European painting and sculpture, but the museum is small, which conveniently allows her to seek all sorts of ancient treasures. In the most recent novel, *Trojan Gold*, the treasure is Schliemann's Trojan gold, which was lost from the National Museum in Berlin during the Nazi evacuation of the city in 1945. Vicky's ongoing bête noire and lover is John Smythe, a sophisticated art thief, with whom she constantly engages in a contest of wills and wits as they search for missing artifacts.

Jacqueline Kirby, who was born of the feminist movement, is a much less endearing personality. She, like all Peters's heroines, is gorgeous—in this case, a glorious redhead. An ex-librarian, she has recently become a romance writer. She had attended a romance writers' convention and decided to write a spoof of the form; the spoof was taken seriously, became a best-seller, and now, to her lasting surprise, Kirby is a romance writer. She has become a more human and emotional individual in the latest work in this series, *Naked Once More*, which is one of Peters's best written and crafted novels.

In my opinion, Peters's finest series in terms of quality of writing, richness of character development, and thematic content is the Amelia Peabody series. One can see why this took longer to develop into a series; in *Crocodile on the Sandbank*, Peters wrote a novel that, while it contained elements of comedy, suspense thriller, and romance, was nevertheless an aberration. It was set in the late nineteenth century, and therefore required a highly skillful blending of contemporary and nineteenth-century cultural expectations with late-twentieth-century gender roles as well as the basic Peters ingredients of comedy, suspense, and romance. Moreover, to complicate matters, Peters married Peabody to Emerson at the conclusion of the novel *and* left Amelia pregnant. No other Peters novel appears to be as conclusive.

However, the tides of literary and political tastes began to shift. In the United States, at any rate, the Victorian era became popular; societal expectations turned once again to the family as a valued way of life and the image of the liberated woman broadened to include those who were not only professional career women but could also successfully incorporate career and family into their life-style. Moreover, the image of the masculine ideal changed. It became acceptably male to engage in active, participatory fatherhood and house-husbandhood while encouraging one's wife to pursue advanced degrees and career. Suddenly, Amelia Peabody and Radcliffe Emerson were off and running straight to Egypt, especially since the movie *Raiders of the Lost Ark* had also reminded America about the aura of archaeological treasure.

The Peabody-Emerson series consists of at least seven novels, in each of which the Peabody-Emerson team pursues mystery (and, occasionally, archaeology) in Egypt, Africa, or England. The two are usually accompanied by their linguistically precocious son, Ramses, and the cat, Bastet. Sleuthing has become a familial function, and much of the reader's delight stems from the awareness that Amelia's ability for ratiocination is at least matched by that of her husband, her son—and her cat.

Amelia Peabody is intelligent, independent, and stubborn. She is not only a role model for the twentieth-century American woman, she is an affectionate spoof of the wealthy and intrepid British women who traveled with their husbands throughout the Near East and Africa in the late nineteenth century. A few of these prototypes even engaged in archaeological excavations.

Radcliffe Emerson is a similarly well-rounded personality; for example, the Egyptians call him "The Father of Curses" because of his linguistic abilities in Arabic. Short on patience but passionate about Egyptology, he spends much of each season attempting to excavate while Amelia is busy sleuthing (often popping buttons off his shirt in frustration when she gets into too much trouble). Then, he jumps in with equal enthusiasm and they sleuth together. When they both strike catastrophe, it is usually Ramses who rescues his parents.

Peters also plays with nineteenth-century literary motifs taken from Rider Haggard, Arthur Conan Doyle, and other sources. Therefore, *Crocodile on the Sandbank* deals with a peripatetic mummy; other novels sport a "master criminal" or discover long-lost civilizations. The books are unabashed comic romps.

However, there is a serious theme in the series. The Emersons succeed as a couple and, ever so gently, Peters indicates that, although humorous, this is not always easy. Amelia, independent and stubborn though she is, is always supportive of Emerson, especially in public. Emerson, in turn, is sensitive of Amelia's thoughts and feelings, often to a greater degree than she herself. Nonetheless, there are tensions and blind spots, notably in that classical matrimonial area, jealousy. This, of course, also contributes to the comedy, for Amelia tends to be blithely unaware, as in *The Mummy Case*, that Emerson is lividly jealous of what he insists is a purely hypothetical master criminal. In the previous novel, *The Curse of the Pharaohs*, it had been Amelia who had been jealous of the conniving Lady Baskerville (who is not from the Devonshire branch of the Baskervilles).

Readers of Elizabeth Peters may enjoy Anne Perry, Aaron Elkins, and Tony Hillerman.

MYSTERY FICTION

Writing as Elizabeth Peters

The Jackal's Head. Des Moines, Iowa: Meredith, 1968; London: Jenkins, 1969.
The Camelot Caper. Des Moines, Iowa: Meredith, 1969; London: Cassell, 1976.
The Dead Sea Cipher. New York: Dodd, Mead, 1970; London: Cassell, 1975.
The Night of Four Hundred Rabbits. New York: Dodd, Mead, 1971; as *Shadows in the Moonlight*. London: Coronet, 1975.
Legend in Green Velvet. New York: Dodd, Mead, 1976, as *Ghost in Green Velvet*. London: Cassell, 1977.
Devil-May-Care. New York: Dodd, Mead, 1977; London: Cassell, 1978.
Summer of the Dragon. New York: Dodd, Mead, 1979; London: Souvenir, 1980.
The Love Talker. New York: Dodd, Mead, 1980; London: Souvenir, 1981.
The Copenhagen Connection. New York: Congdon and Weed, 1982. London: Souvenir, 1983.
Next Train to Memphis. New York: Warner, 1994.

Vicky Bliss Series

Borrower of the Night. New York: Dodd, Mead, 1973; London: Cassell, 1974.
Street of the Five Moons. New York: Dodd, Mead, 1978.

Silhouette in Scarlet. New York: Congdon and Weed, 1983; London: Souvenir, 1984.

Trojan Gold. New York: Atheneum; London: Piatkus, 1987.

Jacqueline Kirby Series

The Seventh Sinner. New York: Dodd, Mead, 1972; London: Coronet, 1975.

The Murders of Richard III. New York: Dodd, Mead, 1974.

Die for Love. New York: Congdon and Weed, 1984; London: Souvenir, 1985.

Naked Once More. New York: Warner, 1989; London: Piatkus, 1990.

Amelia Peabody Series

Crocodile on the Sandbank. New York: Dodd, Mead, 1975; London: Cassell, 1976.

The Curse of the Pharaohs. New York: Dodd, Mead, 1981; London: Souvenir, 1982.

The Mummy Case. New York: Congdon and Weed, 1985; London: Souvenir, 1986.

Lion in the Valley. New York: Atheneum, 1986; London: Piatkus, 1987.

The Deeds of the Disturber. New York: Atheneum; London: Piatkus, 1988.

The Last Camel Died at Noon. New York: Warner; London: Piatkus, 1991.

The Snake, the Crocodile and the Dog. New York: Warner, 1992.

Writing as Barbara Michaels

The Master of the Blacktower. New York: Appleton, 1966; London: Jenkins, 1977.
Sons of the Wolf. Des Moines, Iowa: Meredith, 1967; London: Jenkins, 1968.
      Republished as *Mystery on the Moors.* New York: Paperback Library, 1968.
Ammie, Come Home. Des Moines, Iowa: Meredith, 1968; London: Jenkins, 1969.
      Film: ABC Television, 1969.
Prince of Darkness. Des Moines, Iowa: Meredith, 1969; London: Hodder and
      Stoughton, 1971.
Dark on the Other Side. New York: Dodd, Mead, 1970; London: Souvenir, 1973.
The Crying Child. New York: Dodd, Mead; London: Souvenir, 1971.
Greygallows. New York: Dodd, Mead; London: Souvenir, 1973.
House of Many Shadows. New York: Dodd, Mead, 1974; London: Souvenir, 1976.
The Sea King's Daughter. New York: Dodd, Mead, 1975; London: Souvenir, 1977.
Witch. New York: Dodd, Mead, 1973; London: Souvenir, 1975.
Patriot's Dream. New York: Dodd, Mead, 1976; London: Souvenir, 1978.
Wings of the Falcon. New York: Dodd, Mead, 1977; London: Souvenir, 1979.
Wait for What Will Come. New York: Dodd, Mead, 1978; London: Souvenir,
      1980.
The Walker in the Shadows. New York: Dodd, Mead, 1979; London: Souvenir,
      1981.
The Wizard's Daughter. New York: Dodd, Mead, 1980; London: Souvenir, 1982.
Someone in the House. New York: Dodd, Mead, 1981; London: Souvenir, 1983.
Black Rainbow. New York: Congdon and Weed, 1982; London: Souvenir, 1983.

Dark Duet. New York: Congdon and Weed, 1983.

Here I Stay. New York: Congdon and Weed, 1983; London: Souvenir, 1984.

The Grey Beginning. New York: Congdon and Weed, 1984; London: Souvenir, 1986.

Be Buried in the Rain. New York: Atheneum, 1985; London: Piatkus, 1986.

Shattered Silk. New York: Atheneum, 1986; London: Piatkus, 1987.

Search the Shadows. New York: Atheneum, 1987; London: Piatkus, 1988.

Smoke and Mirrors. New York: Simon and Schuster; London: Piatkus, 1989.

Into the Darkness. New York: Simon and Schuster; London: Piatkus, 1990.

Scattered Blossoms. New York: Simon and Schuster, 1992.

This Quiet Dust. New York: Simon and Schuster, 1992.

Vanish with the Rose. New York: Simon and Schuster; London: Piatkus, 1992.

Houses of Stone. New York: Simon and Schuster, 1993.

CRITICAL BIBLIOGRAPHY

Larew, Marilyn. "Elizabeth Peters: Barbara Mertz." In *Critical Survey of Mystery and Detective Fiction*, ed. Frank N. Magill. Pasadena, Calif.: Salem, 1988, 3: 1311–17.

McDonald, T. Liam. "Will the Real Author Please Stand Up?" *The Armchair Detective*, 26, no. 2 (1993): 6.

Mussell, Kay. "Peters, Elizabeth." In *Twentieth Century Crime and Mystery Writers*, ed. Lesley Henderson. 3rd ed. Chicago and London: St. James Press, 1991, pp. 844–46.

Nichols, Victoria, and Susan Thompson. "Amelia Peabody and Radcliffe Emerson." In *Silk Stalkings*. Berkeley, Calif.: Black Lizard, 1988, pp. 9–11.

———. "Jacqueline Kirby." In *Silk Stalkings*. Berkeley, Calif.: Black Lizard, 1988, pp. 7–9.

———. "Vicky Bliss." In *Silk Stalkings*. Berkeley, Calif.: Black Lizard, 1988, pp. 184–85.

Telgen, Diane, and Jean W. Ross, "Mertz, Barbara (Gross), 1927–." In *Contemporary Authors, New Revision Series*, ed. James G. Lesniak. Detroit: Gale Research, 1992, 36: 264–70.

JUDITH J. KOLLMANN

ELLIS PETERS (1913–)

The creator of Brother Cadfael was born Edith Mary Pargeter on September 28, 1913, in Horsehay, Shropshire, England. She adopted her most famous nom de plume, Ellis Peters (the name of a favorite brother), in 1959, to be exclusively used in conjunction with her detective fiction.

Peters was educated at Dawley Church of England Elementary School and Coalbrookdale High School for Girls and received an Oxford School Certificate. While working in Dawley as a pharmacist's assistant (1933–

40), Peters began her writing career. At the outbreak of World War II, she left Dawley to serve in the Women's Royal Naval Service. In 1944 Peters was honored by King George VI and presented with the British Empire Medal for her outstanding service in communications.

Peters forthrightly asserts that she welcomed the structure the detective genre imposes on a writer and has found that it affords her more artistic freedom than the non-mystery novel does. Preeminent in her detective fiction, and particularly the Brother Cadfael series, is the absence of archaic language and description. Instead, Peters has chosen to forsake historical linguistic accuracy in favor of contemporary verisimilitude. She feels that archaisms inhibit the reader's ability to relate to the immediacy of the plot. Thus, her novels are characterized by vitality and clarity of speech rather than the stilted dialogue which obscures much historical fiction.

Not only are Peters's novels a popular success, they are critically acclaimed as well. In 1962 she was awarded the prestigious Mystery Writers of America Edgar Allan Poe Award for *Death and the Joyful Woman* (Felse Family) and the Crime Writers' Association Silver Dagger in 1981 (Cadfael).

The first detective series, the Felse Family novels, focuses on the criminal investigations of CID Detective Sergeant George Felse, his wife, Bunty, and their son, Dominic. George Felse, the professional detective, is methodical and rational in his crime solving. Bunty Felse, when drawn into detective work, proves herself to be a woman of uncommon courage and discernment. As an Oxford University graduate in the later novels, Dominic is cast into the role of amateur sleuth and proves as clever and successful as his parents.

In 1977 Peters embarked on her most ambitious and popular series: the Brother Cadfael mysteries, set in twelfth-century Shropshire. The Cadfael novels have thus allowed her to combine her love of history (especially the history of her native Shropshire) and her mystery writing.

In her characterization of Brother Cadfael, Peters has combined spiritual insight, scientific knowledge (Cadfael is the monastery's herbalist), and worldly experience. Although not originally conceived as a series character, Cadfael ignited the imagination of his creator and the reading public. The good brother is a remarkably complex character: a Welshman living in England and a former adventurer living the holy life of a tonsured monk, he is a man of multiplicity. As a former Crusader, Cadfael has lived a full and lusty life in the secular world (one novel, *The Virgin in the Ice*, alludes to an illegitimate son). His experiences have given him a keen insight into human nature, both the dark and the light. Now in his early sixties, Cadfael has been retired for the last fifteen years to the Benedictine Abbey of Saint Peter and Saint Paul at Shrewsbury where he has ably ministered to the sick—and solved crimes on the side.

What sets the Cadfael chronicles apart from Peters's other detective fictions is the intrusion of the political environment on the denizens of Shrewsbury, secular and clerical alike. The continuous battles of King Stephen and the Empress Maud for the throne of England create personal and political tensions that sometimes provide the impetus for the criminal activities besetting the seemingly peaceful community of Shrewsbury.

The Cadfael chronicles often transcend generic conventions. Peters frequently uses the historical time and place to foster social issues. For instance, in *Monk's-hood*, she raises the issues of Welsh land rights and the medieval practice of villenage, exposing the latter for its injustice. *St. Peter's Fair*, while revolving around a crime, converges on the conflicts between the aristocracy and the rising merchant class. In *The Heretic's Apprentice*, theological concerns are foregrounded over the murder investigation. And although female characters are on the periphery in the series, the women are depicted as strong, resourceful, and even formidable people.

Unfortunately, the earlier novels and the Felse Family series are not as accessible to the reading public as the Cadfael novels (although in 1991 Mysterious Press began to reprint the Felse novels). Consequently, a reader interested in Peters's detective fiction will probably begin with the Cadfael series because of their availability and popularity. I would recommend, if at all possible, that the new reader begin the series chronologically. Some key characters are fully developed and thus introduced in the earlier books. For example, the sharp-witted Hugh Beringar, the deputy sheriff of Shrewsbury (who is usually instrumental in Cadfael's crime solving), makes his initial appearance in the second novel of the series, *One Corpse Too Many*, as a possible foil to Cadfael. This particular novel establishes the relationship between the clerical/secular authorities in Shrewsbury that is maintained throughout the series.

Overall, readers who enjoy Peters's detective fiction might also be interested in the works of Catherine Aird, M. C. Beaton, P. D. James, Elizabeth Lemarchand, Ruth Rendell, Josephine Tey, and Pauline Winslow.

MYSTERY FICTION

Writing as Ellis Peters

Death Mask. London: Collins, 1959; New York: Doubleday, 1960.
The Will and the Deed. London: Collins, 1960; as *Where There's a Will*. New York: Doubleday, 1962.
Funeral of Figaro. London: Collins, 1962; New York: Morrow, 1964.

Felse Family Series

Fallen into the Pit. London: Heinemann, 1961 (as by Edith Pargeter).
Death and the Joyful Woman. London: Collins, 1961; New York: Doubleday, 1962.

Flight of a Witch. London: Collins, 1964.

A Nice Derangement of Epitaphs. London: Collins; as *Who Lies Here?* New York: Morrow, 1965.

The Piper on the Mountain. London: Collins; New York: Morrow, 1966.

Black Is the Colour of My True-Love's Heart. London: Collins; New York: Morrow, 1967.

The Grass-Widow's Tale. London: Collins; New York: Morrow, 1968.

The House of Green Turf. London: Collins; New York: Morrow, 1969.

Mourning Raga. London: Macmillan, 1969; New York: Morrow, 1970.

The Knocker on Death's Door. London: Macmillan, 1970; New York: Morrow, 1971.

Death to the Landlords. London: Macmillan; New York: Morrow, 1972.

City of Gold and Shadows. London: Macmillan, 1973; New York: Morrow, 1974.

The Horn of Roland. London: Macmillan; New York: Morrow, 1974.

Never Pick Up Hitch-Hikers! London: Macmillan; New York: Morrow, 1976.

Brother Cadfael Series

A Morbid Taste for Bones. London: Macmillan, 1970; New York: Morrow, 1977.

Rainbow's End. London: Macmillan; New York: Morrow, 1977.

One Corpse Too Many: A Medieval Whodunit. London: Macmillan; as *One Corpse Too Many*. New York: Morrow, 1979.

Monk's-hood: The Third Chronicle of Brother Cadfael. London: Macmillan, 1980; New York: Morrow, 1981.

Saint Peter's Fair: The Fourth Chronicle of Brother Cadfael. London: Macmillan; New York: Morrow, 1981.

The Leper of Saint Giles: The Fifth Chronicle of Brother Cadfael. London: Macmillan, 1981; New York: Morrow, 1982.

The Virgin in the Ice: The Sixth Chronicle of Brother Cadfael. London: Macmillan, 1982; New York: Morrow, 1983.

The Sanctuary Sparrow: The Seventh Chronicle of Brother Cadfael. London: Macmillan; New York: Morrow, 1983.

The Devil's Novice: The Eighth Chronicle of Brother Cadfael. London: Macmillan, 1983; New York: Morrow, 1984.

Dead Man's Ransom: The Ninth Chronicle of Brother Cadfael. London: Macmillan, 1984; New York: Morrow, 1985.

The Pilgrim of Hate: The Tenth Chronicle of Brother Cadfael. London: Macmillan; New York: Morrow, 1984.

An Excellent Mystery: The Eleventh Chronicle of Brother Cadfael. London: Macmillan. New York: Morrow, 1985.

The Raven in the Foregate: The Twelfth Chronicle of Brother Cadfael. London: Macmillan. New York: Morrow, 1986.

The Rose Rent: The Thirteenth Chronicle of Brother Cadfael. London: Macmillan. New York: Morrow, 1986.

The Hermit of Eyton Forest. London: Headline. New York: Mysterious Press, 1988.

A Rare Benedictine. London: Headline, 1988. New York: Mysterious Press, 1989.

The Confessions of Brother Haluin. London: Headline, 1988. New York: Mysterious Press, 1989.

The Heretic's Apprentice: The Sixteenth Chronicle of Brother Cadfael. London: Headline. New York: Mysterious Press, 1990.

The Potter's Field. London: Headline. New York: Mysterious Press, 1989.

The Summer of the Danes. London: Headline. New York: Mysterious Press, 1991.

The Benediction of Brother Cadfael. New York: Mysterious Press, 1993.

The Holy Thief. New York: Mysterious Press, 1993.

Fallen into the Pit. New York: Mysterious Press, 1994.

Writing as Jolyon Carr

Murder in the Dispensary. London: Jenkins, 1938.
Death Comes by Post. London: Jenkins, 1940.

Writing as John Redfern

The Victim Needs a Nurse. London: Jarrolds, 1940.

CRITICAL BIBLIOGRAPHY

Barzun, Jacques, and Wendell Hertig Taylor. [Introduction.] In *Never Pick Up Hitch-Hikers!* New York: Morrow, 1976.

Boyd, Mary K. "Brother Cadfael: Renaissance Man of the Twelfth Century." *Clues*, 9, no. 1 (1988): 39–48.

Christian, Edwin, and Blake Lindsay. "The Habit of Detection: The Medieval Monk as Detective in the Novels of Ellis Peters." *Studies in Medievalism* 4 (1992): 78–88.

Greeley, Andrew M. "Ellis Peters: Another Umberto Eco?" *The Armchair Detective*, 18 (1985): 238–45.

Herbert, Rosemary. "Ellis Peters." *Publishers Weekly*, 9 Aug. 1991, pp. 40–41.

ANITA MARISSA VICKERS

NANCY PICKARD (1945–   )

A resident of Kansas, former newspaper reporter and editor Nancy Pickard is the author of the Jenny Cain mysteries. With the publication of *The 27 Ingredient Chili Con Carne Murders*, Pickard also took over authorship of

the Eugenia Potter series begun by the late Virginia Rich. Pickard has served
as a national board member for Mystery Writers of America and as past
president of the respected writers' group Sisters in Crime. Her awards include the Anthony for *Say No to Murder*, the Macavity Award for the Best
Mystery Novel for *Marriage Is Murder*, the Agatha Award for Best Novel
for *Bum Steer*, and both the Agatha and Macavity awards for *I.O.U.* Her
short stories have appeared in magazines and anthologies. "Afraid All the
Time" was the winner of the Anthony, Macavity and American Mystery
awards for best short story in 1979. In 1991 Pickard received a Shamus
Award for best private eye short story for "Dust Devils."

Pickard's first Jenny Cain novel, *Generous Death*, appeared in 1984.
Following a convention of the cozy, Cain is depicted, not as a professional
detective, but as a gifted amateur near whom murder seems to happen. As
the series opens, Cain is on the brink of her thirtieth birthday. She is established as director of the local philanthropic organization in the coastal
town of Port Frederick, Massachusetts. It is often this position with the
Port Frederick Civic Federation, and the resulting social exposure, that
draw Cain into murder. For example, in *Generous Death* someone is murdering the federation's most generous benefactors, while in *Bum Steer* the
bequest of a Kansas cattle ranch draws Cain into the life and death of a
western benefactor.

An amateur detective like Cain is handicapped by the fact that she has
no claim on resources that the police take for granted. Though free of the
constraints of hierarchy and public policy, she lacks crime labs, data banks,
training, professional colleagues, and potential support from other departments and agencies. Thus, the amateur detective often relies on a social or
personal relationship with a police officer. For Jenny Cain, this comes in
the form of a renewed relationship with a high school comrade, Geof Bushfield. Following a divorce, Bushfield returns to Port Frederick to serve as
homicide detective on the local police force. In the first novel, he and Jenny
begin to date, and in *Marriage Is Murder* they marry. Pickard skillfully uses
her character to provide a romantic interest, access to police information
and insight, and sometimes, help. At the same time, she manages to avoid
presenting Cain as a helpless female in need of masculine rescue. Geof
Bushfield admires and supports Cain, both in her professional life and in
her amateur sleuthing, which he declines to disdain.

Jenny's own family history also affects her relationship with the town
known to its residents as "Poor Fred." Especially in *Say No to Murder* and
I.O.U., this leads to murder and mystery. During her teenage years, Cain
Clams, the family business which had provided employment for many people in the community, collapsed. Though trust funds leave the Cain family
comfortably provided for, her father's inept management has put many
people out of work and created family and community resentments that
continue to impact Jenny's life and work. One of the sufferers is Jenny's

mother, Margaret, who spends the last years of her life in a psychiatric hospital, visited only by Jenny.

Though personal and professional issues play a significant role in Pickard's Cain novels, she also uses the novels to raise or respond to social issues. Jenny Cain's status as director of the Port Frederick Foundation discomforts some of the men with whom she works, and as she gains confidence in her role, she presses her board of directors to support more controversial causes. Cain confronts racism, advocates funding for the local battered-women's shelter, supports abortion rights, and backs controversial arts projects.

I.O.U. seems to move the Jenny Cain series in a new direction. Having answered the questions of what led to her father's loss of the family business and her mother's mental illness, Jenny tells readers, "All of my debts were paid." She finishes the novel free of her own past—free to leave or return to her job at the Foundation and, indeed, reflecting on the fact that she and Geof are free to leave Poor Fred if they wish. The publication of the most recent Jenny Cain novel, *But I Wouldn't Want to Die There*, tells readers that Cain is really not ready to leave Port Frederick and the foundation behind permanently.

Pickard works in a tradition that has always been home to both women mystery writers and female protagonists. It is not surprising that it is the feminist hard-boiled writers who have attracted the greatest attention for aligning the mystery story with changing social attitudes about women. Sara Paretsky's V. I. Warshawski and Sue Grafton's Kinsey Millhone stand out because women as working detectives have been so rare in the hard-boiled school. The changes in her formula that Pickard has effected are subtler but equally significant. In the cozy novels, women served as amateur sleuths in part because women were assumed not to be professionals but only ladies of leisure. Here, however, Pickard has given us a professional woman who is bright, independent, and sexually active, and who holds the opinions and attitudes of a liberal-minded and liberated modern woman.

Readers who want to explore the sources of the cozy formula will find Jenny Cain's roots in the English amateur detectives of Martha Grimes and Agatha Christie. Readers seeking variations on the modern woman as detective may want to consider the hard-boiled developments of Sue Grafton and Sara Paretsky, the police procedurals of Frances Fyfield, or Cain's amateur sisters in the work of Susan Wolfe, Carole Berry, and Julie Smith.

MYSTERY FICTION

Jenny Cain Series

Generous Death. New York: Avon Books, 1984.

Say No to Murder. New York: Avon Books, 1985.

No Body. New York: Scribner's, 1986.

Marriage Is Murder. New York: Scribner's, 1987; London: Collins, 1988.

Dead Crazy. New York: Scribner's, 1988; London: Collins, 1989.

Bum Steer. New York: Pocket Books; London: Macmillan, 1990.

I.O.U. New York: Pocket Books, 1991.

But I Wouldn't Want to Die There. New York: Pocket Books, 1993.

Confession. New York: Pocket, 1994.

Eugenia Potter Series

The 27 Ingredient Chili Con Carne Murders. New York: Delacorte Press, 1993.
   (From a story created by the late Virginia Rich.)

CRITICAL BIBLIOGRAPHY

Marks, Jeffrey. "Nancy Pickard." *The Armchair Detective*, 26, no. 2 (1993): 84.
Nichols, Victoria, and Susan Thompson. "Jennifer Cain." In *Silk Stalkings*. Berkeley: Black Lizard, 1988, pp. 135–37.
Wallace, Marilyn. "Pickard, Nancy." In *Twentieth Century Crime and Mystery Writers*, ed. Lesley Henderson. 3rd ed. Chicago and London: St. James Press, 1991, pp. 855–56.

JEFFREY H. MAHAN

JOYCE PORTER (1924–1990)

Joyce Porter was born in Marple, Cheshire, England, on March 28, 1924, and died on December 9, 1990, of pneumonia while returning from China. She was educated at the High School for Girls in Macclesfield, Cheshire, and earned a B.A. with honors at King's College, London, in 1944. After serving with the British Army (1944–47), she became a career officer in the Women's Royal Air Force, where she remained for fourteen years (1949–63), becoming fluent in Russian and achieving the rank of Flight Officer.

She began writing her first novel at age thirty-six. Her third novel launched her career as a writer when it was accepted for publication shortly after her retirement. Although Porter claimed to dislike reading humorous detective stories, she nevertheless recognized that this subgenre suited her abilities as a writer. The irreverent, iconoclastic humor of her novels is also evident in her comments on writing. She continued to say that writing is easier than working long after she admitted, in a series of humorous articles for the *Writer*, that she held to a daily regimen of writing and found it to be hard, demanding, and lonely work.

Porter's novels are a unique combination of classic, careful plotting and subversion of the genre's conventions. She challenges the reader to match wits with her inept Chief Inspector Wilfred Dover of New Scotland Yard, secret agent Edmund Brown of S.O.D., and amateur detective the Honourable Constance Ethel Morrison-Burke (the "Hon. Con."), and she plays fair in making the same evidence available to her characters and readers alike. At the same time, she distracts the reader's attention to the grotesqueries of her "heroes": to the humorous absurdities of their worlds, in which they have no monopoly on incompetence and venality, and to the incorrect, although reasonable, conclusions that they repeatedly draw from the available evidence with the confident ineptness of a Watson or a Hastings.

More than new twists on conventional mystery heroes, Porter's Dover, Brown, and Hon. Con. are antiheroes who are not only inept but also egocentric and motivated by greed, petty self-interest, and a willingness to sacrifice others in the interest of their own comfort. Moreover, they exist in a world that is indifferent to heroic action, intelligence, and commitment to firm moral principle, whether in the form of justice, fair play, or even "eye for an eye" vengeance. Villains here are distinguishable only by their viciousness—their penchant for violence independent of furthering their own self-interest. Truth is uncovered by chance, and it is likely to take second place to expedience. This potentially bleak vision is nevertheless transformed by Porter's exaggeration, humorous innuendo, and lively sense of the absurd to emerge as highly entertaining reading.

Porter's Dover is a model of lethargy with the low cunning of a survivor. Obese and physically repulsive, boorish and insensitive to everyone around him, and obsessed with his own creature comforts, Dover considers sleeping undisturbed in his office a good day's work. Given a case, his objective is to bring it to a convenient close with as little work as possible: "An instant arrest, that was what was needed. Once you'd picked your victim and got him safely tucked away behind bars, you could always fiddle the evidence a bit to make things fit. Dover had done it dozens of times." A source of tension and additional interest is his working relationship with the long-suffering Sergeant Charles Edward MacGregor. Young, handsome, ambitious, eager to investigate actively, intent upon going by the book, and inclined to be somewhat priggish, MacGregor is impoverished by Dover's constant sponging and hopelessly stuck with the man, despite his repeated requests for a transfer anywhere else. Dover takes pleasure in thwarting MacGregor at every opportunity.

The Hon. Con. is Dover's active, amateur counterpart and a parody of the wealthy dilettante detective. As incompetent, insensitive, and boorish as Dover, she, too, regularly misinterprets evidence, jumps from theory to theory, and tends to inadvertently stumble on the truth. Porter milks humor out of playing the spinster Hon. Con.'s sexual naïveté and repression against abundant suggestions of latent lesbianism. The somewhat ambiguous relationship between the Hon. Con. and her live-in companion, Miss Jones ("Bones"), is, however, less successful than the Dover-MacGregor relationship in providing additional interest.

Porter's reluctant spy, Edmund Brown, is her most sympathetic antihero because he is essentially a victim of circumstances. Brown is just as opportunistic, greedy, and self-interested as her other antiheroes, but this world is peopled with less admirable characters. Brown's ineptitude and misinterpretation of situations is matched only by his ability to save his skin by executing spectacular, usually unnecessary, operations.

Building probably on her experience in the military and her distrust of politicians, Porter is at her best depicting organizational politics in all its pettiness, as in *Dover and the Claret Tappers*. Although each of her series may be read in any order, it is helpful to start the Brown series with the first novel, which recounts his recruitment. Readers who enjoy Porter's humor might also enjoy works by Charlotte MacLeod.

MYSTERY FICTION

Chief Inspector Wilfred Dover Series

Dover One. London: Cape; New York: Scribner's, 1964.

Dover Two. London: Cape; New York: Scribner's, 1965.

Dover Three. London: Cape, 1965; New York: Scribner's, 1966.

Dover and the Unkindest Cut of All. London: Cape; New York: Scribner's, 1967.

Dover Goes to Pott. London: Cape; New York: Scribner's, 1968.

Dover Strikes Again. London: Weidenfeld and Nicolson, 1970; New York: David McKay, 1973.

It's Murder with Dover. London: Weidenfeld and Nicolson; New York: David McKay, 1973.

Dover and the Claret Tappers. London: Weidenfeld and Nicolson, 1976; Woodstock, Vt.: Foul Play Press, 1989.

Dead Easy for Dover. London: Weidenfeld and Nicolson, 1978; New York: St. Martin's Press, 1979.

Dover Beats the Band. London: Weidenfeld and Nicolson, 1980.

Edmund Brown Secret Agent Series

Sour Cream with Everything. London: Cape; New York: Scribner's, 1966.

The Chinks in the Curtain. London: Cape, 1967; New York: Scribner's, 1968.

Neither a Candle nor a Pitchfork. London: Weidenfeld and Nicolson 1969; New York: McCall, 1970.

Only with a Bargepole. London: Weidenfeld and Nicolson, 1971; New York: David McKay, 1974.

The Honourable Constance Morrison-Burke Series

Rather a Common Sort of Crime. London: Weidenfeld and Nicolson; New York: McCall, 1970.

A Meddler and Her Murder. London: Weidenfeld and Nicolson, 1972; New York: David McKay, 1973.

The Package Included Murder. London: Weidenfeld and Nicolson, 1975; Indianapolis, Ind.: Bobbs-Merrill, 1976.

Who the Heck Is Sylvia? London: Weidenfeld and Nicolson, 1977.

The Cart before the Crime. London: Weidenfeld and Nicolson, 1979.

CRITICAL BIBLIOGRAPHY

Dunlap, Susan. "Chief Inspector Wilfred Dover." In *100 Great Detectives*, ed. Maxim Jakubowski. New York: Carroll and Graf, 1991, pp. 84–86.

Kendle, Burton. "Porter, Joyce." In *Twentieth Century Crime and Mystery Writers*, ed. Lesley Henderson. 3rd ed. Chicago: St. James Press, 1991, pp. 857–58.

Nichols, Victoria, and Susan Thompson. "Edmund Brown." In *Silk Stalkings: When Women Write of Murder*. Berkeley, Calif.: Black Lizard Books, 1988, pp. 231–32.

———. "The Honourable Constance Ethel Morrison-Burke." In *Silk Stalkings: When Women Write of Murder*. Berkeley, Calif.: Black Lizard Books, 1988, p. 80.

———. "Wilfred Dover." In *Silk Stalkings: When Women Write of Murder*. Berkeley, Calif.: Black Lizard Books, 1988, p. 40.

MICHAEL J. ROSSI

❦ R ❦

SHEILA RADLEY (1928–   )

Sheila Radley (real name, Sheila Mary Robinson) was born on November 18, 1928, in Cogenhoe, Northamptonshire, England. Earning a B.A. from the University of London in 1951, she served in the Women's Royal Air Force from 1951 to 1960.

Radley began to write in her spare time while working in the post office. In the late 1970s she produced three romantic thrillers. Feeling that she would be better at writing the kind of books she enjoyed reading, Radley retired to write detective fiction full time in 1978, and now lives in Norwich, Norfolk.

Insisting that she pays minimal attention to the details of police work, Radley is most interested in character and motive. Her series detective is a middle-aged, rather conservative, country policeman mired in a conventional and unfulfilling marriage. Douglas Quantrill has more than his share of human foibles. However, he is appealing precisely because of his flaws— he is a decent man who often fails in his attempts to come to terms with middle age, as well as with a world far different from that in which he grew up.

The world Quantrill inhabits is perched between old-fashioned country values and progressive urban ideas, as symbolized by the location of Breckham Market's police headquarters "on the dividing line between the old town and the new." Quantrill represents the last of the old guard: he left school at fourteen, joined the force as a constable, and worked his way up through the ranks. He and his kind will soon be replaced by the likes of Martin Tait—individuals who are young, urban, college-educated, and destined to outstrip Quantrill in rank within a few years. Even more disconcerting to those accustomed to the old ways is the appearance of women like Hilary Lloyd, whose independence and competence, coupled with physical attractiveness, baffle men who *want* in a female associate "someone decorative . . . but not too clever" and who *expect* "a plain-clothes bossy-boots . . . with a hairstyle as rigid as her mind."

The old ways, however, are hardly romanticized in Radley's work, nor is village and rural life in general. Quantrill insists: "Villages can be unpleasant places to live in. I expect you think that country life's idyllic, but you'll soon find that there's a surprising amount of spare hatred about."

These words are directed at Martin Tait, whose attitude toward quaint village life is condescending and whose sense of superiority over Quantrill and the rest of the force emanates from everything he says. He is the consummate opportunist, interacting with everyone in his life—including a prospective fiancée and a beloved aunt—in accordance with their ability to further his ambitions.

When Tait moves up in rank, his replacement is Hilary Lloyd, a promising young female detective. She bears a slightly disfiguring scar that runs from the bridge of her nose through her eyebrow, a constant reminder that her dedication to the job outweighs her vanity. She does, however, bring a feminine perspective to police work: unlike Tait, Lloyd agonizes over the ethical compromises it requires. Befriending unhappy women in order to obtain information on a case may be a necessary part of the job, but it leaves her painfully aware of the cost to her personal relationships.

In the early novels, Radley's female characters are sometimes uncomfortably stereotypical, ranging from a sociopath to a classic shrew and a caricatured feminist with a "strong-boned unpainted face," "untrimmed eyebrows," and "wilting-chrysanthemum fringe." Even WPC Patsy Hopkins, who assists Quantrill in the early novels, is recognized more for her shapely legs than her competence. With Hilary Lloyd, however, Radley seems to have hit on a more reasonable portrayal of a contemporary professional woman. In fact, in the later novels even Quantrill overcomes his infatuation with Lloyd and learns to appreciate her friendship and professional competence.

Although Radley's strong point is characterization, her plots are tightly woven and her murderers, generally quite credible. As in many other village mysteries, the culprits are always ordinary, otherwise decent characters who, for a variety of reasons, have crossed the line. In fact, her two latest novels focus far more on those involved in the crime than on Quantrill and Lloyd. *This Way Out* is a masterful reworking of Patricia Highsmith's *Strangers on a Train*, and the core of *Cross My Heart and Hope to Die* is an unpublished manuscript written by a potential witness.

Readers who wish to trace Quantrill's evolution from a self-pitying sexist hankering after other women to a more enlightened family man and colleague may want to read the books in order. Otherwise, *Who Saw Him Die?* is a good place to start—while all Radley's novels expertly intertwine the main plot with a family subplot, this one is especially touching in that it brings Quantrill and his family to the brink of destruction.

Radley's work is perhaps closest to Ruth Rendell's in that both delve into their characters' psyches. For those interested in Radley's intertwining of the detective's personal and professional lives, another good choice would be Frances Fyfield.

MYSTERY FICTION

Quantrill Series

Death and the Maiden. London: Hamilton, 1978; as *Death in the Morning.* New York: Scribner, 1979; London: Prior, 1981.

The Chief Inspector's Daughter. New York: Scribner's; London: Constable, 1980.

A Talent for Destruction. New York: Scribner's; London: Constable, 1982.

Blood on the Happy Highway. London: Constable, 1983; as *The Quiet Road to Death.* New York: Scribner's, 1984.

Fate Worse than Death. London: Constable, 1985; New York: Scribner's, 1986.

Who Saw Him Die? London: Constable, 1987; New York: Scribner's, 1988.

This Way Out. New York: Scribner's; London: Constable, 1989.

Cross My Heart and Hope to Die. New York: Scribner's; London: Constable, 1992.

CRITICAL BIBLIOGRAPHY

Barnard, Robert. "Ordinary People." *The Armchair Detective*, 25 (Winter 1992): 14.

———. "Radley, Sheila." In *Twentieth Century Crime and Mystery Writers*, ed. Lesley Henderson. 3rd ed. Chicago: St. James Press, 1991, pp. 896–97.

Nichols, Victoria, and Susan Thompson. "Behind the Badge: Douglas Quantrill." In *Silk Stalkings: When Women Write of Murder*. Berkeley, Calif.: Black Lizard Books, 1988, pp. 61–62.

Ross, Jean W. [Interview with Sheila Radley.] *Contemporary Authors*, 131 (1990): 394–97.

KATHLEEN SHINE CAIN

SEELEY REGESTER (1831–1885)

Metta Victoria Fuller Victor was born in Erie, Pennsylvania, and spent her formative years in Ohio. In 1846, by age fifteen, she had already published poetry and her first novel. She and her older sister, Frances Barriett Fuller, were well known as the "Sisters of the West," following the publication of their *Poems of Sentiment and Imagination* (1853). Shortly thereafter, Metta met and married Orville Victor, the creator of the dime novel and an editor at Beadle.

Both prolific and eclectic, Metta Victor wrote poetry, cookbooks, romances, sentimental fiction, humor, adventure stories, and mysteries. The first woman in the United States to write detective novels, Victor penned *The Dead Letter: An American Romance* and *Figure Eight; or, The Mystery at Meredith Place*, both of which she published under the pseudonym, "Seeley Regester."

Reissued in 1979 by Gregg Press, *The Dead Letter* clearly demonstrates Regester's talents. Featuring Mr. Burton, who works for the New York City Police Department as an unpaid plainclothes detective, this suspenseful novel holds the reader's attention. Taking its title from an undelivered letter written in code, the novel begins two years after the murder of Henry Moreland, which remains unsolved.

Burton uses somewhat unusual investigative methods. Unlike Poe's Dupin or Conan Doyle's Sherlock Holmes, logical deduction takes a backseat to psychic powers. Burton himself possesses an uncanny ability to "feel" the presence of a murderer in his midst. Also a master graphologist, he unfailingly and accurately describes the personalities, careers, and physical attributes of anyone whose handwriting he analyzes. A widower, he has an eleven-year-old daughter, Lenore, who is clairvoyant. On occasion, Lenore's gift provides great assistance in unraveling the mystery.

Using flashbacks, Regester sustains the reader's interest by including episodes of robbery, reckless gambling, and apparent supernatural occurrences. Closely linked to the search for the murderer is a romantic subplot. The various strands of the story are skillfully interwoven, and the denouement ties up all loose ends.

As a major contributor to the development of detective fiction, Regester's most far-reaching accomplishment may well be the invention of the "climatic gathering" device. She is the first to place all suspects and interested parties in one room. This group then listens as the detective recounts the circumstances of the crime and, through the weight of evidence, forces the murderer to confess his or her guilt.

This novel holds up quite well for modern readers, especially if they are fans of the detective novels of Anna Katharine Green. Although Green has been honored with the title, "Mother of Detective Fiction," Regester's first novel predates Green's first novel by eleven years. Victor's second detective novel, *Figure Eight*, is now out of print and extremely difficult to acquire. As it lacks the cohesiveness and tight plotting of *The Dead Letter*, few readers will find it as compelling as *The Dead Letter*.

MYSTERY FICTION

The Dead Letter: An American Romance. New York: Beadle, 1867. Rpt. New York: Gregg Press, 1979.
Figure Eight; or, The Mystery of Meredith Place. New York: Beadle, 1869.

CRITICAL BIBLIOGRAPHY

Rahn, B. J. "Seeley Regester: America's First Detective Novelist." In *The Sleuth and the Scholar*, ed. Barbara Rader and Howard Zettler. Westport, Conn.: Greenwood, 1988.

CHERI LOUISE ROSS

RUTH RENDELL (1930–   )

Ruth Rendell was born on February 17, 1930, to Arthur and Ebba Elise (Kruse) Grasemann in London. She attended Loughton High School, and from 1948 to 1952 she worked as a newspaper reporter and subeditor for the *Essex Express and Independent*, but did not find the work completely satisfying. Rendell began writing after the birth of her son. When she submitted a novel for consideration, the publisher rejected the submission but asked if she had written anything else. She then sent in the first Wexford novel, which she had written for fun.

Since the publication of her first mystery in 1964, Rendell has earned three Edgar Awards from the Mystery Writers Association, four Golden Daggers and one Silver award from the British Crime Writers' Association, and a National Book Award from the Arts Council of Great Britain. The *Boston Globe* called her "the best mystery writer anywhere in the English-speaking world," an accolade later echoed in *Time*. Rendell writes three different series or types of mysteries: the Wexford series, psychological "chiller/killers," and novels as Barbara Vine. At the heart a Rendell mystery is a concern with good and evil; thus, it is not surprising that all Rendell's novels deal with the psychological and emotional aspects of human nature rather than forensics or the puzzle. On the whole, Rendell's novels are meticulously plotted with a clear understanding of the deceptive potential of everyday things. She instinctively recognizes triggers of readers' assumptions that will lead them to jump to predictable, and erroneous, conclusions.

The Wexford series has become a classic in the British cozy genre. It features Chief Inspector Reginald Wexford and Inspector Burden of the Kingsmarkham police force and is marked by its provincial settings, its meticulous plotting, and the undeniable appeal of the main characters. Wexford is tall, "thick-set without being fat, fifty-two years old, [and] the very prototype of an actor playing a top-brass policeman." He is addicted to literary quotations and is intuitive and imaginative. His expression is "not so much easy-going as tolerant of everything but intolerance." In contrast, Burden is less imaginative, prim, and handsome—leading to discussions that are "often acrimonious but always fruitful."

A major motif in the Wexford series is family, which is usually presented through two major sets of relationships: those of parents and children and those of husbands and wives. For example, her first novel, *From Doon with Death*, compares couples whose marriages appear stable on the surface. Rendell establishes the outward appearance of the marriages through descriptions of the couples' homes, providing economic and social status—and at least one partner's motivation for murder in each marriage. At other times, the focus is on parent-child relationships. At times, such as in *Murder Being Once Done*, it is obsessive, but frequently it is redemptive. In *A New Lease of Death*, the love and understanding of an adoptive father help a child overcome the stigma of being the offspring of a murderer: " 'She says that it was his love that helped her to bear . . . the stigma of her father's crime when she learned about it at the age of twelve. He followed her progress at school, encouraged her in every way, and fostered her wish to get a County Major Scholarship.' "

Rendell's nonseries, psychological novels are often considered her best. In these novels characterization is a dominant element, and it is an aspect of writing that particularly interests Rendell: "The development of a human personality is what I'm really interested in. I like to work on characters. I want to know what will become of them. . . . I think people can be driven to commit murder, and I'm very interested in the pressures that are put on people and the stresses that they suffer from other people." These novels usually focus on a central character in a state of crisis, which is usually a mixture of circumstance and personal weakness or desire. One of the best is *A Judgment in Stone*, where readers know from the very first page what is to happen ("Eunice Parchmain killed the Coverdale family because she could not read or write") and interest centers on why. Readers watch with fascination as the story unfolds and realize that the motivation is not something extreme but rather is trivial: the Coverdales are a very literate family and their maid is illiterate. Adding to this fascination is the fact that throughout, the novel insists that if someone had acted differently, the murders would never have happened: if the Coverdales had understood Eunice's problem earlier; if Melinda had not smothered her with childishly kind attention; if her television had not broken down, and if she had not met Joan Smith. . . . Readers sit helpless yet fascinated, as possibilities are eliminated one after another. It is gripping, but also undeniably chilling.

In 1986, Rendell was awarded her third Edgar for a novel which was to become the beginning of a new series: *A Dark-Adapted Eye*, written under the pseudonym, "Barbara Vine." During a reading/lecture at the 1993 Southern Festival of Books (in Nashville, Tenn.), Rendell discussed the differences between her psychological thrillers and the Barbara Vine novels. According to Rendell, the psychological novels are faster-paced and the motivation is examined from the perspective of the perpetrator, while the Barbara Vine novels are written in a more feminine voice and the psychology of every character is examined. Further, the Vine novels usually employ the more intimate, first-person point of view and deal with a crime that is a matter of accident rather than intent. A frequent theme of the Barbara Vine novels is that of identity mixed with a lack of knowledge about parentage.

The thing that marks any Rendell novel, whatever the genre, is a sense of irony, a fact that led one reviewer to comment that some of her novels are "ice-cold studies." At times, the irony is fairly typical: the presence of evil in a seemingly peaceful neighborhood or the potential for destruction lurking behind a seemingly demure persona. Through her ironic vision, Rendell presents a world where situational irony abounds, as when Wexford investigates the death of a young woman whose bludgeoning is surrounded by the exuberance and energy of a rock festival or the case of the Coverdale family, in *A Judgment in Stone*:

Four members of this family—George, Jacqueline, and Melinda Coverdale and Giles Mont—died in the space of fifteen minutes on February 14, St. Valentine's Day. Eunice Parchmain and the prosaically named Joan Smith shot them down on a Sunday evening while they were watching opera on television. Two weeks later Eunice was arrested for the crime—because she could not read.

Critics have noted that Rendell "has a mind unusually attuned to the odd, the menacing, the abnormal; that she seizes on the contemporary forms these assume, and turns them into something unnerving yet oddly satisfying." Perhaps this is the secret to Rendell's talent: she recognizes the greatest irony, that readers love to be disturbed.

Rendell is often compared with Patricia Highsmith for psychological insight.

MYSTERY FICTION

Writing as Ruth Rendell

To Fear a Painted Devil. Garden City, N.Y.: Doubleday, 1965; London: Long, 1965.

In Sickness and in Health. Garden City, N.Y.: Doubleday, 1966; as *Vanity Dies Hard*. London: Long, 1965.

The Secret House of Death. London: Long, 1968; Garden City, N.Y.: Doubleday, 1969.

The Face of Trespass. London: Hutchinson, 1971; Garden City, N.Y.: Doubleday, 1974.

One Across, Two Down. Garden City, N.Y.: Doubleday; London: Hutchinson, 1971.

A Demon in My View. London: Hutchinson, 1976; Garden City, N.Y.: Doubleday, 1977.

The Fallen Curtain. Garden City, N.Y.: Doubleday; London: Hutchinson, 1976.

A Judgment in Stone. London: Hutchinson, 1977; Garden City, N.Y.: Doubleday, 1978.

Make Death Love Me. London: Hutchinson, 1979; Garden City, N.Y.: Doubleday, 1979.

The Lake of Darkness. Garden City, N.Y.: Doubleday; London: Hutchinson, 1980.
Master of the Moor. New York: Pantheon; London: Hutchinson, 1982.
The Fever Tree. London: Hutchinson, 1982; New York: Pantheon, 1983.
The Killing Doll. New York: Pantheon; London: Hutchinson, 1984.
The Tree of Hands. New York: Pantheon; London: Hutchinson, 1984.
Live Flesh. New York: Pantheon; London: Hutchinson, 1986.
The Collected Stories. New York: Pantheon; London: Hutchinson, 1987.
Talking to Strange Men. New York: Pantheon; London: Hutchinson, 1987.
The Veiled One. New York: Pantheon; London: Hutchinson, 1988.
The Bridesmaid. New York: Mysterious Press; London: Hutchinson, 1989.
Going Wrong. New York: Mysterious Press; London: Hutchinson, 1990.
The Copper Peacock. New York: Mysterious Press; London: Hutchinson, 1991.
The Crocodile Bird. New York: Crown; London: Hutchinson, 1993.

Reginald Wexford Series

From Doon with Death. London: Hutchinson, 1964; Garden City, N.Y.: Doubleday, 1965.

A New Lease of Death. Garden City, N.Y.: Doubleday, 1967; as *Sins of the Fathers*. London: Long, 1967.

Wolf to the Slaughter. London: Long, 1967; Garden City, N.Y.: Doubleday, 1968.

The Best Man to Die. London: Long, 1969; Garden City, N.Y.: Doubleday, 1970.

A Guilty Thing Surprised. Garden City, N.Y.: Doubleday; London: Hutchinson, 1970.

Murder Being Once Done. Garden City, N.Y.: Doubleday; London: Hutchinson, 1972.

No More Dying Then. London: Hutchinson, 1971; Garden City, N.Y.: Doubleday, 1972.

Some Lie and Some Die. Garden City, N.Y.: Doubleday; London: Hutchinson, 1973.

Shake Hands for Ever. Garden City, N.Y.: Doubleday; London: Hutchinson, 1975.

A Sleeping Life. Garden City, N.Y.: Doubleday; London: Hutchinson, 1978.

Means of Evil. London: Hutchinson, 1979.

Death Notes. New York: Pantheon, 1981; as *Put on by Cunning*. London: Hutchinson, 1981.

The Speaker of Mandarin. New York: Pantheon; London: Hutchinson, 1983.

An Unkindness of Ravens. New York: Pantheon; London: Hutchinson, 1985.

Kissing Gunner's Daughter. Garden City, New York: Doubleday; London: Hutchinson, 1992.

Writing as Barbara Vine

A Dark-Adapted Eye. New York: Viking, 1986.
Fatal Inversion. New York: Viking; Harmondsworth; U.K.: Viking, 1987.

House of Stairs. Harmondsworth, U.K.: Viking, 1988; New York: Harmony Books, 1989.

Gallowglass. New York: Harmony Books, 1990.

King Solomon's Carpet. New York: Harmony Books, 1992.

Asta's Book. New York: Harmony Books, 1993.

CRITICAL BIBLIOGRAPHY

Bakerman, Jane S. "Ruth Rendell." In *Ten Women of Mystery*, ed. Earl F. Bargainnier. Bowling Green, Ohio: Bowling Green University Popular Press, 1981, pp. 124–49.
Budd, Elaine. "Ruth Rendell: Terror Times Two." In *13 Mistresses of Murder*. New York: Ungar, 1986, pp. 105–13.

LYNN M. ALEXANDER

CRAIG RICE (1908–1957)

She was born Georgianna Ann Randolph, but it is as "Craig Rice" that she would gain fame in the 1940s, her most creative and popular period, as one of the most successful writers of "screwball comedy" mysteries.

While working in radio and public relations in the "Windy City," she spent the 1930s unsuccessfully attempting to write poetry, novels, and music. At age thirty, with a shaky marriage ending and a trio of children to support, she finally discovered her true talents in the mystery genre. Her first work, *Eight Faces at Three*, featured the hard-working, hard-drinking Chicago lawyer John J. Malone, teaming up with hotshot press agent Jake Justus and eccentric heiress Helen Brand to discover who killed an unpleasant dowager and why the murderer bothered to make up the beds in the victim's house and stopped all the clocks at exactly 3:00.

By the mid-1940s, after producing six well-selling Malone novels, Craig Rice swirled into the popular cultural mainstream when R-K-O Studios purchased and filmed *Having Wonderful Crime*, with Pat O'Brien as Malone and George Murphy and Carole Landis as the now-married Jake and Helen Justus. That same year, Rice authored her most famous book, the semiautobiographical *Home Sweet Homicide*, which dealt with a young widow, who supports herself and her three children by writing mystery novels, uncovering a neighborhood murder. The Twentieth-Century Fox film version, starring Lynn Bari and Peggy Ann Garner, would become one of the box-office hits of 1945. Rice also coauthored screenplays for the light-hearted and witty *Falcon* film series at R-K-O pictures. By 1946, *Time* magazine, in acknowledging the continual popularity of the mystery novel in postwar America, selected Craig Rice for its cover story.

Humorous hard-boiled detective fiction was her special preserve. The comedy does not rely exclusively on wise-cracking dialogue, although this exists in abundance in the stories featuring the rumpled barrister Malone. Rice also infused comedy of situation into her narrative, often bordering on gallows humor. In *Having Wonderful Crime*, a hung-over newlywed awakens wearing an ill-fitting suit to discover a decapitated bride he has never seen before. Maintaining humor in grisly situations without going overboard was a balancing act that Rice skillfully managed to sustain throughout her books. Her flippancy about death never became indecent, and in her detective farces she cleverly mixed unholy living and heinous dying with an atmosphere of equal parts of excitement and amusement.

Although interesting secondary persons frequently engage the reader's interest, Rice's character of trial attorney Malone is her most famous creation. He is never actually seen in a courtroom, but his exploits are legendary—described in *Trial by Fury* as "pyrotechnical." However, he is no second-rate Perry Mason, nor does his attire approach the sartorial splendor of a Nick Charles or Philo Vance. Short and pudgy, with an uncombed thatch of flaming red hair, cigar ashes adorning his shirt front, and suits that seldom find their way to the cleaner's, he is pugnacious and sarcastic. In his law offices, his frequent companion is a bottle of rye in a filing cabinet marked "personal." While beautiful women often turn his head, his overwhelming passion in life is justice. However, he holds no romantic illusions about the law or his particular role in its wheels. His clients occasionally are the very ones he has himself apprehended or identified. "I'm not an officer of the law," he reveals in *The Wrong Murder*. "My profession has always put me on the other side of the fence. I've never served the cause of justice, but rather the cause of injustice."

Of the dozen Malone/Justuses novels, the early entries, particularly *Trial by Fury*, remain the best. Rice also created a second series, a trio of novels featuring itinerent street photographers Bingo Riggs and Handsome Kusak, who solve murders out of self-preservation. These tales also skillfully blend the horrible with the ludicrous and manage to make both characters the detectives as well as their own inept Watsons. However, the height of Rice's art, and a work that hardly dates at all, is a close-to-home rendition inspired by her own three children, *Home Sweet Homicide*, where her previously hidden reserves of sensitivity are permitted to finally come forth.

MYSTERY FICTION

Writing as Craig Rice

Telefair. Indianapolis; Ind.: Bobbs Merrill, 1942; as *Yesterday's Murder*. New York: Popular Library, 1950.

Home Sweet Homicide. New York: Simon and Schuster, 1944.

Innocent Bystander. New York: Simon and Schuster, 1949; London: Hammond, 1958.

John J. Malone and the Justuses Series

Eight Faces at Three. New York: Simon and Schuster; London: Eyre and Spottiswoode, 1939; as *Death at Three*. London: Cherry Tree, 1941.

The Corpse Steps Out. New York: Simon and Schuster; London: Eyre and Spottiswoode, 1940.

The Wrong Murder. New York: Simon and Schuster, 1940; London: Eyre and Spottiswoode, 1942.

The Right Murder. New York: Simon and Schuster, 1941; London: Eyre and Spottiswoode, 1948.

Trial by Fury. New York: Simon and Schuster, 1941; London: Hammond, 1950.

The Big Midget Murders. New York: Simon and Schuster, 1942.

Having Wonderful Crime. New York: Simon and Schuster, 1943; London: Nicholson and Watson, 1944.

The Lucky Stiff. New York: Simon and Schuster, 1945.

The Fourth Postman. New York: Simon and Schuster, 1948; London: Hammond, 1951.

My Kingdom for a Hearse. New York: Simon and Schuster, 1957; London: Hammond, 1959.

The Name Is Malone. New York: Pyramid, 1958; London: Hammond, 1960.

Knocked for a Loop. New York: Simon and Schuster; as *The Double Frame*. London: Hammond, 1958.

People vs. Withers and Malone, with Stuart Palmer. New York: Simon and Schuster, 1963.

But the Doctor Died. New York: Lancer, 1967.

Once Upon a Time and Other Stories, with Stuart Palmer. Canoga Park, Calif.: Gold Penny Press, 1981.

Bingo Riggs and Handsome Kusak Series

The Sunday Pigeon Murders. New York: Simon and Schuster, 1942; London: Nicholson and Watson, 1948.

The Thursday Turkey Murders. New York: Simon and Schuster, 1943; London: Nicholson and Watson, 1946.

The April Robin Murders. New York: Random House, 1958; London: Hammond, 1959. (Completed by Ed McBain.)

Writing as Daphne Saunders

To Catch a Thief. New York: Dial Press, 1943.

Writing as Michael Venning

The Man Who Slept All Day. New York: Coward McCann, 1942.
Murder through the Looking Glass. New York: Coward McCann, 1943; London: Nicholson and Watson, 1947.
Jethro Hammer. New York: Coward McCann, 1944; London: Nicholson and Watson, 1947.

SCREENPLAYS

The Falcon's Brother (R-K-O, 1942), with Stuart Palmer.
The Falcon in Danger (R-K-O, 1943), with Fred Niblo, Jr.
Mrs. O'Malley and Mr. Malone (M-G-M, 1951), with William Bowers and Stewart Palmer.

CRITICAL BIBLIOGRAPHY

Grochowski, Mary Ann. "Craig Rice: Merry Mistress of Mystery and Mayhem," *The Armchair Detective*, 13, no. 3 (1980): 265–67.
Jasen, David A. "The Mysterious Craig Rice." *The Armchair Detective*, 5, no. 1 (1972): 25–27.
Moran, Peggy. "Craig Rice." In *And Then There Were Nine: More Women of Mystery*, ed. Jane S. Bakerman. Bowling Green, Ohio: Popular Press, 1985, pp. 120–45.

CHRISTOPHER J. WARREN

VIRGINIA RICH (?–1984)

Virginia Rich was born in Sibley, Iowa, a town much like Harrington, which is the site of her first Eugenia Potter mystery, *The Cooking School Murders.* Place is an important part of each of the Eugenia Andrews Potter mysteries, each of which is enriched by the food of the location.

Rich's mysteries are suspenseful enough and Potter, engaging enough to hook readers, but many probably have been drawn to the books for the recipes. In all, Rich includes descriptions of luxurious meals and food tips, as well as how to make substitutions for cooks who are not fortunate enough to live within walking distance of a lobster pound. Potter entwines her cooking and sleuthing skills, often asking people in to feed and interrogate them at the same time. Inevitably, as with most food mysteries, people are poisoned with food, though in these books they die in a variety of ways.

Feminist readers will be drawn to Mrs. Potter (as she is referred to by the narrator) as a crone who values her knowledge. Usually she is contrasted with another woman of about the same age who is pompous about her station and money, or with a woman who needs protection. As a woman aged sixty and more, Potter acknowledges the prejudices of her youth and has changed in some ways that her contemporaries have not.

Nancy Pickard (whose Jenny Crain mysteries are discussed in this book) was clearly an inspired choice to write the fourth novel from notes and chapter beginnings left by Rich. Pickard says she had corresponded with Rich and that they had interests in common, including ranching; consequently, the editor's request "felt like fate." Certainly, her recipe for Juanita Ortega's Chili Rellenos is wonderful, and the voice of Mrs. Potter is immediately recognizable in the opening conversation when she is recalled to her 15,000-acre ranch in Wind Valley, Arizona. Pickard offers new menus, a circle of old friends who must contend with murder, a new landscape with as much beauty to be appreciated as the first three, and lots of Spanish, unobtrusively translated. Potter still slips in little cooking hints with her musings, and she is still introspective and determined to stay cheerful.

In addition, perhaps in recognition of problems readers might have with some of the omissions of early books, Pickard reconnects Potter with her children and grandchildren. Furthermore, Pickard allows her to recall losses in earlier books and to reflect on those experiences more than she has before.

MYSTERY FICTION

Eugenia Potter Series

The Cooking School Murders. New York: Ballantine Books, 1982.

The Baked Bean Supper Murders. New York: Dutton, 1983.

The Nantucket Diet Murders. New York: Dell Publishing, 1985.

Pickard, Nancy. *The 27 Ingredient Chili Con Carne Murders: Based on Characters and a Story Created by Virginia Rich*. New York: Delacorte Press, 1993.

CRITICAL BIBLIOGRAPHY

Nichols, Victoria, and Susan Thompson. "Mrs. Potter." In *Silk Stalkings*. Berkeley, Calif.: Black Lizard, 1988, pp. 256–57.

GEORGIA RHOADES

MARY ROBERTS RINEHART (1876–1958)

Mary Roberts Rinehart was born in Allegheny, Pennsylvania, in 1876. Her family was what modern readers would consider lower-middle-class;

her mother took in sewing and her father worked as a sewing machine salesman and did other sales work until his death by suicide in 1895. Mary graduated high school in the liberal studies curriculum and went on to study nursing. Upon her graduation from nursing school in 1896, she married Dr. Stanley Rinehart and they had three sons. Although Mary's health was extremely poor during the early years of their marriage, she took to writing to add to the family income. Her early stories and poems sold for ten to forty dollars apiece, but by the end of her career she could command thousands of dollars for one story. In 1920, her highly successful mystery play, *The Bat*, was produced on Broadway, and it finally grossed over nine million dollars, exploding the myth of her merely augmenting the family income. Several of her stories and novels were purchased for motion picture production in the 1920s and 1930s. Her relationship with the *Saturday Evening Post* continued nearly until her death in 1958 of heart disease.

Her literary career, begun of necessity with quickly written short stories in the early twentieth century, took off in 1908 with the publication of *The Circular Staircase*. This novel, as well as all but one of her others, was first published in serial form. It was hailed as a critical success and became a financial success as well. Its most important feature was the narrator, Rachel Innes, a middle-aged spinster who admits to leading a sheltered life. The novel is both suspenseful and comic, taking place in a summer colony, as many of Rinehart's novels were to do. In many ways, the much later *Episode of the Wandering Knife* seems like a parody of this first novel, with its satirical comment on the life-styles of the wealthy and the characters' bumbling attempts to cover up for one another.

Rinehart is best known as the writer of "had I but known" novels, which are usually defined as having a naive narrator, usually young and female, who looks back on an experience and remarks on how she would have done things differently had she but known what was going to happen next. However, although Rinehart often employs a first-person narrator, they are not always young and female (as they are in *Episode of the Wandering Knife*, *The Wall*, and *The Swimming Pool*). In many cases, they are middle-aged women, like Rachel Innes of *The Circular Staircase*, and in some cases, the narrator is a young and naive male, as in *The State vs. Elinor Norton*. These narrators do not remain naive for long, since Rinehart novels tend to feature multiple, and sometimes bloody, murders. In spite of her novels' bloodthirsty aspects, however, romance is always a possibility, and not always only for the young.

Rinehart also used these narrators, no matter what their age or gender, to comment on upper-class society. While one of her major concerns in her early fiction is the threat to society caused by people marrying above themselves, her longevity as a writer is due in part to her ability to adjust her standard to a changing world. Part of this adaptability may be due to the fact that Rinehart herself was a newcomer to upper-class society; while she apparently enjoyed the trappings of wealth in her later years, including her house in Bar Harbor, Maine, and being photographed as a glamorous grande dame in pearls and furs, she was certainly not brought up in such splendor, and the early years of her marriage were certainly not luxurious. Money is always a concern to a Rinehart narrator, no matter how well-born. In fact, her well-born narrators frequently express concern about how to maintain their life-styles in financial straits, and Marcia Lloyd in *The Wall* describes her financial difficulties—she must retain the old servants, even though she cannot really afford them.

Rinehart developed one series character, although that series is not what she is best known for today. Hilda Adams appears primarily in short stories and novellas, although there is one full-length Hilda Adams novel, *Haunted Lady*. Hilda is a nurse who acts as an undercover investigator for police detective George Patton. Rinehart chose a nurse, not only because of her own knowledge of nursing, but because nurses were not bound by oaths of confidentiality.

Rinehart always described the mystery novel in terms of the "buried plot." She claimed that the surface plot of the novel served to conceal the plot of the mystery beneath. The novel's end and the solution of the mystery resulted in the revelation of the plot, which had been buried all along. The difficulty, of course, was in making the two plots come together at the end and in handling the denouement. Rinehart explicitly mentions the buried plot in her novel *The State vs. Elinor Norton*, in which the narrator refers to the story of Elinor's life as buried. This novel makes a somewhat different use of the buried plot, since there is no mystery about whether Elinor committed the crime she is being tried for.

Rinehart used a number of settings in her mysteries, although many of her novels are set in various summer colonies in the East. She often used a factual basis for her stories, although she frequently had to fictionalize these facts to make them palatable for her audience in the early part of the century. *The Confession* is based on a written confession to some murders in a brothel that a telephone repairman found near Rinehart's home (the brothel was transformed into a family home in the novel). *The After House* is based on some ax murders on a lumber schooner; although the ship in the novel has been turned into a luxury yacht, the plot is essentially the same. Rinehart's own objective interest in spiritualism is also shown in novels such as *The Red Lamp*.

Readers of Rinehart's fiction would probably enjoy Agatha Christie and Ngaio Marsh for the depictions of small communities of characters and the sometimes ironic descriptions. The works of Daphne duMaurier and Victoria Holt would appeal to those who prefer the more romantic "had I but known" variety.

MYSTERY FICTION

The Circular Staircase. Indianapolis, Ind.: Bobbs-Merrill, 1908; London: Cassell, 1909.

The Man in Lower Ten. Indianapolis, Ind.: Bobbs-Merrill; London: Cassell, 1909.

The Window at the White Cat. Indianapolis, Ind.: Bobbs-Merrill, 1910; London: Nash, 1911.

The Case of Jennie Brice. Indianapolis, Ind.: Bobbs-Merrill, 1913; London: Hodder, 1919.

The After House. New York: Houghton, 1914; London: Simpkin, 1915.

Sight Unseen, and The Confession. New York: George H. Doran; London: Hodder, 1921.

The Red Lamp. New York: George H. Doran, 1925; as *The Mystery Lamp*. London: Hodder, 1925.

Two Flights Up. Garden City, N.Y.: Doubleday, Doran; London: Hodder, 1928.

The Door. New York: Farrar and Rinehart; London: Hoddler, 1930.

The Album. New York: Farrar and Rinehart; London: Cassell, 1933.

The State vs. Elinor Norton. New York: Farrar and Rinehart, 1934; as *The Case of Elinor Norton*. London: Cassell, 1934.

The Wall. New York: Farrar and Rinehart; London: Cassell, 1938.

The Great Mistake. New York: Farrar and Rinehart, 1940; London: Cassell, 1941.

The Yellow Room. New York: Farrar and Rinehart, 1945; London: Cassell, 1949.

Episode of the Wandering Knife. New York: Rinehart, 1950; as *The Wandering Knife*. London: Cassell, 1951.

The Swimming Pool. New York: Rinehart, 1952; as *The Pool*. London: Cassell, 1952.

The Frightened Wife and Other Murder Stories. New York: Rinehart, 1953; London: Cassell, 1954.

Hilda Adams Series

Miss Pinkerton. New York: Farrar and Rinehart, 1932; as *The Double Alibi*. London: Cassell, 1932.

Haunted Lady. New York: Farrar and Rinehart; London: Cassell, 1942.

PLAY

The Bat, with Avery Hopwood. New York and London: French, 1932.

CRITICAL BIBLIOGRAPHY

Cohn, Jan. *Improbable Fiction: The Life of Mary Roberts Rinehart*. Pittsburgh: University of Pittsburgh Press, 1980.

———. "Mary Roberts Rinehart." In *Ten Women of Mystery*, ed. Earl F. Bargainnier. Bowling Green, Ohio: Bowling Green State University Press, 1981, pp. 183–220.

Davis, Robert H. *Mary Roberts Rinehart: A Sketch of the Woman and Her Work*. New York: George H. Doran, 1925.

Doran, George H. "Mary Roberts Rinehart." In *Chronicles of Barabbas: 1884–1934*. New York: Harcourt, Brace, 1935, pp. 187–94.

MacLeod, Charlotte. *Had She But Known: A Biography of Mary Roberts Rinehart*. New York: Mysterious Press, 1994.

Overton, Grant. "The Vitality of Mary Roberts Rinehart." In *When Winter Comes to Main Street*. New York: George H. Doran, 1922, pp. 102–17.

MARY P. FREIER

❦ S ❦

DOROTHY L. SAYERS (1893–1957)

Had she never written a single detective story, Dorothy Leigh Sayers would have still been renowned as a scholar, feminist, translator of medieval romances, lay theologian, Christian apologist, innovative advertising copywriter, and religious playwright. Today, however, she is remembered chiefly for her twelve detective novels, eleven featuring Lord Peter Wimsey, an aristocratic "great detective" of the Golden Age of detective fiction, which Sayers, as novelist and critic, both defined and transformed.

Born June 13, 1893, in Oxford, England, the only child of Reverend Henry Sayers (headmaster of the Choir School of Christ Church College), Sayers spent her childhood in an isolated rectory in the Fen country she described so evocatively in *The Nine Tailors*. There she was educated privately by her family and governesses, acquiring fluency in Latin and French and an abiding passion for literature, intellectual puzzles, romance, and dressing-up.

Sent to school at fifteen, she was miserable among the conventional hockey-playing girls and resented the imposed evangelical piety. In 1912 she went up to Somerville College, Oxford, where she delighted in the intellectual and aesthetic stimulation, the friendship, and the fun of college life (to which she paid homage in *Gaudy Night*), earning a First-Class Honours degree in modern languages in 1915.

During and immediately after World War I, Sayers worked at various publishing and teaching jobs in England and France. While struggling to support herself in bohemian Bloomsbury, London, in 1920, she wrote a detective novel in the prevailing puzzle-story mode. Thus was born Lord Peter Wimsey, mingling the silly-ass characteristics of P. G. Wodehouse's Bertie Wooster, the wit of E. C. Bentley's Philip Trent, and the intellectual omniscience of Sherlock Holmes. He dominated Sayers's life over the next two decades, just as Sayers, a founding member and president of the Detective Club and a distinguished critic and editor of detective fiction, dominated the upscale detective literature scene, bringing the prestige of her considerable erudition, wit, and poetic skill to the classic detective novel.

In 1926 Sayers married Oswald Atherton Fleming, a dashing, divorced journalist and war hero twelve years her senior. Mac, as she called him, was shattered by the war in both body and spirit; Sayers gallantly supported him until his death in 1950.

After 1938 Sayers wrote few stories and no novels, for by the end of World War II her attention had shifted to theater, theology, and Dante, where it remained until her death in 1957. Nonetheless, her work in diverse genres reveals an extraordinary consistency of purpose. Certain themes recur in her essays, fiction, criticism, and plays: the sacramental nature of work, and the need to be true to one's work and to accept the consequences of pursuing truth.

Although from his first appearance Wimsey shared Sayers's love of literature and intellectual games, she endowed him with other qualities that she then lacked: worldly knowledge, amorous experience and, above all, great wealth. As the series progressed during the next two decades, so did Sayers's own experience, much of which found its way into the novels, which evolved from puzzle stories into complex novels of manners, with detection integrated into other themes. Wimsey's character, too, gained in complexity, while his somewhat irritating mannerisms in the early novels were later rationalized as disarming camouflage or emotional defenses.

In *Whose Body?* a corpse dressed only in a pince-nez appears in the bathtub of an innocent architect. Enter Lord Peter (sporting a monocle), second son of the fifteenth Duke of Denver, graduate of Eton and Balliol (First-Class Honours in modern history), distinguished war record, cricketer, collector of rare editions, accomplished musician, and amateur detective, supported by his man, Bunter; his mother, the dowager duchess; and his friend, Inspector Charles Parker of Scotland Yard. Wimsey, who turned to detection as a distraction from having been shell-shocked and jilted during the war, suffers from ambivalence: why should he get murderers hanged because he enjoys detecting crime?

His ambivalence is in abeyance during *Clouds of Witness* when he defends his brother, the Duke of Denver, in the House of Lords on a charge of having murdered his sister Mary's fiancé, but returns in Sayers's nastiest novel, *Unnatural Death* which, like most of her books, is a "howdunit" rather than a "whodunit." Aware that his "interference" has precipitated further murders, Wimsey worries about the consequences of his search for truth, a concern that recurs as a major theme in *The Nine Tailors* and *Busman's Honeymoon*.

Wimsey's ambivalence mirrored Sayers's own. In *Strong Poison* she introduced a "love interest" with every intention of getting rid of Wimsey by marrying him off to Harriet Vane, a detective novelist accused of murdering her lover. (Like Harriet, Sayers, too, suffered from her bohemian indulgence in sexual passion; in 1921 she secretly bore a son out of wedlock whom she supported, educated, and later "adopted.") Sayers found, however, that marriage between the two characters based on gratitude would be humiliating for Harriet and shocking to herself, so she set about transforming Wimsey into a real flesh-and-blood character fit for Harriet to marry.

Three more novels chronicle their relationship. In *Have His Carcase* (set in a seaside resort) and *Gaudy Night* (set in Sayers's beloved Oxford) Harriet and Peter collaborate in solving crimes. While Harriet struggles with her sense of inferiority, resentment of gratitude, and fear of emotional involvement, Peter reveals his vulnerability and demonstrates his refusal to deny Harriet responsibility for her own life. *Busman's Honeymoon* (based on a play coauthored with Muriel St. Clare Byrne) both celebrates and tests their marriage: Harriet must accept the legitimacy of Wimsey's work, just as he has accepted hers. "The Haunted Policeman" and "Talboys" (in *Striding Folly*) describe scenes from their married life, while an unpublished fragment, titled "Thrones, Dominations," continues the Wimsey-Vane saga.

Sayers, like Harriet, believed that she mucked up emotional relationships but was true to her work. Work, for Sayers, was sacred and professional competence fascinated her. Her knowledge of advertising is brilliantly deployed in *Murder Must Advertise*. *The Five Red Herrings*, her only strictly puzzle-type story, tells more than readers want to know about Scottish fly-fishing, oil painting, and railway timetables. In *The Nine Tailors*, her finest novel, Sayers provides a thorough dissertation on campanology (the art of bell ringing) within a poetically rendered pastoral meditation on truth and consequences.

Readers either love or loathe *The Documents in the Case*, Sayers's only non-Wimsey novel. Told through letters and documents from various viewpoints, and written in homage to Wilkie Collins's narrative technique in *The Moonstone*, it is a complex tale of suburban passion and poison, interweaving many of Sayers's favorite themes with the detective problem.

Her only non-Wimsey detective is Montague Egg, a commercial traveler (salesman) for Plummett and Rose, wine merchants, who appears in eleven of Sayers's short stories.

The Wimsey novels should be read in order, unless pre-Vane Wimsey proves annoying, in which case readers should skip to *Strong Poison*. Many readers (myself included) find *The Five Red Herrings* tedious; others dislike *The Documents in the Case* (which I find excellent). Readers seeking similar authors should try Margery Allingham, Ngaio Marsh, and Amanda Cross.

MYSTERY FICTION

The Documents in The Case, with Robert Eustace [Robert Eustace Barton]. London: Benn; New York: Brewer, 1930.

Lord Peter Wimsey Series

Whose Body? London: Unwin; New York: Boni, 1923.

Clouds of Witness. London: Unwin, 1926; as *Clouds of Witnesses.* New York: McVeagh, 1927.

Unnatural Death. London: Benn, 1927; as *The Dawson Pedigree.* New York: McVeagh, 1928.

The Unpleasantness at the Bellona Club. London: Benn; New York: Payson, 1928.

Lord Peter Views the Body. London: Gollancz; New York: Payson, 1929.

Strong Poison. London: Gollancz; New York: Brewer, 1930.

The Five Red Herrings. London: Gollancz, 1931; as *Suspicious Characters.* New York: Brewer, 1931.

Have His Carcase. London: Gollancz; New York: Brewer, Warren, 1932.

Murder Must Advertise. London: Gollancz; New York: Harcourt, 1933.

The Nine Tailors: Changes Rung on an Old Theme in Two Short Touches and Two Full Peals. London: Gollancz; New York: Harcourt, 1934.

Gaudy Night. London: Gollancz, 1935; New York: Harcourt, 1936.

Busman's Honeymoon: A Love Story with Detective Interruptions. London: Gollancz; New York: Harcourt, 1937.

Lord Peter: A Collection of All the Lord Peter Wimsey Stories, ed. James Sandoe. New York: Harper, 1972.

Striding Folly, including Three Final Lord Peter Wimsey Stories. London: New English Library, 1973.

Montague Egg Series

Hangman's Holiday. London: Gollancz, 1937; New York: Harcourt, 1933.

In the Teeth of the Evidence. London: Gollancz; New York: Harcourt, 1940.

COLLABORATIVE NOVELS

The Floating Admiral, by Certain Members of the Detection Club. London: Hodder, 1931; New York: Doubleday, 1932.

Ask a Policeman, with Anthony Berkeley, Milward Kennedy, Gladys Mitchell, John Rhode, and Helen Simpson. London: Baker; New York: Morrow, 1933.

Double Death: A Murder Story, with Freeman Wills Crofts, Valentine Williams, F. Tennyson Jesse, Anthony Armstrong, and David Hume. Supervised and with a preface and prologue by John Chancellor. London: Gollancz, 1939.

CRITICAL BIBLIOGRAPHY

Bander, Elaine. "Dorothy L. Sayers and the Apotheosis of Detection." *The Armchair Detective*, 10 (1977): 362–65. Rpt. and abr. in *Twentieth Century Literary Criticism*, 2 (1979): 537–38.

Brabazon, James. *Dorothy L. Sayers: A Biography*. Preface by Anthony Fleming, foreword by P. D. James. London: Gollancz, 1981.

Christopher, Joe. "Dorothy L. Sayers: Duchess of Redonda." *The Armchair Detective*, 17, no. 4 (1984): 418–19.

Coomes, David. *Dorothy L. Sayers: A Careless Rage for Life*. Oxford: Lion, 1992.

Dale, Alzina Stone, ed. *Dorothy L. Sayers: The Centennial Celebration*. New York: Walker, 1993.

Dunkin, Mary Brien. *Dorothy L. Sayers*. Twayne's English Authors Series no. 281. Boston: Twayne, 1980.

Gaillard, Dawson. *Dorothy L. Sayers*. New York: Ungar, 1981.

Gilbert, Colleen B. *A Bibliography of the Works of Dorothy L. Sayers*. London: Macmillan, 1978.

Hall, Trevor H. *Dorothy L. Sayers: Nine Literary Studies*. London: Duckworth; New York: Shoe String, 1980.

Hannay, Margaret P., ed. *As Her Wimsey Took Her: Critical Essays on the Work of Dorothy L. Sayers*. Kent, Ohio: Kent State University Press, 1979.

Harmon, Robert B., and Margaret A. Burger. *An Annotated Guide to the Works of Dorothy L. Sayers*. New York: Garland, 1972.

Heilbrun, Carolyn G. "Sayers, Lord Peter and God." *American Scholar*, 37 (1968): 324–34. Rpt. in *Lord Peter: A Collection of All the Lord Peter Wimsey Stories*, ed. James Sandoe. New York: Harper, 1972, pp. 454–69.

Heldreth, Lillian M. "Breaking the Rules of the Game: Shattered Patterns in Dorothy L. Sayers' *Gaudy Night*." *Clues*, 3, no. 1 (1982): 120–27.

Hone, Ralph E. *Dorothy L. Sayers: A Literary Biography*. Kent, Ohio: Kent State University Press, 1979.

Kenney, Catherine. "Detecting a Novel Use for Spinsters in Sayers's Fiction." In *Old Maids to Radical Spinsters: Unmarried Women in the Twentieth-Century Novel*, ed. and introd. Laura L. Doan. Urbana: University of Illinois Press, 1991.

———. *The Remarkable Case of Dorothy L. Sayers*. Kent, Ohio: Kent State University Press, 1990.

Klein, Kathleen Gregory. "Dorothy Sayers." In *Ten Women of Mystery*, ed. Earl F. Bargainnier. Bowling Green, Ohio: Popular Press, 1981.

Merry, Bruce, "Dorothy L. Sayers: Mystery and Demystification." In *Art in Crime Writing: Essays on Detective Fiction*, ed. Bernard Benstock. New York: St. Martin's, 1983.

Reynolds, Barbara. *Dorothy L. Sayers: Her Life and Soul*. London: Hodder, 1993.

Reynolds, William. "Dorothy L. Sayers' Detective Short Fiction." *The Armchair Detective*, 14, no. 2 (1981): 176–81.

———. "Literature, Latin and Love: Dorothy L. Sayers' *Gaudy Night*." *Clues*, 6, no. 1 (1985): 67–78.

Sayers, Dorothy Leigh. "Gaudy Night." In *Titles to Fame*, ed. Denys K. Roberts. London and New York: Nelson, 1937. Rpt. in *The Art of the Mystery Story*, ed. and introd. Howard Haycraft. New York: Simon, 1946.

Youngberg, Ruth T. *Dorothy L. Sayers: A Reference Guide*. Boston: Hall, 1982.

ELAINE BANDER

SARAH SHANKMAN (?–   )

Sarah Shankman was born in the northeastern part of Louisiana, where people are expected not to dance, drink, or have fun. She was studying for a Ph.D. in English at Emory University when she realized that storytelling interested her more than research. When she was twenty, Shankman taught night school at Georgia State College and worked during the day at *Atlanta* magazine with Anne Rivers Siddons, William Diehl, and Pat Conroy, who encouraged her to write fiction. After working briefly in New York as a trade-publishing and magazine editor, Shankman moved to San Francisco and taught high school English. Later, she returned to New York and began her fiction writing career. She published two nonmystery novels before starting to publish the Samantha Adams series.

Shankman is a member of the executive board of the International Association of Crime Writers, a former national board member and national secretary of Mystery Writers of America, and a member of PEN and Sisters in Crime.

As Marilyn Wallace says of Shankman's amateur detective in *Sisters in Crime 3*, "Samantha continues to explore the social foibles of the new South." On the dust jacket for *The King Is Dead*, Sarah Shankman has been described as "Elmore Leonard with a Southern accent" and as a portrayer of the "joyous eccentricity of the American South."

The Samantha Adams novels present the protagonist as a variation of the southern belle. Adams rejects the traditional life-style (she wanted a car instead of a debut) and becomes an independent investigative reporter. She feels ambivalent about her place in upper middle class society—realizing it to be phony in some ways, but nonetheless understanding the people among whom she grew up.

Shankman's mysteries are stories about one location: the South. Except for a brief sojourn at the Miss America pageant in *She Walks in Beauty*, the Samantha Adams novels occur in Georgia, Louisiana, and Mississippi. The heart of these stories is the evolution of the New South from the Old South, and its effects on the inhabitants. The crimes arise out of family and business relationships. Corrupt attorneys and sheriffs, and con men all appear. These novels fit Mary Morman's definition of Malice Domestic mysteries: "Books and stories . . . involve the protagonist not in a professional capacity but through home relationships. They involve sisters, brothers, friends and lovers." The South that Shankman creates is itself a good entry in *American Weird*, a book that Adams is researching in *The King Is Dead*. One character in *Now Let's Talk of Graves* plans the first flight of his hot-air-balloon lawn chair as the ultimate media event. The Elvis Presley culture depicted in *The King Is Dead* is worthy of its own chapter.

One of the effects of the New South is the changed racial order. Shankman handles the racial angle very well, and her black characters are three-dimensional. For instance, Peaches is Uncle George's cook-housekeeper, but she is also the founder of an adult literacy program. Lavert Washington, Harry's best friend, works as a chauffeur to an Italian wise guy, but he is also a gourmet cook with plans to open his own restaurant.

Shankman's forte is her depiction of character, and even her minor portraits appear fully fleshed out. Readers learn more about them than the one or two points necessary to advance the story line. The only minor charaters who remain two-dimensional are those members of Adams's social class who refuse to realize that times have changed. The main trait that her three-dimensional characters share is that they are all good storytellers, and readers will become as interested in the tale being told as Adams. Shankman deftly describes the correct behavior of both the storyteller and the audience.

These stories are written from the omniscient point of view, with a light touch and acerbic humor, although many of society's current ills are in evidence. Indeed, spouse abuse, anorexia, bulimia, alcoholism, drugs, organized crime, serial killings, rape, fraud, and blackmail are what Adams uncovers.

Shankman uses many aspects of her own life in the Adams novels. Like Shankman, Adams attended Emory University, and Shankman and Adams were both born in what Shankman refers to as the "real South." Adams's research for *American Weird* allows Shankman to display American popular culture of the southern variety. Readers of Shankman will probably enjoy the books of Barbara D'Amato and Karen Kijewski.

MYSTERY FICTION

Samantha Adams Series

First Kill All the Lawyers. New York: Pocket Books, 1988 (as by Alice Storey). New York: Pocket Books, 1988 (as by Sarah Shankman); Bath: Firecrest Books/ Chivers Press, 1991 (as by Alice Storey).

Then Hang All the Liars. New York: Pocket Books, 1988 (as by Alice Storey).

Now Let's Talk of Graves. New York: Pocket Books, 1990.

The King Is Dead. New York: Pocket Books, 1992.

She Walks in Beauty. New York: Pocket Books, 1992.

He Was Her Man. New York: Pocket Books, 1993.

LINDA R. HARRIS

DOROTHY SIMPSON (1933–   )

Dorothy Simpson was born on June 20, 1933, in Blaenavon, Monmouth-shire, Wales. After receiving her B.A. with honors from the University of Bristol, as well as her teaching certificate, she taught English and French in Kent, where she married a barrister in 1961. She has two sons and a daughter. From 1969 to 1982 she returned to work outside the home as a marriage guidance counselor. Both her experience as a counselor and her own family life have clearly influenced the positive treatment of marriage in her novels and her focus on human relationships and motivation. Familiar characteristics of Kent form the basis of her imaginary Kentish town of Sturrenden and its surroundings.

Simpson's strengths lie in her superb multiple plotting and her in-depth exploration of the psychological complexities of ordinary lives and relationships. Winner of the 1985 Silver Dagger Award of the British Crime Writers' Association for her fifth Luke Thanet novel, *Last Seen Alive*, she began writing in 1975. Her first novel, *Harbingers of Fear*, was an immediate success. When her next three psychological thrillers were rejected by a variety of publishers, she redirected her efforts to the murder mystery. As Simpson explains, she recast the heroine of her most recently rejected thriller as the murder victim and set out to develop an attractive detective suitable for the focus of a continuing series. The result was *The Night She Died*. A blend of the "whydunit" with the police procedural and the cozy, it introduces Detective Inspector Luke Thanet at the center of a fully drawn cast of supporting characters and relationships.

These relationships include Thanet's highly productive and comfortable partnership with Sergeant Michael Lineham, Thanet's relationship with his wife, Joan, and Lineham's marriage to Louise. In each, Simpson shows her characters facing such common and potentially destructive challenges as differences in personality and temperament, conflicting needs, the temptation to selfish domination, and simple insensitivity. One situation that is carried over in several of the novels involves Thanet's worry that Joan's desire for a career reflects some inadequacy on his part and threatens an indefinable future loss to him; another involves Lineham's much-regretted decision to seek promotion to satisfy Louise's frustrated ambition. Issues of control, autonomy, and responsibility similarly imbue the parent-child relationships in the novels, including the Thanets' relationship with Bridget and Ben, Lineham's problems with his domineering and manipulative mother, and Thanet's more positive relationship with his mother-in-law. Additional relationships emerge in Thanet's personal circle and are revealed in the circles of those whose lives have become entwined in murder, forging an essential link between both groups, and between plot and subplots, ultimately informing the solution of the crime.

Thanet is an appealingly ordinary, decent man who likes his family, job, and community. Less than perfect, he struggles with his personal limitations and with the conflicting pressures of contemporary society. His outstanding qualities are empathy, imagination, and a critical self-awareness born of the same analytic, psychological scrutiny that he uses to penetrate the defenses and deceptions of people encountered in his murder investigations. For Thanet, knowing the "why" of a murder leads to its solution, and the victim is the key: "Thanet believed that, random victims of violence apart, murder victims carried in themselves or in their lives the seeds of their own tragic destiny. Something in their circumstances, past or present, or something in their character had finally led to that moment of ultimate violence, and it was his job to find out what it was." The pieces regularly fall into place for Thanet when he achieves a partly intuitive synthesis of the facts and personalities revealed in his investigations.

Simpson's novels speak strongly for positive human values and uphold the human ability—the necessity, even—to establish harmony and order within a chaotic and threatening world. She avoids preaching, however. Instead her novels provide positive and negative examples of interpersonal relations and of the long-range consequences of individual actions. Thus, Simpson suggests an underlying unity of human experience that is at once encouraging and unsettling, as her characters shape their individual worlds and fates, for good or ill, through their everyday choices.

To appreciate fully the subtle growth of individual characters and relationships as well as Simpson's gradual buildup and resolution of domestic issues over several books, readers should read the Luke Thanet series in order. *The Night She Died* gives the series a strong start with an absorbing puzzle, double plotting, and an impressively detailed and developed presentation of Thanet's domestic circle. Readers who enjoy Simpson's work might also enjoy works by M. C. Beaton, Catherine Aird, and Sheila Radley.

MYSTERY FICTION

Harbingers of Fear. London: Macdonald and Janes, 1977.

Inspector Luke Thanet Series

The Night She Died. London: Michael Joseph; New York: Scribner's, 1981.

Six Feet Under. London: Michael Joseph; New York: Scribner's, 1982.

Puppet for a Corpse. London: Michael Joseph; New York: Scribner's, 1983.

Close Her Eyes. London: Michael Joseph; New York: Scribner's, 1984.

Last Seen Alive. London: Michael Joseph; New York: Scribner's, 1985.

Dead on Arrival. London: Michael Joseph; New York: Scribner's, 1986.

Element of Doubt. London: Michael Joseph, 1987; New York: Scribner's, 1988.

Suspicious Death. New York: Scribner's, 1988; Leicester, U.K.: Ulverscroft, 1990.

Dead by Morning. New York: Scribner's 1989; Leicester, U.K.: Ulverscroft, 1991.

Doomed to Die. New York: Scribner's, 1991; London: Michael Joseph, 1992.

Wake the Dead. New York: Scribner's; London: Michael Joseph, 1992.

No Laughing Matter. New York: Macmillan, 1993.

CRITICAL BIBLIOGRAPHY

Bakerman, Jane S. "Simpson, Dorothy." In *Twentieth Century Crime and Mystery Writers*, ed. Lesley Henderson. 3rd ed. Chicago: St. James Press, 1991, pp. 963–65.
Hill, Reginald. "Simpson, Dorothy." In *Twentieth Century Crime and Mystery Writers*, ed. John M. Reilly. 2d ed. New York: St. Martin's, 1985, pp. 803–4.
Melling, John Kennedy. [Foreword.] In *Harbingers of Fear*, by Dorothy Simpson. Black Dagger Crime Series. London: Chivers Press, 1987.
Nicholas, Victoria, and Susan Thompson. "Luke Thanet." In *Silk Stalkings: When Women Write of Murder*. Berkeley, Calif.: Black Lizard Books, 1988, pp. 59–60.
Ross, Jean W. "Simpson, Dorothy." *Contemporary Authors* (new revision series), 30 (1990): 405–6.

MICHAEL J. ROSSI

GILLIAN SLOVO (1952–   )

Gillian Slovo was born in Johannesburg, South Africa, in 1952. Her parents, the antiapartheid activists Joe Slovo and Ruth First, were forced into exile in 1964 and the family then settled in London where Gillian Slovo still lives. Over the years she has worked as a journalist and a film producer. The author of three Kate Baeier mystery novels, Slovo has, since the assassination of her mother in 1982 in Mozambique, turned her attention increasingly to fiction dealing explicitly with the struggle against apartheid in South Africa (*Ties of Blood, The Betrayal*). Her family was the subject of the widely acclaimed film, *A World Apart*.

The Kate Baeier series articulates Gillian Slovo's political positions. Kate sees London through the lenses of socialism and feminism, and the solutions to the mysteries derive from the analyses afforded by her ideology. As a woman, Kate is particularly sensitive to the dynamics of power in her society, and much of her investigative work has to do with dissecting personal, economic, and social webs of control. Although single, Kate has a long-standing relationship with Sam, a divorced mathematician who is more interested in poetry than the abstruse algebraic problems of his thesis;

Sam's young son, Matthew, visits on weekends and demonstrates admirably the joys and frustrations of life with an energetic child. Over the course of the series Slovo delineates the ups and downs of Kate's relationship with Sam, and the vicissitudes of their relationship comment on the social and cultural relationships that Kate encounters in her investigations.

In *Morbid Symptoms* the plot revolves around an alleged conspiracy between the South African government and the junta of Argentina to construct nuclear weapons. It reveals the paranoid existences, both of those plotting international conspiracies and of those intent on exposing them.

In *Death by Analysis* Slovo parallels Kate's investigations of the psychoanalysis of others with flashbacks of her own sessions. Kate's efforts to come to grips with life in Britain in the 1980s parallel those of a group of former radicals, and the solution to the mystery of Paul Holland's death reaffirms that the personal is, necessarily, the political.

In the double plot of *Death Comes Staccato* Kate finally has her own detective agency, run jointly with Carmen, a black single mother whom she met in the previous novel. Kate's personal and business connections with Carmen enable Slovo to explore race relations in Britain; Kate's work for the Weatherbys opens up the stresses of contemporary family life, and her probing of the affairs of Jarvis' firm exposes the cruelty of contemporary capitalism.

In the Kate Baeier series Gillian Slovo writes politically engaged mysteries. Kate shares the commitment, perseverance, and independence of other 1980s female investigators, like Sara Paretsky's V. I. Warshawski and Sue Grafton's Kinsey Millhone, though there is less overt violence in the Baeier series.

MYSTERY FICTION

Kate Baeier Series

Morbid Symptoms. London: Pluto Press, 1984; New York: Dember Books, 1985.

Death by Analysis. London: Women's Press, 1986; New York: Doubleday, 1988.

Death Comes Staccato. London: Women's Press, 1987; New York: Doubleday, 1988.

CRITICAL BIBLIOGRAPHY

Smith, Penny. "Slovo, Gillian." In *Twentieth Century Crime and Mystery Writers*, ed. Lesley Henderson. 3rd ed. Chicago and London: St. James, 1991, pp. 969–70.

ROBERT P. WINSTON

JOAN SMITH (1953–   )

Born in 1953 in London, Joan Smith received her education at Reading. In 1978, she was hired at a Manchester radio station where she worked on such newsbreaking items as the Yorkshire Ripper and was hired by the *London Times* in 1979. She has worked as a free-lance journalist since 1984.

Beginning with her first Loretta Lawson novel, *A Masculine Ending*, Smith establishes a premise that follows throughout the series: power corrupts. Any institution with an extremist position is suspect in the eyes of the London University professor and amateur detective, Loretta Lawson.

This skepticism holds true for feminist extremist positions as well as for patriarchal positions. Lawson's attempt to find a middle-ground, conservative stance leads her to Paris to defend feminism against the radical separatist ideals that threaten to tear apart the feminist academic world. While in Paris, Loretta stumbles on her first case, and, in each subsequent novel, murder victims find her at the most inopportune moments.

As an amateur detective, Lawson does not have to play by the rules of the professional: since she is not a recognized detective, she takes on her investigations without the help of local law enforcers. Similarly, Smith makes every effort to disregard the rules of the traditional detective formula: justice in all three novels occurs outside the law. Unlike the traditional detective novel, here, order is not neatly restored simply because Smith is challenging the need to restore the currently corrupt social order.

The ramifications of such corruptibility are analyzed in Smith's second novel, *Why Aren't They Screaming?* Once again enmeshed in a murder by virtue of her feminist concerns, Loretta discovers that local law officials are quick to cover up the illegal actions of the political domain. To disclose the cover-up publicly is impossible for Loretta because of her powerless position as a woman at the mercy of a capitalist society. In essence, Joan Smith's novels are a cynical look at the reality of life; frequently, powerful culprits go unpunished while the powerless assume the blame.

Finally deciding to play by the system, in *Don't Leave Me This Way*, Lawson's mistrust of police protection is justified. While investigating the murder of a member of her long-disbanded support group, Loretta actively petitions the help of the local authorities, only to be jeopardized by the bumblings of the police department. Ironically, Loretta's attempt to comply with the rules of a system which should be able to protect her leaves her unprotected. Haunted by the reminder of her vulnerable position, Lawson makes a break from this memory by moving. Not only is this move necessary for her survival, it seems to indicate Lawson's complete disillusionment and mistrust of the justice system's ability to protect her and, by extension, any powerless individual within society.

Reminiscent of the writings of Amanda Cross, Joan Smith's novels deal with the tension of living in an all-too-corrupt society while participating in the fantasy world of academia—a world in which the greatest concerns are publishing, syllabi, theory, and tenure. Although the series can be read in any order, I suggest that the reader begin with the first novel in order to watch the progression of Lawson's mistrust of institutions, which culminates with her total isolation.

MYSTERY FICTION

Loretta Lawson Series

A Masculine Ending. London: Faber and Faber, 1988; New York: Fawcett, 1989.

Why Aren't They Screaming? London: Faber and Faber, 1989; New York: Fawcett, 1990.

Don't Leave Me This Way. New York: Fawcett; London: Faber and Faber, 1990.

What Men Say. London: Chatto and Windus; New York: Fawcett Columbine, 1993.

TAMMY AIELLO

JULIE SMITH (1944–   )

Born in Savannah, Georgia, and educated at the University of Mississippi, Julie Smith served feature writing apprenticeships for the New Orleans *Times Picayune* and the San Francisco *Chronicle* before becoming a general assignment reporter covering a beat that included police and crime news. While the latter provided her with knowledge that she has put to good use in her three series of novels, the former gave her a breadth of social and sociological knowledge that gives her work depth and verisimilitude. More to the issue of Smith's reputation, however, is the progress in character complexity and stylistic command that her work has developed as the series progress.

Rebecca Schwartz is the protagonist of four of the nine novels that Smith had published by mid-1993. The thirty-something, borderline yuppie-with-liberal sympathies lawyer is involved with cases that, in content, lie somewhere between hard-boiled and "aha! the birthmark!" Rebecca is courageous, nimble-witted, and resourceful in her research. Perhaps the most interesting—and, maybe, the most typical—of the novels is *The Sour-*

dough Wars, in which the murder motive is a well-guarded recipe for sourdough which is coveted by a cast of suspects. The tracing of the crime's
genesis in some misdeeds of the past (à la Ross Macdonald) and the ultimately intellectual solution of the case are clever. If the characters are of
interest only as objects to reflect Rebecca's sleuthing acumen, that is no
real problem; like Smith's first detective hero, Sherlock Holmes, it is Rebecca's performance that counts.

Paul Macdonald, protagonist of *True-Life Adventure* and *Huckleberry
Fiend*, is an ex-reporter and fairly unsuccessful writer of mysteries. He sup-
plements his income writing reports for a private eye, whose death impels
Macdonald into sleuthing. *Huckleberry Fiend* concerns a manuscript of
Twain's classic: is it *the* original? Although she professes affection for Macdonald, Smith has said: "I think I've stopped writing the Paul Macdonald
series now because they weren't very successful. It turned out nobody
wanted to read a woman writing about a man."

The publication of *New Orleans Mourning*, featuring "Crescent City"
policewoman Skip Langdon, gave Smith an Edgar Award and established
her in the upper echelons of women hard-boiled writers. The action is
colorful: a Mardi Gras Krewe King is killed on his float during a parade
and the sniper is spotted wearing a Dolly Parton costume and wig. Langdon, whose academic, sorority, and social credentials give her entrée to
club circles, knows the victim and his family, and is thus assigned to the
case. She is her social-climbing parents' worst nightmare: a woman police
officer who lives in the French Quarter rather than living as a well-married
southern belle in the Garden District. Thinking of herself as an unambitious
underachiever who lacks the attractiveness men admire (she is tall and a
little overweight), Langdon is nevertheless driven to prove herself to her
superiors, move up the ranks to detective, and solve the murder. Along the
way she engages in a heated romance with a young tourist-filmmaker. The
reader is quick to realize that Skip is in no way as inept as she thinks. She
earns the grudging respect of her colleagues (though she is not treated like
"one of the boys"), has male relationships, and banters with her campy,
gay landlord. She even smokes a little marijuana. She is at once rebellious
and authoritative; it is a nice combination, full of tensions that Smith explores and exploits.

In *The Axman's Jazz*, she joins the investigation into the seeming reappearance of a legendary serial killer, and the case involves attending a number of twelve-step programs undercover. The interactions of the
"twelve-steppers" and the startling discovery that her own mother attends
a group provide the most interesting psychological aspects of the novel,
while its most memorable character is the aged father of a suspect, an
irascible old man who might have stepped out of the better pages of John
Kennedy Toole's or Donald Demarest's New Orleans novels. Moreover,
Skip seems to be developing a new edge of toughness. *Jazz Funeral* takes

place during the New Orleans Jazz Festival and involves Skip in the murder of a music producer. It allows Smith to develop a number of show-business "types" and to further secure Skip's perspicuity.

Smith's New Orleans is less kindly rendered than that of M. K. Shuman or Tony Fennelly. Its darkness is part of its deepest being, and its citizens are not sympathetically drawn. However, in the character of Skip Langdon, a hard-boiled heroine whose toughness and resourcefulness surprise even her, Smith has taken aspects of that city's specific culture and melded it with traditional aspects of the genre to create a particularly satisfying character study.

MYSTERY FICTION

Rebecca Schwartz Series

Death Turns a Trick. New York: Walker, 1982.

The Sourdough Wars. New York: Walker, 1984.

Tourist Trap. New York: Mysterious Press, 1986.

Dead in the Water. New York: Ivy, 1991.

Paul Macdonald Series

True-Life Adventure. New York: Mysterious Press, 1986.

Huckleberry Fiend. New York: Mysterious Press, 1987.

Skip Langdon Series

New Orleans Mourning. New York: St. Martin's, 1990.

The Axman's Jazz. New York: St. Martin's, 1991.

Jazz Funeral. New York: Fawcett Columbine, 1993.

New Orleans Beat. New York: Fawcett Columbine, 1994.

CRITICAL BIBLIOGRAPHY

Wallace, Marilyn. "Smith, Julie." In *Twentieth Century Crime and Mystery Writers*, ed. Lesley Henderson. 3rd ed. Chicago: St. James Press, 1991, pp. 970–71.

HERBERT V. FACKLER

SUSANNAH STACEY

Susannah Stacey is Jill Staynes and Margaret Storey, a collaboration begun at St. Paul's Girls' School in England. Staynes, who went to Oxford and worked in advertising, became a teacher, as did Storey, who attended Cambridge and had worked in publicity. Both have written stories for children, with Storey producing fourteen books and Staynes, one. They now write full time in London.

The Inspector Bone series of five books, beginning with *Goodbye, Nanny Gray* through *The Late Lady*, features strong, witty writing. When he first appears, Robert Bone, a detective-superintendent in Tunbridge Wells, is recently widowed (his wife and son were killed in a car accident) and devoted to his daughter Charlotte, who is recovering her speech and the use of a damaged leg (also from the accident). This relationship is central to all the books as Charlotte works toward social and physical health and Bone learns how to be a single parent. For many readers, what matters most in these books will be Bone's story as a father, Charlotte's recovery, and Bone's gradual interest in life outside his work and Charlotte.

The books make sense to new readers in any order, with background information conveyed subtly. Reading in order, however, the reader gains a sense of a community. These characters show Bone connected to a society that values him as a person, apart from his work.

As a detective, Bone likes research, and (unlike Dorothy Simpson's Luke Thanet) he does not seem to mind paperwork or have many troubles with his coworkers. Attractive, like P. D. James's Adam Dalgliesh and Margery Allingham's Roderick Alleyn, he thinks of himself as being "frozen" by his wife's death. Because he likes to talk to interesting people, he dislikes imposing on himself the official role that his work demands. He is funny in standing jokes with Charlotte and his colleague Steve Locker, yet he is often surprised when others respond to him warmly. While he is always successful in these books, he does not revert to a formula to figure out the cases or assemble the suspects for a dramatic encounter. Stacey's style does not shock the reader in some conventional ways (Frances Fyfield and Ruth Rendell, for example, seem enamored of women murderers, though statistically they are rare). All Stacey's books center on at least one murder.

Stacey's crimes show a range of motives, including greed, obsessive love, and fear of loss. The victims are not predictably the most expendable character; in fact, in at least three of the books the reader is able to share Bone's anger at the waste of a character's death. In every book, along with Bone as the central, reliable witness to events and their meaning, Stacey offers characters whose perspective seems correct. When one of these characters is, eventually, murdered, the reader feels the loss of that voice. The perspectives of the murderers are presented without sentimentality for the trauma of their own lives but also without unnecessary horror of the kind that Patricia D. Cornwell usually evokes. While Tunbridge Wells, neighboring villages, and the wider world of London are the usual settings, these are not cosy British mysteries. They do, however, evoke English life in such a way as to satisfy my Anglophilia.

The political messages are subtle: in two of the books, one of which suggests through characterization that homophobia makes a person unlikable, Stacey presents loving gay relationships. Evil is not identified as male or female or as belonging to any particular class or race (though these characters are primarily white). As a feminist father, Bone is a strong statement on what good parenting should be (without having all the answers, especially in *The Late Lady*, where Charlotte gains a boyfriend). Though he has part-time household help, he thinks about what food is in the refrigerator as he drives home. His appeal as a sensitive man is underscored when he meets Grizel Shaw in *A Knife at the Opera* and slowly begins a relationship with her. One of the most reliable perspectives, Grizel clearly likes Bone and recognizes him as someone who accepts her work and its importance. While theirs is not a work relationship, its development is intriguing without turning the novels into mystery/romances.

Aside from Bone's complex wisdom, the writers in the narrative offer much wisdom of their own. One of their most interesting themes is in how we perceive both others and the world and how that perception is not often identical to the perceptions of others. Their stories focus on a decent person and how he is trying to create a good life within his work and home.

MYSTERY FICTION

Bone Series

Goodbye, Nanny Gray. New York: Pocket; London: Bodley Head, 1987.

Body of Opinion. New York: Pocket; London: Bodley Head, 1988.

A Knife at the Opera. New York: Pocket, 1988.

Grave Responsibility. New York: Summit; London: Barrie and Jenkins, 1990.

The Late Lady. New York: Pocket; London: Random Century, 1992.

GEORGIA RHOADES

DOROTHY SUCHER (1933–   )

Dorothy Sucher was born in Brooklyn, New York, on May 18, 1933. Her father, Henry, was an accountant, and her mother, Shirley Hankin Glassman, worked as a medical secretary. On August 6, 1952, Dorothy married Joseph Sucher, a physicist, and they eventually had four children. She received a B.A. degree from Brooklyn College in 1954 and an M.M.H. degree from Johns Hopkins in 1975. Sucher was a contributing editor of the *Greenbelt News Review* from 1959 until 1970. Later, she worked as a psychotherapist for Group Health Association in Washington, D.C. (1975–80) and maintained a private practice in Greenbelt, Md. (1978–85).

Rather than a single detective, Sucher's books provide a pair of sleuths whose traits charmingly complement each other. Sabina Swift, the owner of a detective agency in Georgetown, is a methodical workaholic. Married to Bruno Herschel, a theoretical physicist, she is a thoroughly independent woman who insists on her own name. Like Sherlock Holmes, Sabina is acutely perceptive but not always willing to share her insights with her subordinate, Victor Newman. This second detective serves as the self-effacing narrator of Sucher's novels and frequently displays his youthful impetuosity. Orphaned as an adolescent, "Vic" studied psychology and subsequently worked as a used-car salesman and an aide in a psychiatric hospital. Now he makes better use of his training as Sabina's chief assistant, but he sometimes describes himself as a "frustrated shrink." More casual than Sabina in his style of detection, Vic does not always read the clues as quickly as she, but his loyal support sometimes rescues her from peril.

In her first novel, *Dead Men Don't Give Seminars*, Sucher focuses on theoretical physicists. After an acrimonious estrangement, two scientists whose joint work once won them the Nobel Prize come together again to present seminars at the Lake Champlain Physics Institute. When one drinks a poisoned cocktail, the other becomes a murder suspect. Sucher's cast includes characters with burdensome emotional baggage and many possible motives for murder. The narrative touches on several difficult social issues—homophobia, the debilitating effects of chronic illness, and a parent's problems in rearing a mentally retarded child.

Sucher's first book follows the classic formula of identifying a killer from a group of known suspects assembled in one place. On the other hand, *Dead Men Don't Marry* is more tightly plotted and describes a suspenseful manhunt. The task here is tracking down a serial killer who marries middle-aged women and then arranges for their (accidental-appearing) deaths. Skillfully mixing suspense and psychological realism, this novel displays the lasting effects of child abuse, the vulnerability of lonely middle-aged women, and the traumatic grief of a parent after the loss of a child.

Sucher's work has been compared to that of P. D. James in that her criminals are emotionally scarred from past events, but unlike James, the former's tone is frequently humorous. To appreciate the interaction of Sucher's detectives, a new reader should begin with her first novel.

MYSTERY FICTION

Sabina Swift and Victor Newman Series

Dead Men Don't Give Seminars. New York: St. Martin's Press, 1988.
Dead Men Don't Marry. New York: St. Martin's Press, 1989.

ALBERT E. WILHELM

❦ T ❦

PHOEBE ATWOOD TAYLOR (1909–1976)

Phoebe Atwood Taylor was born in Boston in 1909. She was graduated from Barnard College in 1930, and she published her first novel, *The Cape Cod Mystery*, the following year. Taylor lived for most of her life in Massachusetts, the primary setting for her books. She died in 1976.

An immediate clue to the tone of Taylor's mysteries can be found in her titles, many of which contain outrageous puns or sly jokes. *Dead Ernest* indeed presents a corpse named Ernest; *Out of Order* turns on a misplaced grocery order; *The Perennial Boarder* may or may not be the victim in the book of that name. Similarly, the titles *Figure Away*, *The Deadly Sunshade*, and *Death Lights a Candle* offer playful but significant clues to an alert reader. These tales offer adequate puzzles in detection, but their foremost pleasure is laughter. Beyond wordplay, Taylor's stories glean humor from eccentric characters in farcical predicaments as well as from a subtle vein of social satire.

Under her own name, Taylor chronicles the investigations of Asey Mayo, Cape Cod's wry answer to Sherlock Holmes and Philo Vance. Mayo is a fantastical figure, whose biography emerges piecemeal through the novels. When first met, Asey is comfortably retired, working when it suits him as a jack-of-all-trades handyman. In later books, however, he helps run Porter Motors, supervising wartime tank production and eventually serving on the board of directors. This diverse practical experience helps attune Asey to clues as homely as a bicycle clip, a pincushion, or a batch of nasty-tasting jelly. Even more important, perhaps, is the social mobility his colorful past affords him. He can also keep suspects off-guard by shifting disarmingly between the speech patterns of a yokel and those of an educated gentleman.

The Mayo novels were published between 1931 and 1951, and it is worth some effort to read them in roughly chronological order. The early books are narrated by middle-aged spinsters or widows; smart and brave themselves, their admiration for Asey helps establish his extraordinary talents, which characters simply take for granted in the later, omnisciently narrated, books. Too, Taylor provides precise, often surprising, details about times now past. (I should mention that their characters occasionally utter ethnic epithets we now find offensive, but the novels themselves are never mean-spirited.) The early books reflect consequences of the Great Depression. Plucky, young—and not so young—women of once prosperous families are suddenly faced with the need to earn a living; many a man is daunted by financial losses. For Taylor, economic hard times serve as proving grounds for moral fiber. Similarly, the World War II novels suggest the social upheaval of those years. Notably, women now wear trousers and run businesses, often more successfully than their absent male kinfolk had managed. The last few novels document a postwar disappointment: contrary to wartime expectations, peace has not proved idyllic. Throughout this series, Taylor writes as someone who loves Cape Cod and admires its inhabitants without losing sight of the pettiness and xenophobia that village life can foster. Her sharpest satire is reserved for pretensions and affectations of all sorts—the antithesis of Asey's matter-of-fact common sense.

Writing as Alice Tilton, Taylor recounts the exploits of Leonidas Xenophon Witherall, a retired professor and (later) headmaster of the Meredith Academy in a fictional suburb of Boston. The most distinctive fact about this sleuth is his likeness to Shakespeare. The resemblance is professional as well as physiognomic. Unknown to his companions in adventure, Shakespeare's look-alike writes popular books and radio serials featuring a dashing figure of derring-do, Lieutenant Haseltine. Something of a recurring joke is the fact that everyone—from gangsters to secretaries to society dowagers and minor celebrities—turns out to be a Haseltine fan. The Witherall books share the satirical edge of the Mayo series; here an unflattering portrait of suburban life is combined with rollicking slapstick and frequent literary allusions.

Like any humorist, Phoebe Atwood Taylor is not for everyone. People are likely to enjoy her work to the extent that they appreciate Taylor's particular sense of the ridiculous and her sharp eye for human foible. One might begin with *The Mystery of the Cape Cod Tavern* and *Banbury Bog* (Mayo) and *The Cut Direct* (Witherall). Readers hooked by this sampling can look forward to hours of amusement in Taylor's zany world.

Taylor's books are now easy to find, thanks to the paperback reprint series from Foul Play Press. Fans of Asey Mayo and Leonidas Witherall will also enjoy Charlotte MacLeod's New England mysteries, especially her Peter Shandy extravaganzas and the wild romps of the Grub-and-Stakers (writing as Alisa Craig). Also sharing Taylor's exuberance are Dorothy Gilman and Elizabeth Peters.

MYSTERY FICTION

Writing as Phoebe Atwood Taylor

Asey Mayo Series

The Cape Cod Mystery. Indianapolis, Ind.: Bobbs-Merrill, 1931.

Death Lights a Candle. Indianapolis, Ind.: Bobbs-Merrill, 1932.

The Mystery of the Cape Cod Players. New York: Norton, 1933; London: Eyre and Spottiswoode, 1934.

The Mystery of the Cape Cod Tavern. New York: Norton, 1934; London: Eyre and Spottiswoode, 1935.

Sandbar Sinister. New York: Norton, 1934; London: Gollancz, 1936.

Deathblow Hill. New York: Norton, 1935; London: Gollancz, 1936.

The Tinkling Symbol. New York: Norton; London: Gollancz, 1935.

The Crimson Patch. New York: Norton; London: Gollancz, 1936.

Out of Order. New York: Norton, 1936; London: Gollancz, 1937.

The Annulet of Gilt. New York: Norton, 1938; London: Collins, 1939.

Banbury Bog. New York: Norton, 1938; London: Collins, 1939.

Figure Away. New York: Norton, 1937; London: Collins, 1938.

Octagon House. New York: Norton, 1937; London: Collins. 1938.

Spring Harrowing. New York: Norton; London: Collins, 1939.

The Criminal C.O.D. New York: Norton; London: Collins, 1940.

The Deadly Sunshade. New York: Norton, 1940; London: Collins, 1941.

The Perennial Boarder. New York: Norton, 1941; London: Collins, 1942.

The Six Iron Spiders. New York: Norton, 1942; London: Collins, 1943.

Three Plots for Asey Mayo (novelettes). New York: Norton, 1942.

Going, Going, Gone. New York: Norton, 1943; London: Collins, 1944.

The Asey Mayo Trio (novelettes). New York: Messner; London: Collins, 1946.

Proof of the Pudding. New York: Norton; London: Collins, 1946.

Punch with Care. New York: Farrar Straus: 1946; London: Collins, 1947.

Diplomatic Corpse. Boston: Little, Brown; London: Collins, 1951.

Writing as Alice Tilton

Leonidas Witherall Series

Beginning with a Bash. London: Collins, 1937; New York: Norton, 1972.

The Cut Direct. New York: Norton; London: Collins, 1938.

Cold Steal. New York: Norton, 1939; London: Collins, 1940.

The Left Leg. New York: Norton, 1940; London: Collins, 1941.

The Hollow Chest. New York: Norton, 1941; London: Collins, 1942.

File for Record. New York: Norton, 1943; London: Collins, 1944.

Dead Ernest. New York: Norton, 1944; London: Collins, 1945.

The Iron Clew. New York: Norton, 1947; as *The Iron Hand.* London: Collins, 1947.

Writing as Freeman Dana

Murder at the New York World's Fair. New York: Random House, 1938.

CRITICAL BIBLIOGRAPHY

Dueren, Fred. "Asey Mayo: 'The Hayseed Sherlock.' " *The Armchair Detective*, 10 (1977): 21–24, 83.
Hart, Carolyn G. "Leonidas Witherall." In *100 Great Detectives*, ed. Maxim Jakubowski. London: Xanadu; New York: Carroll and Graf, 1991, pp. 231–32.

SUSAN BAKER

JOSEPHINE TEY (1896–1952)

Very little biographical information is available on this reclusive Scotswoman. During her lifetime, Josephine Tey (born Elizabeth MacKintosh in 1896) rebuffed all attempts to interview her. She was born in Inverness, Scotland, attended the Royal Academy there (majoring in the humanities), and continued her education at Anstley Physical Training College in Birmingham, England. Upon graduation she taught physical education in various English schools. In 1926 she gave up teaching and returned to Inverness to care for her ailing father.

During this period MacKintosh wrote a novel, a number of short stories, and plays under the name of Gordon Daviot. *Richard of Bordeaux* (produced in 1932) studied Richard III, a subject that would continue to intrigue her throughout her life and become the locus of her most critically acclaimed novel, *The Daughter of Time.*

In 1929 MacKintosh (still using the Daviot pen name) wrote her first mystery novel which featured the witty and cultivated police detective Alan Grant. She adopted the pen name of Josephine Tey in 1936, the name under which she authored seven more detective novels. Like her most famous sleuth, Alan Grant, Tey never married, preferring the company of a few close friends. Her outside interests, theater-going, horse racing, and fishing, are often reflected in her novels. After a lengthy illness, Tey died in London on February 13, 1952.

Tey is known as one of the preeminent writers of the Golden Age of crime and mystery writing. Part of her popularity with new generations of mystery aficionados is due to her reluctance to rely on formula (the bane of many detective fiction writers). Choosing instead to foreground human psychology, Tey's novels appeal to readers who ordinarily eschew mysteries. In a Tey novel, the crime commission and solution are filtered through the eyes of Grant and others like him, students of the human condition. Often cited for excellence are her carefully limned characterizations. Unlike other sleuths of the Golden Age, the Tey detectives are not infallible. Rather, they are complex men and women drawn into the human drama which unfolds within the novel.

Surprisingly, each of the eight detective fictions is unique in its construction and development. The Grant series, however, is probably the most widely read of all Tey's works, as the erudite Scotsman is a most mesmerizing sleuth.

Alan Grant, whose inheritance frees him from the need to earn a living, has chosen his profession out of love—and aptitude. A keen observer and student of human nature, Grant has earned the respect of his colleagues. Like his creator, little is known of his background. His work is his life.

One of Grant's foibles (as ascertained by his superiors) is his "flair," the intuitive leap he makes from the examination of hard evidence to his intangible, yet accurate, conclusions. Many times Grant himself finds the "flair" disconcerting, causing him to shunt aside subconscious feelings until he can no longer disregard them. In contrast to the genteel Grant is his partner, Sergeant Williams, a man who is preoccupied with details. Unlike the Sherlock Holmes/Dr. Watson relationship, the Grant/Williams partnership is based upon mutual respect. Williams, unlike Watson, is more than a mere hero worshiper. Sergeant Williams is, indeed, in awe of Grant's genius, but Grant heavily relies upon Williams' attention to detail to aid him in his detection.

Grant was introduced as a richly developed character in *The Man in the Queue* but was not reintroduced in Tey's detective fiction for seven years and then not again until the end of the author's career. Instead, Tey chose to diversify her use of character. In *Miss Pym Disposes* the detective is a retired French teacher turned best-selling author. Miss Lucy Pym, at the request of her old friend Henrietta, now the head mistress at Leys Physical Training College, has returned to academe to lecture. When an unpopular student dies of a skull fracture under mysterious circumstances, the redoubtable Miss Pym uses her knowledge of psychology to investigate the death. *Miss Pym Disposes* superbly delineates the characters of a large cast of characters.

In *Brat Farrar* the impersonator of the dead son of an affluent British family becomes the detective in order to redeem himself. *The Franchise Affair* focuses on the investigation conducted by lawyer Robert Blair at the behest of his client, Marion Sharpe. Especially noteworthy in this latter work are the complex characterizations of Blair's Aunt Lin and Mrs. Sharpe.

However, arguably, Tey's masterpiece is *The Daughter of Time*. (The title is taken from the old proverb, "Truth is the daughter of time.") In the previous Grant mysteries, *The Man in the Queue*, *A Shilling for Candles*, *To Love and Be Wise*, CID Grant is actively engaged in crime solving as a member of Scotland Yard. *The Daughter of Time*, however, has Grant incapacitated, having ignominiously broken his leg while chasing a petty thief. Fractious because of his inability to work, Grant asks his friend Martha Hallard, an actress, to bring him prints. (Grant enjoys "reading" faces.) One of these prints is the portrait of the infamous Richard III at the National Gallery in London. After constant scrutiny, Grant determines that this is not the face of Shakespeare's villain. Grant's Richard has the sensitive and intelligent face of a judge, a man who must make morally difficult decisions. Engaging the assistance of an earnest American graduate student, Brent Carradine, Grant conducts from his hospital bed an investigation of the centuries-old murder of the princes in the Tower. Carradine, the consummate researcher, delivers the writings of Sir Thomas More and other historians to Grant. Other "informants" range from the nurses, the porter, and even friends. Tey deftly interweaves history and detective work, enabling Grant to provide a powerful exoneration of the maligned Richard. (Grant deduces that the real murderer is Richard's successor, Henry VII.) Unfortunately, Grant and Carradine discover that their "findings" are not new; historians since the 1600s have posited such a theory.

Tey's last novel, *The Singing Sands*, is set in her beloved Scottish Highlands. Grant, now suffering from fatigue and claustrophobia, has returned to his native land to recuperate. (Tey's descriptions of the countryside are stunning, evoking the charm of the terrain.) His shaky psychological state conversely aids him to conclude an ex officio investigation, which, in turn, helps him regain emotional equilibrium. His Scotland Yard career is brought to an end.

Because the novels differ in form and structure, it is not necessary to read them in chronological order. For example, I have taught *The Daughter of Time* in undergraduate courses, where it has been enthusiastically received. College students are particularly intrigued by Tey's manipulation of historical analysis in this novel.

Readers who enjoy Tey's detective fiction might also be interested in the works of Catherine Aird, M. C. Beaton, Elizabeth Lemarchand, Ellis Peters, Ruth Rendell, and Pauline Winslow.

MYSTERY FICTION

Miss Pym Disposes. London: Davies, 1946; New York: Macmillan, 1948.
The Franchise Affair. London: Davies, 1948; New York: Macmillan, 1949.
Brat Farrar. London: Davies, 1949; New York: Macmillan, 1950; as *Come and Kill Me*. New York: Pocket, 1951.

Alan Grant Series

The Man in the Queue. London, Methuen, 1929, as *Killer in the Crowd*. New York: Spivak, 1954 (originally as by Gordon Daviot).

A Shilling for Candles: The Story of a Crime. London: Methuen, 1936; New York: Macmillan, 1954.

To Love and Be Wise. London: Davies, 1950; New York: Macmillan, 1951.

The Daughter of Time. London: Davies, 1951; New York: Macmillan, 1952.

The Singing Sands. London: Davies, 1952; New York: Macmillan, 1953.

CRITICAL BIBLIOGRAPHY

Charney, Hanna. *The Detective Novel of Manners: Hedonism, Morality, and the Life of Reason*. Cranbury, N.J.: Fairleigh Dickinson University, 1981.
Davis, Dorothy Salisbury. "On Josephine Tey." *New Republic*, 20 Sept. 1954, pp. 17–18.
Rollyson, Carl. "The Detective as Historian: Josephine Tey's *The Daughter of Time*." *Iowa State Journal of Research*, 53 (1978): 21–30.
Roy, Sandra. *Josephine Tey*. Boston: Twayne, 1980.
Smith, M. J. "Controversy: Townsend, Tey, and Richard III, a Rebuttal." *The Armchair Detective*, (Oct. 1977): 317–19.
Talburt, Nancy Ellen. "Josephine Tey." In *Ten Women of Mystery*, ed. Earl F. Bargainnier. Bowling Green, Ohio: Bowling Green University Press, 1981, pp. 40–76.
Townsend, Guy M. "Richard III and Josephine Tey: Partners in Crime." *The Armchair Detective*, (July 1977): 211–24.

ANITA MARISSA VICKERS

JUNE THOMSON (1930–   )

June Thomson's knowledge of, and affection for, the scenery and people of Essex is vividly expressed in her seventeen police "whydunits" featuring Detective Chief Inspector Jack Finch of the Chelmsford CID. Born in 1930, Thomson grew up and received her early schooling in a small village near Chelmsford. Thomson was married soon after receiving an honors degree in English from Bedford College of London University in 1952.

After becoming divorced, she taught only part time in a secondary school so she could devote more time to writing. In 1983, Thomson won the forty-eighth award of the Prix du Roman d'Aventure.

Because of their interest in character over action women detective writers in Britain are largely responsible for the transformation of the whodunit into the "whydunit" in the years following World War II. Thomson stated: "Women are interested in relationships. That's basically why women are good at writing crime fiction. That's why I write. The detective novel gives me a way of considering different types of relationships."

Thomson occupies a prominent place in the distinguished group of post-World War II English women detective novelists—including P. D. James, Sheila Radley, Ruth Rendell, and Dorothy Simpson—who began publishing police whydunits in the mid-1960s and 1970s. Although all feature a ranking police officer and his sergeant as principal characters, and although considerable attention is paid to the extended police team and their procedures in the novels, actually (except for James's novels), a classical Holmes/Watson partnership exists under the trappings of police routine. Moreover, the solution to the puzzle, usually arrived at by a combination of intuitive insight and logical deduction by the senior detective, only becomes clear when the culprit's motive is identified.

In many of Thomson's novels the police team, with its detailed official routine, is much in evidence. However, it is often Finch's imaginative insight sparked by a random fact or coincidental detail which leads him to rearrange the evidence in a new pattern and hence to understand how the crime was committed and by whom.

Finch's reconsideration is usually based on intuitive insight into the relationships of the principal characters and their motives of behavior. Psychological analysis in the Maigret tradition leads directly to the solution in *Death Cap*, *The Long Revenge*, *Deadly Relations*, and *To Make a Killing*.

Thomson's middle-aged sleuth, Detective Inspector Jack Finch, looks more like a farmer than a policeman with his ruddy complexion, short stocky frame, wrinkled tweed suit, shabby old mackintosh, and unpolished shoes. In the early novels, Finch registers irritation, anxiety, and disappointment by biting his thumbnail. More characteristic is his stance: he puts his hands in his pockets and hunches his shoulders when he is angry, discouraged, morose, or merely contemplative.

He has a low-key, conversational interviewing style and frequently listens with his head cocked to one side to encourage confidences. He dislikes the forthright question-and-answer type of interview and instead prefers to present himself like a family friend come around for a good gossip. Turning casually as he is leaving an interview, Finch often poses the final important question from the doorway catching the subject at a disadvantage after he has relaxed thinking the interview concluded.

The past is a powerful influence in Thomson's work and often Finch traces the origins of a crime to events or actions which occurred years previously or to unhealthy resentments and festering feelings preserved into the present which finally explode into violence. Sometimes there is a need to cover up past events.

A frequent figure among the constellation of characters in Thomson's books is that of the outsider who threatens the community, as Patrick Vaughn does in *Alibi in Time*, or is intolerantly perceived as a threat, like Smith in *Not One of Us*. Thomson shows the villagers' suspicions and fears of an incomer and their instinct to close ranks against him. She also depicts the impulse for vigilante justice lurking under the surface of community life, which masks the desire to destroy the unfamiliar. The outsider can be a stranger or a misfit—someone of a different social stratum or sexual orientation.

Thomson is widely acclaimed for her beautifully rendered settings, especially landscape. The treatment of landscape embodies exquisite selection of detail, sensitive depiction of color and texture, artful composition, evocative interpretation of the viewer's response—thereby revealing character—and finally, sheer love of the beauty of the natural world in all its moods. She explained: "I love doing the setting. I like the challenge of writing descriptive passages. One has to find the words to make a scene live. They have to be short but they must capture the spirit of a place."

Thus, her focus on motivation for crime with its concomitant character development and her use of setting to reveal character and communicate theme identify Thomson as one of the women writers in post–World War II Britain who have helped to shape the "whydunit," and in so doing, to lift the detective novel from formula fiction toward mainstream literature.

It is not necessary to read Thomson's novels in consecutive order to enjoy them or gain a sense of her craft, but it helps provide understanding of the changes in Finch's personal and professional life. Among Thomson's best are *Not One of Us*, *Death Cap*, *Deadly Relations*, *To Make a Killing*, and *Sound Evidence*.

MYSTERY FICTION

Finch (Rudd) Series

Not One of Us. New York: Harper, 1971; London: Constable, 1972.

Death Cap. London: Constable, 1973; New York: Doubleday, 1977.

The Long Revenge. London: Constable, 1974; New York: Doubleday, 1975.

Case Closed. London: Constable; New York: Doubleday, 1977.

A Question of Identity. New York: Doubleday, 1977; London: Constable, 1978.

Deadly Relations. London: Constable, 1979; as *The Habit of Loving*. New York: Doubleday, 1979.

Alibi in Time. London: Constable; New York: Doubleday, 1980.

Shadow of a Doubt. London: Constable, 1981; New York: Doubleday, 1982.

To Make a Killing. London: Constable, 1982; as *Portrait of Lilith*. New York: Doubleday, 1983.

Sound Evidence. London: Constable, 1984; New York: Doubleday, 1985.

A Dying Fall. London: Constable, 1985; New York: Doubleday, 1986.

The Dark Stream. London: Constable; New York: Doubleday, 1986.

No Flowers by Request. London: Constable; New York: Doubleday, 1987.

Rosemary for Remembrance. London: Constable; New York: Doubleday, 1988.

The Spoils of Time. London: Constable; New York: Doubleday, 1989.

Past Reckoning. London: Constable; New York: Doubleday, 1990.

Foul Play. London: Constable, 1991.

CRITICAL BIBLIOGRAPHY

McAleer, John. "The Social-Domestic World of June Thomson's Detective Chief Inspector Jack Finch/Rudd." In *The Sleuth and the Scholar*, ed. Barbara Rader and Howard Zettler. Westport, Conn.: Greenwood, 1988.
Nichols, Victoria, and Susan Thompson. "Rudd/Finch." In *Silk Stalkings*. Berkeley, Calif.: Black Lizard, 1988, pp. 56–57.
Smith, Penny. "Thompson, June." In *Twentieth Century Crime and Mystery Writers*, ed. Lesley Henderson. 3rd ed. Chicago and London: St. James, 1991, pp. 1013–14.

B. J. RAHN

MASAKO TOGAWA (1933–   )

Masako Togawa was born in Japanese-occupied Manchuria in 1933 and repatriated to Japan at the conclusion of the Pacific War (as the Japanese term World War II). Her father was killed in the war, accounting for the persistent anti-Americanism evident in her writing. *The Master Key* (1962) won the Eighth Edogawa Rampo Mystery Award, the most prestigious award in Japanese crime writing. Togawa is now a popular media figure in Japan.

Like her contemporary Shizuko Natsuke, Togawa is a second-generation practitioner of the "social detective school" of crime writing, developed and popularized by Seicho Matsumoto, which emphasizes postwar social and political change rather than the *pazuraa* or puzzle style favored by earlier *misteri* (mystery) writers. Reflecting many of the difficulties in her own earlier life, Togawa focuses on the lives of the losers and misfits of

Tokyo's mean streets rather than depicting the comfortable middle-class existence of Natsuke's stories. The traditional Japanese interests in fantasy, eroticism, the bizarre, and the supernatural are also more apparent in her writing than that of other crime writers and can be considered a defining characteristic. A clear example can be found in her only short story available in English, "The Vampire," which mixes illusion with reality to highlight corruption in contemporary business practices.

Togawa's first novel of psychological suspense, *The Master Key*, focuses on the lonely, often bizarre, lives led by many women in contemporary Japanese society. As study in group dynamics, it details the interaction of the elderly residents of a Tokyo woman's hotel scheduled for demolition. The triggering agent in the tragedy, however, is a thoughtless decision by an American soldier to dump his Japanese wife. Reflecting Togawa's own anti-Americanism, *The Master Key* ends with the soldier's indifference to the consequences of his action.

The mean streets of Tokyo and the bars of the Ginza are the setting of *The Lady Killer*. In this tale with its classic Japanese theme of revenge, a businessman with a rare blood type realizes that he is being framed for murder. While illustrating the clash between modern society and tradition as well as the low status of women, *The Lady Killer* reflects a sympathy for a social system in which Togawa, in spite of her own singing talent, would be just another geisha in the Ginza. *The Lady Killer* has been adapted to both film and television. It was "the break-out" novel that established Togawa as a popular mainstream writer.

Togawa combines the post-war social detective school's focus on motivation and contemporary problems with the traditional interests of history and eroticism in *A Kiss of Fire*. Chopped into sections, each with different character's perspective, *A Kiss of Fire* is difficult to read and does not cross the Pacific cultural divide well.

All three Togawa novels are brilliantly translated by Simon Grove, and convey a sense of the culture. Togawa emerges a reporter of the status quo rather than proponent of change. She is often misleadingly hyped as the P. D. James of Japan. Her writing, with its emphasis on the bizarre is, however, very different from James's conventional mysteries. Togawa's stories are an acquired taste and distinctively her own.

MYSTERY FICTION

The Master Key. New York: Dodd, Mead, 1985; London: Century Hutchinson, 1984.

The Lady Killer. New York: Dodd, Mead, 1986; London: Century Hutchinson, 1985.

A Kiss of Fire. New York: Dodd, Mead; London: Chatto and Windus, 1988.

CRITICAL BIBLIOGRAPHY

Apostolou, John L. "Japanese Mystery Fiction Revisited." *The Armchair Detective*,
    15, no. 2 (1982).
Stone, Nancy-Stephanie. "Death under the Rising Sun." *Drood Review*, 9, no. 5
    (May 1989): 1.

NANCY-STEPHANIE STONE

MARGARET TRUMAN (1924–   )

Margaret Truman was born in Independence, Missouri, on February 17, 1924, the daughter of President Harry S Truman. After earning her B.A. from George Washington University in 1946, she sang professionally until 1954. She has written several nonfiction books, including well-received biographies of President Truman and of her mother, Bess Truman.

Dubbed the "Mistress of Capital Mayhem" by a *Washington Post* reviewer, she has placed her eleven murders at famous landmarks and in neighborhoods of the capital, in what was soon called the "Capital Crime Series." Such a rubric is somewhat misleading, though, for each novel presents a new cast of heroes, usually assigned by the Metropolitan Police Department, the agencies involved, or the local media.

In 1989, however, *Murder at the Kennedy Center* introduced a new investigating couple, law professor Mackensie Smith and art gallery owner (and former lawyer) Annabel Reed, who grow professionally and intellectually with each subsequent adventure and are already married when the next murder happens, at the National Cathedral. In the tradition of Agatha Christie's Prudence and Tommy Tuppence and Dashiell Hammett's Nick and Nora Charles, Mac and Annabel, with their Great Dane, Rufus, admirably hold their own in an affectionate and bantering style. Tony Buffalino, a former good cop turned bad, is given a second chance through his recurring role as a gruff, competent private detective.

Truman presents murders that are challenging, but their solution is not her foremost priority. Of first importance to her is the presentation of the protagonists, often in witty and sharp detail, along with quirky secondary characters who are equally well drawn.

Second, Truman researches her topics thoroughly in order to give an authenticity that adds immeasurably to the stories' sense of place and enjoyment. Her insider's look behind the scenes at personalities and events is made all the more interesting thanks to her suspenseful narrative style. If there is one criticism that can be voiced, it is that beginning with her second work she, along with other practitioners of the mystery and romance genres, indulges in too many descriptions of clothes, food, and drink that add little to the atmosphere or to understanding the characters.

Finally, except for *Murder in the White House*, the one common thread which links all Truman's novels, including the three in the Smith-Reed series, is the evidence of a menacing conspiracy, often masked by patriotism and Cold War rhetoric. Rather than in presidents or cabinet secretaries, real power, it seems, rests in the military-industrial complex and in the deadly world of espionage.

Since the crimes occur in various Washington buildings and milieus, each book can be read independently and in no specific order, with the (minor) exception of Truman's last three. Her intimate knowledge about the workings of the White House probably makes her first murder story an easy choice. Margaret Truman's mystery readers may also enjoy novels by Amanda Cross, Antonia Fraser, and perhaps Helen McInnes as well.

MYSTERY FICTION

Murder in the White House. New York: Arbor House, 1980.
Murder on Capitol Hill. New York: Arbor House, 1981.
Murder in the Supreme Court. New York: Arbor House; London: Severn House, 1982.
Murder in the Smithsonian. New York: Arbor House; London: Severn House, 1983.
Murder on Embassy Row. New York: Arbor House, 1984.
Murder at the FBI. New York: Arbor House, 1985.
Murder in Georgetown. New York: Arbor House, 1986; as *Murder in Washington*. London: Severn House, 1986.
Murder in the CIA. New York: Random House; London: Severn House, 1987.

Mackensie Smith and Annabel Reed Series

Murder at the Kennedy Center. New York: Random House; London: Severn House, 1989.

Murder at the National Cathedral. New York: Random House; London: Severn House, 1990.

Murder at the Pentagon. New York: Random House, 1992.

Murder on the Potomac. New York: Random House, 1994.

CRITICAL BIBLIOGRAPHY

Browne, Ray B., and Alicia R. Browne. "Bad Blood on the Potomac: Margaret Truman's Washington Novels." *Clues*, 3, no. 2 (1982): 100–103.

PIERRE L. HORN

❦ U ❦

DOROTHY UHNAK (1933–)

Dorothy Uhnak was born in 1933 in Bronx, New York, where she grew up next to a police station. Aspiring in her teenage years to be a social worker, Uhnak instead joined the police force at age twenty, battling her way to Detective First Class in the jealously male ranks of the New York Police Department during the pre-feminist 1950s. She married and has one daughter, now an attorney. Although awarded two medals for heroism, one after single-handedly disarming a serial rapist twice her size who was holding a gun to her head, she was demoted back to patrol rank for taking pregnancy leave. After fourteen years on the force, Uhnak quit to finish college and pursue a full-time writing career. Two of her best-sellers, *Law and Order* and *The Investigation*, were made into television movies by Paramount. In 1968 her novel, *The Bait*, received the Edgar for best first mystery from the Mystery Writers of America. The protagonist, Christie Opara, became the prototype for the short-lived *Get Christy Love* television series.

Uhnak is not a fan of most crime fiction and does not like being classified a genre novelist. Valuing realism and detailed characterization, she trades on milieus she knows well: the Bronx, police work, and urban ethnic frictions—which she experienced firsthand as the offspring of a Jewish father and Irish-Catholic mother when disapproval of such unions ran high.

Uhnak's female felons come close to upstaging her law-enforcing heroines. Elena Vargas of *The Ledger*, and Kitty Keeler of *The Investigation*, are the inverse reflections of Detective Opara and her ilk: unconventional women who overcame personal tragedy to succeed in male-dominated criminal milieus by force of personality. As Uhnak's writing has matured, her vision has become darker. In her later novels the guardian of law is often unable to reestablish order: murderers elude institutional justice and corruption in high places continues unabated.

Uhnak's Christie Opara bears the distinction of being one of the first fictional female police detectives. The focus in the series is the interplay between the squad members, particularly the ambivalent, sexually toned relationship between Opara and her chief, Assistant District Attorney Casey Reardon, who is alternately frustrated and bemused by Opara's stubborn, independent style. The novels chronicle her rite of passage, from which she does not emerge unscathed.

Since terminating the Opara series, Uhnak has eschewed a recurring protagonist. *The Investigation* is one of Uhnak's few first-person narratives, told in the persona of Joe Peters, world-weary veteran detective who becomes obsessed with doubt about the guilt of the enigmatic Kitty Keeler, accused child-murderer. This book, Uhnak's most financially successful, draws heavily on the atmosphere and conventions of the classic noir novel, including the ambiguous lure of a dangerous woman, disillusion with the criminal justice machine, and the detective's reliance on his own existential code.

False Witness, also told in the first person, is narrated by Lynn Jacobi, an ambitious female assistant district attorney. Having to contend with the same male attitudes as Christie Opara, but from a position of authority, she gives an impressive demonstration of how to wield command, as she treads her way through the political and personal minefield of a high-profile rape and attempted murder case. Uhnak develops several strong female characters in this book, in a complex web of rivalries, victimization, betrayal, and bonding, which forms a parallel plot to the criminal investigation. Like *The Investigation*, it takes a jaundiced view of the official system of justice and of the political pressures that distort it.

Victims concerns an Afro-Hispanic policewoman investigating a stabbing which superficially resembles the Kitty Genovese incident. The mood of anxiety and uncertainty builds to a feverish pitch, culminating in a dreamlike confrontation with a nemesis of archetypal dimensions.

I would recommend *The Investigation*, *False Witness*, and *Victims*, which generate more suspenseful involvement than the Opara series. The tension comes from a brooding miasma of uncertainty, initially around the prime suspect's guilt, but eventually contaminating the protagonist's personal relationships.

Uhnak is currently writing a mystery featuring a woman attorney who investigates a violent interracial crime; the working title is *Questions of Integrity*. Readers who like Dorothy Uhnak's novels might also enjoy works by Lillian O'Donnell, Patricia D. Cornwell and Liza Cody.

MYSTERY FICTION

Policewoman: A Young Woman's Initiation into the Realities of Justice. New York: Simon and Schuster, 1964.

Law and Order. New York: Simon and Schuster; London: Hodder and Stoughton, 1973.

The Investigation. New York: Simon and Schuster, 1977; London: Hodder and Stoughton, 1978.

False Witness. New York: Simon and Schuster, 1981; London: Hutchinson, 1982.

Victims. New York: Simon and Schuster, 1985; London: Century Publishers, 1986.

Christie Opara Series

The Bait. New York: Simon and Schuster; London: Hodder and Stoughton, 1968.

The Witness. New York: Simon and Schuster, 1969; London: Hodder and Stoughton, 1970.

The Ledger. New York: Simon and Schuster, 1970; London: Hodder and Stoughton, 1971.

CRITICAL BIBLIOGRAPHY

Budd, Elaine. *13 Mistresses of Murder*. New York: Ungar Publishers, 1986, pp. 115–24.

Dove, George. "Dorothy Uhnak." In *And Then There Were Nine: More Women of Mystery*, ed. Jane S. Bakerman. Bowling Green, Ohio: Popular Press, 1985, pp. 80–99.

Mitterling, Philip I. "Dorothy Uhnak: The Development of a Novelist." *Journal of Popular Culture*, 16, no. 1 (1982): 88–98.

Nichols, Victoria, and Susan Thompson. "Christie Opara." In *Silk Stalkings*. Berkeley, Calif.: Black Lizard, 1988, pp. 28–30.

PAUL LEON BAIL

❦ W ❦

PATRICIA WENTWORTH (1878–1961)

Patricia Wentworth was born Dora Amy Elles in 1878 in Musoorie, in the foothills of the Himalayas. She attended Blackheath High School for Girls in London. Twice married, her second husband, Lt. Col. George Oliver Turnbull, assisted her with the preparation of manuscripts for publication. She had one daughter. Wentworth wrote sixty-five mysteries, several romances, and three volumes of poetry before her death in 1961. She wrote a number of nonseries thrillers, eight of which were recently reprinted by Warner Books. Most of these feature young women who must investigate crimes ranging from blackmail and murder to espionage. The best of them are *Mr. Zero, Fear by Night*, and *Rolling Stone*. However, Wentworth is best known for the forty novels featuring Miss Maud Silver, private detective.

Silver has emerged from years as a governess, living in other people's houses and teaching their children—a position she "disliked extremely"—with only a pittance on which to retire. However, she realizes that "human nature shows itself very plainly in the schoolroom. The Child is father of the Man." Thus, she has an excellent foundation for her new career as a private detective. She works from her modest apartment at 15 Montague Mansions. Wentworth outfits the flat with as much distinctive character as 221B Baker Street. Throughout the series the reader is comforted to return to the peacock blue carpet, the Victorian chairs and engravings, the photographs of students and clients, and the large writing table on which are piled the note books in which she takes notes on each case.

Many of her cases begin in London when a client, referred by a friend or a relative, seeks her services. (She does not advertise.) Invariably she insists that her clients be open with her. She quotes her favorite writer, Lord Tennyson, "And trust me not at all or all in all." Some cases are set in London and do not depart from the city. The best of these are *Miss*

Silver Deals with Death, Grey Mask, and *The Girl in the Cellar.* More often, the investigations lead her to villages and country estates where, in the guilty vicarage tradition, a closed set and a finite number of characters offer full play to Wentworth's skills at intricate plotting. Wentworth seems particularly fond of pools, brooks, and wells as crime scenes, and though blackmail, theft, and jealously factor into many of her mysteries, murder is clearly her crime of choice. She is especially effective with suspense, at thrusting the reader into a riveting situation in the opening pages. Good examples are *The Benavent Treasure* and *The Girl in the Cellar.*

In the country setting, gossip is critical for her work. She depends on it for exposition, clues, and even judgment of character. Her method consists of careful observation, questioning, and the analysis of clues. Sometimes she takes great risks to secure evidence, even to the extent of breaking and entering, as in *Lonesome Road.*

Certain characters recur in the Miss Silver mysteries, most notably various members of the police with whom she has had long acquaintance. For example, Chief Constable Randall March was once a student of hers. In *Pilgrim's Rest* March comments on her method: "She comes to very close quarters with people—gets at them from the inside where we only get an outside view. . . . We don't see people being natural as she does." Detective Inspector Frank Abbott of Scotland Yard respects her greatly and consults her often. In addition, like a surrogate nephew, he often has a bit of fun with her, misquoting her beloved Tennyson and challenging her to correct him. His superior, Chief Inspector Lamb, shares Abbott's admiration and even sees Maud's powers as bordering on the supernatural.

In *Wicked Uncle,* Abbott describes "Maudie" as practical, resolute, intelligent, inflexible in her morality, kindly, and prim. She knits her way through all the complications of her cases, making coats and stockings for a host of relatives, most often her niece, Ethel Burkett, and Ethel's several offspring. Her own dowdy outfits are evidence of her thrift and provide protective coloring as she pursues her craft.

Evidence of Wentworth's early interest in the romance genre is apparent. Virtually all her mysteries feature a couple whose bumpy relationship is resolved along with the crimes. To give her credit, not all the couples are young (*Through the Wall*), and they do not always live happily ever after (*Pilgrim's Rest*).

Miss Silver's clients, and indeed many of her murderers, are women. Young girls seem to hold special attraction for Wentworth, perhaps because she was educated at a girls' school, or possibly because of her own daughter. The heroines are generally plucky and attractive, though always qualified as not quite beautiful. Her advice to them, and to all her clients, is direct and hard hitting, but delivered often in lines from the *Book of Common Prayer* or the poems of Lord Tennyson.

Readers of Wentworth will also enjoy E. X. Ferrars, Phoebe Atwood Taylor, and Agatha Christie's Miss Marple series.

MYSTERY FICTION

The Astonishing Adventure of Jane Smith. London: Melrose, 1923; Boston: Small, 1923.

The Annam Jewel. London: Melrose, 1924; Boston: Small and Maynard, 1926.

The Red Laquer Case. London: Melrose, 1924; Boston: Small and Maynard, 1925.

The Black Cabinet. London: Hodder and Stoughton, 1925; Boston: Small and Maynard, 1926.

The Dower House Mystery. London: Hodder and Stoughton, 1925; Boston: Small and Maynard, 1925.

The Amazing Chance. London: Hodder and Stoughton, 1926; Philadelphia: Lippincott, 1928.

Anne Belinda. London: Hodder and Stoughton, 1927; Philadelphia: Lippincott, 1928.

Fool Errant. London: Hodder and Stoughton, 1927; Philadelphia: Lippincott, 1929.

Hue and Cry. London: Hodder and Stoughton, 1927; Philadelphia: Lippincott, 1927.

Will-O'-the-Wisp. London: Hodder and Stoughton, 1928; Philadelphia: Lippincott, 1928.

Beggar's Choice. London: Hodder and Stoughton, 1930; Philadelphia: Lippincott, 1931.

The Coldstone. London: Hodder and Stoughton, 1930; Philadelphia: Lippincott, 1930.

Kingdom Lost. Philadelphia: Lippincott, 1930; London: Hodder and Stoughton, 1931.

Danger Calling. London: Hodder and Stoughton, 1931; Philadelphia: Lippincott, 1931.

Nothing Venture. London: Cassell, 1932; Philadelphia: Lippincott, 1932; New York: Warner Books, 1990.

Red Danger. London: Cassell, 1932; as *Red Shadow.* Philadelphia: Lippincott, 1932.

Seven Green Stones. London: Cassell, 1933; as *Outrageous Fortune.* Philadelphia: Lippincott, 1933.

Walk with Care. London: Cassell, 1933; Philadelphia: Lippincott, 1933.

Devil-in-the-Dark. London: Hodder and Stoughton, 1934; as *Touch and Go.* Philadelphia: Lippincott, 1934.

Fear by Night. London: Hodder and Stoughton, 1934; Philadelphia: Lippincott, 1934.

Red Stefan. London: Hodder and Stoughton, 1934; Philadelphia: Lippincott, 1935.

Blindfold. London: Hodder and Stoughton, 1935; Philadelphia: Lippincott, 1935.

Dead or Alive. London: Hodder and Stoughton, 1936; Philadelphia: Lippincott, 1936.

Hole and Corner. London: Hodder and Stoughton, 1936; Philadelphia: Lippincott, 1936.

Down Under. London: Hodder and Stoughton, 1937; Philadelphia: Lippincott, 1937.

Mr. Zero. London: Hodder and Stoughton, 1938; Philadelphia: Lippincott, 1938.

Run! London: Hodder and Stoughton, 1938; Philadelphia: Lippincott, 1938.

The Blind Side. London: Hodder and Stoughton, 1939; Philadelphia: Lippincott, 1939.

Rolling Stone. London: Hodder and Stoughton, 1940; Philadelphia: Lippincott, 1940.

Who Pays the Piper? London: Hodder and Stoughton, 1940; as *Account Rendered*. Philadelphia: Lippincott, 1940.

Unlawful Occasions. London: Hodder and Stoughton, 1941; as *Weekend with Death*. Philadelphia: Lippincott, 1941.

Pursuit of a Parcel. London: Hodder and Stoughton; Philadelphia: Lippincott, 1942.

Silence in Court. Philadelphia: Lippincott, 1945. London: Hodder and Stoughton, 1947.

Miss Silver Series

Grey Mask. London: Hodder and Stoughton, 1928; Philadelphia, Lippincott, 1929.

The Case Is Closed. London: Hodder and Stoughton, 1937; Philadelphia, Lippincott, 1937.

Lonesome Road. London: Hodder and Stoughton, 1939; Philadelphia, Lippincott, 1939.

In the Balance. Philadelphia: Lippincott, 1941; as *Danger Point*. London: Hodder and Stoughton, 1942.

Miss Silver Deals with Death. Philadelphia: Lippincott, 1941; as *Miss Silver Intervenes*. London: Hodder and Stoughton, 1944.

The Chinese Shawl. London: Hodder and Stoughton; Philadelphia, Lippincott, 1943.

The Clock Strikes Twelve. Philadelphia: Lippincott, 1944; London: Hodder and Stoughton, 1945.

The Key. Philadelphia: Lippincott, 1944; London: Hodder and Stoughton, 1946.

She Came Back. Philadelphia: Lippincott, 1945; as *The Traveller Returns*. London: Hodder and Stoughton, 1948.

Pilgrim's Rest. Philadelphia: Lippincott, 1946; London: Hodder and Stoughton, 1948; as *Dark Threat*. Popular Library, 1951; as *Pilgrim's Rest*. New York: HarperCollins, 1993.

Latter End. Philadelphia: Lippincott, 1947; London: Hodder and Stoughton, 1949.

Wicked Uncle. Philadelphia: Lippincott, 1947; as *Spotlight*. London: Hodder and Stoughton, 1949.

The Case of William Smith. Philadelphia: Lippincott, 1948; London: Hodder and Stoughton, 1950.

Eternity Ring. Philadelphia: Lippincott, 1948; London: Hodder and Stoughton, 1950.

The Catherine Wheel. Philadelphia: Lippincott, 1949; London: Hodder and Stoughton, 1951.

Miss Silver Comes to Stay. Philadelphia: Lippincott, 1949; London: Hodder and Stoughton, 1951.

The Brading Collection. Philadelphia: Lippincott, 1950; London: Hodder and Stoughton, 1952.

Through the Wall. Philadelphia: Lippincott, 1950; London: Hodder and Stoughton, 1952.

Anna, Where Are You? Philadelphia: Lippincott, 1951; London: Hodder and Stoughton, 1953; as *Death at Deco End.* New York: Pyramid, 1963.

The Ivory Dagger. Philadelphia: Lippincott, 1951; London: Hodder and Stoughton, 1953.

Watersplash. Philadelphia: Lippincott, 1951; London: Hodder and Stoughton, 1953.

Ladies' Bane. Philadelphia: Lippincott, 1952; London: Hodder and Stoughton, 1954.

Out of the Past. Philadelphia: Lippincott, 1953; London: Hodder and Stoughton, 1955.

Vanishing Point. Philadelphia: Lippincott, 1953; London: Hodder and Stoughton, 1955.

The Benevent Treasure. Philadelphia: Lippincott, 1954; London: Hodder and Stoughton, 1956.

The Silent Pool. Philadelphia: Lippincott, 1954; London: Hodder and Stoughton, 1956.

The Listening Eye. Philadelphia: Lippincott, 1955; London: Hodder and Stoughton, 1957.

Poison in the Pen. Philadelphia: Lippincott, 1955; London: Hodder and Stoughton, 1957.

The Fingerprint. Philadelphia: Lippincott, 1956; London: Hodder and Stoughton, 1959.

The Gazebo. Philadelphia: Lippincott, 1956; London: Hodder and Stoughton, 1958; as *The Summerhouse.* New York: Pyramid, 1967.

The Alington Inheritance. Philadelphia: Lippincott, 1958; London: Hodder and Stoughton, 1960.

The Girl in the Cellar. London: Hodder and Stoughton, 1961; New York: Harper-Collins, 1992.

CRITICAL BIBLIOGRAPHY

Klein, Kathleen. "Wentworth, Patricia." In *Twentieth Century Crime and Mystery Writers*, ed. John M. Reilly. New York: St. Martin's Press, 1980, pp. 1462–63.

Wynne, Nancy Blue. "Patricia Wentworth Revisited." *The Armchair Detective*, 14, no. 1 (1981): 90–92.

VIRGINIA S. HALE

BARBARA WILSON (1950–   )

Born in Long Beach, California, on October 17, 1950, Barbara Ellen Wilson has lived in Seattle, Washington, since 1974. Her activities as fiction writer, translator, lesbian feminist, and editor mark developments begun in the anti–Vietnam War period of student political dissent. In addition to five mysteries, she has published four volumes of short fiction, two nonmystery novels, and translations of fiction by the Norwegian writers Cora Sandel and Ebba Haslund. As co-owner of the Seal Press, she has significantly facilitated the publication of women writers.

In her detective novels Wilson's issues are many (including Third World strife, international feminism, homophobia, male violence, child prostitution, pornography, women's collectives, and sexual transformation), and her character typology mirrors the human and ideological diversity within feminism. Her narrative skill and sensitivity to the details of culture produce a fiction of felt experience. Generally avoiding polemic and sheer documentary, Wilson presents distinctly transitional characters.

The series detective Pam Nilsen figures in three mysteries. As in Wilson's political novel *Ambitious Women* (1982), here crime obliterates the status quo and serves as catalyst of self-discovery and cultural redefinition. The novels work out the changes for the identical twins Pam and Penny Nilsen; as young adults committed to liberal ideals, they nonetheless live in the house and operate the printing business they have inherited from their parents. The baby sister (by minutes), Pam has always felt inferior and afraid of self-authenticating behavior. By the third novel Pam has identified her true lesbianism, fallen in love, and moved out of the old Nilsen house.

As neutral facilitator of a merger discussion, Pam opens *Murder in the Collective* in the centrist position that is characteristic of her in the series. At issue is the joining of two collectives, Best Printing (of male and female membership) and B. Violet (a separatist lesbian printshop). The murder of her associate Jeremy pushes Pam toward activity as an amateur detective to preserve the survival of Best Printing. The sense of the collective permeates her detecting in which her aides are not inferior confidants but co-equals, if not sometimes her superiors in knowledge and insight. Pam's encounters with members of B. Violet introduce her to the lesbian subculture, her own coming-out, and a love affair with Hadley. The investigation into her associate, Zee, an ultrafeminine Filipina, introduces Pam to the plight of Third World women, the corruptions of the Ferdinand Marcos government, and Zee's anti-Marcos activities and guilt in the murder of Jeremy. Because of his unsavory life as an informal double agent, Pam and Hadley choose to serve ideal justice by refusing to inform on the Filipina woman.

Sisters of the Road turns to the subject of child prostitution in following Pam's efforts to save a child, Trish, from street life after her friend Rosalie is murdered. The novel is perhaps the most successful of the series because of the organic manner in which documentary enters into Pam's awakening to the horrors of Trish's life. Piercing the child's self-evasions, she traces out the girl's victimization by a stepbrother, Wayne; and in the closing, Wayne's rape and near-murder of Pam reify the spiritual sisterhood of the two women.

Dealing with the issue of pornography at large and sadomasochism within the lesbian community, *The Dog Collar Murders* suffers somewhat from Wilson's overuse of Pam as the convenient voice of information and an unconvincing representation of her sexual innocence. However, the narrative effectively provides suspense about the identity of the feminist-intellectual Loie Marsh's murderer, and the final scenes of discovery and the near-murder of Pam by the fundamentalist Sonya are a foray into the grand style of mystery suspense.

In *Gaudi Afternoon* Wilson offers a new series character, the Irish-American lesbian Cassandra Reilly, a translator of Spanish magic realism, sometime detective, and sophisticate of the world. Here the crime is parental kidnapping of the child Delilah by Ben, who is really the mother Bernadette. Cassandra is employed by a woman, Frankie, who is the surgically transformed father. The comedy of transsexuality grows to include other characters and plunges Cassandra into bewilderment. Motifs of search, disguise, and transformation recur in the novel. The comedy of self-absorption ends with Cassandra's discovery of the missing child, Delilah, who wishes only for parents who love each other, regardless of their sexual identity.

Gaudi Afternoon promises well for Wilson's second Cassandra Reilly novel *Trouble in Transylvania*. Wilson's readers may also find an interest in the detective and thriller fiction of Elisabeth Bowers, Rosie Scott, and Maria-Antonia Oliver.

MYSTERY FICTION

Pam Nilsen Series

Murder in the Collective. Seattle, Wash.: Seal Press; London: Women's Press, 1984.
Sisters of the Road. Seattle, Wash.: Seal Press; 1986, London: Virago, 1987.
The Dog Collar Murders. Seattle, Wash.: Seal Press; London: Virago, 1989.

Cassandra Reilly Series

Gaudi Afternoon. Seattle, Wash.: Seal Press, 1990; London: Virago, 1991.

Trouble in Transylvania. Seattle, Wash.: Seal Press, 1993.

CRITICAL BIBLIOGRAPHY

Decure, Nicole. "Pam Nilsen, 'Some Kind of Commie Feminist.' " *Women's Studies International Forum,* 16, no. 2 (March-April 1993): 181–91.
Pykett, Lyn. "Wilson, Barbara." In *Twentieth Century Crime and Mystery Writers,* ed. Lesley Henderson. 3rd ed. Chicago and London: St. James, 1991, pp. 1097–98.
Reddy, Maureen. "The Feminist Counter-Tradition in Crime: Cross, Grafton, Paretsky, and Wilson." In *The Cunning Craft,* ed. Ronald Walker and June Frazer. Macomb: Western Illinois University Press, 1990.
Schwartz, Patricia Roth. "Barbara Wilson." In *Twentieth-Century Western Writers,* ed. Geoff Sadler. Chicago: St. James Press, 1991.

BILL BRUBAKER

CHRIS WILTZ (1948–   )

Chris Wiltz was born in New Orleans on January 3, 1948, and has lived and worked for most of her life in the city that now serves as the locus of her mystery fiction. Attending several universities in Louisiana before earning her B.A. from San Francisco State College in 1969, Wiltz held a variety of jobs (including advertising, grant writing, bookselling, and short-order cooking) before embracing her calling as a writer. The mother of a teenaged daughter, Wiltz draws on her regional background to create her rich fictional milieu.

Her three mystery novels constitute a series featuring Neal Rafferty, an ex-police officer who left the New Orleans police force out of aversion to its corruption and ineptitude, striking out on his own as a private detective. The son of a cop and the product of an Irish Catholic upbringing, Rafferty wrestles with a past that has shaped and constrained him. In *The Killing Circle,* Wiltz introduces Rafferty who is attempting to resolve a troubled relationship with his father, a man of the old school who cannot condone Rafferty's departure from the force or his self-imposed exile from the familial neighborhood.

Rafferty is portrayed with a blend of hard-boiled and sensitive qualities. As a detective, he is well versed in the seamy side of New Orleans life. His now-dead former lover was a prostitute, and his cases take him into the grim underworld of the city, where the governing institutions (politics, business, social structures) are rife with vice and duplicity. In *Killing Circle,*

Neal delves into the death of a man who restores rare books. His romantic involvement with one of the suspects raises complex questions about professional and sexual ethics that Rafferty addresses head-on.

A Diamond before You Die broadens Rafferty's investigative terrain to include municipal politics and the pornography industry. He confronts a contemporary mystery involving prominent politicians engaged in a range of illicit activities, and resolves a prior crime, the murder of his lover. During his inquiry, Rafferty meets and teams up with a female PI, and their brief affair allows Wiltz to show his evolving sensibility. Unlike many of his tough-guy counterparts such as Philip Marlowe, Sam Spade, or Travis McGee, Rafferty eschews misogynist attitudes and cynical alienation. He works to achieve empathy with women, and his New Orleans roots go too deep for the kind of detachment and dislocation that the others live out. As Wiltz herself has said, "No one can be a loner in New Orleans."

The most fully realized of the three novels is *The Emerald Lizard*, in which Rafferty comes to the aid of a childhood friend who is being hounded by a racketeer to pay off a past debt. The case quickly escalates into murder, and Rafferty's probe uncovers a criminal conspiracy that reaches deep inside the city's police department. Beyond its noir themes of greed, lust, and retribution, the novel addresses the environmental spoliation of the Gulf waters ecosystem by industrial interests, a theme that gives the novel added currency.

Wiltz's novels offer an evocative portrait of her native city, and in Neal Rafferty, she has created an appealing protagonist whose complexities carry him beyond the usual constraints of the hard-boiled formula. Admirers of this series (which should be read in order) will enjoy other New Orleans mystery writers such as James Lee Burke, Julie Smith, and O'Neil Denoux.

MYSTERY FICTION

Neal Rafferty Series

The Killing Circle. New York: Macmillan, London: Collier, 1981.

A Diamond before You Die. New York: Mysterious Press, 1987.

The Emerald Lizard. New York: Dutton; London: Penguin, 1991.

CRITICAL BIBLIOGRAPHY

Babener, Liahna. "Murder in New Orleans: Interview with Mystery Writer Chris Wiltz." *Clues*, 10 (Fall/Winter 1989): 1–20.

Hobson, Linda Whitney. "A Place to Write: The New Orleans Literary Scene." *New Orleans Magazine*, March 1990, pp. 40–45, 95–96.

Liahna Babener

MARY WINGS (1949–   )

Born in Chicago, Illinois, on April 14, 1949, Mary Wings attended San Francisco State University and Shimer College in Illinois. She worked from 1983 to 1986 as a graphic designer for feminist research projects at Transnational Institute in Amsterdam. In 1974 Wings started her writing career in the comic genre. She currently lives in San Francisco, California.

She Came Too Late and *She Came in a Flash* present the exploits of series character Emma Victor, a perspicacious, freewheeling, likable, and witty lesbian who adds new dimensions of realism and an unapologetic, confident representation of lesbian identity to the crime fiction genre.

As amateur sleuth, Emma is a bold, confident, spontaneous person, but she is also an opportunist who takes great risks. Her illegal, and often thoughtless, excursions into other people's homes and lives; her blindness to the obvious; and her penchant for alcohol, drugs, and chance encounters often lead her into trouble and make her simultaneously a compelling and reckless heroine. In spite of her blundering, Emma proves wily, competent, and resilient in her search for answers. Her most attractive characteristics are her wit, complete honesty, and ability to see humor in even the most difficult situations.

Very soon in her adventures, Emma becomes involved in a love affair with Dr. Frances Cohen, an equally outspoken lesbian feminist activist. The detective and romantic plots intertwine, allowing the exploration of feminist/lesbian issues through the conflicts of several relationships.

In *She Came in a Flash*, Emma Victor is more centrally concerned with the pursuit of crime. The plot unravels through a series of mysterious events centered around three story lines. Though Emma bungles a drug bust and comes up with the wrong solution, her exploits do help unravel the case.

Not as well conceived as *She Came Too Late*, this novel is marred by some startling implausibilities in the heroine's actions and reasoning but contains Wings's most fascinating portrayal of women characters. More important, both novels serve as a vehicle for numerous feminist/lesbian issues. Ultimately, Mary Wings provides an uncompromising lesbian heroine who nevertheless is entangled with the threat of violence perpetrated against women and the serious problems that women face in forging identities and finding acceptance in contemporary society—all much needed developments in detective fiction.

Readers who like the Mary Wings novels might also enjoy novels by Katherine V. Forrest, Vicki P. McConnell, Valerie Miner, and Barbara Wilson.

MYSTERY FICTION

Emma Victor Series

She Came Too Late. London: Women's Press, 1986; Freedom, Calif.: Crossing Press, 1987.

She Came in a Flash. London: Women's Press; New York: New American Library, 1988.

CRITICAL BIBLIOGRAPHY

Kaveney, Roz. "Wings, Mary." In *Twentieth Century Crime and Mystery Writers*, ed. Lesley Henderson. 3rd ed. Chicago and London: St. James, 1991, pp. 1101–2.

JACQUELYN L. JACKSON

SARA WOODS (1922–1985)

Sara Bowen-Judd, née Hutton, was born in Bradford, Yorkshire, England, on March 7, 1922, and died in Toronto, Ontario, Canada, on November 6, 1985. Before she began to write mysteries in the early 1960s, Bowen-Judd had a varied career, working in a bank and a solicitor's office during World War II and later as a pig breeder and a university registrar. While the vast majority of her novels have English settings, she wrote all of them in Canada, where she lived with her husband, Anthony Bowen-Judd, for the last thirty years of her life.

Bowen-Judd wrote fifty-three novels over twenty-five years: while six feature the characters Jeremy Locke, Stephen Marryat, and Richard Trenton, the rest concern the urbane solicitor Antony Maitland who, although reserved and at times moody, never hesitates to come to the aid of the falsely accused. Maitland typically finds himself defending a suspected murderer whose case seems hopeless out of obligation to friends or pity for the accused's family. The narrative often focuses on Maitland's own curiosity and uncertainty about the case in question.

Set in the 1960s and 1970s, the plots are clever and require careful attention on the part of the reader to follow the full cast of characters, particularly at the beginning. Woods prefers cases in which either the crime or the motive for the crime occurred years before, obliging Maitland to sift through a trail of often irrelevant clues. The titles of her books are taken from Shakespearean quotations and are highly appropriate for the intrigue. Woods's writing is very clear, with realistic dialogue. Most satisfying is her careful tying up of loose ends.

Many of the novels culminate in dramatic courtroom scenes, with Maitland cleverly demonstrating his exceptional knowledge of English law and legal procedures—Woods's experience in a solicitor's office has enabled her to describe realistic legal entanglements and loopholes, making for interesting reading. Maitland's sparring with often-inept judges brings to mind John Mortimer's Rumpole. The legal obstacles that often face Maitland serve as surprisingly effective vehicles of suspense.

While Woods has stated that she favors the development of character over the exposition of plot in her novels, this preference is not evident. Most of the characters—solicitors, victims, suspects, and witnesses alike— generally maintain a stereotypical British calm and detached demeanor, making for at times a dry narrative. The sangfroid is so prominent, even in the exposed murderer, that he or she seems incapable of committing such a violent crime. As Woods's customary preface declares: "no excuse can be considered necessary for the villainy or folly of the people appearing in this book. It seems extremely unlikely that any one of them should resemble a real person, alive or dead." Unfortunately this assessment proves to be all too true—motivation for the characters' oftentimes rash actions is entirely absent.

Maitland's devoted wife, Jenny, and his acerbic uncle, Sir Nicholas Harding, are recurring characters who are among the few people who can influence the intensely private Maitland and in whom he is willing to confide. Despite their apparent closeness, little affection is seen between them, however. Although Maitland judges Jenny as illogical, he seems to find great solace in her "serene" attitude.

Maitland seems to suffer from an inner angst but very rarely reveals his emotions: as his client in *Most Deadly Hate* tells him, "You haven't always found life easy, but your experiences have left you . . . with a penetrating eye for other people's idiosyncrasies." Only in extreme cases does Anthony Maitland demonstrate anger and that is usually done by speaking with a negligible stutter.

Woods's best mystery, *The Taste of Fears* (retitled as *The Third Encounter* in the United States), is exceptional due to the personal presentation given to Anthony and his wife, Jenny. The reasons for Anthony's injured shoulder and for the couple's childlessness are explained, leading to a better understanding of the couple's overall character. The novel's description of Maitland's wartime experiences offers an explanation for the austere behavior seen in the other novels.

While Woods's books resemble each other, they are all expertly composed and always provide intrigues which entertain. Earlier ones, such as *Bloody Instructions* and *This Little Measure*, offer the most ingenious plots and should be read by any fan of the classic British mystery.

MYSTERY FICTION

Writing as Sara Woods

Antony Maitland Series

Bloody Instructions. London: Collins; New York: Harper, 1962.

Malice Domestic. London: Collins, 1962.

Error of the Moon. London: Collins, 1963.

The Taste of Fears. London: Collins, 1963; as *The Third Encounter.* New York: Harper, 1963.

This Little Measure. London: Collins, 1964.

Trusted like the Fox. London: Collins, 1964; New York: Harper, 1965.

Though I Know She Lies. London: Collins, 1965; New York: Holt Rinehart, 1972.

The Windy Side of the Law. London: Collins; New York: Harper, 1965.

Enter Certain Murderers. London: Collins; New York, Harper, 1966.

The Case Is Altered. London: Collins, 1966; New York: Harper, 1967.

Let's Choose Executors. London: Collins, 1966; New York: Harper, 1967.

And Shame the Devil. London: Collins, 1967; New York: Rinehart, 1972.

Knives Have Edges. London: Collins, 1968; New York: Holt Rinehart, 1970.

Past Praying For. London: Collins; New York: Harper, 1968.

Tarry and Be Hanged. London: Collins, 1969; New York: Holt Rinehart, 1971.

An Improbable Fiction. London: Collins, 1970; New York: Holt Rinehart, 1971.

The Knavish Crows. London: Collins, 1971.

Serpent's Tooth. London: Collins, 1971; New York: Holt Rinehart, 1973.

They Love Not Poison. London: Macmillan; New York: Holt Rinehart, 1972.

Yet She Must Die. London: Macmillan, 1973; New York: Holt Rinehart, 1972.

Enter the Corpse. London: Macmillan, 1973; New York: Holt Rinehart, 1974.

Done to Death. London, Macmillan, 1974; New York: Holt Rinehart, 1975.

My Life Is Done. London: Macmillan, 1975; New York: St. Martin's Press, 1976.

A Show of Violence. London: Macmillan; New York: McKay, 1975.

The Law's Delay. London: Macmillan; New York: St. Martin's Press, 1977.

A Thief or Two. London: Macmillan; New York: St. Martin's Press, 1977.

Exit Murderer. London: Macmillan; New York: St. Martin's Press, 1978.

The Fatal Writ. London: Macmillan; New York: St. Martin's Press, 1979.

Proceed to Judgement. London: Macmillan; New York: St. Martin's Press, 1979.

They Stay for Dinner. London: Macmillan; New York: St. Martin's Press, 1980.

Weep for Her. London: Macmillan, 1980; New York: St. Martin's Press, 1981.

Cry Guilty. London: Macmillan; New York: St. Martin's Press, 1981.

Dearest Enemy. London: Macmillan; New York, St. Martin's Press, 1981.

Enter a Gentlewoman. London: Macmillan; New York: St. Martin's Press, 1982.

Most Grievous Murder. London: Macmillan; New York: St. Martin's Press, 1982.

Villains by Necessity. London: Macmillan; New York: St. Martin's Press, 1982.

Call Back Yesterday. London: Macmillan; New York: St. Martin's Press, 1983.

The Lie Direct. London: Macmillan; New York: St. Martin's Press, 1983.

Where Should He Die. London: Macmillan; New York, St. Martin's Press, 1983.

The Bloody Book of the Law. London: Macmillan; New York: St. Martin's Press, 1984.

Defy the Devil. London: Macmillan, 1984; New York: St. Martin's Press, 1985.

Murders Out of Tune. London: Macmillan; New York: St. Martin's Press, 1984.

Away with Them to Prison. London: Macmillan; New York: St. Martin's Press, 1985.

An Obscure Grave. London: Macmillan; New York: St. Martin's Press, 1985.

Most Deadly Hate. London: Macmillan; New York, St. Martin's Press, 1986.

Nor Live So Long. London: Macmillan; New York: St. Martin's Press, 1986.

Naked Villain. London: Macmillan; New York: St. Martin's Press, 1987.

Writing as Anne Burton

Richard Trenton Series

The Dear Departed. Toronto: Raven, 1980.
Where There's a Will. Toronto: Raven, 1980.

Writing as Mary Challis

Jeremy Locke Series

Crimes Past. Toronto: Raven, 1980.

Writing as Margaret Leek

Stephen Marryat Series

The Healthy Grave. Toronto: Raven, 1980.
We Must Have a Trial. Toronto: Raven, 1980.

CRITICAL BIBLIOGRAPHY

Nichols, Victoria, and Susan Thompson. "Antony Maitland." In *Silk Stalkings*. Berkeley, Calif.: Black Lizard, 1988, pp. 141–43.

Rodgerson, Gillian. "Woods, Sara." In *Twentieth Century Crime and Mystery Writers*, ed. Lesley Henderson. 3rd ed. Chicago and London: St. James, 1991, pp. 1104–6.

MARGARET BROOM HARP

L. R. WRIGHT (1939–   )

Laurali Wright was born in Saskatoon, Saskatchewan, on June 5, 1939. After studying in a number of Canadian universities (the University of British Columbia, Carleton University, Banff School of Fine Arts, and the University of Calgary), she was an actress for a short time and then joined the *Calgary Herald*, where she worked as a journalist and editor from 1968 until 1977. She then turned to free-lance writing, publishing her first novel in 1979. After publishing three novels, she produced her first work of detective fiction, *The Suspect*, in 1985. The work received the Edgar award in the best novel category; Wright was the first Canadian to be so honored. Since then, she has published another general novel, and four more detective novels. Wright, who now lives in Vancouver, had been married for many years but is now separated, and has two grown daughters.

The nonmystery novels deal with a variety of concerns. *Neighbors* is almost a thriller, centered around a very disturbed woman. *The Favorite* deals with the complexity of family life, especially the father-daughter relationship. *Among Friends* portrays three women alone, at turning points in their lives, while *Love in the Temperate Zone* is about divorce and the difficulties of learning to love again. Some of the same concerns also appear in the detective novels.

In the first and best of Wright's five mysteries, *The Suspect*, the reader witnesses the murder and sympathizes with the murderer: the question is whether he will be caught. In the second, *Sleep while I Sing*, the deaths are explained by abnormal psychology, a subject in which Wright has also shown an interest in her nonmystery writing. Similarly, the plot of *A Chill Rain in January* depends on the highly abnormal behavior of an apparently normal individual. Though both these novels contain much excellent writing and a great deal of tension, the explanations for the deaths that occur are not entirely convincing. *Fall from Grace* and *Prized Possessions*, like *The Suspect*, deal with essentially normal individuals pushed by circumstances into unaccustomed behavior and, perhaps for this reason, are more satisfying.

All Wright's detective novels have three distinctive features. First, they have as their central voice Karl Alberg, staff sergeant of the local Royal Canadian Mounted Police detachment. His concerns and personal difficulties are a resonant part of each novel. Second, the main setting is the fictionalized small town of Sechelt, on British Columbia's sunshine coast, north of Vancouver. The town itself, and many of the personalities who live there, are central presences in the books. Third, a focal point of all four novels is the diversity and complexity of human motivation; the question is why, not who, "dunnit."

Alberg is appealing as a detective/central consciousness because of his vulnerabilities, which are reminiscent of, though very different from, those of Charlie Salter of the Toronto police department, a creation of fellow Canadian Eric Wright (no relation). Alberg lives alone in Sechelt, having been separated and later divorced from his wife, Maura, and having left his daughters, Diana and Jane, at college in Calgary. He is trying to find the courage to love again in an on-again-off-again relationship with the local librarian, Cassandra Mitchell. His secretary, Isabella, is concerned about his diet. His own frailties give him a certain understanding and even sympathy for the murderers he must pursue and bring to justice, while his training and dedication to his job, as well as his sympathy for past and potential future victims, make him relentless in his pursuit.

By somehow managing to create a sure sense of the physical nature of Sechelt, the writer makes it a living presence. The small size of the town, along with the sense of community and the resulting lack of privacy, are also important. Alberg generally knows the victims and the suspects intimately, which makes it both easier and more difficult to investigate them.

Wright's interest in human motivation has led some reviewers to compare her work with that of the British writers P. D. James and Ruth Rendell. In two of her novels the murderers are truly abnormal, while in the other three it is more a question of basically normal individuals who give way to an impulse when pushed too far by those who become their victims. The latter cases make for more effective detective fiction, since the reader may feel cheated when a murder is committed by someone who appears normal on the surface but is acting under the influence of a powerful, hidden, abnormal psychological need. More appealing to most readers is the basically normal individual with whom they can identify—who is pushed too far and gives way in a moment of stress.

Wright's novels are perhaps best read in the order in which they were written, if only because one of their major pleasures is the evolution in Alberg's life in his relationships with Cassandra, Maura, Diana, and Jane. Her first novel, *The Suspect*, is still the best.

MYSTERY FICTION

Alberg Series

The Suspect. Toronto: Doubleday Canada; New York: Viking; London: Hale, 1985.

Sleep while I Sing. Toronto: Doubleday Canada; New York: Viking; London: Collins, 1986.

A Chill Rain in January. Toronto: Macmillan of Canada; New York: Viking; London: Macmillan, 1990.

Fall from Grace. Toronto: Seal Books; New York: Viking, 1991; London: Macmillan, 1992.

Prized Possessions. Toronto: Doubleday Canada; New York: Viking, 1993.

CRITICAL BIBLIOGRAPHY

Barry, Carol. "Wright, L. R." In *Twentieth Century Crime and Mystery Writers*, ed. Lesley Henderson. 3rd ed. Chicago and London: St. James, 1991, pp. 1110–11.

ELIZABETH NEILD

❧ Y ❧

MARGARET YORKE (1924–   )

British crime writer Margaret Yorke, born January 30, 1924 (as Margaret Beda Larminie, the name she has most recently used for nonliterary matters), has written over thirty-five novels since 1957 (usually one a year). Divorced, with a son and a daughter, she lives in an English village and has been chairman of the British Crime Writers' Association (1979–80).

Yorke's major strength is plot, and readers usually remain gripped throughout her books. Though often not left long wondering whodunnit—they find out quite early—they are, instead, likely to be intrigued in observing what happens to all the characters introduced. Though her focal interest seems to be middle class, Yorke's novels include a wide variety of vivid character portraits. Her plots frequently start with several groups from disparate levels of society playing out their familiar routines which, though in many cases outwardly respectable, usually fail to strictly adhere to all of the ten commandments. Individuals who were quite unconnected are drawn gradually together and then made to collide in a moment of terrible tragedy. Throughout, a sense of general insecurity prevails: people, for example, are watched and plotted against unawares, with the narrative darting rapidly back and forth between the minds of predators, victims, and observers. Suspense and terror accrue through dramatic irony as evil designs mature, while victims become increasingly vulnerable and observers, ever more impotent. In the process, staid, respectable, middle-class people come to sudden and, for them, quite unanticipated grief. Yorke's intricate narratives pulsate with family secrets, hidden conflicts, and murders; they demonstrate how easily horror can lurk beneath the surface of mundane lives.

Her novels belong loosely to the English country house detective genre, the houses often decayed and impoverished like their inhabitants; her successive detectives are largely undeveloped, except in the Patrick Grant novels. Yorke clearly outlines one kind of life in one kind of place—England, with its class distinctions, its concern for what is called face, its obsession with privacy and respectability. It is late-twentieth-century England in the throes of deep social change, where relics of the old landed gentry are forced into frequent contact with new arrivals whom they often resent and despise. These are novels permeated with characteristically English nostalgia for snob rule, for the time when the antecedents of characters with whom the reader seems induced to identify possessed unchallenged prosperity and prestige. Nonetheless, though the novels are redolent of regret that the good old days have departed, they also contain hints suggesting that those days were not, in fact, all that good. Their actions characteristically take place in small villages not far from urban sprawl, villages threatened by in-filling and social insecurity—they are novels reminiscent of Barbara Pym and the John Mortimer of *Paradise Postponed* in exploring the currents of passion pulsing under outwardly placid lives. Yorke's books stir up frissons of horror as readers imagine their own secure middle-class privacy ruthlessly invaded—for example, by anonymous late-night telephone calls to vulnerable ladies alone in isolated houses, calls that include sighing but no message (*Find Me a Villain*) or by a stranger holed-up in a building opposite a home, observing its inhabitants' lives and snooping into their intimate secrets (*The Small Hours of the Morning*).

Her works collectively suggest that something is radically wrong with contemporary England. The action is rarely seen from the reassuring viewpoint of the investigator who is featured in book after book—indeed, when Margaret Yorke attempts to create such a character in the protagonist of her Dr. Patrick Grant mysteries, which are somewhat reminiscent of the adventures of Amanda Cross's academic detective Kate Fansler, she seems less successful than usual. Rather than create a sense of ultimate security, Yorke's books indicate just how fragile is the skin of everyday normalcy, calm, and certainty—an attitude with which contemporary suburban Britons, with their chronic obsession with security, can readily identify. The suggestion is that people met casually in home or street may have terrible skeletons in their closets and may well be rapists or burglars or murderers in mufti.

In particular, Yorke likes portraying dissatisfied women who have been, for the most part, ignored by the patriarchy. Among her main characters one often encounters women who are newly aware of their underprivileged existences, whose attempts to do something decisive to ameliorate their circumstances have ultimately disastrous consequences. As in Pym's work, the women who are featured seem puzzled by their social impotence. Having begun an inadequate training for a business career, they have abandoned it for marriage and then been victimized by their mates. Less often, it seems, the women themselves go astray—the adulterous June Titmuss in *The Small Hours of the Morning*, for example—however, in such cases, the men are likely to be weak and offer little help in solving problems. Also like Pym, Yorke seems particularly interested in documenting the frustrations of women who are becoming increasingly aware of the negative effects of their marginalized status. Other favorite characters include troubled young people, mainly females prone to disastrous relationships—she dwells particularly on flawed marriages, her works suggesting that most marriages are imperfect. One characteristic Yorke type is the respectable, solitary middle-class woman—for example, the widow Lydia Cunningham, the impoverished gentlewoman protagonist of *Evidence to Destroy*. Eccentric and reminiscent of Dorothy Simcox, the vicar's wife in Mortimer's *Paradise Postponed*, she is thoroughly respectable and longs for the secure, socially stratified England of the past, but she has been the victim of a bad marriage. Evidence convincing her that she will have to reveal her hidden secret— that her daughter is not her husband's—drives her, by agonizing degrees, to the very edge of insanity.

MYSTERY FICTION

Summer Flight. London: Robert Hale, 1957; Guilford, Conn.: Ulverscroft, 1988.
Pray Love Remember. London: Robert Hale, 1958.
Christopher. London: Robert Hale, 1959; Guilford, Conn.: Ulverscroft, 1986.
Deceiving Mirror. London: Robert Hale, 1960.
The China Doll. London: Robert Hale, 1961; Boston, Mass.: G. K. Hall, 1985.
Once a Stranger. London: Hurst and Blackett, 1962.
The Birthday. London: Hurst and Blackett, 1963.
Full Circle. London: Hurst and Blackett, 1965.
No Fury. London: Hurst and Blackett, 1967.
The Apricot Bed. London: Hurst and Blackett, 1968; Boston, Mass.: G. K. Hall, 1987.
The Limbo Ladies. London: Hurst and Blackett, 1969.
No Medals for the Major. London: Geoffrey Bles, 1974; New York: Penguin, 1987.
The Small Hours of the Morning. New York: Walker, 1975.
The Cost of Silence. New York: Walker, 1977.
The Point of Murder. London: Hutchinson; New York: Walker, 1978, as *The Come-On*. New York: Harper, 1979.
Death on Account. London: Hutchinson, 1979; and New York: Penguin, 1988.
The Scent of Fear. London: Hutchinson, 1980; New York: St. Martin's Press, 1981.
The Hand of Death. London: Hutchinson, 1981; New York: St. Martin's Press, 1982.
Devil's Work. London: Hutchinson; New York: St. Martin's Press, 1982.
Find Me a Villain. London: Hutchinson; New York: St. Martin's Press 1983.
The Smooth Face of Evil. London: Hutchinson; New York: St. Martin's Press, 1984.
Intimate Kill. London: Hutchinson; New York: St. Martin's Press, 1985.
Safely to the Grave. London: Hutchinson, 1987; New York: St. Martin's Press, 1986.

Evidence to Destroy. London: Century Hutchinson; New York: Viking Penguin, 1987.

Speak for the Dead. London: Century Hutchinson; New York: Viking Penguin, 1988.

Crime in Question. London: Century Hutchinson; New York: Viking Penguin, 1989.

Admit to Murder. London: Century Hutchinson; New York: Viking Penguin, 1990.

A Small Deceit. London: Century Hutchinson; New York: Viking Penguin, 1991.

Criminal Damage. London: Century Hutchinson, 1992; New York: Mysterious Press, 1993.

Dangerous to Know. New York: Mysterious Press, 1993.

Dr. Patrick Grant Series

Dead in the Morning. London: Geoffrey Bles, 1970; Guilford, Conn.: Ulverscroft, 1990.

Silent Witness. London: Geoffrey Bles, 1972; New York: Walker, 1975.

Grave Matters. London: Geoffrey Bles, 1973; Guilford, Conn.: Ulverscroft, 1990.

Mortal Remains. London: Geoffrey Bles, 1974; Guilford, Conn.: Ulverscroft, 1990.

Cast for Death. London: Geoffrey Bles, 1975; New York: Walker, 1976.

CRITICAL BIBLIOGRAPHY

Fredriksson, Karl G. "Yorke, Margaret." In *Twentieth Century Crime and Mystery Writers*, ed. Lesley Henderson. 3rd ed. Chicago and London: St. James, 1991, pp. 1115–17.

CYNDY HENDERSHOT AND ANTONY OLDKNOW

Appendix A

THE EDGAR AWARDS

Among writers of mystery, nothing quite compares with the awarding every spring by the Mystery Writers of America (MWA) of the Edgar Allan Poe Awards, the Edgars. Since 1953, when Charlotte Jay was presented with the first Edgar for her novel *Beat Not the Bones*, the statuette of Poe has been eagerly sought and highly prized. Begun as an attempt to provide recognition to the genre, the Edgar has become the most important symbol of acknowledgment in the world of mystery writing and reading.

Although Poe was a lifelong American, the prize given in his name has become an international one. While the Crime Writers' Association, the MWA's British counterpart, has seldom given the Gold Dagger Award (for the best novel of the year) to a non-British writer, the Edgar has never been exclusively American. Australia's Arthur Upfield was nominated in 1957, and the first foreign winner was British writer Celia Fremlin, in 1959. Since then, Edgars have been sent to all parts of the world. In fact, between 1959 and 1965 only one American won the prize (Donald E. Westlake for *God Save the Mark*). The winners in those years, including John LeCarré's *The Spy Who Came in from the Cold* (1964) and Nicolas Freeling's *King of the Rainy Country* (1966), beat such other major non-Americans as Ngaio Marsh, Mary Stewart, and P. D. James. American nominees during that period included such important names as Dell Shannon, Ross Macdonald, Ellery Queen, and Chester Himes.

Edgar winners have been as varied as the genre itself. There have been fewer domestic, cozy winners than one might expect (the last was L. R. Wright's *The Suspect* in 1985), but the range of recipients remains wide. Several of the books have come from the world of the thriller, including Frederick Forsyth's *Day of the Jackal* (1971) and William Bayer's *Peregrine* (1981). Espionage is represented by LeCarré and by Eric Ambler's *The Light of Day* (1963). A surprising number have been set in unusual, if not always exotic, locales: Tony Hillerman's *Dance Hall of the Dead* (1973) is one of the early Joe Leaphorn novels set on the Navajo reservation in New Mexico; Maj Sjowall and Per Wahloo, the only married couple honored for Best Novel, won in 1970 for *The Laughing Policeman*, one of their ten books set in Sweden and starring Martin Beck; and Stuart Kaminsky's *A Cold Red Sunrise* (1988) takes place in Moscow and features police inspector Porfiry Rostnikov. The police procedural format has been represented by J. J. Marric (John Creasey) in *Gideon's Fire* (1961) and Julie Smith in *New Orleans Mourning* (1990). Comic crime has also been recognized, in particular in the work of Donald E. Westlake.

As notable as the breadth of the prizewinners is the absence of female Edgar winners. After British writer Ellis Peters received the prize for *Death and the Joyful Woman* (1962), it would be nine years before another woman writer would win (when Sjowall and Wahloo's *The Laughing Policeman* was selected in 1971) and more than a decade more before a single woman author would receive the prize (when Canadian L. R. Wright won for *The Suspect* in 1985). The wait between American women winners was even longer. Charlotte Armstrong, with *A Dram of Poison* (1956), was the only American woman to win an Edgar for best novel for over thirty years. However, Julie Smith's *New Orleans Mourning*, in 1990, marked the return of American women to that height.

Though women have not received the prize, throughout the years they have been nominated. Margaret Millar, who won in 1955 for *Beast in View*, received several nominations for her later books. Other women nominees have included Dell Shannon, Mary Stewart, Patricia Moyes, P. D. James, and Nancy Pickard, some of whom have received several nominations; after four nominations, Ruth Rendell (writing under the pseudonym Barbara Vine) finally won in 1986 for *A Dark-Adapted Eye*. In 1987, when the award was presented to Aaron Elkins for *Old Bones* (which featured his anthropologist-hero Gideon Oliver), three of the five nominees were women: Linda Barnes, B. M. Gill, and Charlotte MacLeod.

Much like the Academy Awards, the Edgars have also been notable for the writers who have never won for best novel. Dorothy Salisbury Davis, Ngaio Marsh, Ross Macdonald, and John D. Macdonald are among a long list of great authors who have never won the prize, though all have been nominated. Other major figures have even escaped nomination for the Edgars. That fact is, in some measure, excused by their receipt of the Mystery Writers' Grand Master Award. Since this tribute began with Agatha Christie in 1954, the Grand Master has been given to many of the form's greatest names. Despite that recognition, however, many major figures in the mystery field have never received. nominations for best novel Edgars, much less won the award. These include Sue Grafton, Joseph Hansen, Sara Paretsky, and Bill Pronzini, among currently recognized names.

An important aspect of any literary award is the recognition it provides the winners, books as well as authors. The Mystery Writers of America has been criticized for its selection of little-known writers and less-than-outstanding books to receive the Edgar Award. After reviewing the award's entire forty-year history, however, an analyst should be convinced that most of the nominations have been given to significant books in their year. Whether these books *remain* among the best is, of course, a very different matter. Furthermore, despite quarrels over which nominee ought to have won, there are surprisingly few winning authors who remain completely unknown or books that go entirely unremembered. The Edgar has, it must be admitted, maintained a high standard through the years. The larger problems only appear in broad overview, and not in a narrow, year-to-year examination.

The Edgars do not simply honor a single book as the best novel of the year. There are also awards for the best first novel by an American author and the best paperback original novel. The prize for best first novel has been awarded to a large number of then-new writers who have since become well known: Ira Levin, Harry Kemelman, John Ball, Ross Thomas, Dorothy Uhnak, Joe Gores, Rex Burns, Stuart Woods, and Jonathan Kellerman all won for their first books. Other nominees have included Patricia Highsmith, Dell Shannon, Amanda Cross, Tony Hillerman, Martin Cruz Smith, and Elizabeth George. The winners for best paperback include Bill Granger, Teri White, and Sharyn McCrumb; among the nominees have been Roger L. Simon, Lawrence Block, James Ellroy, Stuart Kaminsky, and Lillian Jackson Braun. Other categories include "Best Fact Crime," "Best Critical/Biographical Study," "Best Juvenile Mystery," and "Best Motion Picture."

The Edgar selection process is a year-long one in which publishers send copies of books that they wish to have considered to members of the appropriate prize committee. (This has grown to a massive task, including scores, and even hundreds, of titles annually.) The committee then winnows down the field to a small number of final nominees (usually four or five), and every member reads (or rereads) the nominated books before arriving at the year's prizewinner.

Despite its flaws, the obvious annual mistakes, and any long-term oversights, the Edgar Awards remain a symbol of the mystery form as it is practiced in America and around the world. They have provided outsiders with a way in which to enter the circle of readers, while readers can gauge their own beliefs and favorite styles and titles against other lists and opinions. In the end, everyone involved in the form, from publishers and booksellers to critics and fans, has gained from the annual presentations when the best books of the year are announced. The Edgar indeed has lived up to its founders' expectations.

In the following list of women nominees, winners are marked with an asterisk.

1953   *Charlotte Jay—*Beat Not the Bones* (other nominees not listed)

1955   *Margaret Millar—*Beast in View*

Patricia Highsmith—*The Talented Mr. Ripley*

1956   *Charlotte Armstrong—*A Dram of Poison*

Margot Bennett—*The Man Who Didn't Fly*

1957   Marjorie Carleton—*The Night of the Good Children*

1958   Dorothy Salisbury Davis—*A Gentlemen Called*

1959   *Celia Fremlin—*The Hours before Dawn*

1961   Anne Blaisdell—*Nightmare*

Suzanne LeBlanc—*The Green Stone*

1962   *Ellis Peters—*Death and the Joyful Woman*

Jean Potts—*The Evil Wish*

Shelley Smith—*The Ballad of the Running Man*

1963   Elizabeth Fenwick—*The Make-Believe Man*

Dorothy B. Hughes—*The Expendable Man*

1964   Margaret Millar—*The Fiend*

Mary Stewart—*This Rough Magic*

1965   Dorothy Salisbury Davis—*The Pale Betrayer*

Mary Stewart—*Airs above the Ground*

1966   Ngaio Marsh—*Killer Dolphin*

1967   Charlotte Armstrong—*The Gift Shop*

Charlotte Armstrong—*Lemon in the Basket*

1968   Heron Carvic—*Picture Miss Seeton*

Dorothy Salisbury Davis and Jerome Ross—*God Speed the Night*

1969   Emma Lathen—*When in Greece*

Dorothy Salisbury Davis—*Where the Dark Streets Go*

1970   *Maj Sjowall and Per Wahloo—*The Laughing Policeman*

Margaret Millar—*Beyond This Point Are Monsters*

Patricia Moyes—*Many Deadly Returns*

1971   P. D. James—*Shroud for a Nightingale*

1972   Ngaio Marsh—*Tied up in Tinsel*

1973   Jean Stubbs—*Dear Laura*

P. D. James—*An Unsuitable Job for a Woman*

1975   Maggie Rennert—*Operation Alcestis*

1978   Ruth Rendell—*A Sleeping Life*

1979   Ruth Rendell—*Make Death Love Me*

1980   B. M. Gill—*Death Drop*

1984   B. M. Gill—*The Twelfth Juror*

1985   *L. R. Wright—*The Suspect*

        Ruth Rendell—*An Unkindness of Ravens*
        Ruth Rendell—*The Tree of Hands*

1986   *Ruth Rendell (writing as Barbara Vine)—*A Dark-Adapted Eye*

        P. D. James—*A Taste for Death*

1987   Charlotte MacLeod—*The Corpse in Oozak's Pond*

        B. M. Gill—*Nursery Crimes*

        Linda Barnes—*A Trouble of Fools*

1989   Frances Fyfield—*A Question of Guilt*

1990   *Julie Smith—*New Orleans Mourning*

1991   Lia Matera—*Prior Convictions*

        Nancy Pickard—*I.O.U.*

1992   *Margaret Maron—*Bootlegger's Daughter*

        Liza Cody—*Backhand*

1993   *Minette Walters—*The Sculptress*
        *Marcia Muller—*Wolf in the Shadows*

REFERENCES

"The 1990 Edgar Awards." *The Armchair Detective*, 22, no. 3 (Summer 1990):
    365.
"The 1991 Edgar Awards." *The Armchair Detective*, 23, no. 3 (Summer 1991);
    374.
"The 1992 Edgar Awards." *The Armchair Detective*, 24, no. 3 (Summer 1992):
    354.
"The 1993 Edgar Awards." *The Armchair Detective*, 25, no. 3 (Summer 1993):
    354.
Steinbrunner, Chris, and Otto Penzler, eds. *Encyclopedia of Mystery and Detection.*
    New York, McGraw-Hill, 1976, p. 301, "Organizations."

Strosser, Edward, ed. *The Armchair Detective Book of Lists*. New York: *The Armchair Detective*, 1989.
Zeman, Barry T., and Angela Zeman, "Mystery Writers of America, Inc.: An Abbreviated History." *The Armchair Detective*, 26, no. 2 (Spring 1993): 36.

FRED ISAAC

Appendix B

THE AGATHA AWARDS

Established in 1989, MALICE DOMESTIC™* is an annual convention held in metropolitan Washington, D.C., to salute the "mysteries of manners"—works best typified by the books of Agatha Christie. Works in the genre usually feature an amateur detective and no excessive gore or violence, and they emphasize character, setting, and relationships among the characters.

Each year, the Agatha Awards—named for Christie—are presented for the best novel, best first novel, and best short story in the genre for the previous year. In 1993, the first Best Nonfiction Agatha also was presented for the best 1992 biography, essay collection, bibliography, or other such book centered on the Malice theme, a Malice-eligible author, or the detective(s) of a Malice-eligible series.

The convention attendees vote for the awards, while the oversight for the awards process is performed by the Agatha Award Committee, which suggests candidates for nominations, reviews nominations for suitability, and tallies the final votes. Eligible books must be published by a living author in the United States between January 1 and December 31 of the year before the MALICE convention. Agatha winners receive teapots with MALICE's skull-and-crossbones emblem on the side. Agatha nominees receive certificates recognizing their achievement.

Women Nominees:

1988
Best Novel
†*Something Wicked*, Carolyn G. Hart
The Widow's Club, Dorothy Cannell
Mischief in Maggody, Joan Hess
Paying the Piper, Sharyn McCrumb
Dead Crazy, Nancy Pickard

Best First Novel
†*A Great Deliverance*, Elizabeth George
The Killings at Badger's Drift, Caroline Graham
The J. Alfred Prufrock Murders, Corinne Sawyer
Goodbye Nanny Grey, Susannah Stacey
Dead Men Don't Give Seminars, Dorothy Sucher

1989
Best Novel
†*Naked Once More*, Elizabeth Peters
The Siren Sang of Murder, Sarah Caudwell
A Little Class on Murder, Carolyn G. Hart
Corpus Christmas, Margaret Maron
Philly Stakes, Gillian Roberts

Best First Novel
†*Grime and Punishment*, Jill Churchill
Working Murder, Eleanor Boylan
A Question of Guilt, Frances Fyfield
The Mother Shadow, Melanie Johnson Howe
The Mark Twain Murders, Edith Skom

Special Agatha for Lifetime Achievement: Phyllis Whitney

1990
Best Novel
†*Bum Steer*, Nancy Pickard
Real Murders, Charlaine Harris
Deadly Valentine, Carolyn G. Hart
The Face of a Stranger, Anne Perry
The Potter's Field, Ellis Peters

Best First Novel
†*The Body in the Belfry*, Katherine Hall Page
Screaming Bones, Pat Burden
Catering to Nobody, Diane Mott Davidson
Sea of Troubles, Janet L. Smith

1991
Best Novel
†*I.O.U.*, Nancy Pickard
The Christie Caper, Carolyn G. Hart
An Owl Too Many, Charlotte MacLeod
The Last Camel Died at Noon, Elizabeth Peters

Best First Novel
†*Zero at the Bone*, Mary Willis Walker
Carpool, Mary Cahill
Just Desserts, Mary Daheim
The Bulrush Murders, Rebecca Rothenberg
Flowers for the Dead, Ann Williams

1992

Best Novel

†*Bootlegger's Daughter*, Margaret Maron
Southern Ghost, Carolyn G. Hart
The Hangman's Beautiful Daughter, Sharyn McCrumb
Defend and Betray, Anne Perry
The Snake, the Crocodile, and the Dog, Elizabeth Peters

Best First Novel

†*Blanche on the Lam*, Barbara Neely
All the Great Pretenders, Deborah Adams
Thyme of Death, Susan Wittig Albert
Decked, Carol Higgins Clark
The Seneca Falls Inheritance, Miriam Grace Monfredo

1993

Best Novel

†*Dead Man's Island*, Carolyn G. Hart
O Little Town of Maggody, Joan Hess
Fair Game, Rochelle Krich
Southern Discomfort, Margaret Maron
To Live and Die in Dixie, Kathy Hogan Trocheck

Best First Novel

†*Track of the Cat*, Nevada Barr
Goodnight, Irene, Jan Burke
A Share in Death, Deborah Crombie
Death Comes as Epiphany, Sharan Neuman
Child of Silence, Abagail Padgett

NOTES

*MALICE DOMESTIC™ is a registered trademark of MALICE DOMESTIC Ltd.
†Indicates winner.

BETH FOXWELL

Appendix C

SISTERS IN CRIME

Sisters in Crime (SIC) is an advocacy group for women who read, write, publish, sell, or review mysteries. Since its founding in 1986, the organization has had an important effect on the treatment of women in the mystery-writing profession.

SIC grew out of concerns that women had expressed for a number of years. In 1985, Phyllis Whitney wrote to the Mystery Writers of America (MWA) pointing out that it had been fifteen years since their most prestigious award had gone to a woman. This sparked discussion within MWA about whether discrimination exists in the treatment of books by women, both in MWA and in the publishing world itself. At the same time, readers were distressed by an increased use of a thin mystery plot as an excuse to depict extremely brutal and graphic sadism toward women and children. Public controversy over this and other questions relating to women in the genre became quite heated.

In October 1986, Sara Paretsky organized a breakfast for women at a Baltimore crime writers' convention to see whether interest and energy existed to work actively on these and other issues. Twenty-six women came to that Baltimore breakfast, and they left with a desire to form a networking and advocacy organization. The following spring, after membership had grown to about one hundred, the women voted to call themselves Sisters in Crime. The original steering committee included Dorothy Salisbury Davis, Susan Dunlap, Betty Francis, Charlotte MacLeod, Kate Mattes, Sara Paretsky, and Nancy Pickard.

SIC's 1993 membership was about 1600. Most members are in the United States, but there are also active chapters in Canada, Germany, and Britain; some Japanese women and people in other western European countries also belong. The organization permits male members but its purpose is as an advocacy group for women.

SIC's first projects were directed at the professional status of women in crime writing. While women have been distinguished writers of the form from its inception, they have often found themselves being slighted or even ridiculed at professional meetings. Moreover, their books did not stay in print as long as books by men. They received proportionately fewer reviews than men, and thus had less opportunity to succeed as writers because neither libraries nor bookstores were aware of their work.

An early SIC project analyzed a year's worth of data on book reviews in the major publications that libraries use to make their buying decisions. After publicizing the data, SIC found many papers discussing—in print— this project and their review policies. After seven years, women's visibility on most review pages had improved, although is still not at parity with their representation in the profession.

Another early project was a booklet, "Shameless Promotion for Brazen Hussies," intended to help women publicize and promote their books. Additionally, SIC's "Books in Print" goes annually to bookstores and libraries to make them aware of works by members, and SIC has a presence at the American Bookseller's Association and American Library Association meetings. These activities have bypassed the problem of reviews and publisher-based publicity: they have made readers aware of what SIC is doing and generated enough demand for books by members that many mystery specialty stores have a separate wall for SIC books. As one reader said: "I hadn't read a mystery since I outgrew Nancy Drew because I didn't think there were any books out there for a reader like me. SIC has introduced me to a new world of books."

Marilyn Wallace left the Baltimore breakfast fired with the idea of showcasing women writers through a short story collection, *Sisters in Crime*, which currently includes five volumes. The series provided a chance for many women to appear in print for the first time and brought women's work to an ever-growing audience. Austrian SIC member Helga Anderle produced a similar volume showcasing Eastern European and African women writers (her book, *Da werden Weiben zu Hyanen*, has unfortunately not found an English-language publisher).

The result of SIC's work since 1986 has been to provide a place where women support each other, both as writers and as readers. The group has made a serious commitment to challenge damaging stereotypes about women, whether in print or in person. As a result, women no longer find themselves segregated at professional meetings, asked such demeaning questions as, "How do you write when your kitty-cat jumps on your word processor?" or told, "How nice that you have this hobby [writing] to occupy you while your husband is at work."

In its earliest days, SIC members endured a certain amount of calumny from parts of the mystery-writing establishment. That hostility has diminished as women's voices have taken on their rightful weight in the field.

SIC has also changed publishers' attitudes toward books by women with women heroes. SIC's grass-roots success in bringing more women readers into the genre has sparked a major interest by publishers in women-centered books.

SIC has been more successful at addressing needs of writers than of readers because writers' problems are easier to pinpoint and address through group action. For example, the organization still wrestles with the issue of the image of women in crime fiction. A study to analyze that image has been promised by a member of the Cornell University Sociology Department. However, it is not yet an active project. SIC is struggling with finding ways in which an organization based in the United States and run by volunteers can represent overseas women. Furthermore, SIC would like to start breaking down the color line in mystery publishing.

Despite these pressing issues, at less than a decade old, the organization is proud of its accomplishments and of the free-floating democracy that allows all its members a voice. For more information on Sisters in Crime, write Beth Wasson, Executive Secretary, Box 442124, Lawrence, Kans., 66044–8933.

SARA PARETSKY

Appendix D

PUTTING OUT THE WORD: ALTERNATE ACTIVITIES FOR MYSTERY FANS

The bad news for avid mystery readers is that one cannot read *all* the time. The good news is that because even birds of a crooked feather yearn to flock together, crime fiction fans have established many networking activities through which to keep in touch. Enthusiasm and good fun are elements common to all these events, which range from the intricate and pricey to the simple and almost cost-free. Fans can, therefore, choose their own poison, according to the limits of their passions or their purses.

Apart from commercial ventures such as mystery cruises, weekends, or evenings during which a crime is acted out and guests (usually paying guests) compete to solve the mystery, other activities include community reading groups and micro-mini conventions: the best sources of information about these activities are one's local newspaper, radio, and television stations. Fans whose communities seem devoid of such criminous activities might wish to consider organizing one. The task is fun (it's also addictive and a tremendous amount of work). Above all, it guarantees one will meet lots of friendly, well-informed folk who tend to be very generous about sharing tips and readings lists. Local ventures like these are a handy way to satisfy one's "mystery habit" as well as have a wonderful time.

The best way to learn about mystery conventions ("cons"), of course, is to attend one. They come in various sizes but similar shapes; some are peripatetic, while others stay put, and they fall into two very general categories, the *fan-author-centered* and the *academic*. Happily for all concerned, academics who love mysteries yield to no one in their *fan*aticism, so all these gatherings are generally informal in tone as well as informative.

Standard elements of *fan-author-centered* cons are the panels, the book room, the signing room, the fan lounge, and the poker game. In discovering the location of the game, you're on your own; I'm no squealer. However, if you stay alert during cocktail hours and between-session coffee klatches, you may pick up the clues you need to locate the game (so I'm told). However, surely our primary interests are the other basic components of mystery cons.

The motives for conferees' attendance, like everything else associated with mystery fandom, are simultaneously the same and very different. Fans come to view and meet their favorite writers as well as learn about other authors whose works may appeal. Almost every event—whether scheduled or coincidental—contributes to this goal. Writers come to meet and greet—or, at least, to encounter—their established fans and enlist new ones. Almost every event contributes to this goal. Both fans and authors, however, benefit considerably from the interaction with their peers, and lasting friendships are frequently a nice bonus of these gatherings.

A tremendous amount of networking goes on among attending writers. The beginner can gain "how-to" tips during formal sessions, and during presentations many audience members take notes furiously (this is because numerous attendees are actually aspiring writers who have gone undercover as fans). Because agents and editors as well as writers attend almost all these meetings, some people see conferences as an opportunity to acquire agents for themselves or to catch the attention of an editor (or an established author who might recommend them to an agent or editor), and they work hard at these goals. Such happy eventualities do sometimes occur, but like all miracles, they are not very common.

Nevertheless, writers can gain important primary support at these gatherings. Moreover, they sometimes can acquire a mentor (or several) among more established writers. Fans' comments can be helpful; moreover, the information shared among peers is often extremely useful, and the opportunities for boosting one's morale are plentiful. It is sustaining to exchange ideas with those whose struggles match your own and very inspiriting to hear from readers who enjoy your work.

Panels (usually lasting about an hour) are the basis of mystery conventions and theoretically encapsulate the primary reasons for attendance. Well-conducted panels simultaneously allow fans to see and hear their favorite writers, satisfy the desire of would-be writers to glean tips about how to go about their tasks, and offer authors a chance to charm and entertain established fans and win new admirers. Panels are generally composed of a moderator (who may be a writer, editor, critic, or fan) and four to six panelists (who tend to be writers, editors, or agents), all of whom speak on an assigned topic, the subject of the panel. Topics vary, of course, but there are some perennial favorites—such as breaking into print, uses and propriety of humor in mystery fiction, writing and rewriting, and the importance and value of setting—that appear again and again, thus providing a minor diversion for frequent attendees who can evaluate the cleverness and uniqueness of the various program committees' rephrasing of these familiar, but always relevant, topics. The committees' success demonstrates that creativity in the mystery community is not limited to the writers.

Certainly, a well-chosen topic is crucial to a panel's success (and most cons solicit ideas for topics from their patrons). Equally important, however, is the skill of the moderator who must facilitate full participation by all panel members, keep the discussion on track, and ensure (at most conventions) that a good portion of the time allotted for the panel is reserved for questions from the audience. Interesting panelists are, of course, a must, and most writers meet these requirements handily; generally, they are forthcoming, genuine, and frank in their observations, and they remain mindful of the fact that though fans attend to become acquainted with and admire writers, another major goal is cracking the code of how to write successful mysteries. If, occasionally, an author's ego (or desire to promote a new title) inspires loquaciousness or if shyness suddenly strikes, the moderator can usually handle the situation; smoothly done quelling and drawing out are parts of the task, after all. Of course, if a panelist resists control, one can always avoid her or his appearances in the future.

The book room is a salesroom. Dealers come from near and far (when the Bouchercon convention was in London, a number of American dealers conducted business alongside their British colleagues) with a broad array of new and used editions, and frequently, representatives of various journals and fanzines maintain booths for signing up new subscribers. Naturally, titles of the authors appearing at the convention are prominent and sell briskly. Many booksellers also carry auxiliary items such as mugs, T-shirts, sweatshirts, or notepaper, which prove to be popular souvenirs, and sometimes local artisans offer mystery-related craft items. Most dealers take credit cards and checks; it turns out that mystery fans are an honest lot. Here, as everywhere, conversations are wonderful. People recommend titles to one another; readers establish mail-order contacts with dealers, and a good time really is had by all—repeatedly. No one visits the book room only once.

Unsurprisingly, the signing room benefits hugely from the book room. In the signing room, authors appear solely for the purpose of autographing books (some purchased in the book room and some lovingly carried from home) and exchanging a few words with individual fans. An immensely popular venue, the signing room often houses long lines and requires considerable waiting, but the conference committees' efforts at crowd control (which can include posting the times of the authors' appearances or limiting the number of copies to be signed at any one encounter, for example) are quite successful. Here, too, conversation with fellow autograph seekers is usually enriching.

As a rule, the fan lounge is an area reserved for informal exchange, putting up one's feet, consuming cups of coffee or tea, and, sometimes, seizing the opportunity to volunteer one's help at the next year's meeting.

The following commentaries identify well-established annual conventions that rank among the most popular and most interesting and that draw on a national U.S. audience. Unless otherwise noted, all present the basic components successfully. Other conventions, some singletons and some intermittent, spring up constantly. News of these meetings is generally found in mystery journals and fanzines.

Bouchercon (named for Anthony Boucher) is the largest (over 1,000 members) and best-known mystery convention. It meets in autumn and the venue changes; the convention includes a formal banquet at which writers are honored (with the Anthony Award) for various achievements. There is a great book room. Exchanges with very well-known writers are somewhat limited for the average fan, but nonetheless, Bouchercon is very popular, and rightly so. Bouchercon also hosts meetings of related groups: these include such organizations as Sisters in Crime, Private Eye Writers of America, and Mystery Readers International. The 1995 convention will be held in Nottingham, England. Watch journals for dates and addresses for this and subsequent meetings.

Malice Domestic™ is devoted to the cozy mystery. It meets in spring in Bethesda, Md. Enrollment is limited and includes a formal banquet and tea, to which some participants wear costumes. Organizers swear that each year's "Ghost of Honor" also attends this spirited event, but the ghosts' garments, like the ghosts themselves, are invisible. Awards called Agathas to honor Christie are given for various authorial achievements. This convention boasts the most varied book room of the lot, with wares usually including crafts, antique jewelry, and vintage clothing. Exchanges between major names and fans are nowadays much more limited than at its inception, but there is still a welcoming environment. The convention keeps enrollees informed with its own newsletter, *The Usual Suspects*. Write Malice Domestic Ltd., P.O. Box 3117, Bethesda, Md., 20824–1137.

Mid-Atlantic Mystery Book Fair and Convention is small but choice. Held in autumn in Philadelphia, Pa., it seems to attract fewer "big names" than other conventions, but many authors do attend, and exchanges between them and fans abound. There is an excellent book room. The convention is well organized and very congenial, with lots of surprise treats. It also capitalizes nicely on its locale. Write Deen Kogan, Society Hill Playhouse, 507 South 8th Street, Philadelphia, Pa., 19147, (215) 923–0211.

Left Coast Crime is relatively new and never attended by this writer, but it has been warmly commended by a good many fans. Held in winter in California (specific locales will be announced), the attendance is limited. It includes panels with information about forensics and other practical background material. Watch journals and fanzines for information.

To date, annual academic conferences that emphasize crime fiction stem from the Popular Culture Association (PCA), whose national meeting (spring) and regional meetings (i.e., the Popular Culture Association of the South and the Midwest Popular Culture Association, both of which meet in autumn, and the Far West Popular Culture Association, which meets in winter) pay considerable attention to mysteries and mystery writers. Here, presenters deliver analytical or critical papers centering on such topics as a writer's work, various types of crime writing, notable patterns that emerge or fade, and influences of one writer or era on another. Generally, PCA sessions last about seventy-five to ninety minutes and include as many as four formal papers (of no more than fifteen minutes each; moderators are expected to hold firmly to this limit) and a question-and-answer session with the audience. Like audiences at fan-author-centered meetings, these participants are very well informed and exchanges are lively and friendly. Most of the papers are entertaining, and humor illuminates a surprising number.

The mystery/detection caucus conducts two special events at the national PCA. Participants hand in questions (and answers), and a game of "Criminal Pursuits" ensues during one noon hour. All in attendance are divided into teams, and competition is fierce; although the prizes are inconsequential, honor is at stake. An event called "Read Any Good Books Lately?" occurs during another lunch hour. Here, readers gather to mention and praise the best of the mysteries they have read during the preceding year. The moderator provides copies of the list developed at the previous meeting, and members leave armed with plenty of ideas for future reading. These are very informal and popular sessions. Both lunch-hour events are well worth packing a lunch for, and they reveal a good deal about the hospitality of the mystery/detection caucus. Newcomers are most welcome; indeed, one award that the caucus presents, the Earl, honors the best paper given by a first-time participant. The Dove, the other award, goes annually to someone who has contributed significantly to the scholarly study of crime fiction. For information about national and regional meetings, write Ray Browne, Popular Culture Association, Bowling Green State University, Bowling Green, Ohio, 43403. (The PCA also sponsors meetings abroad, which take place every other summer; information is available from the same source.)

It seems that devoted fans also like to read *about* what they read, for between conferences, many rely on journals and fanzines to stay current with criminous affairs. As varied as the conferences, these periodicals serve a variety of purposes, chief among them being sheer enjoyment. Though some of the periodicals discussed here include or even feature fiction, they also devote considerable space to reviews, articles, and letters, in contrast to such magazines as *Ellery Queen's Mystery Magazine* and *Alfred Hitchcock's Mystery Magazine,* which are both very interesting but include little discussion of crime writing, instead concentrating on fiction. Because today's short story markets are so limited, these periodicals serve an important need, but nonetheless they are different from the journals we are emphasizing here.

The oldest of the periodicals of interest is the highly respected, much-loved *The Armchair Detective*, a quarterly that offers mystery buffs a little of everything. Full-color covers, well-planned layouts, and a good many illustrations enhance a wide variety of articles and columns. *TAD* publishes some fiction, generally two short stories per issue. Typical among its nonfiction selections are author interviews, critical/analytical studies, and feature articles, which are all eminently readable. Regular columns include reports on upcoming activities and events, information about collecting mysteries, comments on new writers, a vigorous letters section, reviews by the journal's founder, Allen J. Hubin, discussions of mysteries by newcomers to the field, television and film criticism, and still other reviews by a wide variety of *TAD* readers. Advertisements, want ads, and checklists of new publications round out the offerings. The contributors are well informed; many hold very firm opinions and most have readable styles. In fact, crime writing devotees can hardly afford to do without this journal. Subscriptions cost $26.00 for one year and $42.00 for two years. Write *The Armchair Detective*, 129 West 56th St., New York, N.Y., 10019.

Janet Rudolph, who writes "Murderous Affairs," the indispensable roundup of fanzines and conventions for *TAD*, also founded Mystery Readers International (MRI) and its house organ, the quarterly *Mystery Readers Journal*, whose thematic issues always deal with timely topics. Some articles may be written by crime writers whose work falls within the scope of the theme, and reader/members are also encouraged to submit material. This is a lively group. U.S. membership (which includes the journal) is $22.50 per year. For further information about MRI and the *Mystery Readers Journal*, write Mystery Readers International, P.O. Box 8116, Berkeley, Calif., 94707.

Well established and warmly regarded despite some rough times in 1992, the *Drood Review of Mystery* is edited and published by Jim Huang. Now appearing bimonthly, *Drood* includes not only profiles of crime writers and their work, but also reliable, fairly detailed reviews, as well as "Capsules," which are brief reviews. Attractively presented and easy to read, *Drood* costs $20.00 for twelve issues and $36.00 for twenty-four. For subscriptions, write *The Drood Review*, Box 1293, Brookline, Mass., 02146; for editorial inquiries, write *The Drood Review*, 5047 West Main, no. 110, Kalamazoo, Mich., 49009.

A Canadian quarterly, the *Mystery Review*, began its second year of publication in the fall of 1993. Handsomely presented and well-edited, the *Review* publishes interviews, articles, and reviews; profiles bookstores; does some retrospectives; runs some classifieds; and gives brief commentaries about recent releases. There is even the occasional puzzle. Rates are $21.50

(including tax) in Canada; the subscription cost for U.S. fans is $20.00 (U.S.) annually. Write *The Mystery Review*, P.O. Box 233, Colborne, Ontario, K0K 1S0, Canada.

Hardboiled, a quarterly, publishes original fiction, reprints, nonfiction, and some reviews. It also features wonderful covers. For subscriptions ($20.00 for six issues), write Gryphon Publications, P.O. Box 209, Brooklyn, N.Y. 11202.

New Mystery publishes some fiction but also includes numerous book reviews, long and short; audio reviews; commentaries about bookstores; and a letters column. A four-issue subscription costs $17.77. Write *New Mystery*, Flatiron Building, 175 Fifth Ave., no. 2001, New York, N.Y. 10010.

Mystery News, which appears in a polished, folio-sized, newspaper format, is a welcome newcomer. Loaded with useful reviews, it also includes author interviews. The writing is lucid *and* appealing. The journal publishes six issues annually for $15.00. Write *Mystery News*, P.O. Box 1201, Port Townsend, Wash., 98368–0901.

Traditionally, letters have been crucial components in mystery fanzines. Robert S. Napier ("Cap'n Bob") capitalizes on fans' yearning for correspondence in *Mystery and Detective Monthly*, "The Magazine of Great Letterature," which is approaching publication of its one-hundredth issue. Some regulars write for almost every issue. They respond to questions, support or argue with one another, and discuss some topics at great length. Some do a little lobbying for their own publications or those of their friends. Other subscribers are almost—or wholly—silent, finding their pleasure from observing rather than debating. In addition to letters, the magazine includes some classified ads and a very useful, detailed listing called "New Releases," by Robert Samoian. Subscriptions cost $16.50 for six issues and $30.00 for eleven issues; make checks payable to Bob Napier. To subscribe, write *Mystery and Detective Monthly*, 5601 N. 40th Street, Tacoma, Wash., 98407.

Two academic journals deserve mention here. First, *Clues, A Journal of Detection* is published at Bowling Green State University. Featuring scholarly articles (many are versions of papers given at meetings of the Popular Culture Association), *Clues* also includes numerous reviews of current mystery fiction and some reference and scholarly materials. For information, write Pat Browne, Popular Press, Bowling Green State University, Bowling Green, Ohio, 43403.

The other academic journal, *Murder Is Academic*, the brainchild of B. J. Rahn, is the newest publication discussed here. This newsletter is designed to serve people who teach crime fiction, and features include listings of upcoming events, reviews of mystery-related activities, "Scholars' Bookshelf"—reviews of new books, brief course descriptions, and some letters. Currently, Professor Rahn is preparing a collection of course syllabi contributed by her readers. For information, write *Murder Is Academic*, c/o B. J. Rahn, Department of English, Hunter College, 695 Park Ave., New York, N.Y. 10021.

Such a richness of gatherings and publications verify what fans feel in their bones: crime fiction is not only alive and thriving, it is also generating a host of enjoyable offshoots.

JANE S. BAKERMAN

Appendix E

DOROTHYL: MYSTERY ON-LINE

Do you find Susan Silverman's habits annoying? Have you ever had intimate dreams about Rumpole of the Bailey? Do you care who killed Roger Ackroyd? Moreover, do you have an e-mail account?

Then you're a prime suspect—you, too, could be a DOROTHYL'er. Named for British mystery author Dorothy L. Sayers (1893–1957), DOROTHYL is an electronic mail (e-mail)–based discussion group for fans of the mystery genre. "It was founded for fun and interesting discussion of mystery reading," said Diane Kovacs, who is cofounder, co–list owner, and often technical editor (a volunteer position) of DOROTHYL.

Kovacs and several other librarians started the group in 1991 and named it "in honor of one of the great women mystery writers of the century," as the mission statement explains. "Agatha Christie and Josephine Tey were strong contenders, but Dorothy L. Sayers had a LISTSERV-blessed middle initial." LISTSERV is the software used to distribute messages to participants worldwide across Bitnet and Internet, the two major public computer networks. These run via high-speed telephone lines; electronic mail is the feature on which "lists"—and there are thousands—like DOROTHYL run.

Anyone with access to a Bitnet or Internet e-mail account can "subscribe" to DOROTHYL at no cost. Send a message (check your system's procedure) to LISTSERV@KENTVM (Bitnet) or LISTSERV@KENTVM.KENT.EDU (Internet). Leave the "Subject" line blank; write the message, SUB DOROTHYL. It may take a few days to process, but soon, your "mailbox" will show the message, "Welcome to DOROTHYL . . ." This contains all the information about the group: its history, technology, etiquette, and instructions for sending messages.

Every few days you will receive a group of mail messages from DOROTHYL. The number varies with the list's activity—you may have fifteen to one hundred or more. These messages are sent by other subscribers to a central address, DOROTHYL@KENTVM (Bitnet) or DOROTHYL@-KENTVM.KENT.EDU (Internet), which then routes them to the group. Your mail directory allows you to choose what to read: each message has a "Subject" line, such as "Mysteries Set in Boston." You may send messages to the whole group by writing to the central address or reply to individuals privately, as every message includes the address of its sender. Although the recipient's computer receives the message in a few minutes, you should allow a few days for the note to be read and for further response.

Each subscriber receives a guide to e-mail etiquette; the primary rule is courtesy. Suggestions include being tolerant of newcomers and opinions, using descriptive "Subject" lines, and clearly labeling humor and sarcasm. Messages that reveal key plot points or endings should carry warnings such as, "SPOILER ALERT."

Any "mysterious" topic is fair game—authors, books, reviews, films, awards, conventions, readings. For instance, DOROTHYL'ers have debated the conclusion of *The Nine Tailors*, mysteries as literature, and the pros and cons of the Robert Parker character Susan Silverman. "Nowhere else do I converse with intelligent people about mysteries," said a participant, who found no fellow fans in her own locale. "My family and friends think I'm morbid."

The group is an excellent resource. For example, through DOROTHYL members, I was able to contact two authors and several reviewers and obtain information for my academic research. Are you wondering who created Modesty Blaise? Looking for mysteries featuring canals—or cats—or New England towns? At least one (and probably twenty) of over 900 DOROTHYL'ers will know the answer.

DOROTHYL is an enjoyable and educational way to keep up with mysteries. "It can be a valuable readers advisory tool for librarians; it could be used as a tool for serious research," said the list's coordinator, Kara Robinson. "But I guess what's most important is that it's fun."

BRENDA HADENFELDT

Appendix F

SPECIALTY BOOKSELLERS

This is just a sampling of bookstores in the United States and Canada that cater to mystery fans. Many have newsletters and sell by mail. This list is excerpted from *Sisters in Crime Newsletter*, 5, no. 3 (September 1993): 7–8.

Booked for Murder
2701 University Ave.
Madison, WI 53705
(608) 238–2701

The Book Sleuth
2513 W. Colorado Ave.
Colorado Springs, CO 80904
(719) 632–2727

Centuries and Sleuths
744 Garfield
Oak Park, IL 60304

Deadly Passions Bookshop
157 South Kalamazoo Mall
Kalamazoo, MI 49007

Fickes Crime Fiction
1471 Burkhardt Ave.
Akron, OH 44301
(216) 773–4223

Footprints of a Gigantic Hound Bookstore
16 Broadway Vlg.
123 S. Eastbourne Dr.
Tucson, AZ 85716
(602) 326–8533

Foul Play
302 W. 12th St.
New York, NY 10014

Foul Play
6072 Busch Blvd.
Columbus, OH 43329
(614) 848–5583

Foul Play Mystery Books
1465 Second Ave.
New York, NY 10021
(212) 517–3222

Fountain of Mystery Books
1119 Prospect St.
Indianapolis, IN 46203
(317) 635–2583

Grave Matters
P.O. Box 32192
Cincinnati, OH 45232

Gravesend Books
P.O. Box 235
Pocono Pines, PA 18350

Grim Reader
P.O. Box 790682
San Antonio, TX 78279
(210) 341–0640

Grounds for Murder
P.O. Box 60325
San Diego, CA 92166
(619) 284–4436

Haven't Got a Clue
1823 Western Ave.
Albany, NY 12203
(518) 464–1135

It's a Mystery to Me
4900 Main St.
Yorba Linda, CA 92686
(714) 970–9695

It's Just a Matter of Crime
200 John Knox Rd.
Tallahassee, FL 32303
(904) 422–3453

Kate's Mystery Books
2211 Massachusetts Ave.
Cambridge, MA 02140
(617) 491–2660

Killing Time Mystery Books
2821 NE 55th
Seattle, WA 98105
(913) 842–1325

Murder and Mayhem
6412 Carrollton Ave.
Indianapolis, IN 46220
(317) 254–8273

Murder for Fun Mystery Books
2006 Fairview Rd
Raleigh, NC 27608
(919) 755–0013

Murder, They Wrote
1001 Wilson Blvd. Ste 604
Arlington, VA 22209
(703) 841–1615

Murder Unlimited: A Mystery Store
2501 San Mateo Pl. NE
Albuquerque, NM 87110
(505) 884–5491

Mysteries and More
1139 N. IH35 "176
Austin, TX 78753

Mysteries by Mail
P.O. Box 679
Boonville, CA 95415
(707) 895–3822

Mysteries to Die For
2940 Thousand Oaks Blvd.
Thousand Oaks, CA 91362
(805) 374–0084

Mysteries Unlimited
18820 Aurora Ave. N
Seattle, WA 98133

The Mysterious Bookshop
129 W. 56th St.
New York, NY 10019

The Mysterious Bookstore
6906 Snider Plaza
Dallas, TX 75205

Mysterybooks
1715 Connecticut Ave. NW
Washington, DC 20009

Mystery Bookshop Bethesda
7700 Old Georgetown Rd.
Bethesda, MD 20814

Mystery Books of Merion
405 Andrews Rd.
Merion, PA 19066

Mystery Hound
13416 Santa Fe
Lenexa, KS 66215
(913) 842–1325

Mystery Lovers Bookshop
514 Allegheny River Blvd.
Oakmont, PA 15139
(412) 828–4877

Mystery Lovers Ink
8 Stiles Rd.
Salem, NH 03079
(603) 898–8060

Mystery Loves Company
1730 Fleet St.
Baltimore, MD 21231

Once Upon a Crime
604 W. 26th St.
Minneapolis, MN 55405
(612) 870–3785

Prime Crime Books
891 Bank St.
Ottawa, ON K1S 3W4
Canada

Scotland Yard Books, Ltd.
556 Green Bay Rd.
Winnetka, IL 60093
(708) 446–2214

Seattle Mystery Bookshop
117 Cherry St.
Seattle, WA 98104

The Poisoned Pen
7100 E. Main St.
Scottsdale, AZ 85251

The Raven Bookstore
8 E. 7th St.
Lawrence, KS 66044
(913) 749–3300

The Rue Morgue
946 Pearl St.
Boulder, CO 80302

Secret Staircase Bookshop
2223 Broadway
Redwood City, CA 94063
(415) 366–1222

Sleuth of Baker Street
1595 Bayview Ave.
Toronto, ON M4G 3B5
Canada

Snoop Sisters
566 N. Indian Rocks Rd.
Belleair Bluffs, FL 34640
(813) 584–4370

Spenser's Mystery Bookshop
314 Newbury St.
Boston, MA 02115

KATHLEEN GREGORY KLEIN

Appendix G

FOURTEEN CATEGORIES OF
MYSTERY FICTION:
LISTS FOR READERS

Caveat: Attempts to categorize mystery fiction are filled with danger. Use the following lists at your own risk.

Classic/Golden Age: The focus is on ratiocination; these were typical in 1920s and 1930s but also continue into the present; common theme is the restoration of order. Examples: Christie, Sayers.

Allingham, Campion series except *The White Cottage Mystery, The Crime at Black Dudley, Mystery Mile, Look to the Lady, Sweet Danger, Traitor's Purse, The Beckoning Lady, The Mind Readers, Cargo of Eagles.*

Arnold, all (except *Desperate Measures, Sinister Purposes*).

Brand, *Death in High Heels.*

Caudwell, all.

Christie, *The Mysterious Affair at Styles, Murder on the Links, The Mystery of the Blue Train, Murder in Three Acts, Cards on the Table, Appointment with Death, The Patriotic Murders, Murder in Retrospect.*

Daly, all.

Disney, *Appointment at Nine, Did She Fall or Was She Pushed?, Find the Woman, Fire at Will, Here Lies . . . , Murder on Target, Straw Man.*

Ford, *All for the Love of a Lady, The Bahamas Murder Case, The Clue of the Judas Tree, False to Any Man, Honolulu Story, Ill Met By Moonlight, Murder in Maryland, The Murder of an Old Man, Old Lover's Ghost, The Philadelphia Murder Story, Reno Rendezvous, The Simple Way of Poison, The Strange Death of Martin Green, Three Bright Pebbles, Washington Whispers Murder, The Woman in Black.*

Fraser, *Quiet as a Nun, Oxford Blood.*

Heyer, *Why Shoot a Butler?, The Unfinished Clue, Death in the Stocks, They Found Him Dead, Duplicate Death.*

Kallen, *Piano Bird, A Little Madness.*

Mitchell, all.

Sayers, all.

Tey, *Miss Pym Disposes, The Franchise Affair, Brat Farrar.*
Thomson, Holmes short stories.

Comic/Caper: These are mostly funny; there are improbable settings, crimes, or characters. Example: MacLeod.
Babson, *Cover Up Story, Murder on Show, Murder Murder Little Star, The Cruise of a Deathtime, Reel Murder, Encore Murder, In the Teeth of Adversity.*
Brand, *The Three-Cornered Halo.*
Davis, *Death of an Old Sinner, Old Sinners Never Die.*
Disney, *The Day Miss Bessie Lewis Disappeared, Family Skeleton.*
Ford, Mr. Pinkerton series, *The Black Envelope, The Eel Pie Murders, The Hammersmith Murders, Homicide House, The Man from Scotland Yard, The Murder of the Fifth Columnist, Scotland Yard Can Wait, Two Against Scotland Yard.*
Gill, *Nursery Crimes* (black comedy).
Hess, Malloy series, Hanks series, Bloomer series.
Heyer, *Behold Here's Poison, A Blunt Instrument, No Wind of Blame.*
MacLeod, Shandy series, Kelling/Bittersohn series, Rhys series, Grub-and-Stakers series.
McCrumb, MacPherson series, Omega series.
Porter, Dover series, Hon Con series.
Rice, all.
Taylor, writing as Tilton, all.

Great Detective/Great Police Officer: Featured is an overpowering protagonist, whether amateur or police officer; these usually are set in the first third of the twentieth century. Examples: Christie's Poirot, Marsh's Roderick Alleyn, Sayers's Peter Wimsey.
Brand, *Heads You Lose, Green for Danger, The Crooked Wreath, Death of Jezebel, London Particular, Tour de Force.*
Christie, *Curtain.*
Marsh, Alleyn series.
Moody, Wanawake series.
Papazoglou, writing as Haddam, Demarkian series.

Hard-Boiled: These involve mean streets and crime for criminals. Examples: Grafton, Paretsky.
Barnes, Carlyle series.
Bowers, Lacey series.
Davis, *The Pale Betrayer, The Little Brothers, A Death in the Life, Scarlet Night, Lullaby of Murder, The Habit of Fear.*
Dunlap, O'Shaughnessy series.
Grafton, Millhone series.
Grant-Adamson, *Too Many Questions.*
Kijewski, Colorado series.
McDermid, Brannigan series.
Muller, McCone series.

Paretsky, Warshawski series.
Wiltz, all.

Lesbian: This is a separate subcategory with connections to other categories; recognized separately because of small press output, it features a lesbian protagonist and, typically, a women-centered crime. Examples: Wilson, Forrest.
Baker, all.
Cross, *Death in a Tenured Position*, *The Players Come Again* (modified).
Forrest, all.
McDermid, Gordon series.
McNab, all.
Wilson, all.

Locked Room: Just what it says.
Cross, *In the Last Analysis*, *Poetic Justice*, *The Theban Mysteries*, *Death in a Tenured Position*.
D'Amato, *The Hands of Healing Murder*, *Hard Tack*.
Fraser, *A Splash of Red*.

Police Procedural: This type involves police (usually in the plural) working as teams or, at least, pairs; often they are following more than one case, although cases are often related. Example: Linington.
Aird, all.
Butler, Coffin series; writing as Melville, Daniels series.
Cornwell, all.
Dunlap, Smith series.
George, Lynley/Havers series.
Gill, *Victims*.
Haymon, all.
James, Dalgleish series.
Kellerman, Decker/Lazarus series.
Linington, all (except *Nightmare*).
McGown, all (except *An Evil Hour*, *The Stalking Horse*).
Nabb, all.
O'Donnell, Mulcahaney series.
Peters, Ellis, Felse series.
Stacey, all.
Tey, Grant series.
Thomson, Finch/Rudd series.
Uhnak, all (except *Policewoman*).

Puzzle: The focus is on plot, timetables, alibis, and lists of suspects. Example: Sayers's *Five Red Herrings*.
Borthwick, all.
Christie, *The Murder of Roger Ackroyd*, *Peril at End House*, *Thirteen at Dinner*, *Murder in the Calais Coach*, *Death in the Air*, *The A.B.C. Murders*, *Murder in Mesopotamia*, *Death on the Nile*, *And Then There Were None*, *Evil Un-*

der the Sun, The Body in the Library, Remembered Death, Hickory Dickory Death, Cat among the Pigeons, The Clocks, A Caribbean Mystery, At Bertram's Hotel, Third Girl, By the Pricking of My Thumbs, Elephants Can Remember, Sleeping Murder.

Cross, A Trap for Fools.

Gilman, The Clairvoyant Countess.

Grant-Adamson, Guilty Knowledge, Wild Justice.

Green, all.

McGown, The Stalking Horse.

Moyes, all.

Natsuke, Innocent Journey.

Regester, The Dead Letter, Figure Eight.

Soft-Boiled: The protagonist is a private eye or police officer; these involve less violence than the hard-boiled variety. Example: Wright.

Barnes, Sprague series.

Cody, Lee series.

Dunlap, Haskell series.

Gosling, Monkey Puzzle, Backlash, Death Penalties, The Body in Blackwater Bay.

Grant, all.

James, Gray series.

Maron, all.

McGown, An Evil Hour.

Meek, all.

Meyers, all.

Slovo, all.

Truman, all.

Wright, all.

Suspense/Had-I-but-Known: These mysteries are often connected with the psychological but usually focus on investigation; typically, they follow the point of view of an innocent (or even naive) protagonist. Examples: Armstrong, Millar.

Armstrong, all.

Arnold, Desperate Measures, Sinister Purposes.

Christie, The Secret Adversary, The Man in the Brown Suit, The Secret of Chimneys, The Secret Dials Mystery, The Boomerang Clue, N or M?, They Came to Baghdad, So Many Steps to Death, Passenger to Frankfurt, Postern of Fate.

Clark, all.

Clarke, The Mystery Lady, Last Seen in London, Murder in Writing.

Cross, The Question of Max.

Davis, Enemy and Brother.

Disney, Cry for Help, The Departure of Mr. Gaudette, Don't Go into the Woods Today, Heavy Heavy Hangs, The Hospitality of the House, Look Back on Murder, The Magic Grandfather, Method in Madness, My Neighbor's Wife, Night of the Clear Choice, No Next of Kin, Should Auld Acquaintance.

Ford, By the Watchman's Clock, The Girl from the Mimosa Club, In at the Death,

Invitation to Murder, Murder Comes to Eden, Murder Is the Payoff, Murder with Southern Hospitality, The Road to Folly, The Town Cried Murder.
Fraser, *The Wild Island, Cool Repentance.*
Gill, *Dying to Meet You, Time and Time Again.*
Gilman, all (except Mrs. Pollifax series and *The Clairvoyant Countess*).
Gosling, *Fair Game, The Zero Trap, Solo Blues, The Harrowing, Woman in Red, The Wychford Murders.*
Grant-Adamson, *Threatening Eye, Curse the Darkness.*
Highsmith, Ripley series.
Kelly, all.
Millar, all.
Papazoglou, *Sanctity, Charisma.*
Rinehart, all.

Thriller/Psychological: These often depict a crime without a detective; more attention is paid to the criminal than the investigation. Examples: Rendell; Highsmith's nonseries novels.
Allingham, *The Crime at Black Dudley, Mystery Mile, Sweet Danger, Traitor's Purse, Coroner's Pidgin, More Work for the Undertaker, The Tiger in the Smoke, The Mind Readers, Cargo of Eagles, Other Man's Danger, Rogues' Holiday, The Shadow in the House.*
Babson, *Pretty Lady, The Lord Mayor of Death, Queue Here for Murder.*
Brand, *The Rose in the Darkness.*
Clarke, all (except *The Lady in Black, The Mystery Lady, Last Seen in London, Murder in Writing, The Whitelands Affair, The Case of the Paranoid Patient*).
Cody, Wylie series.
Cross, *Your Royal Hostage.*
Davis, *A Gentle Murder; Black Sheep, White Lamb; God Speed the Night.*
Disney, *The Chandler Policy; Do Not Fold, Spindle or Mutilate; Do Unto Others; Enduring Old Charms; The Last Straw; Money for the Taking; Only Couples Need Apply; Prescription: Murder; That Which Is Crooked; Three's a Crowd; Trick or Treat; Two Little Children and How They Grew; Voices from the Grave; Who Rides a Tiger?; Winifred.*
Gill, *Death Drop.*
Grant-Adamson, *The Face of Death.*
Hess, *The Playroom, Half Light.*
Highsmith, all (except Ripley series).
Hughes, all.
Natsuke, *The Third Lady, The Obituary Arrives at Two O'Clock, Portal of the Wind.*
Rendell, all (except Wexford series).
Simpson, *Harbingers of Fear.*
Togawa, *The Master Key, The Lady Killer, A Kiss of Fire.*

Village/Domestic/Traditional (British): This is a classic style of detective novel involving a village or rural setting and a closed circle of suspects. Example: Christie's Miss Marple series.

Allingham, *The White Cottage Mystery*, *The Beckoning Lady*.
Babson, *Unfair Exchange*, *The Stalking Lamb*, *Murder Sails at Midnight*, *There Must be Some Mistake*, *Tightrope for Three*, *So Soon Done For*, *The Twelve Deaths of Christmas*, *Dangerous to Know*, *Death Warmed Up*, *Death beside the Sea*, *A Fool for Murder*, *A Trail of Ashes*, *Death Swap*, *Death in Fashion*, *Fatal Fortune*, *Murder on a Mystery Tour*, *Guilty Party*, *Tourists Are for Trapping*, *Past Regrets*.
Christie, Miss Marple series.
Clarke, *Letter from the Dead*, *We the Bereaved*.
Ferrars, all.
Gill, *Seminar for Murder*, *The Fifth Rapunzel*.
Giroux, all.
Grant-Adamson, *Death on Widow's Walk*.
Grimes, Jury series.
Kenney, *Garden of Malice*.
Lemarchand, all.
Peters, Ellis, Brother Cadfael series.
Radley, all (except *This Way Out*).
Rendell, Wexford series.
Wentworth, all.

Village/Domestic/Traditional (American): This is the same as the British version, but with a Yankee flavor. Example: Pickard.
Carlson, all.
Conant, all.
Cross, *The James Joyce Murder*.
Davis, *The Judas Cat*, *The Clay Hand*, *A Town of Masks*.
Kallen, *Introducing C. B. Greenfield*, *The Tanglewood Murder*, *No Lady in the House*.
Kenney, *Graves in Academe*.
Langton, all.
Papazoglou, Pay McKenna series.
Pickard, all.
Rich, all.

"Whydunit": The focus is on motive; the murderer is known or suspected from outset and the actual criminal is less important than the motivation. Example: Thompson.
Cross, *Sweet Death, Kind Death*; *No Word from Winifred*.
Davis, *Shock Wave*.
Natsuke, *Murder at Mt. Fuji*.
Simpson, all (except *Harbingers of Fear*).
Thompson, all.

COMPILED BY KATHLEEN GREGORY KLEIN

AUTHOR/PSEUDONYM INDEX

TITLE INDEX

ABOUT THE EDITOR AND CONTRIBUTORS

KATHLEEN GREGORY KLEIN is the author of the award-winning book *The Woman Detective: Gender and Genre* (1988 [tran. 1994], rev. ed. forthcoming in 1995) and editor of *Women Times Three: Writers, Detectives, Readers* (forthcoming), as well as numerous articles on detective fiction. She teaches English and Women's Studies at Southern Connecticut State University.

TAMMY AIELLO has presented papers on the influences of the maternal in *The Autobiography of St. Therese*, June Arnold's use of contraries in *Sister Gin*, and the reproduction of mothering in Mickey Spillane's *The Killing Man*.

LYNN M. ALEXANDER is an associate professor of English at the University of Tennessee at Martin, where she teaches courses in the British novel and women's literature. A regular participant in the Mystery and Detective Fiction division of the Popular Culture Association meetings, she received her Ph.D. from the University of Tulsa in 1986.

THERESA PERRI AMMIRATI teaches English at Connecticut College, where she is also Director of the Writing Center. She has served as a scholar/keynote speaker for the Southern Connecticut Library Council's "Poisoned Pen" book series and has also been a scholar/facilitator for other book series in libraries throughout the state.

LIAHNA BABENER is Associate Professor and Head of the English Department at Montana State University. Her interests include popular culture, regionalism, film studies, and feminist theory; she has written and published in all of these areas. She is currently at work on a study of regional autobiography and a feminist reappraisal of the films of Alfred Hitchcock.

PAUL LEON BAIL is a forensic psychologist consulting to the criminal courts and an Instructor at Fitchburg State College. He reviews nonfiction for *Criminal Justice and Behavior* and fiction for the *Drood Review of Mystery*, and has contributed to the *Encyclopedia of Criminology*. He has four children and 1,700 books.

SUSAN BAKER, Professor of English at the University of Nevada, wrote the essay on E. X. Ferrars for *And Then There Were Nine* and contributed several entries to *Twentieth Century Crime and Mystery Writers*. She coedited *In Another Country: Feminist Perspectives on Renaissance Drama* and has published essays about Shakespeare.

JANE S. BAKERMAN, Professor Emerita, Indiana State University (and inveterate conference-goer), publishes widely about crime fiction in both popular and scholarly journals. Currently, her review column, "The Criminal Element," appears in *Clues: A Journal of Detection*, and she presents a monthly book review program on the Wabash Valley's ABC television network.

ELAINE BANDER, who was born in New York in 1946, received her B.A. and Ph.D. degrees from McGill University in Montreal, where she teaches English, including a course on detective fiction, at Dawson College. She has published articles on various aspects of detective fiction.

BARBARA BOEHNKE is a librarian at the State University of New York at Buffalo.

BILL BRUBAKER is an Associate Professor in the Department of English at Florida State University, Tallahassee. He has written short fiction, poetry, critical articles, and a book, *Stewards of the House: The Detective Fiction of Jonathan Latimer*. He is currently engaged in a critical book on Latimer's film noir.

ELIZABETH BUCKMASTER has taught at Penn State, Delaware County Campus, for twenty-five years. Her graduate work was in medieval studies. She is coeditor of a yearly bibliography of short story anthologies.

LANDON C. BURNS is Professor Emeritus of English at Penn State University. He publishes an annual cross-referenced index of short-fiction anthologies in *Studies in Short Fiction*, and continues to have an active interest in the short story as well as in historical and mystery fiction.

KATHLEEN SHINE CAIN is Associate Professor of English and director of the Writing Center at Merrimack College, North Andover, Massachusetts. She is the author of several textbooks, including *Exploring Literature: A Collaborative Approach* (with Albert C. DeCiccio and Michael J. Rossi), and has presented papers on women mystery writers and female detectives.

ANN SANDERS CARGILL designs computer software for the South Carolina Student Loan Corporation in Columbia, South Carolina. She has been reading women's mysteries seriously for ten years and has presented her work at the annual meeting of the Popular Culture Association. Her current interest is in southern mysteries.

MILES CLOWERS is Professor of History and Political Science at San Diego City College, where he has taught since 1971. An advocate of fiction as a teaching tool, he has published two works, *Understanding American History through Fiction* and *Understanding American Politics through Fiction*. He has utilized mysteries in teaching both history and political science.

MARY JEAN DEMARR holds a Ph.D. in English from the University of Illinois. She is Professor of English at Indiana State University, where she teaches courses in American literature, women's literature, and popular literature. She publishes regularly in *Clues: A Journal of Detection* and *MidAmerica*.

BARBARA DOUGLAS is a writer living in Branford, Connecticut. She holds an M.A. in English from Southern Connecticut State University. Her field of interest is Irish literature and Gaelic writing. She is an avid Sherlockian and is affiliated with the Society of the Baker Street Irregulars.

HERBERT V. FACKLER, Associate Professor of English at the University of Southwestern Louisiana, has published fiction and poetry as well as literary criticism. Editor and coauthor of *Hard-Boiled Cajun: The Dave Robicheaux Novels of James Lee Burke*, he is also author of the "Spenser" entry for the *Oxford Companion to Crime and Mystery Fiction*.

BETH FOXWELL, vice-chair and a founding director of MALICE DOMESTIC Ltd., is an editor at the American Association of Colleges for Teacher Education in Washington, D.C. She has authored articles on mystery authors such as Elizabeth Peters/Barbara Michaels, Anne Perry, and Dorothy L. Sayers, and edits MALICE's newsletter, *The Usual Suspects*.

MARY P. FREIER graduated from Millikin University with a B.A. in English and philosophy. She received her A.M. and Ph.D. degrees from the

University of Illinois at Urbana-Champaign. She has conducted research on nineteenth-century novels by American women and detective fiction.

HELEN S. GARSON, Professor of English and American Studies, is Professor Emeritus of George Mason University in Fairfax, Virginia. The author of two books and numerous articles about Truman Capote, she has also written about John Le Carré; John Hawkes; Flannery O'Connor; Gothic, spy, and detective novels; pornography; popular culture; and American women novelists.

BRENDA HADENFELDT is a free-lance writer and reviewer based in Nebraska. A frequent contributor to campus literary journals and newspapers, she recently completed a master's program in professional writing and publishing at Emerson College in Boston, where her thesis work focused on the publishing field of mystery and detective fiction.

VIRGINIA S. HALE is Professor of English at the University of Hartford. A specialist in Chaucer and medieval literature, she also teaches courses in detective fiction. She is the author of the two-volume text, *Literature and Film of Other Cultures*, and several articles on detective fiction.

MARGARET BROOM HARP is an Assistant Professor of French at the University of Nevada, Las Vegas. She obtained her doctorate at Tulane University in New Orleans and specializes in literature of the French Renaissance. She has recently begun to research "polars" or French mysteries.

DONNA WALLER HARPER teaches high school in Nashville, Tennessee, and is an adjunct at Middle Tennessee State University in Murfreesboro. Her doctorate is in the field of mystery fiction. She is currently working on a study of women as characters and writers in mystery fiction.

LINDA R. HARRIS is a writing instructor and Writing Lab coordinator for the English department at the University of Maryland, Baltimore County. A recent member of the Popular Culture and American Culture associations, she has presented two papers on her favorite topics from mystery fiction: the academic mystery and the woman detective.

BARRIE HAYNE is Professor of English at the University of Toronto, where he has taught since 1964. His particular interest is American culture between 1865 and 1917; he has published articles on Cooper, Poe, and Dreiser, as well as in American film. A member of the Popular Culture Association since 1973, he has served as its vice-president.

CYNDY HENDERSHOT is a doctoral student at Texas Tech University.

She has articles appearing or forthcoming in *Notes on Contemporary Literature, Clues: A Journal of Detection, University of Mississippi Studies in English,* and the *Victorian Newsletter.* Her book of fiction, *City of Mazes and Other Tales of Obsession,* was recently published by Asylum Arts.

PIERRE L. HORN received his Ph.D. from Columbia University and is Professor of French at Wright State University in Dayton, Ohio, where he also holds the Brage Golding Distinguished Research Professorship. He has written extensively on French literature and culture, including a study of Marguerite Yourcenar and biographies of Louis XIV and Lafayette.

CATHERINE ELIZABETH HOYSER is Assistant Professor and Chair of English at Saint Joseph College (Connecticut). At Indiana University, she was Managing Editor of *Victorian Studies.* She coedited *Woman: An Affirmation* and has presented papers on George Eliot, the new woman, and detective fiction. Currently, she is coediting an anthology on the movie, *Thelma and Louise.*

EDELMA HUNTLEY teaches dramatic literature at Appalachian State University in North Carolina. She has published articles on Restoration Drama and on contemporary American playwrights, as well as on the mystery writers Simon Brett, Leo Bruce, and Julian Symons. She is currently working on an essay on the culinary mystery.

FRED ISAAC is a long-time member of the Popular Culture Association. His interests include northern California mystery writers. He "sunlights" as Head Librarian at the Jewish Community Library, San Francisco.

JACQUELYN L. JACKSON is an Associate Professor of English at Middle Tennessee State University, where she has served as Interim Chair of the English Department and Director of the African-American Studies minor program. She also developed the African-American literature curriculum. Currently, she is an advisor to numerous organizations.

MYRA HUNTER JONES, who belongs to that endangered species, the native Floridian, recently returned home after some years spent translating Russian in Washington, D.C., and doing public relations in North Carolina. She likes literature that crosses boundaries, such as the mystery–science fiction of Douglas Adams. When not reading mysteries, she teaches college composition and literature.

NATALIE HEVENER KAUFMAN, Professor of Government and International Studies at the University of South Carolina, has published four books on international law and human rights. Her article on fictional female detectives appeared in the *International Journal of Women's Studies*, and she has presented papers on this topic at the Popular Culture Convention.

MARTY S. KNEPPER, Professor of English at Morningside College, has served as President of the Popular Culture Association. She teaches a class in detective fiction and has written articles on Agatha Christie, Dick Francis, Amanda Cross, and Dorothy L. Sayers. She is currently writing an essay on Agatha Christie's Miss Marple.

JUDITH J. KOLLMANN is a Professor of English at the University of Michigan-Flint, where she teaches courses in medieval literature, the Old and New Testament, fantasy, and crime fiction. She has published several articles on Charles Williams, as well as articles on John Gardner, Sheridan Le Fanu, and Andrew Greeley's murder mysteries.

JOAN G. KOTKER teaches English and crime fiction at Bellevue Community College in Bellevue, Washington. She is a member of the Popular Culture Association's Mystery and Detection Area and has had essays, articles and reviews published in the *Armchair Detective*. She has been interested in Martha Grimes's Richard Jury series since its inception.

JOSEPH P. LOVERING was born in Calais, Maine, and educated at Holy Cross, Boston, and Ottawa universities. He is the author of two critical biographies on American novelists: *S. Weir Mitchell* and *Gerald W. Brace*. A retired professor from Canisius College, he lives with his wife, Eileen, in Tonawanda, New York.

GINA MACDONALD, of Loyola University, New Orleans, has taught everything from English as a second language to graduate courses in Shakespeare. She regularly writes articles on mystery and detective fiction for Salem Press, Greenwood Press, Bruccoli Press, and St. James Press, and has a chapter on "Scott Turow" in *It's a Print*.

JEFFREY H. MAHAN is Assistant Professor of Practical Theology and Media in Contemporary Culture at Garrett-Evangelical Theological Seminary, Evanston, Illinois. His work on the mystery story includes *A Long Way from Solving That One: Psycho/Social and Ethical Implications of Ross Macdonald's Lew Archer Tales*.

MARYKAY MAHONEY is Associate Professor of English at Merrimack College in North Andover, Massachusetts. She has published articles on "The Adventure of the Copper Beeches" and the teaching of *In Cold Blood*, and has articles forthcoming on Nicholas Blake's novels and the film adaptation of Patricia Highsmith's *Strangers on a Train*.

LOIS A. MARCHINO is an Associate Professor of English at the University of Texas at El Paso, where she has also served as Director of Women's Studies and Director of Literature. Her teaching interests, research, and publications concern primarily literature by and about women, including women in detective fiction.

DENISE M. MARSHALL is a professor of culture and women's studies. She studies comedies, gender bending, and women's images in popular genres. She is working on a biography of Phoebe Atwood Taylor and editing a collection of women's travel letters. Her next project focuses on heroism in comic books, cartoons, and film.

THOMAS MAVOR holds a B.A. from the University of the South and an M.A. in English from Louisiana State University. He currently teaches at Brother Martin High School in his hometown of New Orleans, Louisiana.

JOHN MICHIELSEN obtained a Ph.D. from the University of Toronto and teaches German and Dutch at Brock University in St. Catharines, Ontario. He has published and lectured on German realism, twentieth-century Dutch poetry, feminist literature, and European and American mystery writers.

ELIZABETH NEILD, a New Zealand native, is an aficionado of detective fiction. She holds a Ph.D. in comparative literature from the University of Chicago and has taught at a number of U.S. and Canadian colleges and universities. She is currently a psychiatric social worker in Boston, Massachusetts.

ANTONY OLDKNOW, a British-born writer, is Chair of Languages and Literature at Eastern New Mexico University, Portales. His poems and literary translations have been published in *American Poetry Review*, *Antaeus*, *Poetry*, *Nation*, *Chelsea*, and similar publications. He also authored a critical translation of Francis Jammes's 1899 novel, *Clara d'Ellébeuse*.

SUSAN OLEKSIW is the author of *Murder in Mellingham* and *Double Take*. After earning a Ph.D. in Sanskrit, she compiled *A Reader's Guide to the Classic British Mystery*. She recently completed an interpretive history of the mystery novel.

KATHLEEN OSER is project director for "Connecticut Reading Connections," a grant-funded service of the Southern Connecticut Library Council, and a graduate student in English at Southern Connecticut State University. She presented "The Case of the Missing Phallus: A Feminist Film Critique of *The Big Sleep*" at the Northeastern Popular Culture Association.

LIZABETH PARAVISINI-GEBERT is Associate Professor of Caribbean literature at Vassar College. She has published on contemporary Caribbean, Latin American, and American fiction, is editor of *Green Cane and Juicy Flotsam* (1991) and *Pleasure and the Word: Erotic Writings by Latin American Women* (1993), and authored *Phyllis Shand Allfrey: A Caribbean Life* (forthcoming).

SARA PARETSKY is the author of the award-winning mystery novels featuring hard-boiled private eye V. I. Warshawski. She is also a founding member and former president of Sisters in Crime.

LINDA C. PELZER is Associate Professor of English at Wesley College in Dover, Delaware. A specialist in American literature and women's studies, she earned her Ph.D. at the University of Notre Dame and has conducted research in Britain on a Fulbright Collaborative Research Grant.

KATHY PHILLIPS contributes reviews to the *Drood Review* and *Mystery Scene*, is the buyer for Spenser's Mystery Bookshop, Boston, and sells mysteries through the mail as Time and Again Books. She is a practicing attorney fresh from fifteen years of contracts and computer law as in-house counsel for various major corporations.

BONNIE C. PLUMMER is Professor of English at Eastern Kentucky University in Richmond, where she frequently teaches courses in detective fiction. Her articles on detective fiction have appeared in *Clues* and the *Baker Street Journal*.

SIDNEY POGER is Professor of English at the University of Vermont. He has taught courses in detective fiction for over ten years. Among the subjects of his publications and papers are American literature, modern poetry, Irish literature, introductions to poetry, and detective fiction.

B. J. RAHN is a member of the English Department of Hunter College of the City University of New York. Cofounder and editor of *Murder Is Academic*, she is a member of the Mystery Writers of America, the Sherlock Holmes Society of London, the Dorothy L. Sayers Society, and the Crime Writers Association of the U.K.

GEORGIA RHOADES, an English and women's studies teacher at Appalachian State University, teaches and writes about feminist detective fiction.

She has also written about the political problems of feminist teachers, is cowriting a performance art piece on feminist archetypes, and plans a book on feminist biography.

BETTY RICHARDSON is a Professor of English at Southern Illinois University–Edwardsville. Her books include studies of *Sexism in Higher Education* and *John Collier,* and her articles, reviews, and review essays have appeared in *Papers on Language and Literature, Victorian Britain, British Literary Journals, Clues,* and elsewhere.

JOAN WARTHLING ROBERTS is Professor of English at the State University College of New York at Buffalo, where she teaches courses in Victorian literature, women in literature, detective fiction, and poetry. She is currently working on a literary biography of Anna Katharine Green, "mother of the detective novel."

CHERI LOUISE ROSS received her Ph.D. in English from Purdue University in 1991. Her area of specialization is nineteenth- and early-twentieth-century women writers of the Americas, and she has published articles on Anna Katharine Green and Marietta Holley. She is Assistant Professor at Penn State University, Mont Alto Campus.

JOAN WARCHOL ROSSI teaches nineteenth-century studies, Shakespeare, writing, and children's literature at several New England colleges. She has published articles and frequently presented in these areas.

MICHAEL J. ROSSI is an Associate Professor and Chair of the Department of English at Merrimack College in North Andover, Massachusetts. Coauthor of *Exploring Literature: A Collaborative Approach,* and a mystery addict, he finds inspirational the accounts of successful mystery writers who began their writing careers late in life.

SHARON A. RUSSELL teaches film at the Indiana State University Department of Communication. She is past head of the Detective and Mystery Fiction Area of the Popular Culture Association and has published articles on mystery and horror fiction and film. She is currently editing a collection treating animals in mystery.

MARILYN RYE has taught writing and literature at Rutgers University, New Brunswick, New Jersey, where she was formerly an Associate Director of the writing program and is now a Campus Director at the Learning Resource Center. Rye has written frequently on detective fiction and edited a composition anthology.

ANN MARTIN SCOTT directs the Technical Communications Program at the University of Southwestern Louisiana, where she is Associate Professor. She teaches technical writing and linguistics courses and has published in various professional journals. She has also edited anthologies on collaborative technical writing and Cajun Vernacular English.

MARILYN SPARKS SEVERSON is Associate Professor of French at Seattle Pacific University in Seattle, Washington. A reader of mysteries ever since grade school, when her mother rationed her Nancy Drew books, Severson is currently intrigued by how women writers of mystery fiction portray women in their novels.

FRANK W. SHELTON is Associate Dean for Academic Affairs at the University of South Carolina–Salkehatchie Regional Campus. His research interests include contemporary southern fiction, and he has published essays on contemporary crime fiction set in the South.

CHARLES L. P. SILET teaches courses in film and contemporary culture as well as modern fiction in the Department of English at Iowa State University. He reviews crime fiction and also interviews crime writers. Currently, he is preparing a collection of his interviews for publication.

JENNIFER SMITH is a Ph.D. candidate at Ohio State University, where she is completing her dissertation on the political aspects of romantic love in literature. Her previous critical work has centered on women's roles in mystery fiction. She is also the author of five contemporary romances under the pseudonym of Jennifer Crusie.

MARCIA J. SONGER is Assistant Chair for Undergraduate Studies in the English Department at East Tennessee State University, where she teaches computer-assisted composition, English as a second language, and world literature. She is a frequent presenter in the Detective and Mystery Fiction section of the Popular Culture Association.

NANCY-STEPHANIE STONE has a Ph.D. in government and writes occasional papers on intelligence matters. She is also a staff writer for the *Drood Review* and author of *A Reader's Guide to the Spy and Thriller Novel*. She lives in Cambridge, Mass., but is often found in the other Cambridge (U.K.).

LORENA STOOKEY teaches in the English Department at the University of Nevada in Reno. Her regular course offerings include British literature, poetry, and mythology. She is also interested in the sciences and in language theory. She loves a good book, so her latest mystery novel is never far from hand.

GARY STORHOFF is an Associate Professor of English at the University of Connecticut, Stamford Campus, where he also serves as Associate Director of Campus. His area of research is African-American literature, and his work on Chester Himes led to a study of detective fiction generally.

NANCY ELLEN TALBURT is Associate Vice-Chancellor for Academic Affairs at the University of Arkansas, Fayetteville. Her essays appear in *Twentieth Century Crime and Mystery Writers*, *Dictionary of Literary Biography*, and other collections. She was the editor, with Lyna Lee Montgomery, of *A Mystery Reader*.

ELIZABETH A. TREMBLEY specializes in modern British literature and Gothic and detective fiction. Since obtaining her Ph.D. at the University of Chicago, she has published and presented on Dorothy L. Sayers, Arthur Conan Doyle, medievalism, psychological theory, and film adaptations of literature. She is coediting *"It's A Print!": Detective Fiction from Page to Screen*.

ANITA MARISSA VICKERS is Assistant Professor of English at Penn State University, Schuylkill.

DAVID CONNOR WALLACE, JR., received his B.A. from Rhodes College (formerly Southwestern at Memphis) and his M.A. from the University of Arkansas. He did doctoral work at Auburn University. He is an English Instructor at Jacksonville State University in Jacksonville, Ala., where he teaches a course in detective fiction.

CHRISTOPHER J. WARREN is the founder of Murder by Invitation, Ltd.

THOMAS WHISSEN is Professor Emeritus of English at Wright State University and author of *Isak Dinesen's Aesthetics*, *Components of Composition*, *A Way with Words*, *The Devil's Advocates: Decadence in Modern Literature*, *Classic Cult Fiction: A Companion to Popular Cult Literature*, and the musical comedy, *The Sky's the Limit!*

MARYBETH WHITE, who was born in Illinois and raised in New Mexico, earned a B.A. in English at McMurry College, Abilene, Texas, and two graduate degrees at the University of Arkansas, Fayetteville. She is currently an Assistant Professor of English at Southeast Missouri State University, where she teaches composition, grammar, and mythology.

GWENDOLYN WHITEHEAD is a lecturer in English at Lamar University in Beaumont, Texas. She received her Ph.D. from the University of Southwestern Louisiana with a dissertation on Robert B. Parker's contribution to hard-boiled detective fiction. She has presented papers on detective and other types of fiction at several conferences.

ALBERT E. WILHELM, Professor of English at Tennessee Technological University, has published essays on Thomas Wolfe, Robert Penn Warren, John Updike, John Cheever, and Bobbie Ann Mason. He has also written several commentaries on the novels of Dick Francis. As a Fulbright lecturer, Wilhelm has taught American literature in Poland and South Korea.

ROBERT P. WINSTON is Associate Professor of English at Dickinson College in Carlisle, Pennsylvania. He specializes in American literature before 1914 and in the relationships between popular literatures and national cultures. He is coauthor, with Nancy C. Mellerski, of *The Public Eye: Ideology and the Police Procedural*.

PAULA M. WOODS received her B.A. from Illinois Wesleyan University, her M.A. from the University of Illinois, and her Ph.D. from the University of North Texas. An Assistant Professor of English at Baylor University, Woods has presented conference papers on mystery/detective fiction and published criticism in *Explorations in Renaissance Culture*.

JUANA R. YOUNG is Associate Director of Libraries at the University of Arkansas, Fayetteville. She is coeditor of *Books and Letters*, the library newsletter, and a contributor to library journals. She has coauthored presentations on the woman detective and religion in crime fiction for Popular Culture Association meetings.